The CATHOLIC CHURCH

AND THE

AMERICAN NEGRO

BEING

An Investigation of the Past and Present
Activities of the Catholic Church in Behalf
of the 12,000,000 Negroes in the United
States, with an Examination of the Diffi-
culties which affect the work of the Colored
Missions.

BY

JOHN T. GILLARD, S.S.J.

BALTIMORE
St. Joseph's Society Press
1929
All rights reserved

JOHNSON REPRINT CORPORATION JOHNSON REPRINT COMPANY LTD.
111 Fifth Avenue, New York, N.Y. 10003   Berkeley Square House, London, W. 1

Cum Permissu Superioris:

LOUIS B. PASTORELLI, S.S.J., LL.D.
Superior General

Nihil Obstat:

JOSEPH BRUNEAU, S.S., S.T.D.
Censor Librorum

Imprimatur:

✠ MICHAEL J. CURLEY, D.D.
Archbishop of Baltimore.

December 5, 1929.

———

1479143

To the Sainted Memory of

𝕽𝖊𝖛. 𝕽𝖆𝖞𝖒𝖔𝖓𝖉 𝕽. 𝕸𝖈𝕮𝖆𝖗𝖙𝖞, 𝕾. 𝕾. 𝕵.,

whose pilgrim period of life spent in the Colored Harvest still serves as inspiration in our troublous trudgings along the highways of the saints,

This Book is Reverently Dedicated.

TABLE OF CONTENTS

Preface .... xiii-xv

CHAPTER   PAGE
I. THE PROBLEM 1
   1. Its Existence 1
   2. Nature of the Problem 2
   3. Literature of the Problem 5

PART ONE — *Past Conditions*

II. BEFORE THE CIVIL WAR 10
    1. From 1619 to 1829 10
       A. Conditions in General 11
       B. Maryland 14
       C. Louisiana 16
       D. Kentucky 19
       E. Georgia and Carolinas 20
       F. Virginia 23
       G. Alabama 23

    2. From 1829 to 1866 24
       A. Bishop England 24
       B. Baltimore 27
       C. Washington, D. C. 28
       D. First Church for Negroes 29
       E. Other Places 30

    1. From 1866 to 1871 (Arrival of Josephites) 32
       A. Emancipation 32
       B. Effect on Church 33
       C. Opposition 34
       D. Catholic Reaction 36
       E. Catholic Activities 38
    2. From 1871 to 1900 39
       A. First Organized Effort 39
       B. Situation 42
       C. Important Foundations 43

CONTENTS—*Continued*

PART TWO — *Present Conditions*

CHAPTER   PAGE
IV. SURVEY OF COLORED CATHOLICS 47
    1. National Census of Colored Catholics.... 47
    2. Distribution of Colored Catholics 51
    3. Survey of Exclusively Colored Catholic
       Missions 57
    4. Distribution by Sex 64
    5. Converts and Baptisms 64

V. EXCLUSIVELY COLORED CATHOLIC CHURCHES ... 67
    1. Summary of Survey 67
    2. Necessity and Advantages 68
    3. The Catholic Church and the "Color-Line" 76

VI. PRIESTS OF THE NEGRO MISSIONS 79
    1. Summary of Survey 79
    2. Necessity of Trained Missioners 80
    3. The Question of Colored Clergy.......... 85

PART THREE — *Negro Migration*

VII. IN GENERAL 94
    1. Number of Movements 94
    2. Causes 95
    3. Character 96
    4. Extent 96
    5. Destination of Migrants 99
    6. Adjustment of Migrants 101
    7. Effects on Missions 101
    8. A New Problem 105

VIII. MIGRATION AND THE SOUTH 109
    1. South Atlantic Group 109
    2. East South Central Group 114
    3. West South Central Group 117

IX. MIGRATION AND THE NORTH 121
    1. New England States 121
    2. Middle Atlantic States 122
    3. East North Central States 127

X. MIGRATION AND THE WEST 130
    1. West North Central Group 130
    2. Mountain States 132
    3. Pacific States 132

CONTENTS—*Continued*

PART FOUR — *Education*

CHAPTER   PAGE

XI. A RETROSPECT—Beginnings 134

XII. SCHOOLS OF THE COLORED MISSIONS 147
1. In General 147
2. Non-Catholic Resources 148
3. Catholic Resources 150
4. Summary of Survey 152
5. Rural Schools 158
6. Sisters 162

XIII. EDUCATIONAL ACTIVITIES 166
1. Trends 166
2. College 168
3. High Schools 173
4. Industrial Schools 179
   A. Necessity 179
   B. Catholic Efforts 184

PART FIVE — *Social Welfare Work*

XIV. NEGLECTED AND DELINQUENT CHILDREN 192
1. Causes 192
2. Child-Caring Homes 196
3. Day Nurseries 200
4. Houses of Good Shepherd 201

XV. SOCIAL SERVICE CENTERS 204
1. Necessity 204
2. Care of Sick and Aged 205
3. Social Centers 207
4. Catholic Societies for Negroes......... 209

PART SIX — *Obstacles to Greater Results*

XVI. EXTERNAL DIFFICULTIES 212
1. Prejudice Against the Church.......... 212
2. Discrimination 213
3. Lack of Priests 216
4. Financial 218

XVII. INTERNAL DIFFICULTIES—REMOTE 220
1. Negro Religion 220
   A. Negro Church—Its Rise 220
   B. Emotional Religion 223
   C. Social Religion 226
   D. The Negro Preacher 229

CONTENTS—*Continued*

CHAPTER   PAGE

XVIII.   INTERNAL DIFFICULTIES—REMOTE (Continued) 234
- 2. Negro Morality 234
  - A. Heredity and Morality 234
  - B. Environment and Morality 237
  - C. Poverty and Morality 240
  - D. Emotion and Morality 243

XIX.   INTERNAL DIFFICULTIES—IMMEDIATE 246
- 1. Two Idealisms 246
- 2. Emotional Tendency of Catholic Negroes.. 247
- 3. Lack of Social Life in the Church 249
- 4. Secret Societies 250
- 5. Mixed Marriages 251
- 6. Class Distinctions Within the Race 252
- 7. Race Consciousness 254
- 8. Irregularity in Church Attendance....... 256

XX.   DEFECTIONS FROM THE CHURCH 258
- 1. Leakage 258
  - A. Existence 258
  - B. Extent 259
- 2. Causes—Past 259
- 3. Causes—Present 262
  - A. Where no special priests are assigned. 262
  - B. Where special priests are assigned.... 263
    - (a) Migration 263
    - (b) Environment 265
    - (c) Mixed Marriages 265
    - (d) Insufficient Instruction 267
- 4. Inefficiency in Schools 268
- 5. Conclusion 271

XXI.   CONCLUSION 273
- 1. General 273
- 2. Recommendations 284

Bibliography 291

Index 302

TABLES

TABLE   PAGE

1. Catholic Colored Population by Archdioceses and Dioceses 48
2. Catholic Colored Population by Sections and States 50
3. Distribution of Colored Catholics in Relation to Population 52
4. Summary of Exclusively Colored Missionary Work, *Insert facing* 58
5. Colored Missionary Work according to States...... 59
6. Summary of Government Statistics (1926 Survey) 61
7. Number of Churches, Membership, Value of Edifices, Debt on Edifices, Value of Parsonages, and Number of Sunday School Scholars, for Urban and Rural Communities of the United States for 1926; with comparative figures for 1916 and 1906, (Government Census, 1926).... 62
8. Distribution of Colored (1920) 97
9. Concentration of Negroes in Districts........... 99
10. Concentration of Negroes in Cities 100
11. Distribution of Negroes in New York City 124
12. Colored Catholics in Archdiocese of Philadelphia... 126
13. Colored Catholics in Archdiocese of Cincinnati 127
14. Educational Activities according to States........ 152
15. Educational Activities according to Dioceses...... 155
16. Institutions in Charge of Seculars 158
17. Mission Schools Conducted by Lay Teachers 160
18. Summary of Sisterhoods and Work in Their Charge 164
19. Catholic High Schools for Negroes, *Insert facing*.. 179
20. Catholic Child-Caring Homes for Negro Children.. 198
21. Houses of Good Shepherd 202
Map Showing Proportion of Negroes in the Total Population of each State, 1920 53
Graph Showing Baptisms and Converts (Josephite Missions, 1913-1928) 65

xi

PREFACE

Time was when we were admonished to let not the right hand know what the left hand did. Today, whether we will or not, we tabulate, we index, and we file the good which we do, for a sceptical world demands that Religion pass its pragmatic test. Indeed, in the mission field these things we must do if we would remain true to the divine command to teach all nations, for with the increasing complexities of modern life our mission methods must be enlarged adequately to meet situations which inevitably arise in a changing and challenging world. Since complete fulfilment of our obligation towards the "other sheep" of Christ involves intelligent study of our mission problems, we must not neglect a single activity which may be of service in giving the fullest measure of the Gospel to those entrusted to our care. Wherefore, we must bring to our missionary work supreme intelligence, eagerness to learn, and readiness to improve. Of primary importance, if we would interpret aright prevailing conditions and adopt methods and policies to them, is a knowledge of the facts. The *Catholic Church and the American Negro* professes to supply such knowledge of the Colored Missions.

As to the need of such a book, there is little to be said. Heretofore the Catholic Church has not generally been considered a force in the solution of America's most vexing problem. One of the disconcerting things about current literature on the Negro is the consistent inaccuracy of information on the work which the Catholic Church is doing in his behalf, most writers on the subject assuming that it is doing nothing, while such as occasionally do notice its work are usually inaccurate and misleading. The fault is our own, because heretofore we have had no source of any considerable authority which we might present to seekers after the truth.

Today, with the Negro question assuming a deserved importance, the Catholic Church must take its right place as a power worthy of serious consideration and as having something valuable to contribute towards a solution of the so-called race problem. But to get this recognition it must give "a sign" such as Christ gave to the credulous disciples of St. John the Baptist.

The present Survey of Catholic Missionary Activity in Behalf of the 12,000,000 Negroes in the United States is an attempt, feeble though it be, to study the problem of the Negro as it relates to the Catholic Church. In the first five parts statistics are gathered and data compiled; they are accurate and exhaustive so far as our knowledge goes. Our faith in chancery figures, however, may be challenged. While it is certain that chancery statistics are not always to be accepted without question, generally speaking our correspondence with diocesan officials has been of a satisfactory nature, several having gone to extremes to insure a maximum accuracy. Most of our information, however, was supplied by individual missioners in the field. Where possible, statistics were cross-checked. While it is difficult to obtain desirable accuracy in all information, we believe that the law of averages works towards reliable general statistics. Without claiming finality in our findings, we are convinced that our figures, on the whole, are deserving of credence. At the same time, if we have overlooked any of the works or workers in the Colored Mission field, we crave indulgence and shall welcome correction.

Part Six (Difficulties Affecting the Work of the Colored Missions) is an effort to discover, if possible, why the Catholic Church has not made greater progress in Negro evangelization. There are those, perhaps, who would favor elimination of this section on the ground that it contains inflammable and controvertible material. Others there may be who would relegate the statistical parts of the book to an appendix and enlarge upon the discussion of difficulties. Manifestly there is much room for personal opinion in the matter.

To our mind it would seem only fair to present both sides of the question. Those of us who are familiar with the work of the Colored Missions know that while Catholics as a whole are making a tremendous contribution to the welfare of the Negro race, there is room for improvement. The Catholic Church is divine; its members are human, and as such are susceptible to the defects and faults of mankind. While all our readers may not be in accord with the opinions expressed and the conclusions drawn (they represent only our personal opinions and conclusions), readiness to differ will be at least a first step towards a disposition to act. Sometimes irritation is not a bad thing; and we have known instances in which it has begotten activity along desired lines.

Thoroughly aware of the limitations of this investigation, our hope is that it will go at least a short way towards filling a long-felt need—a literature of the Colored Missions—and, at the same time, encourage those who are better gifted by age, wisdom, and grace to put on paper the thoughts which are in their hearts; for at present the lack of anything like scientific literature on the work of Colored Missions is perhaps the chief difficulty in the way of greater achievement and ultimate solution of "America's responsibility."

We wish to express our sincere thanks to all those who in any way co-operated with us in the collection and preparation of our material; particularly are we indebted to the Rev. Thomas Duffy, S.S.J., whose patient kindness and continued encouragement have given us an experience beyond our years and a perseverance beyond our powers.

THE AUTHOR.

CHAPTER I

THE PROBLEM

1. Its Existence.

In 1888, the year for which the first statistics for colored
Catholics are available, the report of the Commission for
Catholic Missions among the Colored People and Indians estimated the total colored Catholic population in the United
States to be 138,213. This figure was an estimate based upon
the reports from dioceses in which colored mission work was
being done at the time. Four years later Cardinal Gibbons,
than whom there is no better authority, placed the colored
Catholic population of the United States at 160,000. In a
letter which he wrote to Cardinal Vaughan under date of
April 14, 1892, he stated, "there are now eight millions of
the black fold, of which but two per cent are Catholics, and
of the rest the vast majority have no religion." The report of the Commission for Catholic Missions Among the Colored People and Indians for that year substantiates the approximate correctness of the figure, giving the total Catholic
Negro population as 152,692, with no returns from Cincinnati,
St. Louis, or San Antonio. Taking 160,000 as a fair estimate of
the colored Catholic population in 1890, and 204,000 [1] for 1928,
the numerical gain in colored Catholics is 44,000, or 27.5
per cent.

The Federal Census for the year 1890 gave the total Negro
population of the United States as 7,500,000, in round figures.
According to the latest figures, [2] in 1926 there were 11,600,000
Negroes in the United States. This represents a gain
of 4,100,000, or 54.7 per cent.

It would seem, then, that although the colored population
in this country during the past forty years has increased

---

[1] cf. National Census, infra, p. 48.
[2] Survey of Negro Colleges and Universities, Bureau of Education,
Section of Bulletin, 1928, no. 7, p. 33.

54.7 per cent, by natural increase alone, the Catholic colored population has increased by only 27.5 per cent. The large difference between these figures would indicate that the Catholic Church is not even keeping pace with the growing colored population of the country, much less making the progress which might reasonably be looked for.

Apart from the positive fact that the increase in the number of converts has not been proportionate to the increase in population, consideration must also be given to the negative fact of leakage from the Church. While there are no reliable figures available to prove the contention, one familiar with the conditions which existed previous to and for some time after the emancipation of the slaves is inclined to believe that if we go back to the year 1863, when the Emancipation Proclamation was issued, the proportionate and actual loss of colored Catholics would be much greater. At one time it was reported that many thousands had lost the Faith for want of priests to care for them. While today the leakage is not so great, it is, nevertheless, a fact which must be given due consideration.

Population statistics, however, give only quantitative data. Qualitative data deserve attention even in a brief statement of the situation. This is afforded by the statistics herein given of the number of Negro churches, schools, priests, teachers, and pupils in the schools. They show what is being done for the Negroes. For instance, there is a Catholic school in nearly every Negro parish. Is this the case for white parishes? In some respects, then, the situation is not quite so tragic as it might seem at first glance.

Why is it that, even with due allowance for work done, the Catholic Church has not made a greater advance in the evangelization of the Negroes in the United States? In the following pages it is proposed to study this problem. Three questions are asked: namely, what has been done, why has not greater progress been made, and what can be done to insure greater progress in the future? The method of investigation will be:

(1) An investigation of past conditions; this is fact finding.

(2) An investigation of present conditions; this also deals with facts, and includes a survey of the present condition of Catholic effort in behalf of the Negro: religious, educational, and sociological.

(3) An investigation of the difficulties affecting Catholic missionary activity in behalf of the Negro.

(4) A final chapter in which some helpful suggestions are made for the future development of our missionary program.

2. NATURE OF THE PROBLEM

Today the problem of the Negro is a subtle, intangible part of our national life. While friction between two races living side by side, as here in America, is not unique, the majority of Americans would seem to think that a solution may be found in refusal to recognize the problem. Although the theory that the difficulties between the two races might be ignored has been found to be untenable, Catholic scholars, with notable exceptions, are surprisingly slow to recognize that the very presence of the Negro in the United States constitutes an opportunity for and a challenge to our best Catholic thought. In a recent issue of *America,* a writer in "Books and Authors" comments as follows upon a new Catholic sociology: "In view of the wide range of matters discussed, it is a little strange that no reference at all is made to two of the most fundamental of all our American problems: that of the Negro and that of rural life, nor to any of the agencies concerned therewith." [1] As a matter of fact, the problem of the Negro, even as it affects the Catholic Church, is religio-sociological, the religious and social phases of his life being inextricably bound together.

While no one has yet given a definition of sociology which is entirely acceptable, it would be a mistake to suppose that it restricts itself to the study of social evils. Sociology "must study social evils, as they are a part of social life; but it must also study the higher social relationships resulting from or tending to shape political, economic, or *religious* life; it cannot neglect the family, the state, or the *church;* it must

---
[1] May 25, 1929, p. 167.

search into man's aptitudes, characteristics and virtues; it must recognize man's threefold relationship—*to God*, to his fellow man and to himself."[1] If religion and morality may not be separated from sociology, then any plan for the betterment of the social and economic condition of the Negro in the United States containing no reference to spiritual and moral elements would be neither accurate nor complete; in other words, any attempt at social and economic betterment of the Negro must neglect none of his higher faculties or his relationship to his Creator. Conversely, any attempt at the religious improvement of the Negro must keep him in mind as he actually is, with all his social, economic, and educational needs.

As far as the American Negro is concerned, it will be almost impossible to raise him to a high spiritual and moral level unless at the same time we try to develop the home and the school, to increase his industrial efficiency, and to assist his contributing to literature, science, art, and philosophy. The social and the religious betterment of the Negro must go hand in hand; wherefore, if our conception of the Negro missionary movement be something more than the mere erection of mission chapels,—if, for example, it takes in the 6,000,000 non-church-going Negroes,—then we must make our preaching and acting as broad as life itself.

It is obvious, then, that effective missionary methods must work close to the common ground of this world. While secondary to religion, an improved social order is a necessary outcome of true religious progress. As the Jesuit, Spalding, notes: "Wherever the Gospel was preached there not only resulted a higher moral life, but everywhere there was an increase in the knowledge of those things which tend to premote social and civic progress. In fact, the missionaries generally began with social work; and it was only after they had gained the good will and confidence of the neophytes by patience and service that they brought to them the higher truths of Christianity."[2]

[1] Muntsch, S.J., Albert, and Spalding, S.J., Henry, *Introductory Sociology*, p. 78.
[2] *Chapters in Social History*, p. 378.

Protestant missionary societies are following this method, and owing to it they have reaped a harvest among the Negroes. They have expended enormous sums of money in building primary, secondary, and higher educational institutions, hospitals and social centers, and have proved by their superior methods that Christianity has something worth while to give to the Negro.

In this age of materialism the tendency is to emphasize material assistance and comfort, and more or less to draw apart from the spiritual. The true concept of sociology, however, is to use the rendering of material aid, the furnishing of worldly relief to sickness and want, as a means of establishing a basis of confidence upon which to build up the spiritual edifice and lead to the practice of religion. To the Catholic all things are seen in relation to eternity. As Rev. Doctor P. H. Furfey, of the Catholic University, in *Some Trends in Modern Sociology*, correctly observes: "For him, applied sociology is not an end in itself but a means to a higher end—the salvation of human souls. For this reason the philosophical approach, taking account as it does of moral values, will always be exceedingly important in the eyes of the Catholic." [1] This is particularly true of the work which the Catholic Church is doing for the Negroes in the United States.

While much of the work which the Catholic Church is doing in behalf of the Negro is social work in the strict sense of the term, all such missionary endeavor may be properly classed as social work in the broader sense; viz., that whatever betters a man spiritually should produce a favorable reaction socially, for while "missionary work must have for its primary object the conversion of the unbeliever to the religion of Christ, there must result from this message of salvation a higher social order." [2]

3. LITERATURE OF THE PROBLEM

The absence of anything like an adequate literature of Catholic missionary activity in behalf of the Negroes in the United States has long been felt to be a major difficulty in

[1] *American Catholic Philosophical Association*, Fourth Annual Meeting, p. 69.
[2] Spalding, *Chapters in Social History*, p. 392.

the way of greater missionary activity and ultimate solution
of the problem of the Negro.   So far we have been working
more or less in the dark.

There are those who speak with scorn or sarcasm about
statistical methods in missionary activity.   Rev. William
Kerby, Ph.D., LL.D., in *The Social Mission of Charity*, notes
this unfriendly attitude towards statistical methods in charity,
but the same is true of all statistics. As Doctor Kerby very
pointedly observes, however, ridicule is not the customary
weapon of well-informed men.   The scholarly mind endeavors to find wherein statistics may be of aid in the faithful
performance of its duty.   We have only impressions about
facts which are vital to our work "until investigators place
in our hands well-tested tables indicating clearly the facts
as trained minds can find and classify them.   The world recognizes and respects statistics and statisticians and grate-
fully uses their work while making due allowance for elements
of error which must be expected. The case for statistics and
every resource of art and ingenuity in enabling us to visualize
facts and movements of facts is strong enough to be dismissed." [1]

The relation of facts to Catholic work and the Negro
may not be dismissed so readily, Our literature of Investigation, that is, exact information on Catholic missionary
activity on the Negro Missions in the United States, is very
meagre.   In this field there is probably not a single investigation of such scope and accuracy as would enable us to
answer authoritatively the many and varied questions which
invariably arise in a discussion of the practical attitude of
the Catholic Church toward the so-called "race question" in
the United States.   For instance, the statement has been often
made and as often denied that Catholic missionary activity
for the Afro-American is not as intensive as it should be.
Missionaries engaged in the work have their own impressions,
but such must remain nebulous until substantiated by indisputable corroboratory facts.   As long as we lack a scientific
compilation of statistical facts we shall fall far short of the
achievement that would come from a fuller knowledge of

[1] pp. 149, 150.

all the multitudinous phases of the Negro problem as it affects the Catholic Church. Indeed, the advantages which would accrue from a literature of Investigation are too obvious to require expatiation.

In the years that are gone, it would seem that the missioners engaged in the work of the Colored Missions have been, in the words of Doctor Kerby, "so busy serving the poor whom we found that we had no time to count those whom we served or those who had need of our services. It may be that those who might have been investigators were so much engaged in actual duties of relief that none had the leisure and knowledge required for work of this kind. It may be that many who might have done such work refrained from it in the belief that it was useless or opposed to the spirit in which charity should be dispensed. Whatever the explanation, conditions now urge upon us the task of developing ability to conduct investigations. Critical methods are orthodox." [1]

Facts as such are only "symptoms of processes whose meanings lie beneath the surface"; hence, we need also a literature of Interpretation. Facts may arouse us, but only critical interpretation of those facts will reveal them in their true light and enable us to deal with them fruitfully. While statistics may not reach the spiritual world with which the missioner has to deal, they do reach the natural life upon which is built the supernatural life of the colored people. As Doctor Kerby points out, preaching and teaching the law of God must be done in the light of clearest understanding of social processes and adequate information about facts and processes of life. "The religious leader who knows conditions, and interpretations of social investigators working in the field of feeble-mindedness in relation to immorality ought to be far wiser as teacher and shaper of policies than one who preaches on sin and repentance alone and has no critical information beyond." [2] The same is true of the missioner to the Negro who is in possession of an interpretative literature on his work.

---

[1] Kerby, *op. cit.*, p. 152.
[2] *Ibid.*, p. 156.

Direction follows Interpretation. Once we have found the cause and meaning of the difficulties affecting Catholic missionary activity in behalf of the Negroes in the United States we can adopt methods to situations and work in the light of understanding. If the wisdom of many is of more authority than that of one, then "the fund of experience gathered at much cost in mistakes and experiments is precious." Yet, we have little such literature of Direction concerning the Colored Missions. The priests working on the missions develop methods and traditions in the work they do, but such methods and traditions are personal and local. While they may meet admirably well the immediate needs of individual missioners, a literature to which all would contribute their experiences ought to enrich each.

We have developed much Inspirational literature; in fact, nearly all we have is inspirational. Religious communities devoted to the work of the Colored Missions have stated and re-stated the great inspirational truths of our religion and have derived their standards and inspirations from them. Literature on the work of the Colored Missions is mostly in this class because hitherto there has been too little information of an exact and national nature to have it otherwise.

Of Catholic literature on the work of the Negro Missions that may be said which Doctor Kerby says of Catholic charities: "They are rich in literature of Inspiration. They are fairly well supplied with literature of Direction, yet not in any way proportionately to the magnitude of their activities or the rich experience to be found in them. We have relatively little literature of Investigation and Interpretation. Since the modern world places supreme emphasis on the last three and less on the first named, we find ourselves often lacking in enthusiasm for the three and contenting ourselves with insistance on the field in which we are best equipped; namely, that of Inspiration: discussion and defense of motive, spiritual values and tone." [1]

---

[1] *Ibid.*, p. 160.

PART I.—PAST CONDITIONS

Introduction

The lack of notable progress in the work of Negro evangelization will not cause so great wonder if consideration be given to the conditions affecting the religious life of the Negro prior to the twentieth century. Not before the beginning of this century was there anything like a concerted effort to win the Negro to the Catholic Church, and at least another decade elapsed before the effort gave unmistakable signs of success. For a proper appreciation of the position of the Catholic Church as regards colored missionary activity it is necessary to take past conditions into consideration.

This investigation of past conditions as they affected Catholic colored missionary activity may be divided into certain definite periods, as follows:

I—Before the Civil War:

    (1) from the beginning of slavery to 1829, the year in which the First Provincial Council was held in Baltimore.

    (2) from 1829 to 1866, when the Second Plenary Council was held in Baltimore.

II—After the Civil War:

    (1) from 1866 to the coming of the Josephite Fathers, in 1871.

    (2) from the arrival of the first Josephites to 1900.

CHAPTER II

BEFORE THE CIVIL WAR

1. FROM 1619 TO 1829

The Negro has been a factor in American history from the beginning. Spaniards were the earliest explorers and colonists of what is now the southern portion of the United States. In their expeditions they were accompanied by Negroes in the capacity of servants and slaves, since at that time Negro slavery was permitted by the law of nations. The earliest Spanish colonies of what is now the United States were not successful, and the advent of the Negroes was therefore only transient. They either returned to Spanish America or perished in the failure of the colonies. African slaves were with the expedition of Hernando de Soto. Probably the first Negroes to set foot on the soil of the United States were those who landed with the Spanish settlers at Chicora, in 1526, on what is now the coast of South Carolina. Negroes accompanied the colonizing expedition of Vasquez de Ayllon at the founding of the settlement at Guandape, in 1526, near the site where eighty-one years later the English built Jamestown. The unfortunate expedition, led by Panfilo de Narvaez, in 1528, had with it the Negro slave, Estevan, or Stephen. Narvaez perished in the waters of the lower Mississippi; and Stephen, with three other survivors, after years of suffering and wandering across what is now the southeastern part of the United States, reached Petatlan, in Sinaloa, in 1536.[1] Stephen's later adventures and death, at the hands of the Zuni Indians, form an interesting episode in the early history of what is now Arizona and New Mexico.[2]

[1] John Gilmary Shea, *The Catholic Church in Colonial Days*, p. 110; Booker T. Washington, *The Story of the Negro*, vol. I, p. 88.
[2] Elizabeth Dickens, "Estevan Early American Negro", *The Commonweal*, Aug. 14, 1929, gives an interesting account of this Negro.

10

A. Conditions in General

Before the introduction of slavery in 1619 the number of Negroes in this country was comparatively small. From that time, however, an increasing number of slaves was brought from Africa to the various colonies along the Atlantic seaboard. In the eighteenth century the importation of slaves received an impetus due to the great demand for cheap labor, particularly in the South where the Negro could be used to advantage on the large plantations.

In early colonial days the Established Church refused to permit the baptism of slaves on the ground that a Christian could not be held in bondage. Baptism of the slaves would, consequently, result in their manumission, and this was very undesirable from a pecuniary point of view. The Nonconformists held to the same opinion. To the credit of Catholics, and later, of the Quakers, be it said that they alone felt the obligation to teach the Negroes what they could of Christianity. The Spanish and French missionaries, the first to grapple with the problem, set an example which influenced the other Churches in their dealing with the Negroes. As Woodson states the matter: "Put to shame by this noble example of the Catholics, the English colonists had to find a way to overcome the objections of those who, granting that the enlightenment of the slaves might not lead to servile insurrection, nevertheless feared that their conversion might work manumission. To meet this exigency the colonists secured, through legislation by their assemblies and formal declaration by the Bishop of London, the abrogation of the law that a Christian could not be held as a slave. Then, allowed access to the bondmen, the missionaries of the Church of England, sent out by the Society for the Propagation of the Gospel among the Heathen in Foreign Parts, undertook to educate the slaves for the purpose of extensive proselyting."[1]

During the whole time of slavery the Catholics and the

[1] Woodson, Carter G., *The Education of the Negro Prior to 1861*, p. 3; An interesting account of this phase of the question is given in Brackett, J. R., *The Negro In Maryland*, p. 28. *et sq.; cf. also* Hughes, S.J., Thomas, *History of the Society of Jesus in North America*, vol. II, p. 116, *et sq.*

Quakers continued to promote religion and education among the colored in those places where they had opportunity. Even the reactionary movement in the early part of the nineteenth century failed to swerve them from their course. The opportunities for doing good, however, were rather few: in several southern colonies, later, states, the Catholics were denied access to the Negroes, even where they sought to work among them as missionaries. Special laws were enacted in some states to prevent the influx of such Christian workers.[1]

The laws governing the education of slaves varied according to time and place. For a long time there was no general exclusion of slaves from the privileges of education; those were the halcyon days when ability to read and to write was considered essential to the teaching of religion. Later, beginning in South Carolina in 1740, prohibitive legislation was enacted making religious instruction almost impossible except by the questionable process of verbal instruction. The first prohibitive and punitive laws were directed against unlawful assemblage of slaves; subsequently, of free Negroes and mulattoes, as their influence in exciting discontent or insurrection was to be guarded against. Afterwards legislation became more general throughout the South, prohibiting meetings for the teaching of reading and writing. In some states it was unlawful for the Negroes to meet even for religious worship unless a white man was present.[2]

Catholics frequently defied the laws and instructed the slaves regardless of consequences. The same may be said of the Quakers. Severe and general as were the laws against the education of the Negroes, they rarely applied to or were seldom enforced against the teaching of individuals or groups on plantations or at the homes of owners. Often the mistress of the household or her children taught the house servants; on Sundays others were included in the classes.[3] Catholics were bound to take at least this means of instructing the slaves, as is evident from the many Pontifical utterances of the Popes, from Pius II down.

---

[1] Woodson, *op. cit.*, p. 183.
[2] "Virginia Code", quoted by McConnell, J. P., *Negroes and Their Treatment in Virginia*, p. 107.
[3] Curry, J. L. M., *Education of the Negroes Since 1860*, p. 8.

The religion of the master usually determined the religion of the slaves. Often enough, however, the master was incapable of giving the slaves any religious instruction and, in many cases, was opposed to others doing so. Some masters, on the other hand, allowed their slaves to join societies of their own, more or less under the supervision of the regular church organizations. Other masters preferred the slaves to attend the white churches in their company; in such churches a place was always reserved for them, sometimes in the back of the church, but more often in the gallery. Catholic masters usually saw to it that their slaves attended church with regularity, in some cases even having special chapels built for them. An interesting example of solicitude on the part of masters is that of a certain Mr. West, a Protestant, be it noted, of Petersville, Md. In 1825, Mr. West gave a piece of land for a church, apparently for the benefit of the slaves, for the small log church, erected in 1826, was attended almost entirely by colored Catholics who were visited regularly by the Jesuits from Frederick. [1]

While decrying the general conditions of neglect as they existed at the time, we cannot fail to take cognizance of the oft-repeated but untrue charge that the Catholic Church totally neglected the welfare of the colored people. The fact is that during the whole period of slavery the moral and spiritual welfare of the slaves demanded a slow development due to the difficulties encountered. The activities of the Catholic Church were always necessarily limited owing to the smallness of its numbers and the weakness of its influence. Besieged by enemies from without and torn asunder by schisms within, the wonder is that the Church survived those times at all. Even in settlements in which Catholics had some standing, and despite the good will of the Church, lack of priests and means with which to carry on an extensive missionary program prevented any notable advance in the evangelization of the Negroes.

In the period before 1829 all Catholic effort was neces-

---

[1] *The Catholic Church In The United States*, edited by "The Catholic Editing Company," and undertaken to celebrate the Golden Jubilee of His Holiness, Pope Pius X, (Cardinal edition), vol. III, p. 85.

sarily individual. There is abundant evidence that during this period Catholics did admirable work in behalf of the Negroes, but Maryland and Louisiana (later Kentucky) were the only localities in which the Church was free to do anything like effective work.

B. Maryland

Originally a Catholic colony, Maryland did not long remain under Catholic control; it was, nevertheless, one of the few places in which Catholics were at all numerous. That Catholics of Maryland, priests and laity, were interested in the welfare of the Negroes is evident from the readiness with which Protestants identified them with the Negroes when rebellion was feared. Beginning in 1689, and lasting as long as the Maryland colony was in control of the Protestants, there were rumors and suspicions that the Indians and Negroes were in league with the priests and were plotting against the government of the Province. The "Romanists" and Negroes were, as a consequence, kept under the watchful eye of the government. In 1708, for instance, the sheriffs of the counties of Maryland were ordered to send to the Governor within a few weeks the number and names of "papists"—not merely of masters and families, but of the households, servants, and slaves baptized in the Roman faith. In 1745, one of the many times the "Romanists" were under suspicion, Governor Bladen wrote to one of the Catholic leaders that the religious duties of Catholics should be fulfilled, as they surely might be, without such large meetings of people as might give suspicions of designs other than religious exercises. "Nothing," wrote the Governor, "could give greater alarm to good subjects of King George than such frequent meetings of whites and Negroes under pretence of divine worship." [1]

That Catholicism made good headway among the colored people of Maryland is evident from the "Relation of Religion in the United States" which Father John Carroll, later Archbishop of Baltimore, forwarded to Cardinal Antonelli in 1785. Father Carroll wrote: "There are in Maryland about 15,800

[1] Brackett, op. cit., p. 92, et sq.

(Catholics); of these there are about 9,000 freemen, adults or over twelve years of age, children under that age about 3,000; and about that number of slaves of all ages of African origin, called Negroes. There are in Pennsylvania about 7,000, very few of whom are Negroes." [1]

In Maryland the Negroes were fortunate in having the Jesuits and, later, the Sulpicians to look after their interests. During the whole period of slavery the Jesuit Fathers labored zealously in the cities and counties of Maryland for the salvation of the Negroes. As far back as 1636, Leonardtown had been settled by the English. In that year Mass was said for them and some colored Catholics by a Jesuit from Newton. [2] While the Jesuits themselves owned slaves, they were slaves in name rather than fact. They were called "Priest's Negroes," as descriptive of the enviable treatment they received; the Fathers always referred to them as "servants" rather than as "slaves." [3] That the Jesuits had success in their work among the Negroes is evident from a statement of a certain Father Mosley who, in answer to a query about the religion of the slaves, wrote: "The Negroes that do belong to the (Catholic) gentlemen of our persuasion are all Christians, and instructed in every Christian duty with care." [4] Of the non-Catholic Negroes he had this to say: "The Negroes of all other persuasions are much neglected, as you imagine; and few ever christened." [5]

At the time of the San Domingan revolution, in the last decade of the eighteenth century, a large number of colonists fled from the island to the United States. The Annals of Baltimore note that on July 9, 1793, fifty-three vessels arrived at that port, bearing about one thousand whites and five hundred Negroes. [6] Unable to speak the English language, they were taken care of by the Sulpician Fathers of St. Mary's Seminary. Special services were held for the

---

[1] Shea, John G., *Life of Archbishop Carroll*, p. 257.
[2] *History of the Catholic Church in the U. S.*, op. cit., vol. III, p. 99.
[3] *cf.* Hughes, *History of the Society of Jesus in North America*, pp. 559-562.
  for description of the good treatment of the slaves.
[4] *Ibid.*, p. 564.
[5] *Ibid.*
[6] De Courcy, Henry, and Shea, John G., *Catholic Church in the U. S.*, p. 74.

Negroes, all of whom were Catholics,[1] in the chapel of the Seminary. By their constant solicitude for the welfare of the colored people of Baltimore, the Sulpician Fathers, though seminary professors by calling, have earned for themselves an enviable place in any history of Catholic missionary labors for the Negroes.[2]

In 1796, M. William Valentine Dubourg, afterwards Bishop of New Orleans, started a catechism class for the refugees. At his departure from Baltimore the work was taken over by M. Tessier, later second superior of the Sulpicians in the United States. The paternal care which Father Tessier gave to these colored refugees is one of his principal claims for immortality.

In 1810, when Father Tessier was elevated to the presidency of the Seminary, the work was handed over to Reverend James Hector Nicholas Joubert de la Muraille, more commonly known as Nicholas Joubert, who had only that year been ordained to the priesthood. Father Joubert had previously escaped from the uprising at San Domingo and had reached Baltimore in safety, where he studied for the priesthood. Such were the difficulties of catchising the Negroes that, with the consent of Father Tessier, he organized, in 1828, a little society of colored women to assist him in the work. The following year, 1829, they were officially established as a religious community—the Oblate Sisters of Providence. It is worthy of note that this event took place thirty-four years before the abolition of slavery.[3]

C. Louisiana

In the territory of Louisiana the work in behalf of the colored race was begun early in the eighteenth century, when the Jesuits devoted themselves especially to the care of the

[1] *Catholic Church in the U. S., op. cit.*, vol. III, p. 18.
[2] One of the few externs buried in the Sulpician graveyard at St. Mary's Seminary is Henrietta Blackstone, the faithful cook of the Seminary. Born a slave in 1807, she must have been freed before she came to the Seminary, because the wage paid her is recorded. When she died, the Sulpicians buried her as they did their other friends, near and with themselves and with all the honors of the Church. She died in 1903, at the age of 96.
[3] Herbermann, C. G., *The Sulpicians In The United States*, pp. 230-236.

Indians and the Negroes. In this section of the country the instruction and Christianizing of the Negroes was always facilitated by the liberal attitude of the French towards them. While the French were in control of Louisiana, the Code Noir, promulgated by M. Bienville in 1724, and in force until 1803, provided that masters should take their slaves to church and have them instructed and baptized in the Catholic religion.[1] The Code allowed the slaves time for their religious duties and rest, not only on Sundays, but on all the festivals of the Church, which at that time were more numerous than now.

The "Jesuit Relations" inform us of the care given to the welfare of the slaves by the Jesuits. Typical is the entry concerning the French village of Cascakias: the "Relations" note that the Fathers were very exact in the fulfillment of their duties, "to which must be added the instruction of the Negroes and savages, slaves of the French, to prepare them for Baptism and the reception of the other sacraments."[2] On Sundays and feasts the slaves were gathered together with the white settlers; the exercises opened with prayer, followed by spiritual reading, after which "two instructions in the catechism were given, one for the French children and the other for the black slaves and the savages."[3] If a large number of slaves was found in a community, they were given separate services and instructions.[4]

In the years following 1716, and especially after 1726, when the great demand for cheap labor was being met by the Law Company's large importation of slaves, the "Relations" give several instances of the instruction of slaves by French Catholics.[5] Le Petit wrote, in 1730, that he was "settled to the instruction of the boarders, the girls who live without, and the Negro women."[6] It is also noted that "the Jesuits had upon their estate a hundred and twenty or a

---

[1] For description of the treatment of slaves in a typical religious house, the Ursuline Convent, New Orleans, La., cf. *Catholic History of Alabama and the Floridas*, by a Member of the Order of Mercy, pp. 73-76.
[2] Vol. LXX, p. 233.
[3] *Ibid.*
[4] *Ibid.*, vol. V, p. 62.
[5] *Ibid.*, vol. LXVII, pp. 259, 343.
[6] *Ibid.*, vol. XLVIII, p. 201.

hundred and thirty slaves," and it is asked, "ought not the care of instructing and governing these give some of the missioners enough to do?"[1] In 1750, Father Vivier, S.J., wrote in the "Relations": "New Orleans is inhabited by French, Negroes and some savages (Indians) who are slaves; all these together do not, it seems to me, number more than twelve hundred persons."[2] It was the zeal of the Jesuit missioners in Louisiana, as we have previously noted, which forced non-Catholic denominations to find a way out of their scruples concerning the baptism of slaves, "lest the Catholics whom they derided as undesirable churchmen should put the Protestants to shame."[3]

After the revolution in San Domingo about two thousand Negroes fled to New Orleans. They spoke the French language, were Catholics, and some educated their children in France, the northern states, or in private schools at home. Thus there came to exist in New Orleans a colored society unlike any other in the country. Victor Sejour, a native quadroon of this settlement in New Orleans, later became private secretary of Louis Napoleon and a famous dramatic writer of Paris.

An event of more than ordinary interest at the close of this period was the founding of the Christian Doctrine Society of New Orleans. This society of colored people was founded in March of 1818 by Bishop Dubourg, and was specially privileged by two Popes. Little is known of the real founder except that he was a Capuchin Father. Attached to the Cathedral of St. Louis, the association at first admitted to membership only men; about half a century later, women were made eligible. At times the society has had as many as two hundred members.

The primary object of the society was promotion of the spiritual well-being of its members by the practice of good works and the development of Christian virtues. The second aim was to honor in a particular manner the Most Blessed Virgin, Mary, in her Immaculate Conception, and also to

---

[1] *Ibid.*, vol. LXX, p. 245.
[2] *Ibid.*, vol. LXIX, p. 211.
[3] Woodson, *op. cit.*, p. 42.

foster a particular devotion to St. Joseph and St. Louis. The third aim of the Society was to help its members to walk firmly in the path of virtue, aiding them to avoid all that is evil and offering them all possible aid and encouragement to progress in spiritual perfection; the practical work adopted as the means of furthering this object was the evangelization and spiritual care of the Negroes. As such, the Society is said to have been a powerful instrument. It is only of recent years that the Society has ceased to function.

D. Kentucky

In 1738 a movement to colonize the West spread over the Atlantic seaboard. From several parts of Maryland, Catholics had begun to move towards Kentucky as early as 1774. In 1785 twenty-five of a league of sixty families set out from St. Mary's County to settle on lands which they had taken up at Pottinger's Creek. The following year another party of Catholics settled at Hardin's Creek. In 1787 Bardstown was the home of another cluster. Nicholas Miles, whose son later became Bishop Miles, the Father of the Church in Tennessee, settled at Froman's Creek, about six miles northeast of Bardstown, in 1796. We are told that Miles took his slaves with him, a dozen or more, and it is not improbable that other settlers also had slaves. [1]

We are assured that the most cordial relations existed between masters and slaves in the Diocese of Louisville. "Many of the wealthier Catholics owned slaves who attended the mission with their masters, kneeling along side of them at the confessional and the altar rail to receive Holy Communion........ The pious custom of saying family prayers at morning and night existed very generally; and when the head of the house owned slaves they, too, were required to be present at these exercises. All knelt together in the same room and the father or mother of the family gave out the prayer and the others answered. Before or after these exercises the master would frequently enter into conversation with his slaves concerning the health of this one or the occu-

---

[1] O'Daniel, O.P., V.F., *The Father of the Church in Tennessee*, pp. 37, 39.

pation of another . . . Between Catholic master and slave there most generally existed real sympathy and affection." [1] Nor can we pass over in silence the admirable solicitude for the Negroes of such men as Badin, [2] Flaget, [3] and Nerinckx. [4] Father Nerinckx was the founder of the "Little Society of the Friends of Mary, Under the Cross of Jesus". This community of white sisters opened a school at Loretto, Ky., which "will become an asylum or shelter for old age, and decrepit and useless slaves". [5] As we shall see later, it was Father Nerinckx who gave the veil of religion to the first colored girls to enter a convent in the United States. [6] Bishop Miles too, while still a young priest stationed at St. Rose's Convent, Springfield, Ky., had a reputation for kindness to the Negroes, and he numbered among his penitents not a few colored people. [7] In 1833, when Kentucky was stricken by a terrible plague, of Father Miles it is writen that "the poor colored people were the objects of his special solicitude." [8]

E. Georgia and the Carolinas

Passing from Maryland, Louisana, and Kentucky, we leave behind us the only sections of the country in which Catholics had any influential status at all. Typical of the conditions which prevailed in non-Catholic settlements are those of Georgia and the Carolinas. In 1821, when Bishop England arrived at his See of Charleston, there were but a few hundred Catholics scattered over his entire ecclesiastical territory, which included both the Carolinas and Georgia; nearly all who had once been Catholics had abandoned the Faith. For a long time before this the Catholics of North and South Carolina, as also of Georgia, had but one priest—a native of France who had accompanied the San Domingan refugees

---

[1] *Records of the American Catholic Historical Society*, vol. XXV, no. 4, p. 341.
[2] Spalding, M. J., *Kentucky Sketches*, p. 116; *Life of Bishop Flaget*, p. 81.
[3] *Records of the American Catholic Historical Society*, Vol. XXXV, No. 2. pp. 114, 115; Spalding, *Life of Bishop Flaget*, pp. 108, 138, 276.
[4] Spalding, *Life of Bishop Flaget*, pp. 91, 93; *Kentucky Sketches*, p. 139.
[5] Maes, C. P., *Life of Rev. Charles Nerinckx*, p. 269.
[6] *Vide*, p. 135.
[7] O'Daniel, *op. cit.*, p. 160.
[8] *Ibid.*, p. 241.

in their flight. Nor could the Gospel be preached to the slaves who followed in the footsteps of their masters, embraced his religion if he had any, and dared not join any other church without his consent, which he was not likely to give as far as the Catholic Church was concerned. The slaves were "believed generally to be without souls; they were regarded as chattels......... As a necessary result their moral condition may be imagined but never can be described."[1]

In Georgia the slave holders almost to a man were Protestant. Though few in number, the Catholics did what they could for the Negroes. The few colored Catholics in the state were, in all probability, brought there by Catholic migrants from Maryland. The records of the Church of Georgia, which are in the possession of the Bishop of Savannah and date back to the year 1790, show that at that time an Abbe La Moine was pastor of a small band of Catholics at a place about fifty miles from Augusta: in Shea's History the place is called Maryland. A party of Catholics from Maryland had settled at locust Grove, Wilkes County, which is the location mentioned by Shea.[2] They must have had some slaves, the number of whom was augmented by the slaves brought from San Domingo by the French refugees. There were also some Catholics to be found at the settlements of Athens and Brunswick: mostly Irish from New York and French from San Domingo, who, no doubt, had a limited number of slaves.

Extant church records indicate the baptism of a number of slaves, some of whom were infants and children of larger growth. Occasionally these baptisms took place *en masse*, a priest being called to baptize twenty or thirty at a time. Usually the slaves were registered by their Christian names only, the name being written in the register with the name of the owner; care was always exercised to indicate whether the person was slave or free. The records of the marriages of slaves show that the dignity of the Sacrament of Matrimony was impressed upon their minds. Among the interesting entries made by a certain Rev. le Mercier is one of freeing the infant child of a slave in recognition of

---

[1] O'Connell, O.S.B., J.J., *Catholicity in the Carolinas and Georgia*, p. 44.
[2] *The Catholic Church in the United States, op. cit.*, vol. III, p. 195.

the faithful service of the mother. Notice of the emancipation
was made in the baptismal register at the request of a Mme.
de Prevot.[1]

The first item in the history of the Catholic Church in
the Carolinas is the tarring and feathering of two Irish
Catholics charged with the crime of tampering with the Negroes.[2] Some idea of the deplorable conditions under which
the slaves lived may be obtained from Carroll, the non-Catholic author of *Historical Collections of South Carolina*. After
referring to the inhuman treatment of the slaves under the
English, he writes thus of their spiritual condition: "One
thing is very certain, that the Negroes of that country, a few
excepted, are to this day as great strangers to Christianity,
and as much under the influence of pagan darkness, idolatry
and superstition, as they were at their first arrival from
Africa........ Masters of slaves under the French and
Spanish jurisdiction are obliged by law to allow them time
for instruction, and to bring them up in the knowledge and
practice of the Catholic Religion........ Even Catholics of
Spain pitied the condition of Negroes living among the Protestant colonies and, to induce them to revolt, proffered them
the advantages of liberty and religion at St. Augustine."[3]

The fact is slaves were forced to live under such terrible
conditions that the Catholics of St. Augustine did harbor
refugees, being careful, however, to give pecuniary recom-
pense to the English slave holders. Slaves thus rescued from
the cruel domination of the English colonists in Georgia formed an important item in the Catholicity of St. Augustine.[4]

[1] *Ibid.*
[2] O'Connell, *op. cit.*, p. 140.
[3] *Catholic Church in U. S.*, *op. cit.*, vol. III, p. 240.
[4] *Vide*, *Journal of Negro History*, vol. XII, no. 4, p. 666, *et sq.*, for an account of the Negro settlement at Mose. Among the principal grievances set forth in a report to the South Carolina House of Commons
on the Oglethorpe Expedition was the carrying off and harboring of
their slaves, of which a number of instances are enumerated. In
the seige of St. Augustine by Oglethorpe, "The Spanish authorities
of St. Augustine sent emissaries to the borders of Carolina to entice
away Negroes, promising them freedom and protection. Many Negroes had gone to them from time to time, a sufficient number, it
is said, to form a regiment which was placed on the same footing
as the Spanish regular."

F. Virginia

In Protestant Virginia, prior to 1776, the exercise of the Catholic religion was prohibited under severest penalties. As late as 1775, we are informed, a certain minister, Benjamin Fawcett by name, addressed the Christian Negroes of Virginia in the following strain: "Rejoice and be exceeding glad, that you are delivered either from the Frauds of Mohamet, or Pagan Darkness, and Worship of Daemons; and are not now taught to place your Dependence upon those other dead Men, whom the Papists impiously worship . . . Read and study the Bible for yourselves; and consider how Papists do all they can to hide it from their fellows...... You may perhaps be tempted very unjustly to renounce your Fidelity and Obedience to your Old Masters, in Hope of finding new ones, with whom you may live more happily. At one time or other it will probably be suggested to you that the French will make better Masters than the English. But I beseech you to consider that your Happiness as Men and Christians exceedingly depends upon your doing all in your Power to support the British Government, and that kind of Christianity which is called the Protestant Religion; and likewise in opposing, with all your might, the Power of the French, and the delusions of the Popish Priests, and all the Rage and Malice of such Indians as are of the French Interest." [1]

G. Alabama

Early in the History of Alabama appeared the Negro. In the early part of the eighteenth century Jean Chastang, a white French physician, lived on the Bluff now named after him, and there grew about him the colored Creole [2] settlement of Chastang, which to this day represents his family. A large tract of ground was granted to him and his two brothers by the Spanish Government. Jean Chastang married a slave; the other two brothers married white women. The doctor had his slaves instructed, and his whole family re-

---

[1] Woodson, *op. cit.*, pp. 351, 352.
[2] The word "Creole" has various interpretations in the South. As applied in this section of Alabama a Creole has some Negro blood.

mained true to the Church. Before the Civil War the Afro-Latin Creoles of this section of Alabama were highly respectable freeman, often owning slaves, as did the rich Negroes themselves, but socially keeping aloof from the Negro population.[1] Practically all these Creoles of Alabama, as well as their numerous slaves, were Catholics, but apart from these colored Catholics were few. Even to this day in Alabama a careful distinction is made between Negroes and Creoles, some missions finding it necessary to maintain separate schools for each group.

2. FROM 1829 TO 1866

Before this period there was no opposition to giving the Negro some kind of education. With the climax of the insurrectionary movement (about 1835) there was a reversal of attitude. The industrial revolution, consequent upon the introduction of improved methods in spinning and weaving, resulted in an increased demand for cotton fiber and gave rise to the plantation system in the South, with its consequent demand for a greater supply of slaves. With such change came the rise of the Abolition Movement and consequent uprisings among the Negroes. As a result, most southern people came to the conclusion it was impossible to cultivate the minds of the Negroes without arousing a dangerous self-assertion.[2]

A. Bishop England

John England, Bishop of Charleston, stands out prominently at this time as champion of the cause of the Negro; it is doubtful if the Negro in the United States ever had a greater and better friend than he. In an historical account of the Catholic Church in the United States, written in 1833, Bishop England stated that there were 40,000 slaves in the city of Charleston alone, and that of these only about 5,000 were Catholics.[3] Most of these slaves were from Maryland or

---

[1] A Catholic History of Alabama and Florida, by a Member of the Order of Mercy, p. 340.
[2] Woodson, op. cit., p. 2.
[3] Guilday, Ph.D., Rev. Peter, Life and Times of John England, vol. II, p. 191. The statistics of Bishop England have been seriously questioned.

San Domingo, or were descendants of such slaves. Of the plight of the Negroes and his plans for their betterment, Bishop England wrote in a letter to the Cardinal Prefect of Propaganda: "Its boundaries (the Diocese of Charleston) enclose nearly two million inhabitants, of whom about one half are Negro slaves. In all this population there are but little more than ten thousand Catholics...... Probably one thousand are slaves belonging to Protestant masters. For the Catholics are generally too poor to possess this or any other property...... About three years ago three women asked my permission to take religious vows. I encouraged them to form a congregation to instruct the black girls, as also the poor white girls........... I also wish to establish in my diocese a congregation of young men who, bound by religious vows and leading a community life under regular discipline, may attend to the instruction of poor boys, free and slaves, and teach them the ways of commerce and the industrial trades. [1]

In South Carolina the slave code forbade the teaching of slaves but permitted the education of the free Negroes. To stop the great leakage of free Catholic Negroes who lost their Catholic Faith while attending sectarian schools, Bishop England opened schools for them in Charleston. Since there were several other such church schools in the city he anticipated no trouble in this move. The attendance rapidly increased and was the means of bringing back to the Church not only many of the children but their parents as well. All seemed well when the flooding of Charleston with Abolition tracts so incensed a portion of the populace that a near-riot ensued. The outcome of the unfortunate misunderstanding was that Bishop England had to close his schools for the slaves. [2]

Of the conduct of Catholic slaves, Bishop England wrote in 1839: "Several of the Catholic slaves are extremely well instructed and pious; they are fond of entering little sodalities of devotion and of assembling in the afternoon in the church for prayer and singing; they also have a great charity in assisting each other in time of sickness and distress, not only

---

[1] *Ibid.*, vol. II, pp. 526-28.
[2] *Ibid.*, vol. II, p. 151, *et sq.; vide, infra*, p. 136.

with temporal aid if it be required, but by spiritual reading, prayer and consolation; they are exceedingly attentive to have the funeral of an associate respectably attended, and not only have the offices of the Church performed, but to continue the charity of prayer for a considerable time after death for the repose of the souls of their friends." [1]

O'Connell very aptly remarks by way of summation of England's devotion to the colored: "Missionaries from outside were not necessary to remind him of his duty to the slave. They were his first care, and their condition won not only his sympathy, but the tenderest solicitude of his administration; none since has accomplished so much for their salvation and the amelioration of their condition. He began to teach them and founded schools, one under a priest for the males, and the other for girls, under the care of the Sisters of Mercy. He was shortly compelled to desist and his efforts in this direction were blocked by legislation forbidding to teach Negroes to read and write, under severe penalties, apart from social ostracism. He arranged a separate service for the slaves, said Mass for them himself Sunday mornings at seven o'clock, and preached in the afternoons. In relation to similar duties he regarded them of primary importance and gave them the preference before all others." [2] It is related of Bishop England that he was accustomed to preach two Sunday afternoon sermons; if unable, however, to deliver both, he would disappoint the rich and cultured who flocked to hear him, and preach to the poor colored.

That Bishop England loved the slaves and worked energetically for their welfare is evident from numerous entries in his diurnal. Each year, in every town he visited, they were especial objects of his paternal solicitude. We quote a few instances, taken at random from many such: [3] "On this morning, after having attended a Culprit in the Negro conspiracy to execution, etc."........"Heard confessions and in the evening instructed the Negroes and heard confessions again"........"Baptized Anne, an adult slave or Mr. Brad-

---

[1] *Catholic Church in the United States, op. cit.*, vol. III, p. 129.
[2] O'Connell, *op. cit.*, p. 71.
[3] *Records of the American Catholic Historical Society for 1895.*

ford Thompson, her Sponsor, Anne, Slave of Mr. Thompson, Sr., and rehabilitated the marriage of that same woman with Edward, slave also of Mr. B. Thompson, it having been invalid on account of Cultus disparitas"........"Baptized Edward, a black child........I then baptized two black persons, Nathaniel and Mary, the first a slave of Squire ———, the second free........In the evening baptized three black adults........"Baptized....four Negroes belonging to Col. J. Creyon........Afterwards gave private instruction to a colored man, servant to Mr. Gaston"........Baptized Eliza Hanrehan an adult, and Abraham, a slave belonging to Mr. Gaston, and Anne Gillet, a child of seven years of age, the last two under condition"........"Gave some private instruction to two person of color."

B. Baltimore

At Baltimore, in the meantime, the little community of Oblate Sisters of Providence, which M. Joubert had founded, was prospering. After long trials the members of the community were permitted to take the vows of religion. Approved by Archbishop Whitfield, June 5, 1829, they were recognized by the Holy See on October 2, 1831, and thenceforth enjoyed all the privileges and indulgences accorded to the Oblates at Rome. "The Almighty has blessed the efforts of the worthy M. Joubert," wrote Rev. Mr. Odin, in 1834; "there are already twelve of these sisters; their school is very numerous, piety and fervor reign among them, and they render great services to religion." [1] The Sisters at that time had a girls' school with one hundred and thirty-five scholars, and a boys' school with fifty.

At this time the spiritual plight of the Negroes was giving cause for alarm; the clergy, however, was unable to cope with the work to be done. Successive Archbishops of Baltimore deplored their inability to undertake the evangelization of the colored as they would wish. "How distressing it is," wrote Archbishop Whitfield, in 1832, "to be unable to send missionaries to Virginia, where there are five hundred thousand Ne-

---

[1] De Courcy,-Shea, op. cit., p. 115.

groes. It is indubitable that had we missionaries and funds to support them, prodigies would be effected in this vast and untilled field. In Maryland blacks are converted every day, and many of them are good Catholics and excellent Christians. At Baltimore many are frequent communicants, and three hundred or four hundred receive the Blessed Sacrament the First Sunday of every month. It is the same throughout Maryland, where there are a great many Catholics among the Negroes." [1] In 1838, Archbishop Eccleston wrote: "The slaves present a vast and rich harvest to the apostolic laborer. I do not believe that there is in this country, without excepting the Indians, a class of men among whom it is possible to do more good. But far from being able to do what I would desire for the salvation of the unhappy Negroes, I see myself unable to meet the wants of the thousands of whites who, equally deprived of the succors of religion, feel most keenly their spiritual abandonment." [2]

Of the conditions at this time De Courcy has this to say: "This sad state of things has not ceased to exist, for the clergy are still too few to devote themselves especially to the conversion of the blacks. There are many Negro Catholics in Louisiana, Maryland, and New York, but in general it is the fanaticism of Wesley that is preached with success to the colored people, and a part of the slaves follow the superstitious practices of that sect, while a large number preserve the worship of Fetichism." [3]

C. Washington, D. C.

In the parish churches of Washington, D. C., the colored people were made to feel a real welcome. The Commissioner of Education [4] gives glowing encomium to the Catholic Church which "was as free in all its privileges to the black worshipper as to the white, and in the sanctuary there was no black gallery . . . . The colored people in those days, in all the Catholic Churches, not only knelt side by side with

---

[1] *Ibid.*, p. 116.
[2] *Ibid.*
[3] *Ibid.*, p. 116.
[4] *Special Report of the United States Commissioner of Education, 1871,* p. 218.

the highest personages, but the pews were also free to all
. . . this (impartiality) has been the general treatment
which the colored people have received from the Catholic
Church, the cases in which a priest has attempted to make a
distinction having been very few and exceptional."

Conditions were so in St. Patrick's Church, under its
founder, Father Matthew (1804-1854), "who recognized the
poorest and most benighted Negro of his parish as inferior
to none in all the privileges and duties of the church." Father
John Donelan, the first pastor of St. Matthew's Church, was
equally impartial. The Rev. Leonard Neale, later Archbishop
of Baltimore, with his brother, Rev. Francis Neale, the
founder and first pastor of Holy Trinity Church, and Father
Van Lommel are also mentioned by the Commissioner of Education, as being "friends of the poor, showing no distinction
on account of color."[1]

At St. Aloysius', the last church to be built before the
Civil War, the colored people held pews on the same floor with
the whites, and there was a large free female colored school
in the parochial school building connected with the church.
At St. Mary's Church, Alexandria, Va., the same spirit was
manifested, the colored people occupying the same floor and
the free pews with the whites without discrimination. The
parochial instruction in the parish churches always embraced
the colored children.

When the colored people were excluded from all the
Protestant churches of the District in the years of the mobs,
the Catholic people stood firm, allowing no molestation of
their colored worshippers. When the Sunday schools were
broken up in every Protestant Church in the District, every
Catholic Church steadily retained its colored children under
the usual Sunday instruction, and these schools embraced all
ages.

D.   First Church for Negroes

Of special interest is the beginning of the Church of St.
Francis Xavier, Baltimore, Md., the first Catholic Church in
the United States for the exclusive use of Negroes. In the

---
[1] *Ibid.*, p. 217.

year 1859, when the country was wrestling with the problem
of secession, the Rev. Peter L. Miller, S.J., was called to
Baltimore to labor among the colored people of that city.
The whole priestly life of Father Miller, extending over a
period of nearly thirty years, was spent in arduous labor
among the colored people of Maryland, chiefly in Baltimore.
His first charge was among the colored people in the vicinity
of Loyola College. There his work was somewhat limited, and
he was assigned to the counties of Maryland which offered a
wider field for his activity. For a time Father Miller labored
with his confreres in the counties of Frederick and St. Mary.

Eventually, the basement of St. Ignatius' Church, in Baltimore, was remodelled and converted into a chapel for the use
of colored people who had previously attended St. Mary's
Seminary Chapel. It was placed under the patronage of
Blessed Peter Claver. Father Miller was recalled to Baltimore and appointed pastor. With the pastorate went the
chaplaincy of St. Francis' Convent and School, then the
motherhouse of the flourishing community of the Oblate Sisters; the Sulpician Fathers, in accordance with their policy
of disembarrassing the Society of St. Sulpice of extraneous
works had previously given over the direction of the convent
and school to the Jesuits. In a short time Father Miller added
an orphanage to the school. It soon became apparent that a
more spacious church was needed for the rapidly growing
congregation of Blessed Peter Claver's Chapel. Enlisting the
influence of the saintly Bishop O'Connor, who had resigned
the See of Pittsburgh to join the Jesuits, and who now begged
from door to door for money with which to secure a larger
church, an historic old building at the corner of Calvert and
Pleasant Streets was purchased in 1863. This building stands
even to this day as the Church of St. Francis Xavier, and
was the first Catholic Church in the United States officially
and exclusively for the use of the colored people.

E. Other Places

In 1842, Bishop Blanc, of New Orleans, who was deeply
concerned over the wants of the colored people, together with
Father Etienne Rousselon, his Vicar-General, founded the Sis-

ters of the Holy Family, a community of colored sisters whose duty was to care for colored orphans and the aged colored poor. This was the second community of colored sisters founded in the United States before the Civil War.[1]

The first Catholic slave to be brought to Richmond, Va., was taken there from Baltimore in 1846.[2] The following year (1847) Bishop Miles, of Tennessee, in a letter to Propaganda notes that among other works being carried on in his Diocese of Nashville there was a free school for Negroes (opened probably 1840).[3] There are evidences also that there were some Catholic Negroes in Boston, New York,[4] and New Jersey. At Philadelphia, in old St. Joseph's Church, from very early times a number of colored people formed a regular part of the congregation. At the Jesuit Church in St. Louis, Mo., the colored also formed part of the congregation. This was true, too, of the congregation of St. Ann, in Cincinnati, Ohio.

Such was the condition of the colored missionary work in the United States at the outbreak of the Civil War. Of individual interest and zeal for the evangelization of the Negro there is no end of evidence; and this was the sole effort possible previous to the formation of the American Hierarchy in 1808.

---

[1] *Vide,* p. 140.
[2] *Colored Harvest, 1889,* p. 6, gives an interesting account of this slave girl.
[3] O'Daniel, *op. cit.,* p. 423.
[4] Vide, *The Trial of John Ury,* published by M. J. Griffin, Phila., 1899.

CHAPTER III

AFTER THE CIVIL WAR

1. FROM 1866 TO 1871

A. Emancipation

On the afternoon of New Year's Day, 1863, after the
official reception was over, President Lincoln returned to the
Executive Chamber, unfolded upon his desk the manuscript
of the Proclamation of Emancipation, and took up a pen to
sign it.

"Seward," said he, to his secretary, "I have been shaking
hands with people for three mortal hours and my hand trembles. If it trembles when I sign this they will say that I
was afraid to sign it." He laid down the pen. In memory
he went back to September twenty-second of the year just
past. The President had then given to the war-cleft nation
the first monitory proclamation of emancipation to all slaves
within the borders of the states in secession.

"I made a vow to my God," said Lincoln at that time,
"that if Lee were driven back from Maryland, I would issue
this proclamation and not delay it any longer." Two days
previously the battle of Antietam had been written into history, and Lee had retreated across the Potomac into Virginia.
Picking up the pen which he had laid down, Lincoln signed
the document before him.

With the passage of the Thirteenth Amendment and the
subsequent Fourteenth and Fifteenth, it may be said that
never before in the history of mankind had four million slaves,
whose ancestors in former generations had been the children of
ignorance and superstition, received in so short a time the
privileges of citizens, become equal before the law, and entitled
to all the rights, duties, and responsibilities of freemen. Yet,
during the long years of the disgraceful Reconstruction Pe-

32

riod the condition of the Negroes may be said to have been truly deplorable: little attention was paid to their material welfare and less to their spiritual.

B. Effect on Church

The vast majority of slaves had been held in the Protestant sections of the South where the Catholic Church had but meagre opportunity for contact with them. After the war some few Catholic bishops made zealous efforts to spread the elevating influence of the Church among the colored people, but they were rendered helpless by the lack of priests and scarcity of money.

It is now quite generally agreed that while the emancipation was in one sense a great boon to the colored people, the manner in which the majority of them were thrown into an entirely different mode of life caused great evils. It has been said that if Lincoln had lived he would have worked out his plan with greater good to all concerned; as it was, the emancipation came so suddenly that the Negroes were totally unprepared for it. As for Catholic Negroes, there was no one to supply the steadying influence formerly exerted by Catholic masters and mistresses. True, the church was still there, but gone were the masters who saw to it that attendance was regular. The new-found freedom was too much; colored Catholics fell away by the thousands and either joined mere social organizations or formed separate religious organizations with their own church buildings and preachers.

Of the four million slaves in the United States at the time of the emancipation, probably not more than five per cent, certainly less than ten per cent, had Catholic masters.[1] With some notable exceptions,[2] Protestant slaveholders had not been over-zealous about the religious training of their slaves, despite the fact that there were numerous mission organizations in the field. Even making due allowance for the number of slaves who belonged to non-Catholic denominations, the greater number were not bap-

[1] Butsch, S.S.J., Rev. Joseph, "Negro Catholics in the United States," *The Catholic Historical Review*, April, 1917, p. 36.
[2] Woodson, *op. cit.*, pp. 185-194.

tized and had little or no religious training. The same might be said of the free Negro population, which at the time numbered about 500,000.[1]

In the years following the war but a few zealous priests were devoting their time to the colored people. These priests adhered to the idea that the Negro should be educated to grasp the meaning of the Catholic doctrines. Even where a priest was found willing to care for the colored, the work was so different from that in which he had been engaged previously that but meagre success could be realized. The clergy and people did some good work among the Negroes in the cities and at first with a fair degree of success, but at this time the Protestant denominations were fully awakened to the harvest to be reaped among the liberated slaves. Numerous mission organizations were in the field, organizations which had many advantages that the Catholic Church did not have: much money was at their command and they had the advantage of being able to turn out missionaries at a much faster rate than Catholics could educate priests. The Negro preacher of little education had no place in the Catholic Church, and since there was better prospect for promotion in the Baptist and Methodist Churches, to these they went, and with them went the majority of their people.

C. Opposition

The first real stimulus to the religious training of the Negro came from the North. The earliest missionary endeavor began in Virginia in 1861, when the American Missionary Association established Sabbath Schools for Negroes. The New England Freedmen's Aid Society, the Friends, the Con-

---

[1] Among the free Negroes of the South a certain number were planters and slave-holders. Some of these were wealthy. Four or five of them in Louisiana, in 1852, were said to be worth between four and five thousand dollars. Others were small traders, peddlers, blacksmiths, etc. In some of the older cities of the South, like Charleston, S. C., there was a little aristocracy of free Negroes who counted several generations of free ancestors, and who, because of their industry, thrift and good reputation among their white neighbors, enjoyed privileges and immunities not granted to other free Negroes of the South.

gregationalists, the Free Will Baptists, the Presbyterians, as well as other church organizations were soon in the field, first establishing schools and later churches.

Before the close of 1866, the Colored Baptist Churches of the South had formed a number of associations which put themselves in connection with the Northern Baptists. In the American Baptist (African) Missionary Convention which met in Richmond three years after the emancipation nearly all the southern states were represented. Within a few years practically all Negroes had withdrawn from the white churches and numerous denominations entirely free from white control were formed.[1] These newly formed organizations claimed thousands of Negroes who had been Catholics while in slavery, but who found the ways of freedom inconsistent with Catholic morality, or who simply drifted away because there were no priests to care for them as had their Catholic owners. **1479143**

Even what work the Catholic Church could do was strongly opposed by all Protestant denominations. In Alabama, for instance, Fleming notes, in *The Civil War and Reconstruction in Alabama*, that the Catholic Church was opposed "especially by the Northern Methodist Church. It seemed to be dreadful news to the Methodists when it was reported that the Catholic Church was about to open fifteen schools in Alabama for the Negro, where free board and tuition would be given. The American Missionary Association, supported in Alabama mainly by money from the Freedmen's Bureau, used its influence among the Negroes against the Catholic Church, which, the Association stated in a report, 'was making extraordinary efforts to enshroud forever this class of the unfortunate race in Popish superstition and darkness.' "[2]

In 1867, the American Missionary Association in Virginia expressed the fear that the "splendors" of the Catholic Church would appeal to the Negro's "love of display." According to the report of the Association for 1867, the "man of sai" had

---

[1] McConnell, *op. cit.*, pp. 108-9.
[2] p. 646.

already discovered and entered the promising field.[1] In 1872, the Rev. W. B. Derrick, speaking before the Virginia Conference of the A. M. E. Church, offered a resolution condemning the efforts and the means used by the Roman Catholic Church to proselyte the Negroes, and admonished the latter to have nothing to do with Catholicism.[2]

D. Catholic Reaction

Small wonder that the Second Plenary Council of Baltimore, in 1866, had wrung from its heart the pathetic appeal which it couched in the following heart-rending terms: "By the bowels of the mercy of God, we beg and implore priests, as far as they can, to consecrate their thoughts, their time, and themselves wholly and entirely, if possible, to the service of the colored people." "Four million of these unfortunate beings," wrote Archbishop Spalding at the time, "are thrown on our charity, and they silently and eloquently appeal to us for help. We have a golden opportunity to reap a harvest of souls, which neglected may not return." The Third Plenary Council, in 1884, going a step farther, urged on the superiors of seminaries to foster vocations for this mission and ordered that a special annual collection be taken up for the Negro and Indian missions.

In the latter part of 1871, Father Vaughan, later Cardinal, came to America and made a tour through the southern states, everywhere eagerly seeking information on the condition of the colored. He carefully noted down his observations and conclusions. What he saw filled him with pity and compassion. For ignorance and spiritual desolation he was prepared, but it came as a shock to find out how little was being done for the Negro, and how far he seemed to be left outside the area of philanthropic and religious effort. His biographer, Sneed Cox, has this to say: "He now visited all the great centers, and his notebooks show with what great care he collected information as to both the spiritual and temporal conditions of the Negroes in every place he stayed. He quickly

---

[1] *The Journal of Negro History*, vol. XI, no. 3, p. 429.
[2] *Ibid.*

found that slavery had left the Negroes in absolute ignorance of even the elements of Christianity. . . . From the local clergy he appears to have got a somewhat mixed reception. Many of them who worked unceasingly among the whites, regarded the blacks as hopeless, or at any rate outside their sphere of labor. . . . In Memphis he notes: 'Negroes regarded even by priests as so many dogs. . . . I visited the hospital where there were a number of Negroes. Talked to many in it and in the street. All said they had no religion. Never baptized. All said either they would like to be Catholics or something to show that they were not opposed to it. Neither the priest with me nor the Sisters in the hospital do anything to instruct them. They just smile at them as if they had no souls.' " [1]

The deplorable desolation of the large Negro population was epitomized by the Rt. Rev. J. J. Kain, Bishop of Wheeling, West Virginia, when he wrote: "It is an object of deepest concern to all the bishops of the South, on whom mainly rests the duty of providing these millions of souls with the means of attaining a knowledge of our holy religion. Many difficulties must be met and overcome . . . Little progress can be made until separate churches and schools are provided for them, and until men, endowed with the apostolic spirit and familiar with the Negro character, are especially trained for this missionary field." Priests were the crying need of the day, but hardly enough priests were had to keep up the already established work of the dioceses in the South. The Rt. Rev. F. Janssens, then Bishop of Natchez, later Archbishop of New Orleans, voiced this need: "Our priests everywhere in the southern states are devoted to their duty, and willing, too, to work for the colored people as well as for the white. But the work for the one and for the other is quite different, and it is almost impossible to do much good for the salvation of the Negro whilst engaged in the ministry for the whites. Again, all the southern dioceses stand greatly in need of priests to keep up the work that has already been established and needs to be continued. Consequently, it is next to impos-

---

[1] *Life of Cardinal Vaughan*, vol. I, pp. 170, 171.

sible to obtain priests willing, and possessing the necessary requisites, to devote themselves to this peculiar work." [1]

E. Catholic Activities

Of Catholic colored mission work between the emancipation and the coming of the Josephites from Mill Hill, England, we are in much the same ignorance as was the editor of *St. Joseph's Advocate*, the official organ of the English Josephite Fathers. In its first issue, in 1883, Father Green, the editor, wrote: "Who will enlighten us on the work and workers in this special and rugged corner of the vineyard prior to our coming? How gladly would we 'give Caesar his due,' and how becoming would the credits look, passing to the hands of strange and interested successors? All we can be sure of is that the deepest interest in the spiritual well-being of the colored people was manifested by individual ecclesiastics, both religious and secular, for many long years anterior to our advent. Here and now were we to enter into particulars and give names, we would only show our ignorance and run the risk of wounding susceptibilities as much, perhaps, by omission as by assertion, more especially to the honored dead." If one so near to that period felt the inadequacy of the facts at hand for an accurate enumeration of activities, the difficulties are not lessened by the passage of more than fifty years. Speaking in general terms, Jesuits, Redemptorists, Sulpicians, and Seculars may be named as local apostles to the colored people, but only as individuals, not as communities.

Besides the Church of St. Francis in Baltimore, there were several others throughout the country, given over to the exclusive use of the colored people.

In Charleston, S. C., sections of the old Cathedral, St. Mary's, and St. Patrick's had been reserved for the special use of the colored. Bishop Lynch purchased a building, formerly a synagogue, in Wentworth Street, and set it apart for the exclusive use of the colored people of the city in 1867. It was placed under the patronage of St. Peter Claver.

---

[1] *Report of the Commission for Catholic Missions Among the Colored People and Indians*, 1889.

St. Augustine's Church in Washington, D. C., owes its origin to the efforts of Rev. Charles White, D.D., pastor of St. Matthew's Church, who started the parish in 1863. A frame building used as a schoolhouse served also as a chapel where Mass was offered under the patronage of Blessed Martin de Porras, a colored saint of the Dominican Order. The number of colored Catholics rapidly increasing, in 1874, a new church was erected and dedicated under the patronage of the great African Bishop, St. Augustine.

In 1869, St. Augustine's Church, Louisville, Ky., situated on 14th Street and Broadway, was erected with a special view to the needs of the colored Catholics. Rev. John L. Spalding, later Bishop of Peoria, was named pastor. On each Sunday and holyday of obligation two services took place in it: one for the colored people for whom it had been built, and one for the white Catholics living in the neighborhood. This arrangement lasted until the following year when the Church of the Sacred Heart was opened for the white people.

A half dozen churches represented the exclusively colored parishes in the United States when, in 1871, the first four Josephite Fathers arrived in Baltimore from Mill Hill, England.

2. ARRIVAL OF JOSEPHITE FATHERS, 1871 TO 1900

Doctor Guilday, in "The Catholic Question in the United States," notes that: "In spite of its (the Catholic Church's) admirable record in certain localities for the amelioration of the social and moral conditions of the slaves, the first organized effort in the United States to win the souls of the colored people after the Civil War was carried out by the priests of Mill Hill who came here from England in 1871. It was twenty-one years later (1892) before the American Church accepted the whole burden of the spiritual welfare of our colored citizens through the establishment of the Society of St. Joseph." [1]

A. First Organized Effort

The event referred to by Doctor Guilday is the coming of the first four missioners from Mill Hill, England, the first

---

[1] Article XXV.

fruits of the missionary society which five years previously Doctor Herbert Vaughan had founded. In the autumn of 1871, the little society had assigned to it by the Holy See its first sphere of work. Early in the year, Doctor Vaughan, having four priests ordained, went to Rome where, prostrating himself at the feet of Pius IX, he offered his little band to whatever mission His Holiness would assign to them. The decrees of the Second Plenary Council of Baltimore had but lately been approved by Rome. The Council had spoken in most moving terms of the condition of the Negroes in the United States and had appealed for priests to devote themselves exclusively to that neglected race. By the command of Pius IX, Doctor Vaughan communicated with Archbishop Spalding of Baltimore. The result was that in November of 1871 Father Vaughan in company with Fathers Cornelius Dowling, James Noonan, Joseph Gore, and Charles Vigeront sailed from Southampton for Baltimore, where they arrived in December. The first missioners who left Mill Hill were four in number; the vow by which they consecrated their lives may well have recalled the memory of Peter Claver— they had vowed themselves forever to the service of the Negro race.

The little party met with a very friendly reception in Baltimore, and the Archbishop placed at their disposal St. Francis Xavier's Church, which up to that time had been in charge of the Jesuits. This church had been erected for Protestant service in 1836, and had a notable local history: for a time it was used for political conventions; in 1844 Henry Clay was there nominated for the Presidency; during the Civil War a convention was held there for the purpose of deciding whether or not the State of Maryland would secede— it is related that while the convention was in session, the United States soldiers surrounded the church and marched off to Fort McHenry, as prisoners of war, the assembled delegates.

Up to 1887 aspirants for the Negro missions in the new Society of St. Joseph were obliged to go to Mill Hill, England, where the Josephite Fathers had their house of studies. Sending students to England was an expensive and indirect way of reaching the colored population of America; hence, in 1887, by the joint action of Cardinal Gibbons and Bishop Vaughan, then Superior-General of the missionaries, it was resolved to open St. Joseph's Seminary in Baltimore, Md. The old Western Maryland Hotel, Pennsylvania Avenue and St. Mary's Street, was purchased, fitted up, and opened in 1888, with four seminarians. The following year Epiphany Apostolic College was opened at Walbrook, a suburb of Baltimore, with an enrolment of 35 preparatory students. Since then both of these institutions have prospered.

In October, 1872, the Society of the Holy Ghost sent several Fathers from Europe to this country to establish an agricultural and industrial school in the Diocese of Covington, Ky. Unfavorable circumstances retarded the work, and the Fathers were compelled to abandon the undertaking.[1] In 1878 establishments were opened in the Diocese of Little Rock, Ark., to provide for the spiritual needs of immigrants and Negroes. In 1889 the Fathers were called to Philadelphia to do missionary work for the Negroes of that city. In 1895 they accepted the chaplaincy of St. Emma's Industrial and Agricultural School, Rock Castle, Va., which had been opened the previous year.

In 1874, the Benedictine Fathers came to Charleston, S. C., and devoted themselves to the care of the colored. Two priests, Rev. Gabriel Bergier, O.S.B., from France, and Rev. Raphael Wissel, O.S.B., from Italy, collected a congregation of colored people, erected a little frame church at Harris and East Broad Streets, and opened a parish school. When the epidemic of yellow fever broke out in 1876, the community falling victim to the plague, the church was handed over to a secular priest, Father Eckert. Later, in 1877, the Benedictines from St. Vincent's Abbey, Pa., erected a monastery on Skidaway Island, N. C., and in connection with it opened an industrial school for colored boys. This was abandoned in 1887. A small wooden church for the use of the colored people was then built and used until 1890, when a new church, the Church of St. Benedict the Moor, was built for them.

---

[1] *The Catholic Church in the United States, op. cit.,* vol. I, p. 402.

B. The Situation

At the time of the establishment of the American Josephites, (1893) the number of Catholic churches for the colored did not exceed twenty in the whole United States. They formed, as it were, a circle around the old slave states. While the churches in Richmond and Norfolk, Va., Louisville, Ky., and Charleston, S. C., were the only missions in the heart of the South, still there were many congregations in the South composed largely of colored Catholics. Eight of the twenty exclusively colored churches were in charge of the Josephite Fathers; the Benedictine Fathers had several missions under their care and owned the Islands of Hope and Skidaway, North Carolina, by deed in trust for the purpose of educating the colored youth; the Jesuit Fathers were also laboring for the colored in the counties of Maryland, in St. Louis, Mo., in Macon and Augusta, Georgia.

In New Orleans there were 160,000 Negroes, nearly all baptized Catholics, but for various reasons the majority of them had been lost to the Church. Of the 650,000 Negroes in Virginia, only about 500 were Catholics. Of the 650,000 in the Diocese of Mobile, Ala., about 2,500 were Catholics, but these were fast losing the Faith because there were no priests to care for them. In the State of Florida there were 1,200 colored Catholics among a population of 150,000 Negroes. The Bishop of Nashville, Tenn., had to report only 30 colored Catholics out of a total of 400,000 Negroes in his diocese. Other dioceses of the South had much the same sad story to tell.

Usually the school was the first part of the mission unit to be built, the mustard seed, as it were, from which a colored mission would grow. There were at this time nearly a hundred Catholic schools for colored children in the 18 dioceses of the South. In those schools were sisters belonging to the communities of the Holy Ghost, St. Francis, St. Dominic, St. Benedict, Sisters of Mercy, of Charity, of St. Joseph, and of the Sacred Heart, as also the two colored sisterhoods: the Oblates, of Baltimore, and the Sisters of the Holy Family, of New Orleans. To these, as always, must be added the humble country schools conducted by Catholic teachers, chiefly where Religious could not be procured.

C. Important Foundations

The need of an organized national effort to preserve the Faith among the Catholic Negroes and Indians had been voiced by the American Bishops at the Second Plenary Council. It was, however, the Third Plenary Council, in 1884, which actually effected the constitution of a permanent Commission for this object. According to its plan, the Commission was to consist of a Board of Directors composed of three members of the Hierarchy, assisted by a secretary. Its funds were to be derived from an annual collection which the Bishops of the Council ordered to be taken up in every church in the United States on the first Sunday of Lent. These acts of the Council were formally approved by the Holy See, and the Commission, known as "The Commission for Catholic Missions Among the Colored People and the Indians," began to function immediately.

The decree of the Council reads as follows: "Let a special collection be taken up in every diocese of this country on the First Sunday of Lent of each year, and let the proceeds thereof be sent to the Commission which is to be established for these domestic (i. e., Negro and Indian) missions. The distribution of this is to be effected in the following way: The money, which is derived from this collection in the case of dioceses wherein the Society for the Propagation of the Faith already exists, is to be expended by the Commission in the interest of the missions among the Indians and the Negroes."[1] The Commission, of which Rev. J. B. Tennelly, S.S., D.D., is Secretary, still functions; its headquarters are in Washington, D. C.

As far back as 1879 Cardinal Vaughan had proposed that the American Province of the Society of St. Joseph be erected into a distinct society. It was felt that such a move would facilitate the work of the missions. The Cardinal saw the need of a special community for the Negro work in America, a community which would draw vocations from this country. He urged a separation again in 1889 in a public letter to the Bishops then assembled in Baltimore for the centennial of the

---

[1] *Decreta*, Tit. VIII, Cap. II.

American Hierarchy. In May, 1893, with the approbation of both Cardinal Vaughan and Cardinal Gibbons, the final separation was made. Since then St. Joseph's Society of the Sacred Heart (commonly known as "St. Joseph's Society for Colored Missions") has grown exceedingly, and the evolution of the Negro Missions has been healthy. It has always been felt that the salvation of the American Negro is a distinctly American problem and that America can look after the Negroes within its borders; at present there is every hope that America will prove true to its trust.

Another important development in this period of organization was the founding, in 1889, of the Sisters of the Blessed Sacrament, by Miss Katharine Drexel, at Philadelphia, Pa. The purpose of this community is missionary work among the Indians and the Negroes of the United States. Formal approbation of the Holy See was given to the congregation in 1907.

The Rt. Rev. James O'Connor, Bishop of Omaha, acting in conjunction with Miss Drexel, decided with the approval of Most Rev. P. J. Ryan, Archbishop of Philadelphia, to form a new congregation of religious women devoted exclusively to missionary work among the Indians and Negroes. For some years previous to this step, Miss Drexel had been very active in re-establishing and supporting many schools in Indian reservations; the greater portion of the income which she had derived from her father's estate was used in maintaining and furthering these charitable projects. At this period a survey of the field revealed about 250,000 Indians neglected and over 9,000,000 Negroes still trying to find their bearings after the Civil War.

With the approval of Church authorities, Miss Drexel gathered around her young women imbued with the same ideas as she had concerning the care of these neglected people and founded, towards the close of 1889, the nucleus of the new community. The first members made a novitiate of two years with the Sisters of Mercy, after which they continued their period of preparation in the old Drexel homestead, Torresdale, near Philadelphia. Early in 1892, a motherhouse and novitiate was opened at Maud, Pa., near which was erected a manual training and boarding school for colored boys and girls.

The Congregation of the Sisters of the Blessed Sacrament has prospered since its foundation and has exerted tremendous influence in the work of the Colored Missions. [1]

In 1906, at the request of His Holiness, Pope Pius X, of saintly memory, the Archbishops of the country met with Cardinal Gibbons to devise a project whereby additional funds might be raised for the support of the Negro Missions of the South. The annual collection for the Indian and Negro missions was recognized to be insufficient: individual missions were receiving as little as $100, and some nothing at all. Several years earlier the danger to the Indian Missions had been seen and attended to by the establishment of the Catholic Indian Bureau, with headquarters in Washington, D. C. In 1907, Cardinal Gibbons launched the Catholic Board for Mission Work among the Colored People, incorporated under the laws of the State of Tennessee and having for its purpose: "To create and foster the missionary spirit among Catholics and others in favor of the colored people; to preach on this subject in churches and elsewhere; to distribute literature and form associations in aid of the work." Associated with Cardinal Gibbons, President of the Mission Board, were three archbishops and three bishops. Father John Burke, pastor of St. Benedict the Moor's Church, New York City, was chosen as Director General of the newly established Mission Board, and national headquarters were opened in New York City. This Board is solely a collecting agency and has no official connection with any missionary organization in the field.

---

[1] The introduction of other Sisterhoods into the work of the Negro Missions will be noted in subsequent pages.

PART II—PRESENT CONDITIONS

During the past few decades, and despite adverse conditions, considerable progress has been made in the field of Catholic colored missionary endeavor. A most important phase of this progress is the improved and constantly improving means provided for the care of colored Catholics. Today a superior type of colored Catholic is being developed in our churches and schools; their spiritual needs are better provided for than they were forty years ago. At that time, very many were undoubtedly uninstructed, careless, and merely nominal Catholics; the inadequacy of religious facilities and subsequent apostasies show this must have been the case. Today the Catholic Church and its schools are in closer contact with the larger part of Catholic Negroes, the legitimate inference from which is that there must be a great religious improvement, taking Negro Catholics as a body.

Of course, some portions of the mission field have for natural reasons developed more rapidly than others. These can now be regarded as centers of permanent and successful missionary activity. Baltimore, Md., and New Orleans, La., are two such centers, with others, like Mobile, Ala., rapidly coming to the fore. Such centers are evidences of the stability of the work as a whole, and their importance cannot be overestimated.

Until recent years it has not been possible to plan for more than what might be regarded as the bed rock of the mission— its church and school. It has been recognized that other activities and institutions are necessary, but owing to lack of men and funds it has not been within the power of those concerned to build up that extensive system which in more fortunate Catholic situations includes a number of houses devoted to charitable purposes and opportunities to pursue higher education. The priests of the missions have met these obligations so far as they could, but conditions over which they have no control necessarily limit their activities along these lines.

CHAPTER IV

SURVEY OF COLORED CATHOLICS

In this survey, a summary of which immediately follows,
an attempt is made to expose in a brief way the relation of
Catholic religious work to the present condition of the colored
race so as to help in the adjustment of the activities of the
Church to present conditions.

1. NATIONAL CENSUS OF COLORED CATHOLICS

A census of colored Catholics in the United States, cov-
ering every diocese in the country, shows that of the 11,600,-
000 Negroes in the United States only 203,986 belong to the
Catholic Church. This is the first time that a national census
of colored Catholics in the United States has been taken. Previous figures were estimates based upon the Catholic colored
population of those states in which colored mission work was
being done; their inadequacy lies in the fact that they do not
cover the whole ground.

To obtain an accurate enumeration of colored Catholics
would necessitate taking a census in each of the eighteen thousand parishes and missions in the United States. Owing to
present conditions this is manifestly impossible. While a
large number of colored people live in colored parishes and
have their own churches, many others are scattered among the
whites in widely separated parishes where no report is ever
made of the color of members.

In gathering data for our census the Hierarchy of the
United States was appealed to as being most conversant with
conditions in the different dioceses and, therefore, the most
reliable source of information. A letter was sent to each
member of the Hierarchy explaining the purpose of the census and requesting actual or approximate statistics as regards
colored Catholics in each diocese.

About fifty per cent of the Hierarchy, including the most
important dioceses, returned accurate information represent-

ing an actual enumeration of colored Catholics. The others, due mostly to lack of distinction between the whites and the colored in annual reports, could give only approximate figures, but the approximations are as reliable as a census would be since they represent careful estimates. In a few instances the bishops may have been over-generous in their estimates. It is known that others under-estimated the number: such bishops returned figures based on actual count of those attending church, leaving no margin for careless Catholics. The few over-statements offset the under-estimates, so that, on the whole, the results may be considered accurate. The figures herein given may then be taken as the first, official, national census of colored Catholics in the United States January 1, 1928.

Tables 1 and 2 give a summary of results obtained according to archdioceses and dioceses, and the distribution of colored Catholics by sections and states:

TABLE 1. CATHOLIC COLORED POPULATION BY ARCHDIOCESES AND DIOCESES.

ARCHDIOCESES:

Baltimore, Md.	21,927
Boston, Mass.	1,000
Chicago, Ill.	4,000
Cincinnati, Ohio	1,200
Dubuque, Iowa	12
Milwaukee, Wis.	300
New Orleans, La.	35,000 [1]
New York, N. Y.	13,800
Oregon City, Ore.	25
Philadelphia, Pa.	3,000
St. Louis, Mo.	3,000
St. Paul, Minn.	655
San Antonio, Tex.	590
Santa Fe, New Mexico	0
San Francisco, Cal.	1,250

DIOCESES:

Amarillo, Tex.	0
Albany, N. Y.	250
Alexandria, La.	6,258
Altoona, Pa.	30
Baker City, Ore.	6
Belleville, Ill.	200
Bismark, N. Dak.	10
Boise, Idaho	0
Brooklyn, N. Y.	12,000 [2]
Buffalo, N. Y.	250
Burlington, Vt.	0
Charleston, S. Car.	487
Cheyenne, Wyo.	10
Cleveland, Ohio	852
Columbus, Ohio	200
Concordia, Kan.	0
Corpus Christi, Tex.	100
Covington, Ky.	125
Crookston, Minn.	0
Dallas, Tex.	314
Davenport, Iowa	6
Denver, Colo.	900

[1] This estimate would seem to be low, especially if it be compared with that of Lafayette; exclusively colored churches in the Archdiocese of New Orleans account for 34,000.
[2] This estimate is not excessive if it be remembered that 90 per cent of the Negroes in Brooklyn are West Indians, a majority of whom are nominally Catholics.

TABLE 1. CATHOLIC COLORED POPULATION BY ARCHDIOCESES
AND DIOCESES—*Continued*

Des Moines, Iowa	20	Omaha, Neb.	283
Detroit, Mich.	1,100	Peoria, Ill.	25
Duluth, Minn.	50	Pittsburgh, Pa.	1,350
El Paso, Tex.	12	Portland, Maine	0
Erie, Pa.	25	Providence, R. I.	100
Fall River, Mass.	0 [1]	Raleigh, N. Car.	362
Fargo, N. Dak.	0	Richmond, Va.	2,048
Fort Wayne, Ind.	137	Rochester, N. Y.	50
Galveston, Tex.	6,843	Rockford, Ill.	0
Grand Island, Neb.	0	Sacramento, Cal.	150
Grand Rapids, Mich.	60	St. Augustine, Fla.	1,894
Great Falls, Mont.	12	St. Cloud, Minn.	15
Green Bay, Wis.	0	St. Joseph, Mo.	107
Harrisburg, Pa.	158	Salt Lake, Utah	0
Hartford, Conn.	500	Savannah, Ga.	1,300
Helena, Mont.	0	Scranton, Pa.	40
Indianapolis, Ind.	500	Seattle, Wash.	0
Kansas City, Mo.	800	Sioux City, Iowa	25
La Crosse, Wis.	50	Sioux Falls, S. Dak.	0
Lafayette, La.	60,000	Spokane, Wash.	10
Lead, S. Dak.	0	Springfield, Ill.	250
Leavenworth, Kans.	350	Springfield, Mass.	75
Lincoln, Neb.	4	Superior, Wis.	25
Little Rock, Ark.	481	Syracuse, N. Y.	64
Los Angeles, Cal.	2,500	Toledo, Ohio	250
Louisville, Ky.	2,300	Trenton, N. J.	964
Manchester, N. Hamp.	0	Tucson, Ariz.	2
Marquette, Mich.	40	Wheeling, W. Va.	100
Mobile, Ala.	4,200 [2]	Wichita, Kans.	100
Monterey-Fresno, Cal.	0	Wilmington, Del.	292 [3]
Nashville, Tenn.	627	Winona, Minn.	0
Natchez, Miss.	3,582	Belmont Abbey, N. Car.	150
Newark, N. J.	900		
Ogdensburg, N. Y.	0	TOTAL	203,986
Oklahoma, Okla.	959		

[1] In the Diocese of Fall River there are about 4,000 Catholic "bravas",
but these are not "Negroes", strictly speaking.
[2] Mobile includes western Florida.
[3] Includes Eastern shores of Maryland and Virginia.

TABLE 2. CATHOLIC COLORED POPULATION BY
SECTIONS AND STATES

GEOGRAPHIC DIVISIONS:
New England 1,675
Middle Atlantic 32,881
East North Central...... 9,189
West North Central 5,437
South Atlantic 29,526
East South Central 9,768
West South Central 110,545
Mountain 999
Pacific 3,866

TOTAL 203,986

THE NORTH:
New England States:
Maine 0
New Hampshire 0
Vermont 0
Massachusetts 1,075
Rhode Island 100
Connecticut 500

1,675

Middle Atlantic States:
New York 26,414
New Jersey 1,864
Pennsylvania 4,603

32,881.

East North Central States:
Ohio 2,502
Indiana 637
Illinois 4,475
Michigan 1,200
Wisconsin 375

9,189

West North Central States:
Minnesota 720
Iowa 63
Missouri 3,907
North Dakota 10
South Dakota 0
Nebraska 287
Kansas 450

5,437

Total for North.......49,182

THE SOUTH:
South Atlantic States:
Delaware 292
Maryland and the
Dist. of Columbia..21,927
Virginia 2,048
West Virginia 100
North Carolina 512
South Carolina...... 487
Georgia 1,300
Florida 2,860

29,526

East South Central States:
Kentucky 2,425
Tennessee 627
Alabama 3,134
Mississippi 3,582

9,768

West South Central States:
Arkansas 481
Louisiana 101,258
Oklahoma 959
Texas 7,847

110,545

Total for South......149,939

THE WEST:
Mountain States:
Montana 12
Idaho 0
Wyoming 10
Colorado 900
New Mexico 0
Arizona 2
Utah 0
Nevada 75

999

Pacific States:
California 3,825
Oregon 31
Washington 10

3,866

Total for West 4,865

2. DISTRIBUTION OF COLORED CATHOLICS IN RELATION TO POPULATION

In table 3 figures are given for the various elements in those states in which there is some exclusively colored missionary activity. The total population and the colored population for 1928 were computed from the Government census for 1920 and, where available, the state censuses for 1925; the calculations were made only after having taken into consideration the increase or decrease indicated in the Government reports for the past three decennial censuses. In all but a few instances the percentage of Negroes in the total population of southern states is growing less each decade. The figures here given are, perhaps, in several instances, slightly less than they actually should be, the benefit of the doubt having been given to the state so as not to seem to over-rate the Negro problem. The figures for the total number of Catholics are taken from the Official Catholic Directory for the year 1928, while the total number of colored Catholics is computed from the returns made in answer to the questionnaire sent to each member of the Hierarchy.

In the last column of the table each state is given a rating based upon the number of colored Catholics there should be in the state if Negroes belonged to the Catholic Church in the same proportion as they form part of the total population of the state. The State of Mississippi, for instance, is fifty per cent colored. Manifestly, then, half of the Catholic activities in the state should be for Negroes, and, proportionately, half the Catholics in the state, or 12,867, should be Negroes. As a matter of fact, there are only 3,582 Negro Catholics in the state. The proportion between what would be a perfect distribution and what is the actual distribution is: $12,867:100\%$ :: $3,582:27.8\%$. This rating is, of course, a bare statement of the proportion of colored Catholics in a state in relation to the total population, the total Catholic population, and the colored population; it does not take into consideration the difficulties affecting the work of the missions.

TABLE 3.—DISTRIBUTION OF COLORED CATHOLICS IN
RELATION TO POPULATION

	Estimated Total Population, 1928	Estimated Total Colored Population, 1928	Total Catholic Population, 1928	Total Catholic Colored Population, 1928	Colored Catholicity Average
States with 40 per cent or over of population colored:					
Mississippi	1,790,618	895,309	25,725	3,582	27.8
South Carolina	1,863,300	894,384	9,520	487	10.6
Georgia	3,185,716	1,274,286	18,700	1,300	17.3
States with 30 to 40 per cent of population colored:					
Louisiana	1,907,333	667,566	569,297	101,258	50.8
Alabama	2,657,615	930,165	43,019	3,134	19.6
Florida	1,440,593	460,989	56,425	2,860	17.3
States with 20 to 30 per cent of population colored:					
North Carolina	2,878,948	777,315	7,365	512	25.7
Arkansas	1,913,948	516,765	26,319	481	6.7
Virginia	2,533,596	658,734	44,363	2,048	17.8
Dist. Columbia	534,107	122,844	59,098	9,880	69.0
States with 10 to 20 per cent of population colored:					
Tennessee	2,476,654	421,031	25,725	627	14.3
Maryland	1,589,536	238,430	245,043	12,067	34.2
Texas	5,198,214	675,767	611,810	7,847	9.8
Delaware	241,278	28,953	32,255	292	6.9
States with 2 to 10 per cent of population colored:					
Kentucky	2,531,496	177,204	177,964	2,425	19.4
Oklahoma	2,346,688	164,268	54,990	959	24.9
W. Virginia ...	1,684,547	107,072	63,944	100	2.6
Missouri	3,504,417	270,265	565,393	3,907	11.5
New Jersey	3,716,743	148,669	935,027	1,864	49.8
Ohio	6,658,826	266,353	1,065,879	2,502	5.8
Illinois	7,252,752	253,846	1,495,763	4.425	8.4
Pennsylvania ..	9,676,225	290,568	1,908,301	4,603	8.0
Kansas	2,468,921	74,067	182,018	450	8.2
Indiana	3,138,432	94,152	208,777	637	10.7
New York	11,628,272	232,565	3,262,652	26,414	40.4
States with less than 2 per cent of population colored:					
California	4,377,995	65,669	700,370	3,825	36.4
Michigan	4,446,348	72,522	853,483	1,200	8.9
Massachusetts .	4,611,325	52,538	1,638,669	1,075	5.6
Nebraska	1,390,772	14,186	154,716	287	18.2
Minnesota	2,669,405	10,320	482,731	720	38.0

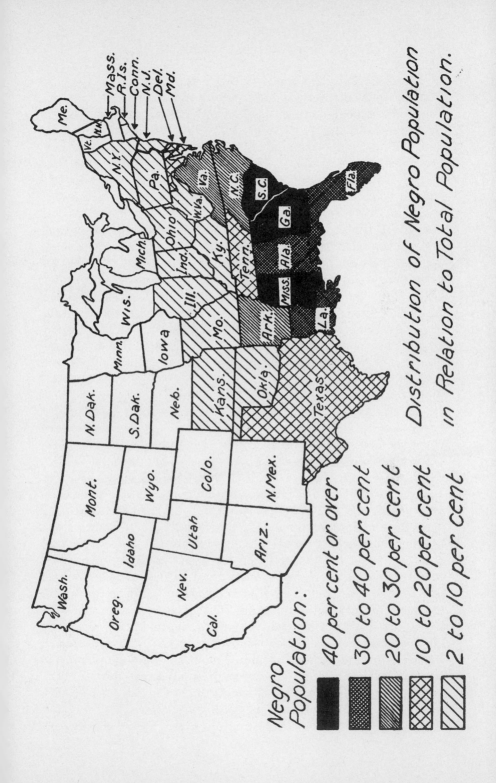

Distribution of Negro Population in Relation to Total Population.

Negro Population:

- 40 per cent or over
- 30 to 40 per cent
- 20 to 30 per cent
- 10 to 20 per cent
- 2 to 10 per cent

The 1920 Federal Census found that out of a total population of approximately 106,000,000 in the forty-eight states, nearly 10,500,000 were classed as "Negroes," that is, people having more or less African blood in their veins. Recent estimations place this figure at 11,600,000. One finds that they are largely concentrated in the South: in 1920 nearly 9,000,000 of the 10,500,000 Negroes in the United States lived in the sixteen southern and eastern states of Delaware, Maryland, Virginia, West Virginia, North and South Carolina, Georgia, Florida, Kentucky, Tennessee, Alabama, Mississippi, Arkansas, Louisiana, Oklahoma, Texas, and the District of Columbia.

The map on page 53 shows how, in 1920, the Negro population compared with the total population of each state. Some importance must be attached to these ratios because they go a long way towards explaining differences in interracial attitudes between the North and South. In the North, where the Negro forms but a slight fraction of the total population, the problems of race relations are necessarily different from what they are in the South where the two groups are more nearly equal.

As a consequence of this distribution of the colored population in the United States, Catholic colored missionary activity is necessarily concentrated in the South. Catholic Negroes live chiefly in those states originally settled in part by Catholics; the larger number dwell in Maryland and the states on the Gulf of Mexico, especially the State of Louisiana. With the exception of Maryland, the southern parts of Louisiana and Alabama, and a small part of Florida, all the southern states are predominantly Protestant. Even along the Gulf Coast the majority of towns which have sprung up in recent years are largely Protestant. An average of little less than six per cent is all that the Catholic Church can claim of the total population of the South: half of the southern states are less than two per cent Catholic; and four, less than one per cent. It is a well known fact that these southern states, with the exceptions noted, are not only non-Catholic but are anti-Catholic. Under such a handicap the work of converting the Negro race to the Catholic Church of necessity is extremely slow and fraught with difficulties.

It is not surprising, in view of what has been said, to find that less than half of the entire colored population of the United States has any church affiliation whatsoever, and it is not without its significance that ninety-eight per cent of the total Negro population does not and never did belong to the Catholic Church. Of denominations exclusively colored, in 1906, there were 2,311,172 members enrolled in Baptist Church bodies; 869,710, in Methodist Church bodies; and 24,165, in other church bodies. In 1916, there were 2,967,085 in Baptist Church bodies; 1,077,324 in Methodist Church bodies, and 38,869 enrolled in other Negro church bodies. Incomplete United States Census figures for 1926 show that in the South alone there were 20,093 Negro Baptist churches, with a membership of 2,700,575. There were 5,601 African Methodist Episcopal churches with a membership of 430,086. The Colored Methodist Episcopal Church had 2,148 churches and a membership of 180,637, while the African Episcopal Zion Church had 2,125 churches and 370,222 members.

Of Negro members in communions having mixed membership, in 1906, Baptist bodies enrolled 43,617 members; Methodist bodies enrolled 312,421; and other bodies enrolled 83,507 members. In 1916 mixed Baptist bodies enrolled 53,842 Negro members; Methodist bodies, 323,713; and other mixed bodies enrolled 103,216 Negroes.

Not only are the Negroes concentrated in the South, but they are concentrated in the rural areas. Two-thirds of all the Negroes in the United States live outside of cities, while in the South this ratio is three out of four; in 1920, no fewer than 6,660,000 Negroes out of the total of 10,500,000 lived in the rural areas of the South. In contrast it is found that relatively few Negroes live in the rural areas of the North: in 1920, the rural Negro population living in northern and western states was 242,396, or only one out of every six. This situation finds the Catholic Church at a disadvantage: it is unable to supply a ministry to innumerable little towns and villages because requirements for the priesthood are very high and apply universally. Unlike many Protestant denominations, the Catholic Church does not find it advisable to send even to rural missions men of little or no training. The fact

that no particular standard of training is required by some of
the evangelical religious bodies enables them to have a minister wherever he is able to eke out an existence; that most of
these ministers are unlettered does not prevent some of them
from being "powerful preachers." In the Catholic Church
conditions are such that even where a priest is assigned to
such a rural charge his work covers such a large territory
that it is well nigh impossible to do anything like efficient
work.   Father Sabino Grossi, S.S.J., for instance, has to cover
a territory of some 2,500 square miles, which technically is
his mission territory of Chastang, Ala.   Within this same
territory there are at least twenty-five ministers engaged in
preaching.   Obviously one missioner is unable to cope success-
fully with such situations.

The recent migration has considerably modified the distribution of America's Negro population.   This migration is
usually thought of as a movement from the South to the
North.   This view is only partially correct.   It is correct in
the sense that during the decade between 1910 and 1920 the
Negro population in cities of the North and West increased
from 830,000 to 1,309,000, or by nearly 480,000.   Since during this decade the total increase in the Negro population in
cities was less than 900,000, it follows that more than
half the Negroes who moved to cities entered northern
cities.   Of equal importance, however, is the fact that during
this same decade the Negro population of southern cities increased by approximately 400,000.   Furthermore, as compared with the number of Negroes who left the South, there
were 1,063,332 Negroes who migrated from one southern
state to another.[1]   In many respects, therefore, it is more
correct to consider the migratory movement as being fom rural
to urban locations rather than as being from South to North.
In 1920, Negro city-dwellers numbered 3,500,000; recent official statistics estimate the number to have increased to
4,000,000, whereas, in 1900, the urban Negro population was
a little over the two million mark.   This would indicate that
during the past quarter of a century the urban Negro pop-

---

[1] *Census, 1920*, Vol. II, p. 623.

ulation of the United States has actually doubled. The scarcity of anything like a sufficient number of Catholic missioners to take care of all the Negroes in the United States makes imperative a continuance of the present policy of concentrating our meagre forces on city work. The above observations prove the wisdom of this procedure.

3. SUMMARY OF SURVEY OF EXCLUSIVELY COLORED CATHOLIC CHURCHES

The general plan adopted for the collection of parish and mission statistics in this survey was that of correspondence with individual priests and sisters engaged in the work, together with such assistance from the Hierarchy and superiors of societies engaged in the work as was deemed necessary and they were willing to give.

In carrying out this plan it was necessary to secure a list, as complete as possible by name and location, of individual parishes, missions, schools, and institutions; for this the religious superiors were chiefly relied upon. For the parishes and missions attended by secular priests, the Official Catholic Directory (1928) was consulted and some information obtained from it. The Directory, it is to be noted, is not exhaustive so far as exclusively colored churches are concerned; some churches which are known to be for Negroes are not so listed in the Directory. In an effort to make the list as complete as possible, the personal acquaintance of missionaries was relied upon, chancery offices written to, and numerous mission periodicals consulted.

With this list as a basis, a questionnaire with a letter of explanation was sent to the pastor of each church and mission. When the letter was returned unclaimed, or no reply was received within a reasonable period of time, other means varying according to circumstances were employed to reach the missionary. In some cases as many as five letters were necessary before a reply was received. If all means failed to elicit a reply such statistics as were available from other sources were accepted and the churches are so listed.

To insure accuracy all items of information contained in

the questionnaires were examined as to consistency and fullness of report. Where necessary, correspondence was carried on with those making incomplete or inaccurate report. Where accurate information could not be obtained such fact is noted. [1]

It is most important to bear in mind that this survey does not represent all the work that the Catholic Church is doing for the colored people of the United States. It is, however, a fair compilation of what is being done in exclusively colored parishes, missions, schools, and institutions. Throughout the South practically every white parish has its quota of colored members. The same is true for many churches in the North. [2]

---

[1] The religious census taken by the Government in 1926, is not yet completed and will not be published for some time to come. The general census taken in 1930 will not be available until about 1934. cf. tables 6 and 7, pp. 61, 62.

[2] Schools and charitable institutions will be reported in their respective places.

Indies. In the Archdiocese of New York there are only two churches listed as exclusively colored: St. Benedict the Moor's and St. Mark's. In the Harlem section of New York it is understood that the white parishes are to care for the colored people living within their boundaries. A very large number of colored people in Harlem attend the Churches of St. Aloysius, Resurrection, St. Thomas, St. Charles, All Saints, and Our Lady of the Miraculous Medal, the last named church being attended by a great many people from Porto Rico and other Spanish-speaking countries.

The State of Arizona with a colored population forming three per cent of its total population has no colored Catholics to speak of and no missionary activity at all in behalf of the 13,500 Negroes living in the State.

TABLE 6. SUMMARY OF GOVERNMENT STATISTICS
1926 SURVEY; CATHOLIC NEGRO WORK

| UNITED STATES | Total of Churches (1) | Number of Members | | Value of Church Edifices | | | Expenditures during year | Sunday School Attendance |
		Total	Average per Church	Number reporting	Amount	Average per Church		
Total..........	147	124,324	846	126	$4,667,378	$37,838	$1,005,645	11,406
Urban........	117	106,839	913	101	4,484,128	44,397	946,469	10,736
Rural.........	30	17,485	595	25	183,250	7,330	59,176	670
Alabama........	13	2,361	184	12	176,150	14,689	61,104	327
Arkansas........	3	347	116	2	34,000	17,000	24,521	......
Dist. of Columbia	7	9,893	1,270	7	964,000	123,428	102,117	1,370
Florida...........	6	1,657	276	6	95,500	15,917	20,979	510
Georgia.........	5	1,203	241	5	118,200	23,640	22,193	558
Kentucky.......	4	2,068	517	3	98,000	32,666	19,330	50
Louisiana........	35	61,615	1,757	29	768,150	26,488	243,669	3,427
Maryland.......	5	7,520	1,504	5	286,500	57,300	42,597	629
Mississippi......	10	2,956	295	9	111,000	12,222	50,723	415
Missouri........	3	1,272	424	2	47,000	23,500	13,695	195
New York.......	4	10,805	2,701	4	420,000	105,000	131,591	510
North Carolina...	5	676	135	5	139,600	27,920	17,893	411
Ohio............	4	1,411	358	3	457,000	152,500	29,772	587
Oklahoma.......	8	1,100	137	7	20,200	2,886	5,511	104
Pennsylvania....	5	3,095	613	3	140,000	46,666	43,573	438
Tennessee.......	4	661	165	1	25,000	25,000	4,878	86
Texas..........	9	6,120	680	9	191,500	21,278	26,605	1,139
Virginia.........	4	1,172	293	2	68,677	34,339	31,350	207
Other States (2)..	13	8,392	645	11	606,901	55,173	113,544	443

(1) Includes parish churches and mission churches.
(2) Includes Delaware 1, Illinois 2, Indiana 1, Kansas 2, Michigan 2, Minnesota 1, Nebraska 1, South Carolina 2, and Wisconsin 1, to avoid disclosing the statistics of individual churches.

TABLE 7.—NUMBER OF CHURCHES, MEMBERSHIP, VALUE OF
EDIFICES, DEBT ON EDIFICES, VALUE OF PARSONAGES, AND
NUMBER OF SUNDAY SCHOOL SCHOLARS, FOR URBAN AND
RURAL COMMUNITIES, OF THE UNITED STATES, FOR
1926; WITH COMPARATIVE FIGURES FOR 1916 AND 1906.
CATHOLIC NEGRO WORK.

ITEM	1926	1916	1906
Number of Churches [1]	147	83	36
Urban	117		
Rural	30		
Members	124,324	51,688	44,922
Urban	106,839		
Rural	17,485		
Value of Edifices	$4,667,378	$1,173,372	$678,480
Urban	$4,484,128		
Rural	183,250		
Debt on Edifices	$851,461	$182,400	$75,650
Urban	$843,711		
Rural	7,750		
Value of Parsonages	$879,906	$273,550	$109,400
Urban	$843,906		
Rural	36,000		
Number of Sunday School Scholars	11,406	9,655	3,151
Urban	10,736		
Rural	670		

[1] Includes mission churches.

During April of 1929 a National Catholic Welfare Conference news article made the rounds of many papers. The
item was captioned "Colored Catholics More Than Triple In
Two Decades." The article in question stated that there were
147 separate local organizations with a membership of 124,324
colored Catholics. It noted, too, that in 1906 the number of
colored Catholics was 44,882, and in 1916 it had grown to
51,688. The conclusion was deduced that the present number
of colored Catholics represent an increase of 140 per cent
within the last decade. This conclusion would be welcome
news were it true. Unfortunately, it is not true.

The article was originally prepared by a former Negro
employee of the Bureau of Census at Washington, who now

conducts the "Capital News Service" for his own race. The statistics were compiled by the Bureau of Census, Department of Commerce, Washington, D. C.

Concerning the 1926 Government statistics for Negro Catholics, two facts are important. The first is that the figure for colored Catholics in exclusively colored parishes, as supplied by the Bureau, is the first for colored Catholics ever procured by the Bureau with any degree of accuracy. After vainly trying to secure from various sources a complete list of exclusively colored Catholic congregations in the United States, the Bureau of Census sent a representative to St. Joseph's Seminary, Baltimore, Md. A complete and accurate list of churches for the exclusive use of Negroes was forthwith compiled and sent to Washington. This entailed some fifty corrections of and additions to the list originally possessed by the Bureau. With its aid, however, the Bureau was enabled to secure an accurate census. Allowing for a difference of a few thousand, the figure 124,324 may then be accepted as accurate for Negroes *attending exclusively colored churches.* [1]

The misleading conclusion arising from the news article is due to the fact that a comparison of this accurate figure was made with the previous decennial statistics which were woefully false. Had those who were engaged in missionary labors among the Negroes been so disposed, they might have seized upon the publicity value which such a misleading conclusion seemed to warrant. They know, however, that the previous statistics on colored Catholics which have been issued by the Government are open to question, and have only been allowed to stand because the missioners have not been in possession of official data with which to substantiate any correction. This erroneous impression concerning their missionary success must not be allowed to prevail, or they will be faced with an embarrassing situation ten years hence when they will be called upon to explain an apparent lack of progress.

The second point essential to a proper understanding of

---

[1] *Cf.* Table 4.

the Government statistics on colored Catholics is that colored Catholics do not all belong to the race churches. The first official census of colored Catholics in the United States which is given in preceding pages shows that of the 11,600,000 Negroes in the United States 204,000 claim membership in the Catholic Church.

By chance the previous figures, which were based upon the Catholic colored population of those states in which missionary work was being done, were fairly accurate; ranging as they did between 200,000 and 300,000. Their lack of authority lay in the fact that they did not cover the whole ground.

Attention is here called to the fact that unless the Bureau of Census makes note of the foregoing corrections (and attention has been called to them) the usual decennial comparisons which will appear in the as yet unpublished statistics on colored Catholics are liable to misinterpretation. This is one case where facts without explanations are positively misleading.

4. DISTRIBUTION BY SEX

There were 110,271 members of exclusively colored congregations reported. Of this number 45,284, or 41 per cent, are men, while 64,987, or 59 per cent, are women. The reported proportion for the Roman Catholic denomination (1926) was: male, 44.9; female, 55.1. This would indicate that the Church does not make a normal impression on the Negro men. On the other hand, however, the Catholic Church has more than the average of Negro women.

5. CONVERTS AND BAPTISMS

There were 2,386 converts reported for last year (1927). This is a remarkably large number if one considers the difficulties of convert-making among the colored people. The true index to any Catholic progress, however, be it missionary or parochial, is the number of baptisms reported. In view of this fact it is very enlightening to note that during the past year (1927) a total of 6,133 baptisms has been reported by the missioners. During the past ten years (1918-1928), 47,999

Baptisms and Converts (Josephite Missions, 1913-1928)

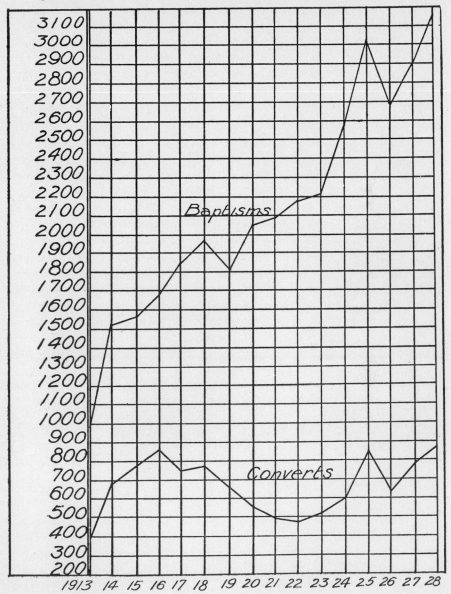

baptisms have been registered. If we could add to this number the fallen-away Catholics who have been reclaimed the number would be much larger; reclamation work is just as arduous work as is convert-making, in many cases, more so.

Taking the Josephite missions as a cross section of the mission field, it is interesting to study the graph on page 65. It will be noted that beginning with the year 1916 and up to the year 1923 the number of converts fell off considerably. There was a corresponding decline, though not so great, in the number of baptisms.

Migration accounts for this. During this period of decline there was as much missionary effort put forth as in previous years, yet the result was anything but encouraging. Practically all the missions suffered, some so much so that their abandonment was seriously considered. In 1923 the urge to migrate had spent itself and a certain permanency of dwelling on the part of the people permitted the missioner to make some progress in the work of conversion. The slump in 1926 cannot be accounted for with satisfaction. It simply denotes a period of depression such as occasionally occurs in the business world when for no apparent reason the results are not in proportion to the effort expended. The same condition is often noticed in particular missions where the increase and decrease in the number of converts and baptisms would seem to move in cycles.

CHAPTER V

EXCLUSIVELY COLORED CHURCHES

1. SUMMARY

At the present time, 47,000 churches are maintained by Negroes, with 5,000,000 communicants, and 46,000 Sunday schools are being conducted with 3,000,000 pupils. These churches contribute $350,000 annually for home missions and $200,000 for foreign missions. They support 200 missionaries. The total value of Negro church property amounts to $100,000,000.[1]

In the United States there are 121 exclusively colored Catholic parish churches,[2] 55 exclusively colored missions, and a dozen or more mission stations where Mass is said occasionally. Chaplaincies are attached to several of the parishes. Exclusively colored missionary work is being carried on in 29 states and the District of Columbia, 46 archdioceses and dioceses, and one abbatia.

Of the exclusively colored parishes, 95 are in the Southern States, nine in the Middle Atlantic States, nine in the East North Central group, while the other eight are scattered. Of the 55 missions, 50 are in the South and one is in the State of Missouri: these are missions properly so called, each having at least a church building. Of the other four missions, three are exclusively colored parishes in the process of formation: Albany, N. Y.,[3] Atlantic City, N. J., and Toledo, Ohio. In Boston the colored people have a special Mass in one of the white churches, this being counted as a mission.

---

[1] *Survey of Negro Colleges & Universities*, Bureau of Ed., Section of Bulletin, 1928, No. 7, p. 1.
[2] Since the completion of this survey, new missions have been opened at Cairo and Peoria, Ill.; Dayton, Ohio; Fort Worth and Washington, Texas; Gary and South Bend, Ind.; Greensboro and Raleigh, N. Car.; Cote d'Afrique and Franklin, La.; Maysville, Ala.
[3] Since built.

2. NECESSITY AND ADVANTAGES

Until the beginning of the twentieth century work on the Colored Missions was hard and success was limited. All effort previous to this was spent on organization. Though auspiciously started, Negro missionary work made little progress, owing to the almost universal custom of forcing the colored people to attend white churches. There, with notably few exceptions, they were given a minimum of attention and were usually assigned a few rear pews totally inadequate for their numbers. All church activities were for the white portion of the congregation only: the church societies admitted white members only, and the sermons were suited only for the more intelligent whites. Usually, the colored portion of the congregation was looked upon as intruders, to be tolerated; wherefore, the Negro, like other backward races, being sensitive of the treatment accorded to members of his race, did not dare to venture where he perceived that he was not welcome. One church for both white and colored people may be necessary and satisfactory where there are a few Negroes, but where the colored population is numerous it is a matter of experience that separate churches are needed.

In many places, even at this advanced stage of the work, the colored are still relegated to an inadequate number of rear pews. Though the priest may be zealous and fair-minded, there is likely to be a class of people in the congregation who resent what they deem to be an intrusion of the colored element. Discrimination and prejudice may then arise. Recently, a missioner from the South related an incident which, though possibly extreme, indicates the feeling still prevalent in sections of the South. He was assigned a mission church which had been built by the colored for their own exclusive use. Owing to circumstances, the white people attended the church and in the course of time had segregated the colored people in a few rear pews in the church. The first Sunday the priest attended the mission, he was waited on after Mass by a delegation of white people. The delegation informed him they did not oppose the colored people attending Mass in the church, but they did object to the Negroes receiving Holy Communion with them. And this in the Negroes' own church!

Experience has amply demonstrated the need and advisability of churches which the colored people can call their own. Without gainsaying the fact that it were better for both races to worship in unison, under the existing social order it is evident that this ideal is not realizable. The Catholic Church is not committed to the policy of separatism, but were a missioner to remain loyal to the best interests of both races, he cannot with safety ignore present racial antipathies and consequent demands for separation. "True friends of the race," observes Doctor Edward Murphy, S.S.J., "would not be false in pointing out to the Negro that even the artificial color line, however sketchy its excuses, has its compensations. It gives a concrete expression to the exclusiveness which a dusky people feels no less than a light. Even if there were no color line, paradoxically, there would still be one. If the whites did not make it the colored themselves likely would." [1] Educated Negroes realize that races separate themselves automatically and that "the fairest, kindliest sentiments in our land cannot erase the differences between black and white, or ignore them without stultification."

At the same time, separate churches are not unmitigated evils. They have their advantages. In the first place, they impose responsibility upon the Negro. No longer a camp follower, the Negro is called upon to exercise leadership in various parish organizations, an opportunity of no little value in race development. Hitherto a subordinate, dependent worshipper in white churches, he is raised to a position of independence in his own church, and therewith is presented a golden opportunity to make of himself a self-reliant man, confident, proud with the pride that comes from doing. As a consequence, leadership is fostered.

Education is best imparted in churches set apart for the use of the colored. Indeed, only where the pastor is entirely devoted to the needs of his colored flock is a decent Catholic education imparted. Elsewhere it is neglected altogether or is very limited. When recent Negro migrants had been well instructed in their Faith there was little fear that they would lose it in seeking a new abode. Migration of well instructed

---

[1] *Commonweal*, January 9, 1929, p. 286.

Negroes spreads the Faith as Christianity was spread in the early days of the Church by the migratory habits of many Christian Romans. Only when Catholic training and education were superficial, either because of neglect or recentness of conversion, was the danger of perversion very great.

More widespread employment of Negroes is a not insignificant consequence of separate churches. Whenever possible, insistence is laid upon the employment of Negroes in the construction, repairs and alterations of churches, schools, convents and rectories belonging to colored congregations. Moreover, colored people are employed about the plant: teachers, housekeepers, sextons, and other help are drawn from the colored race. In some instances, pastors, through their kindly interest, have succeeded in establishing some of their people in business. In this way racial prosperity has slightly increased.

In churches for the use of Negroes there exists an outlet for the talent of the race. Hitherto unsuspected musical powers come to light in the choir, while parish plays, debates, concerts, musical organizations, etc., reveal and foster latent native ability. Father Vincent Warren, S.S.J., has a band for boys and one for girls in connection with his school of Saint Joseph, Norfolk, Va. A few years ago he took the boys' band to Atlantic City, N. J., where in competition with forty bands, some composed of professional musicians, first prize was awarded to Father Warren's boys. Incidentally, Father Warren used his band as a wedge for entrance into non-Catholic rural sections. He advertises a concert; when all have enjoyed the music he takes advantage of the opportunity to address his audience on the Catholic Church and its doctrines. It was on such an occasion that Father Warren was kidnapped by the Ku Klux Klan a few years ago.

In the South the social life of the Negroes is generally centered around the church. The various services, societies, social affairs, and entertainments bring together the members of the parish who, under ordinary circumstances, would remain strangers to one another. Every missioner longs for the day when his mission plant will include a Catholic club wherein the young men and girls of the parish may be brought together in a wholesome atmosphere favorable to Catholic marriages.

Separate churches have won back to the fold many who had left because they could not brook entering houses of worship where they had to accept the indignity of inferiority. Of their own churches the Negroes can say: "These are our own churches; in them we can sit anywhere without fear of a hand being placed upon our shoulder, and of a voice warning us to get back where we belong, back to the rear." Thousands at present attend their duties who would not do so were they compelled to attend white churches. Not long ago a mission was given by way of opening a colored parish on the Gulf Coast. On one day alone, Holy Communion was given to five hundred and forty-five adults. Tears flowed freely from the eyes of many of the women folk; tears of joy at seeing so many of the men receiving Holy Communion after years of neglect. Wives and daughters had long since given up hope of ever again seeing their husbands and fathers approach the altar rail.

In another city where formerly there was no separate church for Negroes, many of them seldom attended services because of prevailing unpleasant conditions. They were, consequently, unknown to one another. When a church was opened, services and social functions brought together several thousands of the faithful and formed them into a powerful body for the first time conscious of its size and strength. A prominent member of this church remarked that until the beginning of the parish he never realized the vast number of colored Catholics there were in that section of the city.

In spite of undoubted success there was much opposition on the part of some Negroes to the apportionment of churches for their exclusive use. Speaking in a general way, it may be said that it is not so much the "color-line" which the Negro resents. "Color-lines" are but the expression of an underlying truth; that the Negroes themselves draw color-lines within their own race reveals how naturally and inevitably the thing is done. Dr. Edward Murphy throws light on the sitation: "If the whites did not make it (the color-line), the colored themselves likely would. That the whites drew it against

them and that it looks like hypocrisy and spite is what angers
our colored population. . . . Social courtesy, as well as common prudence, requires that much expression be either avoided as superfluous or reduced to a minimum as perilous." [1]   To
resent the action of the Church in giving separate churches to
the Negroes was neither fair nor logical, since such action was
brought about by neither hypocrisy nor spite. While we must
be prepared to admit a certain amount of prejudice in many
members and some ministers of the Church, the actu-
ating principle in the beginning of special work for the
Negro was the deep-seated anxiety on the part of bishops for
the salvation of souls.

When the question of separate churches for Negroes was
first agitated, Archbishop Janssens of New Orleans stated the
crux of the difficulty in a letter to the Commission for Mission Work among the Negroes and Indians, published in 1894.
The Archbishop wrote: "It would be desirable to have no discrimination in our churches, so that anyone might occupy any
pew or any seat anywhere in the church, but the feeling between the two races makes such an intermixture impossible.
. . . In a few parishes of the diocese there is no distinction
made between the whites and colored people and they freely
intermingle in the pews and in the church. In the country,
where instructions are given in French, the colored people
have ample accomodation in the churches and would not wish
any separation." [2]

Again the Archbishop wrote: "Our colored Catholics who
speak French (there are few who speak only English) do not
want a church for themselves. They imagine that I wish to
separate the races, and widen the gap which exists between
the white and colored population, and yet they acknowledge
that a great number do not go to church at all, and that
many have lost the Faith. I have several times consulted our
clergy and very few favor the experiment of separate
churches. In some out-of-the-way places where there is no
church as yet, and where the priest comes occasionally, there
exists a great prejudice, and the white Catholics would wish

---

[1] *Commonweal, Ibid.*
[2] Report, 1894, p. 14.

to build churches and exclude the colored people. . . . A church for the colored people alone may deepen ill-feeling and separate still more the two races, which now meet on a common ground in the churches. On the other hand, such is the prejudice and feeling of the white people, that we cannot prudently extend the same privileges of indiscriminate pews, of rank in procession, etc., and some of the colored Catholics use this as a pretext not to come to church."[1]

Mission work among the colored people struggled along until about twenty years ago when the question of separate churches would seem to have been definitely settled. The separation, however, has left its mark of bitterness in the hearts of some who would accuse the missioners who were given charge of such churches of lending aid to racial segregation. Malcontents refuse to see that the Church is not responsible for social conditions which exist in the South. Earnest priests have had to bear the brunt of ill-feeling engendered by this assignment of definite churches to the colored. While no one more than these priests desires to see obliterated all "color-lines" in church matters, yet, because of prevailing social prejudices which they are almost powerless to repress, they find themselves accused of treason to a race the soul of which they choose to save in preference to its social status.

In towns where there are no separate churches for Negroes they continue to attend any Catholic church. Even in those cities where there are several colored Catholic churches many Negroes attend white churches as a matter of convenience. In most northern cities where there is a large Negro population the Negroes by preference have their own churches. In spite of the minority opinion referred to and because of the prevailing inhospitable attitude towards the Negro, coupled with the fact that independent Negro churches of non-Catholic denominations are gradually strengthening their hold on the race, the general tendency at present is towards a distinct decrease in Negro attendance at white churches of any denomination. Then, too, there are the prac-

[1] *Ibid.*

tical difficulties already referred to in the way of any large number of Negroes and whites occupying the same building.

The beginning of the Church of Our Lady of the Blessed Sacrament, Cleveland, Ohio, illustrates the sensible attitude assumed by a majority of Catholic Negroes. In 1922 a movement for a separate church was inaugurated by the colored Catholics in Cleveland. A census revealed as many as a hundred and fifty Catholic colored families living in Cleveland. Bishop Schrembs was requested to grant permission for the erection of a church. The letter which the committee sent to the Bishop is a beautiful testimonial of the faith of the colored people of Cleveland and, indirectly, a high compliment to the missioners of the South who had trained many of them. The letter is considered worthy of reproduction:

Rt. Rev. Joseph Schrembs,
Bishop of Cleveland.

Your Lordship:

Among the divers nationalities that go to make up the Catholic body of this large cosmopolitan city of which Almighty God has been pleased to call you as our shepherd, there are about two hundred persons of Negro birth, who are scattered throughout the various parishes and consequently so over-shadowed and hidden by the countless thousands of other worshippers as to be unknown and almost of no consequence.

The undersigned committee, representing a social and charitable organization composed solely of members of this racial group of your flock, are mindful of the recent unwarranted attack made upon your Lordship by a minority group of colored Catholics, who voiced the sentiment that we do not desire a church of our own in this city, on the supposition that such would in some way militate against the civic well-being of the race.

We protest that such is untrue and unfounded, and do incline to the conviction that a Catholic Church and priest consecrated to the needs and service of our race could be none other than a very potent factor in the material uplift as well as of untold spiritual blessing to the race and to the community.

We hardly deem it necessary to avow that we, as children of our glorious Mother Church, have the same filial love and devotion in all things pertaining to her that characterize all other true Catholic people.

Although these things are true, we are nevertheless deeply conscious of the fact that our usefulness is greatly curtailed. That the holy aspirations which surge within the hearts of our boys to serve as acolytes at the altar of their God, or the virgin longing that inflames the souls of our girls for the loving, devoted service in the various activities of a Catholic parish, is in nearly every case, either smothered in the inception or finally withered away through lack of opportunity and encouragement.

It is by no means in the spirit of pique or resentment that we view these matters; recognizing as we do that the world is not governed by idealistic principles, and that it is part of discretion to deal sanely and wisely with social and economic forces as we find them both within and without the Church.

The Church in her wisdom, although looking ever toward the day when all nations shall be as one, nevertheless realizes that under earthly conditions religion and piety are best developed along ethnological lines and she therefore tolerates the division into racial groups.

With our heart set upon the evangelization of the masses, and looking forward to a greater field of usefulness not only in this diocese but also as an important link in the Catholic chain of educational and spiritual uplift which is surely destined to become a mighty power throughout the land, we therefore humbly implore that Your Lordship may be pleased to approve our resolutions and to grant us such permission and authority as may be necessary to proceed in the establishment of an independent parish organization under your jurisdiction and conformable in every way to your wishes.

Awaiting, as we hope, your favor and blessing, we remain.

Your obedient servants,

(Signed)   Oliver G. Waters, *Chairman*,
Anna Lomax,
Harriet Williams,
John F. Johnson.

The commendable effort of these Catholics to form a congregation of their own met severe opposition on the part of a local colored newspaper. The ludicrousness of an exclusively colored paper opposing the formation of an exclusively colored church did not strike the editor. The very existence of the colored paper was evidence that the particular needs and affairs of the colored race of Cleveland did not receive sufficient attention in the daily papers. The growth and welfare of the race is more properly looked after by the existence of colored churches (as well as of colored newspapers) whose priests (as well as editors) give their whole time and attention to a single end.

On the whole, the principle antagonists of churches for use by colored people are usually those so-called leaders of the race who are willing to sacrifice the vital welfare of countless thousands of their people for what they conceive to be a point in race advancement. The mass of colored people, endowed with a fund of natural logic, are unwilling to be so sacrificed. In this position they find ample leadership in the guidance of those members of their race who take a sane view of the situation and are not blinded by the all-consuming desire for immediate race equality.

3. THE CATHOLIC CHURCH AND THE "COLOR-LINE."

Of sufficient frequency to warrant attention are the insinuations, if not outright accusations, that the Catholic Church fosters the "color line" and is guilty of false pretenses in its solicitude for the colored people. In spite of the very creditable fact that the majority of colored Christians in the world belong to the Catholic Church, picayune race writers fulminate against the Church because every individual Catholic is not Christian enough to inhibit a feeling of aversion. While it is perfectly true that the Church is a divine institution and of a higher order than this world, it is of equal truth that the supernatural is built upon the natural; hence, if some Catholics are devoid of even the rudiments of social decency, the Church can not be obligated to an assumption of responsibility for their lack of supernatural ideals.

The aversion which unlike races feel to social intermingling is a psychological fact due to a spontaneous consciousness of difference. Whenever two races come in contact in sufficiently large masses this consciousness of kind arises. Whether this consciousness is instinctive or dominantly mental is debatable. But whatever its nature, it may be softened by a sympathetic understanding. Unfortunately, mass consciousness is fatal to individual thinking, a probable reason why so few individuals bother to analyse national or racial prejudices. Even so potent a force as religion cannot be expected immediately to break down aversion of different races.

As a proposition considered *in se*, when freed from all

abuses, slavery is not intrinsically opposed to the natural or divine law. This is theoretical, however, since slavery rarely existed without abuses. Historical slavery, with all the abuses which follow in its wake, has ever been condemned by the Church. This is evident from the writings of the Popes from Pius II to Leo XIII. The only ground upon which slavery as it existed in the United States could have been justified was social expediency. But that was no excuse for its continuance longer than necessary, despite the attempted justification of the system by a few Catholic theologians.

Slavery as a social institution was early supported by the laws of all the English Protestant colonies. Although not slave colonies at first, the Protestant colony of Georgia and the Catholic colony of Maryland were later obliged to establish slavery because of the economic pressure exerted upon them by the other colonies. If we except the old Catholic colonies of Maryland, Louisiana, and Florida, Catholics were not very numerous; consequently, at first they could form but a very small part of the slave-holding class. A majority of the Catholics in the country belonged to that class of labor which had immigrated from Europe and which, because of its aversion to competition with the slave labor of the South, was a contributing factor to the Civil War and the consequent Emancipation Proclamation.   Catholics had to struggle to better their own condition in a predominantly Protestant land; they were in no position to fix the status of the Negro. If, under the conditions then and now obtaining, some Catholics, even whole sections of them, have been contaminated by prevailing non-Catholic customs and prejudices, the odium is not to the Catholic Church but to those individual Catholics who fail to square their conduct with the demands of true Christian democracy.

So far as the Church was concerned, it did not create the injustice of slavery. Slavery was a social institution which the Church had to face and gradually demolish, just as it overthrew the slavery of an ancient world. Such revolution, however, cannot be effected immediately. It is only by dealing tactfully with human nature and by persistent efforts that the Church is able to make Christian ideals predominate. Lin-

coln, as President of the United States, was in a position to
take a shorter course for the abolition of slavery. The Emancipation Proclamation forestalled the influence of the only
method which the Church could employ—influencing society
for its transformation through individual souls.

Even where the Catholic Church has some semblance of
power it cannot and does not attempt summarily to abolish
the color line. It does, however, exert a powerful and steady
pressure for the immediate amelioration of the condition of
the colored people and for the ultimate abolition of a system
of caste which even in its mildest form is inconsistent with
the teachings of Christ. In the past the Catholic Church has
accomplished great social reforms by the prudent use of this
social pressure: history amply testifies that where the Catholic Church did have control over such conditions as now prevail in the United States (e. g. Brazil) it was not long in
bringing them into accord with the universal brotherhood
preached by Christ. The policy of the Catholic Church has
never been to accomplish reforms by revolution; such would
inevitably alienate some portion of its flock. On the other
hand, never in history has the Catholic Church failed to
ameliorate the condition of a people who came to it for suc-
cor, and there is no indication that it will fail the Afro-American.[1]

While it is true that the Church cannot be held entirely
responsible for the prejudice and the discriminations practised by its members, the American Church must recognize
some responsibility for the constant and persistent co-operation of her members in discriminations which are objectively
wrong. It would seem that the Church has some obligation
to instruct its members as regards the moral character of
these activities.[2]

---

[1] Cf. Journal of Negro History, Vol. II, no. 4, pp. 393, et sq., for good
article on "The Catholic Church and the Negro", Rev. J. Butsch,
S.S.J.

[2] cf. Gilligan, S.T.D., Rev. Francis, The Morality of the Color Line.

CHAPTER VI.

THE PRIESTS OF THE NEGRO MISSIONS

1. SUMMARY OF SURVEY

In the United States there are 196 priests engaged exclusively in Catholic missionary work for Negroes. Of this number 142 are laboring in the South, while 22 are engaged in college and seminary work, preparing aspirants exclusively for the colored mission field. These institutions are St. Joseph's Seminary, Baltimore, Md., St. Augustine's Mission House, Bay St. Louis, Miss., St. Anthony's Mission House, [1] Tenafly, N. J., and Epiphany Apostolic College, Newburgh, N.Y.

The State of Louisiana claims 39 priests, the largest number wholly devoted to colored missionary work in any state. The District of Columbia has 13 such priests, Maryland has 10 in parish work and 6 at St. Joseph's Seminary, Texas has 11, while Georgia and Pennsylvania have 9 each.

Nine different societies, with a total of 166 priests, are represented in the colored mission field. The remaining 30 priests are from the secular clergy. The representation of the different groups are as follows: [2]

African Mission Society	17 [3]
Benedictines	1
Capuchins	3
Divine Word, Society of the	16
Franciscans	3
Holy Ghost Fathers	38
Jesuits	4
St. Joseph, Society of	80
Vincentians	4
	166
Secular	30
Total	196

[1] St. Anthony's Mission House has since been closed.
[2] Since this report the Passionist Fathers have taken over the missions at Newbern and Washington, N. C., and the Redemptorists have taken over the white mission at Newton Grove, N. C., to which is attached a chapel for the colored. The numbers here given are for January 1, 1928.
[3] The African Mission Society includes the Fathers from the Irish Province, of which there are two in East St. Louis, Ill.

These figures include only priests who devote their whole time to the work of the missions. There are many zealous priests engaged in other activities who can give only a portion of their time to colored missionary work; of such are the Jesuits, who for years have been doing remarkably good work among the colored people in the counties of southern Maryland. While several Jesuit parishes include a large number of Negroes, those only are here listed which are officially for their use. [1]

2. NECESSITY OF TRAINED MISSIONERS

For long the Negro has been defensively secretive; slavery made him that. In the past the instinct was defensive and passive, but with a growing education and a certain kind of leadership this instinct is becoming conscious and self-directive. If the Catholic Church wants the Negro—and it wants him more than he wants it—then it behooves the Church to train priests specially for him, because to get at the real feeling of the Negro one must be acceptable to him. Few "part-time" laborers can pass the required test. Priests devoting their whole lives to the welfare of the Negro should certainly come nearer to a satisfactory understanding of him than can those whose interest and training are matters of indifference. Experience has amply demonstrated that the Negro feels more at home with priests of undivided allegiance: they come to "their priests" with greater freedom for comfort and advice. Beyond doubt the temporal and spiritual welfare of the Negro is better served and his Catholicity more efficiently promoted by a body of specially trained priests.

Occasionally an "arm-chair missioner" bursts into meteoric brilliance across the literary sky. Of very humanitarian impulses, he burns with a zeal but recently enkindled on the fires of an exoteric knowledge and a tyronian experience. He has discovered the Catholic Negro problem. Dismissing as incompetents and laggards those missioners who for the better part of a century have plowed southern fields, he writes

---

[1] *The Official Catholic Year Book* (1929) credits the Jesuits with "24 missions for the Colored in southern Maryland." This number is over-estimated.

his jeremiads as if his pen were first to turn a furrow in fields long ripening to the harvest. In flaming rhetoric he proves to his own satisfaction that millions of Negroes are clamoring at the church-doors of the South. Well, as one white-haired missioner jokingly exaggerated, some are clamoring at the church doors—to get out. These ardent optimists might well be ignored were it not that they increase the tragedy of the race. By writing of race contacts in sciolistic rather than scientific vein they suggest that the brotherhood of man enjoins a free and unrestrained association with all people regardless of conditions in life. Truth is that Negroes of education and means do not admit this fatuity even within the limits of their own race.

The real missioner, on the other hand, studies the needs of this awakening people. With an esoteric knowledge of the difficulties involved in the race question he knows full well that one wave of a mission crucifix, and still less, one flourish of a flippant pen, will never metamorphose a fledgling race into a thoroughly Catholic-minded people. As Doctor Edward Murphy, S.S.J., so well points out: "Without the least sacrifice of social dignity, the white priest lives side by side with his colored charges, helping them to raise themselves. He does not manhandle their characteristics, or try to mold them in the Caucasian image. His purpose is to have them develop and improve themselves according to their racial favors. His approach may well be studied by all those who are interested in Negro welfare and in promoting the harmony of the races."[1]

Pedagogues quite generally agree that proper training of children is a work for teachers of more than average ability. They recognize that a gifted teacher with an astute understanding of child psychology can mold the man in the plastic mind of the child. Failures of manhood often have inception in the kindergarten. The practical thing, therefore, is to place the youngest child under the care of the most skillful teacher. If this is true in pedagogy, why not also in missionology? Yet, with some the idea would seem to prevail that any kind of priest is good enough for backward races. Nothing is more contrary to fact.

[1] *Commonweal*, Jan. 9, 1929, p. 286.

The prospective missioner to the Negro must have a natural adaptability to the "child-like" mentality of this infantine race. He must by practice acquire skill in handling daily difficulties in keeping with the most recent findings of pedagogy. Finally, by diligent study he must constantly acquire a deeper understanding of the soul of the Negro — a soul which has been through the wine-press of sorrow.

The studies and practices of an aspirant to Negro missions must deal with a double content: on the one hand, with the matter he will impart to his people; on the other, with the process of this imparting. Both of these requirements differentiate the priest of the Negro from his fellow-priests. In the first place, his doctrinal training should be more thorough than that ordinarily required of the average parish priest. Like Christ, the missioner to an uncultured race must translate the sublimities and intricacies of dogmatic theology into simplest language. In moral theology, too, he must be an adept, tactfully educating from ignorance to knowledge and skillfully distinguishing between material and formal.

Of equal importance is the process of imparting his knowledge. A thorough understanding of the psychological and educative process is essential. This entails a general familiarity with the field as well as a special knowledge of the particular sections of the country in which he labors. The missionary to the Negro must know the social and historical basis of present conditions, and he must know how to apply this knowledge in its relations to other forces in the lives of his people. He should, therefore, be trained to know his work in its end, its content, its forms and various agencies, and its relations with all the phases of Negro life. In this way he will discover the bond which connects the interests of his ministry with the general interests of the race.

A course in theoretical instruction and practice training, which is part of the curriculum in a missionary seminary, will correlate and connect the student's knowledge and its application. This correlation is essential for even a modicum of success. Seminarians preparing for the work of the Negro Missions find a means for this practical training in their work of visiting hospitals, eleemosynary and penal institutions,

and in catechizing children. This "Claverian work," as it is
called, has a triple advantage. In the first place, theoretical
knowledge acquired in the routine class-work of the seminary
is immediately utilized and thus made an integral part of the
novice-missioner. Secondly, if tactical mistakes must be made
it were preferable that they be made before sacerdotal dignity
adds to their gravity. Finally, when the young missioner is
assigned to a mission, he is able properly to visualize his field;
already he has learned that the congregation which faces him
is neither a university group nor an African tribe. From the
very beginning of his career, therefore, his usefulness is un-
impaired by lack of at least essential experience. Such a training is within the sphere of that seminary alone the special
object of which is to train missioners for the Colored Missions. Only by such training can theory and practice go hand
in hand and their effects extend into the lives of the Negroes
so as to co-operate with the disciplinary training of Catholic
dogmatic and moral theology.

These same points the specially trained priest will bring
into the social education of his colored charges. Working
through individual souls which he will influence for good, his
is no mean contribution to general race uplift. The moral and
social welfare of any people are very closely bound together;
in fact, real social welfare is identical with and follows inevitably from Catholic morality, with this difference, that the
social form adds new problems. The process of social uplift
will function properly if it be focussed upon the totality of the
spiritual treasures of the race. The spiritual treasures, the
transmission of which is a sacred duty to the priest, should
always be rated first in importance and receive the largest
share of attention; whereas the social treasures, the transmission of which is in keeping with the high calling of the race,
should be second in importance and attention; while those,
finally, which are merely useful, should be third.

Moreover, an infinite patience must characterize the priest
of the Negro. Negro churches in the South are centers of
social life more so than in the North where many other distractions are offered. Partly because the social life of the
Negro is so inextricably bound up with his church affairs, it

happens that nearly all social rivalries, jealousies, and feuds are carried over into the church, resulting in the formation of coteries and factions which often split the congregation. One false step by an unsuspecting priest will frequently serve to alienate a large portion of his congregation. Unless the pastor be a trained man skilled in Negro psychology and blessed with a Jobian patience, positive harm will result from his mistakes.

The desirability of a body of clergy specially trained to minister to the wants of the Negro does not mean that the work of his evangelization should be limited to certain missionary organizations. These organizations neither have nor want a monopoly in the field; furthermore, it is not in accord with the mind of the Church, which ordains all priests for the salvation of souls without distinction as to color. A Christlike ministry is absolutely incompatible with a color-line, and a priestly interest which ends with the souls of the more favored races already confirmed in the Faith is scarcely begun. All priests, therefore, can and should be interested in the salvation of the Afro-American, even though all priests are not gifted by either nature or grace to occupy themselves solely with that work.

On the matter of clerical interest, Doctor Murphy has this to say: "She (the Catholic Church) accepts conditions, but always strives to mold them with higher principles. For any of her clergy to let themselves be infected with the prevalent prejudices against the black man would be Satan's triumph, and no true priest in his heart of hearts does anything of the kind. But the impression has somehow been made that not all of them are immune; rendering it essential that even the appearance of such a condition be scrupulously avoided. The priests who are giving everything to the Negro ministry have known the experience of hopes dashed to the ground by misconceptions and misinterpretations on the part of the more educated colored folk—a steadily increasing class—who look for more fairness in the Catholic fold than in others and have a right to do so, but are not always content with what they find. . . . It is unthinkable that a minister of the all-loving

Christ should be even subconsciously fixated in racial aversion, or even open himself to such a suspicion." [1]

The increasing number of secular priests who have taken up colored work is pregnant with possibilities for future advancement in Negro evangelization. That nearly all the secular priests laboring for colored congregations are still in the North does not indicate that there are not to be found in the ranks of the southern clergy zealous priests who would do likewise were the exigencies of work already established less imperative. The very fact that even the secular clergy of the North has taken up the cudgels in behalf of the Negro is an encouraging indication that his evangelization is no longer looked upon as an activity suited only for missionary organizations. This is in itself a tremendous advance. At the same time it must be emphasized that the nature of the work demands the same careful training of secular priests as is demanded of missionary priests.

3. COLORED CLERGY

So far nine colored priests have been ordained and assigned to work in the United States. Rev. Augustus Tolton was the first. [2] Ordained at the College of Propaganda, Rome, in 1888, he opened a mission at Quincy, Ill., in the Diocese of Springfield, to which diocese he belonged. Later he went to Chicago where he was pastor of St. Monica's (now St. Elizabeth's) parish. He remained there until his death in 1902.

Rev. Charles Randolph Uncles was the first colored priest ordained in the United States. He is a member of the Society of St. Joseph. Ordained in the Baltimore Cathedral by Cardinal Gibbons in 1891, since ordination he has been a professor at Epiphany Apostolic College, the Josephite preparatory house of studies.

Rev. John Dorsey, another priest of the Society of St. Joseph, was ordained in the Baltimore Cathedral by Cardinal Gibbons in 1902. For several years he was a member of a mission band. Later he was appointed pastor of St. Monica's Church, Baltimore, Md. He died in 1926.

---

[1] *Ecclesiastical Review*, Nov., 1928, p. 501.

[2] *Vide, St. Joseph's Advocate*, Jan., 1887, for an account of Father Paddington, who was reputed to have been the first Negro priest in America.

Rev. Joseph Plantvigne, also a member of the Society of St. Joseph, was ordained in 1907 by Bishop Curtis in the chapel of St. Joseph's Seminary, Baltimore, Md. He was engaged in giving missions until 1909 when, because of failing health, he was assigned to St. Francis Xavier's Church, Baltimore. He died there in 1913.

Rev. John Burgess was ordained in Paris, France, in 1907. He made his preparatory course of studies at Epiphany Apostolic College under the Josephite Fathers; later he joined the Holy Ghost Fathers. He was engaged in missionary and professorial work until his death in 1922.

Rev. Stephen Theobald was ordained in St. Paul's Seminary, St. Paul, Minn., in 1910. He was the first colored secular priest ordained in the United States. At present he is pastor of the Church of St. Peter Claver, St. Paul, Minn.

Rev. Norman Duckette made part of his preparatory studies at St. Joseph's Catechetical School, Montgomery, Ala., a school in which the Josephite Fathers trained catechists for the Negro missions. He was ordained in Detroit by Bishop Gallagher in 1925, and until recently was pastor of the Church of St. Benedict the Moor, Detroit, Mich.

Rev. Joseph John made his preparatory course of studies at Epiphany Apostolic College under the Josephite Fathers. Later he joined the Society of African Missions (Motherhouse at Lyons, France). He was ordained in 1923 by Bishop Collins, S.J., in the Church of St. Benedict the Moor, New York City. His last American assignment was at Corpus Christi, Texas. Father John left the United States in 1928.

Rev. Augustine Derricks was a member of the Order of the Most Holy Trinity. Ordained in Rome June 9, 1927, he was assigned to the Church of St. Ann (Italian), Bristol, Pa., where he labored until his death, October 22, 1929.

Although there have been only nine colored priests in the United States, this is not due, as has been charged, to lack of opportunity for colored boys to study for the priesthood. While there is no way of ascertaining just how many availed themselves of the opportunities which were open to them in various institutions throughout the country, it is a fact that the number is much larger than is supposed. The records of St.

Joseph's Society alone, as an instance, show that at some time or other about thirty-five colored boys have been in its preparatory college and seminary—of this number only two or three were dismissed. Other seminaries can add considerable to this number of one-time colored students. Besides those at St. Augustine's Seminary, Bay St. Louis, Miss., at present colored students are listed in ten or twelve colleges and seminaries, secular and regular, throughout the country. Such facts lead to the conclusion that unfounded are the charges of those who claim opportunity is denied colored boys who desire to study for the priesthood.

Hitherto colored candidates for the priesthood have been trained in white seminaries. The Society of the Divine Word inaugurated a new experiment, that of training colored students by themselves. In 1920 the Fathers of the Divine Word opened St. Augustine's Mission House, Bay St. Louis, Miss. It is described in the Catholic Directory as "a preparatory Seminary for the education of colored candidates to the Society of the Divine Word, to work as missionaries among their own people at home and abroad." It has received special encouragement from the Holy Father, Pope Pius XI. Upon completion of the regular six-year preparatory course the students spend a year in the novitiate of the Society at Lake Beulah, Wis., after which they teach for one year in the preparatory seminary. Candidates then make first profession in the Society and are ready to enter upon their philosophical studies. The 1929 Catholic Directory lists St. Augustine's Seminary as having 6 novices, 3 scholastics, and 30 students. That the venture is not without its discouraging aspect is seen from the recent statement of Very Rev. Bruno Hagspiel, Provincial: "It is safe to say at this time that if the Society had forseen its present predicament it would not have gone into this venture." [1] Nevertheless, St. Augustine's Seminary is an institution worthy of the continued support of all Catholics interested in the furtherance of the cause of Christ among the Negroes in the United States.

One of the results of the Vatican Missionary Exhibition was the issuance of the Encyclical *Rerum Ecclesiae* by Pope

---

[1] *Report of the American Board of Catholic Missions*, July 1, 1929, p. 174.

Pius XI, "The Pope of the Missions," as he is called. A careful analysis of the mission field is presented and very specific advice is given to missionaries and Prefects Apostolic as regards the training of native clergy and of catechists. A careful perusal of this document, however, leads one to believe that it does not refer to a Negro clergy in the United States. Besides the fact that he expressly mentions the "East" and the "South," it would seem that the Holy Father did not have in mind the unique race conditions prevailing in this country. The social conditions which the encyclical assumes to exist when reference is made to a native clergy find no parallel in the United States. The conclusion that this encyclical had reference directly to the foreign missions alone is strengthened by the subsequent appointment of six native Chinese bishops. The Pope's words relative to a native clergy are, nevertheless, frequently quoted as if they referred to a Negro clergy in our country.

Of the feasibility and advisability of a colored clergy in this country no general empirical conclusions can be drawn because of the paucity of experiments in that direction. The question is so inextricably bound up with what is called "the race question" that it is difficult for even disinterested persons to get a proper perspective. Leaders of the race have insistently and loudly demanded that they be given priests of their own race. There is a possibility, however, that zeal for the cause of race advancement may have made some oblivious of difficulties which are not lightly to be ignored. At any rate, a frank discussion of the problem may help to clear the ground for a better mutual understanding.

Concerning the mental fitness of some Negroes for the priesthood there is no doubt. While the high intellectual requirements for the priesthood immediately eliminate the majority of the race, the increasingly large number of professional men within the race is eloquent proof that many Negroes are capable of advanced learning. Of a still more restrictive nature are the moral requisites of candidacy for priestly rank. However, the unquestioned integrity of the few colored priests and the many colored nuns leaves no doubt as to the moral capacity of some Negroes. A third requirement, and by far a more limiting, is that of priestly vocation. A colored mother recently wrote asking where she could place her twelve-year-old son, as she wishes "to make a priest out of him." Priests are not made that way. God is the Dispenser of vocations, and were the demands for a colored clergy as numerous as the stars in the heavens and as loud as the roaring of the mighty sea, they could not produce one vocation to the priesthood. It might be well in this matter to remind ourselves that the supernatural is built upon the natural; God alone knows when one is prepared for the other.

To the seminary faculty belongs the duty to determine the presence of the three necessary qualities "insofar as human frailty is able to know." If the "call" be given and accepted, the Negro aspirant to the priesthood has all the assurance of vocation and fitness that can be had, granting which there is no reason why there cannot be a colored clergy. Then, surely, both the colored candidate and the colored race have a right not to be discriminated against.

Colored priests will undoubtedly have the advantage of a thorough understanding of the Negro soul. They will have shared the humiliations and trials of their people, and they will know from experience how to reach the motivating forces to energize them to better achievement. This does not mean that the white priests who have labored so well during the heat of the day have failed in a proper understanding of the problems involved or have been lacking in a sympathetic approach to their solution. Not infrequently the very fact of being white is an advantage: there may be times and occasions when the colored priest because of the trees sees not the woods. That white priests in the field have not made more progress is due rather to their pathetically small number. Furthermore, what few colored priests there have been have not produced results any greater than have their white confreres.

Whether or not color has anything to do with priestly results is questionable. In at least one instance a colored priest was met at the railroad station of his home town and told to "keep right on a-going" as the town did not wish to receive him. Another colored priest, a gifted preacher, could literally "pack" the church. His audience always included a number of non-Catholics, yet the number of conversions was few. Pride was in the eyes of his people, but conviction was not in their hearts. White missioners in the same churches made as many as thirty and forty converts. It is a commentary not without its pathos that Father Joseph John found it preferable to leave the United States.

Will the Negro receive, respect and obey a colored pastor? Some will; some will not. Perhaps the future will be kinder than the past.

Properly the question is not *should* there be colored priests. *Unquestionably, there should be.* More pertinent is the question of time and manner. Social conditions largely determine the "when." Experience advises as to the "kind" of colored priest more likely to succeed.

Are social conditions sufficiently tolerable to justify ordaining a colored boy to the priesthood? Prescinding from any of the inevitable practical questions as to his reception by whites or blacks, of far more importance is it that consideration be given to the personal feelings of the colored priest himself. Time, training, and the authority of the Church will satisfactorily dispose of the practical difficulties which stand in the way of his acceptance. Of far more vital and personal importance is the willingness of the colored candidate to accept and live in the conditions which will inevitably form part of his priestly life.

The colored aspirant to the priesthood must realize that in the Roman collar there is no magic power to change social conditions. Neither does the collar give open sesame to any social privilege at present denied him. He who would wear the symbol of priestly rank must, to a degree far greater than is true of his unmarked brother, expect to be discriminated against in quarters and at times least expected, to be insulted in the most insidious as well as outrageous manner, and to be ostracized with a refined cruelty which will drive him dangerously near the madhouse. The writing is on the wall: he may not mix socially with white people, and, for reasons best known to himself, he must not mix uncircumspectly with his own people. A priest as truly as any other priest, a man educated beyond the pale of nine-tenths of his race, he must be willing in a very personal manner to wear without regret a crown of thorns and to bare his back without flinching to the stinging lashes of the whip. Finally, he must be courageous enough to hang upon his cross in desolation and be spat upon by some of the very people whom he would save. Verily, the Negro priest must have the Christian virtue of humility. If at times the world demands in no uncertain terms that these penalties be paid by white priests laboring on the Colored Missions, will it be satisfied with less than a pound of flesh from the colored priest? Crumbs of comfort there are in the thought that the angel of God's grace will refresh him and the authority of God's Church will support him, but unless his own soul can see the humor of the universe and can laugh with the laughter of the saints, then better let him remain a layman. If in death the colored boy sees life, if in the grave he sees the resurrection, then in the name of God ordain him, for then only, in the words of the Pontifical, "he knows what he does."

If the past be an augury of the future, the problem of a Negro clergy will find satisfactory solution in the secular ranks of the northern clergy. It is not without a certain significance that those missionary societies which have experimented with colored priests have learned to be conservative in considering Negro applicants for the priesthood. Men with the good of the race at heart do not lightly follow a policy which would seem to impede progress. When appearances are to the contrary, surely there should be at least a suspicion that rationality influences the course of action. While it is true that the number of colored priests ordained has been too few to support general conclusions, nevertheless, multitudinous experiments are not necessary to arrive at certain satisfactory particular conclusions. One of these conclusions is that the difficulties likely to be encountered in the placement of colored priests belonging to religious societies are sufficiently serious to warrant hesitation in ordaining them. It must be borne in mind that conditions other than willingess to ordain are to be given consideration. All religious societies are dependent upon the bishops for their field of labor and the acceptance of laborers. This dependence alone jeopardizes the assurance of usefulness of colored priests so far as religious societies are concerned. On the other hand, a secular priest by the very fact of his adoption into a diocese has better assurance of opportunity for usefulness since his placement depends solely and directly upon the bishop.

In fairness to bishops it should be said that they must be governed by conditions in their dioceses. Indisputable as is their probity in all things that affect the salvation of souls, be the bodies black or white, yet even the most zealous bishops at times find themselves unable to alter embarrassing situations. For this reason it would seem that if a colored priesthood is to be given ample opportunity for proving its worth (and there is no question of the outcome to many of us), it will be a secular priesthood in the North where prejudice is not so all-pervading or fatal. The only colored priests in the country are working in the North; colored priests who had been in the South found conditions not at all livable. Under the social regime now holding forth below the Mason and Dixon line the idea of a colored clergy is too new and startling to find ready acceptance. It is only after the idea has pervaded the more tolerant North that it will permeate into the South. Like all new ideas it were better first to prove the worth of a colored clergy in friendly territory, for if the North be not friendly, at least it is passive.

To the parents of a race who long to see their sons at the altar let it be kindly said that the gates of the sanctuary are always open to the sons of any race who can pass the universal tests of fitness and vocation. Above all else, let the parents of the Negro race be willing to see their sons bear crosses, golden though they be, far heavier than they themselves have ever borne. A headless prejudice in a heartless land has so decreed. The Catholic Church, the Mother of all, would have it otherwise. In the words of St. Paul, the Church still says: "To every one of us is given grace according to the measure of the giving of Christ. . . . And he gave some apostles, and some prophets, and other some evangelists, and other some pastors and doctors. For the perfecting of the saints, for the world of the ministry, for the edifying of the body of Christ: until we all meet into the unity of faith, and of the knowledge of the Son of God, unto a perfect man, unto the measure of the age of the fullness of Christ."[1] Here breathes the spirit of Christ, here the spirit of His Church, here the spirit of His Vicar, here the spirit of His Hierarchy, here the spirit of His Priesthood, here your spirit and mine.

---

[1] *Ephesians.* IV, 7-13.

PART III—NEGRO MIGRATION

Chapter VII.

THE MIGRATION IN GENERAL

One of the most disconcerting elements in the program of Catholic colored missionary activity is the recent Negro migration. This mass movement has upset the old order of things and has worked untold hardships for the missioners who have been laboring to build up stable missions in the South. It would seem to be no exaggeration to say that this upheaval has set back the work of the Colored Missions at least a decade of years. Whole parishes have been depopulated, the flock ruthlessly scattered, and work everywhere retarded. To have a proper perspective of present conditions on the Colored Missions it is necessary to know something about this migratory movement.

1. NUMBER

Although the recent exodus of Negroes from the South to the North is generally considered as one movement, it took place in two mass movements: that of 1916-1920 and that of 1922-1924. The first of these movements began in 1915, reached its maximum in 1917, and continued at a decreasing rate up to 1920, when, because of economic depression in the North, it almost ceased. At first the movement was from the southeast to the northeast, following main lines of transportation. Soon, however, it became known that the middle West was in a similar need of men; many industries advertised in southern Negro papers. The Federal Department of Labor for a time was instrumental in the transportation of Negroes from the South to relieve labor shortage in other sections of the country; it discontinued its efforts when southern congressmen pointed out that the South's labor supply was being depleted. The second movement, that of 1922-1924, while not so extensive as the first, assumed huge proportions. Since

1924, however, there has been practically no migration; what little there has been since then has been offset by the return of Negroes to the South.[1]

2. CAUSES

The general causes of these migratory movements were the World War and subsequent legislation limiting immigration quotas. With the World War, foreign immigration to the United States stopped. At the same time the Army drafted hundreds of thousands of civilians from every condition and state of life. Simultaneously with this drain on the man power of the country came into existence war industries which made urgent calls upon the already depleted forces of the North. Prior to this time foreign labor filled the unskilled labor field; Negroes were held closely in domestic and personal-service work. The cessation of immigration and the return of thousands of aliens to their mother countries, together with the opening of new industries and the expansion of old ones, created a much greater demand for American labor than heretofore. To meet this emergency the labor supply of the South, largely Negro, was drawn upon.

As far as the Negroes of the South were concerned, the causes of their exodus fall into three main classes: economic, educational and social.[2] They may be subdivided as follows:

(1) *Economic*:

    (a) Ravages of boll weevil.
    (b) Low wages.
    (c) Farmer tenant system.

---

[1] *cf. The Negro in Chicago*, Report of the Chicago Commission on Race Relations; *Negro Year Book; A Century of Negro Migration*, Woodson; *The Negro Migrant in Pittsburgh*, Epstein; *Negro Migration in 1916-1917*, Dillard; "The Negro Migrant," Address of Phil. H. Brown, issued by Dept. of Labor, Sept. 6, 1923; "Negro Migration", article issued by Dept. of Commerce, Dec. 17, 1921; "Recent Northward Migration of the Negro", J. Hill, issued by the Dept. of Labor, 1928; "Negro Migration", article issued by Dept. of Labor, October 24, 1923; "The Negro Migration of 1916-1918", H. H. Donald, in *Journal of Negro History*, Vol. VI, no. 4, p. 383, *et sq.*

[2] *Current History*, Vol. XVIII, no. 6, p. 943; *Cf.* also, *The Negro in Chicago*, Report of the Chicago Commission on Race Relations, pp. 84, 85; *The Negro Year Book*, 1925-1926, pp. 7, 8.

(2) *Educational*:
  (a) Disproportionate expenditures for education of white and Negro school children.
  (b) "Miserable" schoolhouses.
  (c) Large numbers of untrained school teachers.
(3) *Social*:
  (a) Judicial.
      (1) Injustice in the courts.
      (2) Sheriff "fee" system.
  (b) "Jim Crow" cars.
  (c) Lynching and mob law.
  (d) Disfranchisement.
  (e) Ku Klux Klan.

3. CHARACTER

In character this migration is not without precedent and cannot be separated completely from the steady though inconspicuous movement of Negroes from the South to the North that has been in progress since the emancipation. It is estimated that between the years 1865 and 1873 thirty-five thousand Negroes migrated towards the northeastern part of the United States, mostly from South Carolina, Georgia, Alabama and Mississippi.[1] In 1879 a similar movement, though not so great, was reported, when five to ten thousand Negroes from Mississippi, Louisiana, Texas, Alabama, and North Carolina moved to Kansas. In a lesser degree the recent migration also bears a striking resemblance to the movement from Arkansas and Texas in 1888 and 1889.

4. EXTENT

In extent the recent migration of Negroes is one of the greatest mass movements in the history of the United States: it swept on thousands of Negroes from remote sections of the South, depopulated entire communities, drew upon the Negro inhabitants of practically every city in the South, and spread from Florida to the western limits of Texas.[2]

Some idea of the rapid growth of the colored population in the North which resulted from the first wave of migration may

---

[1] Woodson, *A Century of Negro Migration*, pp. 117-120.
[2] Scott, Emmett J., "Negro Migration During the War," article in *The Negro Problem*, Johnson, p. 245, *et sq.*

be seen in that in 1900 there were 911,025 Negroes living in
the North: 10.3 per cent of the total Negro population of the
country, which was 8,833,994 in that year. The Federal Census report for the decade between the years 1900 and 1910
indicates a net loss of 595,703 Negroes for southern states
east of the Mississippi. Of this number, 366,880 were in northern states. The Government census for 1920 indicates a distribution of colored people as shown in Table 8.

TABLE 8.—DISTRIBUTION OF COLORED (1920)

Section	Negro Population			Increase			
	1920	1910	1900	1910-1920		1900-1910	
				No.	Per Cent	No.	Per Cent
TOTAL	10,463,131	9,827,763	8,833,994	635,368	6.5	993,769	11.2
The South [1]	8,912,231	8,749,427	7,922,969	162,804	1.9	826,458	10.4
The North [2]	1,472,309	1,027,674	880,771	444,635	43.3	146,903	16.7
The West [3]	78,591	50,662	30,254	27,929	55.1	20,408	67.5

Normally Negro migration from the South to the North
proceeds at the rate of about 10,000 a year. Estimates made
at the 1916-1920 migration placed the number of Negroes who
went North from 150,000 to 1,000,000. The Government census for 1920, however, shows that the Negroes from the South
actually living in the North at the time of the census had increased by only 330,260 in the whole ten years previously.

Estimates of the number who migrated during the 1922-
1924 movement vary from 100,000 to 500,000. According to
the Negro Year Book (1925-1926), however, if a census were

[1] South Atlantic, East South Central, West South Central divisions.
[2] New England, Middle Atlantic, East North Central, West North Central
divisions. The boundary line between the North and the South is
formed by the southern boundaries of New Jersey and Pennsylvania, the Ohio River and the Southern boundaries of Missouri
and Kansas.
[3] Mountain and Pacific divisions. The West is that part of the country
lying beyond the western boundaries of North and South Dakota,
Nebraska, Kansas, Oklahoma, and Texas.

taken it would show that there were probably not 250,000 more Negroes from the South living in the North and West than there were in 1920. As the Year Book points out, there has been much overlapping in the figures due to the fact that many of the Negroes who went North in the 1922-1924 exodus were persons who had already been in the North but had returned to the South at the time of the economic depression. It is probable that during the past ten years several hundred thousand Negroes have moved from the South to the North and back again.

On the other hand, it was announced by the Secretary of Labor, in a press communication dated October 24, 1923, that 478,700, or nearly half a million Negro migrants, forsook their abodes and occupations in thirteen southern states during the year September 1, 1922, to August 31, 1923. This figure was based on a series of total figures submitted by state, municipal and civic statisticians and authorities, and is believed to be a fairly accurate summary of estimations carefully compiled for Alabama, Arkansas, Florida, Georgia, Kentucky, Louisiana, Mississippi, North Carolina, Oklahoma, South Carolina, Tennessee, Texas and Virginia.

An analysis of the 478,700 total reveals the fact that of Negro migrants for the year noted, Alabama yielded 90,000; Arkansas, 5,000; Florida, 90,000; Georgia, 120,600; Kentucky, 2,500; Louisiana, 15,000; Mississippi, 82,600; North Carolina, 25,000; Oklahoma, 1,000; South Carolina, 25,000; Tennessee, 10,000; Texas, 2,000; and Virginia, 100,000. It may be noted that Georgia yielded the largest, and Oklahoma the smallest quota of Negro migrants.

In commenting upon the migratory movement, the Chambers of Commerce in several cities of the South expressed the opinion that the oncoming winter would cause the return of large numbers of the departees. Other prominent officials were reasonably sure that the yield of their states could be traced to specific areas; hence, that it was not a movement of general proportions. Another feature of the exodus seemed to indicate that the movement was quasi perpetual, inasmuch as departing Negroes were replaced by incomers who, in turn, were continually succeeded, until many of those who first left had returned to their original domicile.

5. DESTINATION

The movement of Negroes to the North is not to that section as a whole; rather to a few industrial centers, about ten in number. The tendency seems to have been to reach those fields offering the highest wages and most permanent prospects. The Negro Year Book (1926) reports that 1,139,505, or 73.4 per cent of the Negro population in the North, was concentrated in ten industrial districts as follows:

TABLE 9. CONCENTRATION OF NEGROES IN DISTRICTS

Indianapolis District	47,550
Detroit—Toledo District	55,918
Cleveland—Youngstown District	58,850
Kansas City District	65,393
Pittsburgh District	88,273
Columbus—Cincinnati District	89,651
St. Louis District	102,607
Chicago District	131,580
Philadelphia District	248,343
New York District	251,340
TOTAL 1,139,505	

In the North, outside the large cities above listed, there is only a small, though a rather widely distributed, Negro population. Out of a total of 1,272 northern counties, there are only 83 which have no Negroes at all, while in 671 other northern counties the number of Negroes is less than 100, making 754 counties—about 60 per cent of the total number—in which there are either no Negroes or fewer than 100. On the other hand, there are only 184 counties in which there are more than 1,000 Negroes. At present there is no indication that any dispersion of Negroes in the North is in progress.

Industrial and commercial cities offered greater opportunities than did the smaller towns or the farms; naturally, they attracted the vast majority of migrants. The tremendous increase in the colored population of such northern and western cities from 1910 to 1920 may be seen from representative cities listed in Table 10: [1]

TABLE 10.—CONCENTRATION OF NEGROES IN CITIES

City	Population of City (1920)			Per Cent of Total Pop. Colored, 1920	Increase in Colored Population (1910-1920)	
	Total	White	Colored		Number	Per cent
Akron, Ohio	208,435	202,718	5,580	2.7	4,923	749.3
Buffalo, N. Y.	506,775	502,042	4,511	0.9	2,738	154.7
Chicago, Ill.	2,701,705	2,589,169	109,456	4.1	65,355	148.2
Cincinnati, Ohio	401,247	371,097	30,079	7.5	10,440	53.2
Cleveland, Ohio	796,841	762,026	34,451	4.3	26,003	307.8
Columbus, Ohio	237,031	214,721	22,181	9.4	9,442	74.1
Dayton, Ohio	152,559	143,495	9,025	5.9	4,183	86.4
Des Moines, Iowa ..	126,468	120,887	5,512	4.4	2,582	88.1
Detroit, Mich.	993,678	952,065	50,838	4.1	35,097	611.3
Gary, Ind.	55,378	50,044	5,299	9.6	4,916	1,283.6
Hartford, Conn.	138,036	133,681	4,199	3.0	2,454	140.6
Indianapolis, Ind. ...	314,194	279,411	34,678	11.0	12,862	59.0
Kansas City, Kan. ..	101,177	86,703	14,405	14.2	5,119	55.1
Kansas City, Mo.	324,410	293,517	30,719	9.5	7,153	30.4
Los Angeles, Cal. ...	576,673	546,864	15,579	2.7	7,980	105.0
Milwaukee, Wis.	457,147	454,824	2,229	0.5	1,249	127.4
Minneapolis, Minn. .	380,582	376,365	3,927	1.0	1,335	51.5
New Bedford, Mass...	121,217	116,142	4,998	4.1	2,113	73.2
New York, N. Y.....	5,620,048	5,459,463	152,467	2.7	60,758	66.3
Newark, N. J.	414,524	379,223	16,977	4.1	7,502	79.2
Oakland, Cal.	216,261	204,004	5,489	2.5	2,434	79.7
Omaha, Nebr.	191,601	181,046	10,315	5.4	5,172	100.6
Philadelphia, Pa. ...	1,823,779	1,688,180	134,229	7.4	49,770	58.9
Pittsburgh, Pa.	588,343	550,261	37,725	6.4	12,102	47.2
Springfield, Mass. ...	129,614	126,799	2,650	2.0	1,175	79.7
Toledo, Ohio	243,164	237,385	5,691	2.3	3,814	203.2
Youngstown, Ohio ..	132,358	125,595	6,662	5.0	4,726	244.1

Within each city there is usually a segregation or concentration of Negroes in certain sections or localities—a Negro quarter. In New York City, for instance, 42.4 per cent of the total Negro population is located in two assembly districts, within which Negroes form, respectively, 35 and 49 per cent of the total population. In Chicago there is one ward which

---

[1] 1920 census. This census does not take into account the added increase of the 1922-1924 migration.

contains 44 per cent of the total Negro population of the city; Negroes form 70 per cent of the total ward population. In Detroit the concentration is not so marked, although there is one ward in which Negroes constitute about 25 per cent of the total population; in another the ward average is nearly 20 per cent.[1]

6. ADJUSTMENT OF MIGRANT

The adjustment of the colored migrant to a new mode of life in the North was not always easy; very frequently it was a dual process, including adjustment of the rural southern Negro to urban northern conditions. Over 70 per cent of the Negro population of the South was rural, which meant that economic and social conditions in northern cities were entirely different from what they had been accustomed to in the South. Meeting these new conditions of life brought joys and disillusionments, and were reflected in the schools, public amusement places, industries, the street cars, etc. Many northern cities, hitherto unaware of a local race problem became color-conscious and drew the color line tighter. While in the South, due to lack of competition in the industrial and professional lines, the Negro had had little competition, in the North colored professional men and skilled artisans were forced into second place, in many cases being obliged to accept menial positions and to live in social strata far inferior to what they had been accustomed to in their southern homes. The great demand in the North was for unskilled labor. While various organizations made serious efforts to accommodate the migrants to their new mode of life, and while the increase in the non-Catholic church membership would indicate that the Negroes themselves made prompt efforts to re-engage in community life and to establish themselves in their new environment, nevertheless, the tragedies and the disillusionments of the migrants were many.

7. EFFECT ON MISSIONS

What migration there was previous to this recent movement did not affect seriously the work of the Colored Mis-

---

[1] "Recent Northward Migration of the Negro", *Monthly Labor Review*, March, 1924, p. 8.

sions; the movement was confined almost entirely to those southern states bordering on the North. But with the tremendous movement of late years no mission is entirely free from loss. One very notable thing about the recent migration is the way it has reached into the far South. As recently as 1910, 48 per cent, or nearly one-half of the southern-born Negroes living in the North came from two states—Virginia and Kentucky; the migration between 1910 and 1920 reduced the proportion born in these two states to 31.6 per cent. On the other hand, the proportion of northern Negroes coming from the far South (the cotton-belt states of South Carolina, Georgia, Florida, Alabama, Mississippi, Arkansas, Louisiana and Texas) increased from 18.2 per cent of the total number of southern-born Negroes living in the North in 1910 to 40.5 per cent of the total in 1920. The absolute number of Negroes in the North who were natives of these states increased from 75,517 in 1910 to 298,759 in 1920, so that there were nearly four times as many in 1920 as there were in 1910.

The missions in some states, as Texas, Louisiana, Arkansas, Oklahoma, and the delta section of Mississippi, where the cotton crop was generally rather good, seem to have suffered less than others. Even in the states most affected by the migratory movement, it would seem that certain sections were harder hit than others: where, for instance, the floods of 1916 destroyed everything in large sections of Alabama and Mississippi; where for several years previously the cotton had been a failure owing to the ravages of the boll weevil, the Negroes had to leave or starve. Naturally these mass movements, including as they did a certain quota of colored Catholics, considerably disorganized the missionary program of the Colored Missions in the South. The exodus carried off not only the unskilled laborers from the farms and industries of the South but also many of the skilled mechanics from the larger cities such as New Orleans, Montgomery, Birmingham, Savannah and Charleston. Many trained workers of lesser skill, and not a few professional men, were caught up in the movement. As regards missions, this was unfortunate, because the loss of such dependable members of the congregation meant financial hard times for the pastor of the colored mission, the expenses of which were not reduced in proportion to the loss of income.

The migrant usually followed the main lines of transportation. Those from Florida, Georgia, North and South Carolina, and Virginia, drifted into the Middle Atlantic and New England States; for the most part they were Protestant. From Louisiana great numbers of Catholic migrants went west to California, particularly to the cities of Los Angeles and San Francisco, where, from reports received, it would seem to be no exaggeration to say that half were lost to the Church. Many of the Louisianian migrants found their way south into Texas, but the loss among these was not so appalling since colored churches were already there to care for them; being still in the South the so-called "freedom" of the North and the West could work no ill-effects upon them. Finally, there were others from Louisiana and Alabama who found their way to the central cities of Chicago, Cleveland and Detroit where priests devoted exclusively to the welfare of the colored held many of them; nevertheless, in spite of untiring efforts countless others unknown to the priests were lost to the Faith.

Not all the effects of the migration are harmful; some good has resulted. In the South there is the changed attitude towards the Negro; in the North and the West it has resulted in a diffusion of the Negro problem to an extent never before equalled. Generally speaking, it has put the burden of humanity and tolerance on increased numbers of the white population of the country. For the first time many northern people have had thrust upon their sympathies the colored man of the South, and the humane instincts of many have been aroused to an effort in his behalf. While this has not always been the case, and unpleasant instances of clashing opinions rise up here and there, Catholic churches in the North should not have to face any embarrassing clashes, for whatever may go on outside the church edifice, Negro Catholics will be given, as always, the rights and privileges of other communicants.

What, however, about the missions in the South? The practical organization and equipment of the colored missions

has been established and directed by the thought that by far
the vast majority of the race would remain in the South. Is
there any ground for worry in the developments which have
resulted from the extent of the migration?

To begin with, even the most generous estimate can hardly
place above a million the total number of Negroes who left the
South. Out of a total of some nine millions an imposing bal-
ance is still left. Just how many colored Catholics left the
South is impossible to say precisely; probably about 20,000
would be a conservative estimate based upon reports at hand,
which cover the years of the migratory movement.

There may be opportunity in the turn of events.
One of the most perplexing problems in the past has been this:
how can the missionary reach the country people? In the
early days of Christianity the Faith grew first in the large
cities and then overflowed into the country districts. Catholicity has been compelled to follow much the same method in
the southern missions. While the migratory impulse affected
many of those living in rural districts, many never advanced
farther than the great cities of the South, where they replaced
northbound labor. The migration, it will be recalled, was two-
fold: from the South to the North, and from southern rural
sections to southern urban centers.

During the ten-year period between 1910 and 1920, the
Negro population of Southern cities increased by approximately 400,000. In 1890 fewer than 1,500,000 Negroes lived
in cities, and as late as 1900 the number was 2,000,000. By
1920 the number had jumped to 3,500,000, and recent official estimations place it as high as 4,000,000. In 1920 there
were no fewer than twenty-four cities having Negro populations of 25,000 each, although New Orleans, Baltimore,
Washington, Chicago, Philadelphia, and New York each had
more than 100,000. Of necessity, then, the colored missionary work of the Catholic Church is chiefly concentrated in
the cities of the South. Lack of anything like a sufficient
number of missionaries necessitates the development of work
in cities where the greatest possible number of people can be
reached. Of course, this means that rural districts must be
somewhat neglected. But with the influx of the country popu-

lation to the city, new avenues of approach are opened to the city missionary. Even though the great majority of the colored population still lives in the rural sections of the South, the migration has brought into the cities an adequate number of Negroes to give the missioners sufficient new material to work on for years to come. Numbers of rural Negroes who had been in total ignorance regarding the Church, many who, before moving, had never even seen an edifice dedicated to Catholic worship have been brought into contact with Catholicity and Catholic Negroes in the southern cities. They may even send their children to a Catholic school. A southern pastor writes: "From time to time colored boys and girls from the country have come into our schools. They are shy and very backward for their age, and they are obliged to enter the lower grades. Yet, their good, sturdy, country habits bring them finally to the top." Thus, by a providential stroke, many members of the colored race whom the Church could not have hoped to reach for some time are brought under the influence of Catholic life and teaching.

The same conclusion holds in reference to those Negroes who have gone North. There they live in large cities where Catholic churches abound and where the Catholic element is a large and influential part of civic activity. Their experience will react for the better on their brethren in the South, to which, it is not improbable, many of the migrants will return. Negroes went North by the trainload; they will return by two's and three's—it is the habit of the colored man when times are dull to go long distances to visit old haunts and kinsfolk. A constantly returning stream will carry back the remembrance of a manly and generous Catholicity. It is not too much to expect that many misconceptions and prejudices will be removed and that the conquest of the race for Christ will be thus made less remote.

8. A NEW PROBLEM

In the North the sudden and abnormal increase in the Negro population of necessity involves a tremendous change and creates a new situation, demanding the immediate attention of Church authorities. The imperative necessity, of course, is to provide for the Catholic migrant. This entails a positive effort to reach him. While some bishops have already done much for him, others are seemingly unaware of his presence. One thing is certain: we may not now without serious error confine colored missionary activity to the South.

During the past fifteen years, as we have already shown, hundreds of thousands of Negroes forsook the land of their birth and resolutely set their faces toward the land of promise in the North. Caught up in this hegira were thousands of Catholic Negroes, some with a long line of Catholic ancestors back of them, others with only a few years of Catholic training to stand by them in their need. The majority of these migrants went to the North, principally to the Middle Atlantic States of New York, New Jersey, and Pennsylvania. In the North, about one of every thirty Negroes belongs to the Catholic Church. In the West, the ratio is about one to twenty. These relatively large ratios are, as we have seen, due to the fact that the Negroes in the North and West are concentrated in cities where much more effective missionary work can be carried on. This does not mean, however, that all colored Catholics are practical Catholics; in most instances it simply means that the presence of so many colored Catholics is known or suspected. Just what success the Church is having in holding them is another matter. In New York State, for instance, there is an estimated colored population of over 250,000 of which over 26,000 are supposed to be Catholics; yet, it is certain that thousands of colored Catholics are swallowed up in the maelstrom of New York City alone. Brooklyn, with an estimated colored Catholic population of 12,000, can claim only about one-tenth of them as being practical. Pennsylvania, with a colored population of 300,000, of which 5,000 are Catholics, can satisfactorily account for only about half of them.

Difficulties peculiar to the North are to be found, but as a rule they are largely local and the situation can be adequately handled by the local ordinaries. That some bishops are coping with the problem is evident from the fact that in the Middle Atlantic and East North Central divisions fifty per cent of the work for Negroes has been started within the past decade. When we consider that of the colored population in the North .035 is Catholic, whereas under the more difficult situation in the South only .017 (proportionately, half as many) is Catholic, we can readily see the necessity of immediate action on the part of northern bishops.

In the meantime the Negro is restlessly searching for improvement and justice. Dissatisfaction with the present unjust order of things is making him go far afield in quest of a solution of his troubles. Does it mean nothing to us Catholics that even some non-Catholic writers gracefully admit "the Catholic Church can bring to the Negro that which no other institution in the world can give him. . . The Catholic Church is the ideal instrument—and it seems to me, the only instrument, that can solve the race problem in the South"?[1] The South, however, is Protestant, and the Catholic Church in the South is poor and insignificant. In the North, on the contrary, it is prosperous and less hampered in its activities. Because of circumstances northern Catholics are more liberal in their views on the color line; then, too, in the North the church and school equipment so necessary for saving souls is well nigh perfect. Let the Church in the North make the Negro feel welcome and he will find therein that peace which neither the world nor any Protestant church can give to the earnest yearnings of his soul.

Those of other faiths are not standing idly by, but have gone forth provided with a host of workers and abundant resources to make proselytes. The 1926 Appeal of the American Hierarchy in Behalf of the Negro and Indian Missions in the United States very pointedly observes that: "Where we give thousands, they (Protestants) give tens of thousands and millions; where we have only hundreds of workers, they have thousands in the field. Sad to say, our organization in this respect compares very unfavorably with theirs; indeed it compares unfavorably even with our own foreign mission organizations. What others are doing we Americans have all the more reason to be doing for the Indians and the Negroes. They stand at our very door, needy, helpless, perishing spiritually for lack of the Water of Life. To these poor, be-

---

[1] Aswell, Edward C., *The Commonweal*, Nov. 21, 1928, p. 68.

nighted people we have a mission and a duty—the same glorious mission and the same sacred duty that were entrusted to the Apostles: 'Going, therefore, teach ye all nations, baptizing them and teaching them to observe all things whatsoever I have commanded you.' "

The 1927 Appeal of the Hierarchy reminds us further that: "chief among our missionary undertakings is the apostolic work among the Negroes and Indians of this country. In fact, this work is the first in time, for it antedates our foreign mission endeavors, and is as yet our greatest and most real achievement. It was our apprenticeship, our first conquest for Christ and the first fruits of our zeal for the spreading of the Kingdom of the Savior, and, therefore, should be first in our affections, our charity and our duty. These races naturally have the first claim upon us, for they dwell amongst us, and charity begins at home. We Catholics must regard them as our wards, and ourselves as their apostles."

If one considers that in two score years there has been in these United States an increase of but four thousand in the number of colored Catholics, one can hardly deny that, to further quote the 1927 Appeal, "They can, in truth, complain of their benighted condition as in some measure due to our spiritual neglect of them." Eleven and a half million Negroes in our country and only a little over two hundred thousand of them Catholic! There is no quibbling with the figures—an episcopal signature stands under every one of them. Here is a problem worthy of our best Catholic thought and action. Are we measuring up to it?

CHAPTER VIII.

MIGRATION AND THE SOUTH

With the scanty data at our disposal it is impossible to make an exhaustive study of the effects directly traceable to migration. But even though information is not at hand for the missions, a satisfactory study may be ma,de from the official reports of the Josephite missions and such other information as is had from the questionnaires returned by missionaries of other societies laboring on the Colored Missions. The missions in charge of the Josephite Fathers number about half of the exclusively colored missions in the South and form a fair cross-section of the ground to be covered.

Of fifty representative Josephite parishes which are studied for a period of time from 1913 to 1928, 31 show a net loss, although only seven indicate an actual loss in numbers.[1] Of 44 accurate reports from missions founded before 1920 and in charge of other societies, only eight report a gain. The other 36 report no increase or show an actual loss over a ten-year period (1918-1928).

1. SOUTH ATLANTIC GROUP

DELAWARE—There is no indication that the State of Delaware was much affected by the migration. There was only one exclusively colored mission in the whole state—St. Joseph's Mission in Wilmington.[2] Reports from this mission would indicate a net loss, although the actual number in the

[1] By actual loss is meant that the number of souls actually in the congregation today is less than in 1913, or than when the mission was begun, if later than that year. By net loss is meant the number of souls unaccounted for by natural decrease. This latter figure was arrived at by adding the number of baptisms reported since 1913 (or later, if the mission was founded later) to the number in the congregation in that year. From this figure is subtracted the number of deaths reported during the same period. The result is what the congregation would have been in 1928 by natural growth. The difference between this theoretical figure and the actual number now in the congregation is the net loss. Some small allowance must be made for defections within the parish during that period, but there is no way of knowing the exact number of these.

[2] A new mission has since been founded at Belvedere.

congregation remained about the same. This apparent loss is due to the fact that formerly there was an orphanage attached to the mission. When the children were discharged from the orphanage they usually went elsewhere; few remained to become members of the parish. The baptisms from the orphanage, however, swelled the figures in the annual reports. The State of Delaware was sufficiently north to share in the opportunities which attracted migrants from more southern states, so there was no necessity for the Negroes of Delaware to seek opportunity elsewhere.

MARYLAND—In the city of Baltimore there are four exclusively colored parishes. Of these parishes, two indicate an actual loss due to movement to other parts of the city; one reports an actual gain but a net loss of over a thousand, due mostly to movement to other sections of the city and consequent attendance at white churches. The Church of St. Peter Claver reports an actual gain of 2,184; natural gain by baptisms accounts for all but 460. Some of the new-comers to St. Peter's are from the counties of southern Maryland, many from other Baltimore parishes, and a few from other states. In the figures from the Baltimore parishes some allowance must be made for migration to points farther North. The number of such migrants, however, is not large enough materially to affect the figures. The two churches which show an actual loss, St. Francis Xavier's and St. Monica's, have been in charge of the Josephite Fathers since their arrival in America in the seventies. Eventually these churches must be re-located in those sections of the city to which their congregations have moved.

The reports at hand being incomplete, it is difficult to say precisely to what extent the missions in southern Maryland have been affected by migration. The questionnaires which were returned indicate some decrease. That the Baltimore parishes have acquired not a few new members from the counties would indicate that the Maryland rural missions have suffered somewhat.

DISTRICT OF COLUMBIA—Of the seven parishes in the District, five have been established as recently as 1920. Only two show a decrease: St. Augustine's, the mother parish of the others, decreased partly because recently two new parishes have been formed from portions of it, and partly because the people are moving to other sections of the city; the Church of the Epiphany also shows a slight decrease. The sections of the District in which these two parishes are located are becoming commercial and white again. The three more recent parishes in the district, St. Vincent's, Holy Redeemer, and Incarnation, show substantial gains.

VIRGINIA—Being a border state, Virginia has always been affected more or less by migration. Most of the Virginia migrants, as has been noted, went to the Middle Atlantic and New England States. Many of the migrants were natives of Virginia, but the bulk of them in all probability came from points further south. In many cases, obstacles had been placed in the way of direct movement to the North, so they tarried for a while at Norfolk and Richmond, whence they made a new start either upon their own initiative or with the aid of labor agents.

St. Joseph's mission in Richmond is just about holding its own, despite the fact that an actual gain of 191 members is reported over a period of fifteen years. This does not mean so much if account be taken of the fact that there have been 1,764 baptisms and only 793 deaths reported in the same period of time. It is true that many of these baptisms were hospital and institution cases, but their number was probably not so large as to account for the leakage of 780. St. Joseph's mission in Norfolk is likewise barely holding its own, although in recent years there have been several convert classes over the hundred mark. While an actual gain of 583 is reported for this latter mission, there is a net gain of only three during a fifteen-year period. There would seem to be no doubt that migration has robbed both Richmond and Norfolk missions of many Catholics. The same conditions prevail at St. Joseph's mission in Alexandria; the people are moving from Alexandria into the District of Columbia just across the Potomac River. Better working conditions is the reason given. This mission has a net loss of 77 over a fifteen-year period.

The country missions in Virginia are suffering even a

worse fate; it has been necessary to close several of them. The Holy Cross mission, Rock Castle, in charge of the Holy Ghost Fathers,[1] reports a substantial net loss and no actual gain. Attached to this mission are the chaplaincies of St. Emma's Industrial School and St. Francis' Academy, both at Rock Castle.

WEST VIRGINIA—In view of the fact that there are hardly 100 colored Catholics in the whole State of West Virginia and no exclusively colored missionary activity, migration from this state cannot affect the colored missions.

NORTH CAROLINA—The Negro migrants from this State have gone principally to points in Virginia, West Virginia, New Jersey, Pennsylvania, and New York. The State of North Carolina was not affected so much as were the states farther south. Many Negroes from the more southern states came into North Carolina and Virginia, and after staying for a short time proceeded to northern destinations. The missions at New Bern and Wilmington report losses; New Bern just about holding its own, while St. Thomas' in Wilmington shows a net loss of 111. In this latter mission there have been 290 baptisms and only 35 deaths reported over the period being studied. The pastor at St. Mark's mission, Newton Grove, reports that, "they move away as fast as I get them." A striking feature of the North Carolina migration is the very large movement within the state; a large number of the residents of the mountains moved into the cotton mill towns, where they remained as operatives, whole families, including children, accepting employment.

SOUTH CAROLINA—In South Carolina reports indicate that heavier migration was felt in the western part of the state than in the eastern. This is particularly true of Abbeyville and Greenville counties. The only other section which suffered heavily was the coastal region around Charleston, into which section the movement of turpentine laborers in Georgia seems to have extended. St. Peter's mission in the city of Charleston reported that because of losses through migration the number in the congregation remained practically unchanged. If the actual number in the congregation

---

[1] Now in charge of the Benedictines.

remained the same, it is very probable that there was a net loss, as there were 290 baptisms reported since 1918. The number of deaths would hardly equal this figure. This represents an almost complete turnover; the congregation numbered only 340 in 1928. The mission of St. James, Catholic Hill, Ritter, reports no gain, which probably means a loss. These are the only two exclusively colored missions in the state.

GEORGIA—Extremely low wages and the appearance of the boll weevil in the southwestern section of Georgia had much to do with starting the migration. The two main centers of movement were in the southern part of the state: one was the boll weevil area in the southwest, and the other was around the city of Savannah on the Atlantic coast. That colored Catholics were among the migrants is evident from the fact that St. Anthony's mission in the city of Savannah shows no increase over a ten-year period. On the other hand, St. Benedict's mission in the same city shows an increase of 300. The exact reasons for this gain were not given in the questionnnaire. In the upper Piedmont section of the central black belt about Macon, Augusta, and Columbus, there was little mass movement of the Negroes reported in surveys, although St. Peter's mission in Macon reported a loss of over a hundred, almost a third of the normal congregation. The Immaculate Conception mission in Augusta indicated a net loss of 375, in spite of the fact that the actual gain in the mission was nearly 400. The pastor of the Immaculate Conception, Rev. Alfred Laube, S.M.A., has built up this parish from the two families he found there eighteen years ago. Its present number is 446.

FLORIDA—In Florida the three exclusively colored missions report that they are just about holding their own. The mission of St. Benedict the Moor, opened in St. Augustine (1915) with a congregation of 315, today has only 380; however, this is normal growth. St. Pius', Jacksonville, shows an actual gain of 168 in the congregation, but a net gain of only 10; this, also, is about normal.

On the other hand, the missions in northwestern Florida report losses. The mission of St. Joseph in Pensacola, Fla.

(Diocese of Mobile), reports that in one year (1927) as many as 200 left the mission for points north. The pastor reports only 18 converts for the year 1927, although in former years he averaged as many as 40. So many Catholic families went north from the missions at Escambia and Cantonment that they were closed. The Holy Family mission at Appalachicola, Fla. (Diocese of Mobile), reports a membership of only 16 in the congregation, although there have been 18 baptisms since its foundation in 1920. Several other churches in the state, two of which are exclusively colored, have a large number of Negroes in the congregation, but no reports were had from them.

2. EAST SOUTH CENTRAL GROUP

KENTUCKY—The extent to which migration affected the Kentucky missions is difficult to state exactly owing to lack of precise information. Of the two exclusively colored missions in the city of Louisville, St. Augustine's reports a gain of approximately 200, while St. Peter Claver's did not answer the question. In as much as there are only 135 members in the congregation, and the number of baptisms reported for the past ten years is over the two hundred mark, it would seem that it is faring badly. St. Peter's mission in Lexington reports that the number of people in the mission is "decreasing; moving elsewhere." Whether this means they are moving to other states or to points within the state is not clear. The congregation is small and made up of a "floating" population, which makes it difficult to obtain exact figures.

TENNESSEE—The exclusively colored missions in Tennessee show a decided disturbance due to migration. St. Anthony's mission at Memphis reports that in the past fifteen years there have been enough new members added to the congregation to form four or five parishes as large as the present one. This is probably due to the fact that Memphis was a point of distribution for migrants from farther south. From other states and from the rural sections of Tennessee they would come as far as Memphis, linger for a few months or a year, until such time as they had saved sufficient money to carry them farther north. This mission shows a net loss of

264, but the turnover was far greater. At present the congregation numbers only 205, although there have been 500
baptisms reported in the fifteen-year period under study.
From this number 68 deaths are to be deducted.

Holy Family mission in Nashville reports a net loss of
111, and St. Joseph's in Jackson a net loss of 23. Both these
missions are in Protestant sections. The latter numbers about
15 adults and 40 children, although there have been 74 baptisms reported during the past ten years.

ALABAMA—All sections of Alabama have been troubled
by migratory movements. The cities of Birmingham and Bessemer, owing to their railroad facilities and peculiar location
in a large coal and iron industrial district, have been most
important points of distribution. A large percentage of the
Negroes who left the black-belt districts in the south-central
sections of the state first purchased tickets to Birmingham,
whence they went to points north and east. Most of the
migrants from the district went to the coal fields in Kentucky,
West Virginia, Virginia, and Pennsylvania, where there was
a constant demand for miners from this district. A large
number from Birmingham made their way to Detroit, Chicago, East St. Louis and other points in Illinois, as also to
Cincinnati, Akron, Cleveland, and Dayton. The places vacated
by these migrants from Birmingham were filled by "boll-
weevil" Negroes and others from the black-belt around Meridian and points east of the Mississippi, as well as from
southwest Georgia and the western part of Florida.

The Immaculate Conception mission in Birmingham shows
a net loss of over 200 in the past decade, with a probable
turn-over five times the normal size of the congregation,
which was never more than 150. The work of convert-making in this mission is rendered more difficult by the fact that
Birmingham is in a distinctly Protestant part of Alabama.
St. John the Baptist mission, Montgomery, is another mission
in a Protestant section. In the past fifteen years this mission
indicates a net loss of 214. At present it has a congregation
of only 186, although reports indicate 404 baptisms and only
91 deaths.

The Mobile missions of the Most Pure Heart of Mary and of St. Peter Claver suffered heavily for the same reason given for the Birmingham loss: Mobile was a point of distribution. Both missions in Mobile indicate a total loss of 1,137. This figure is probably too high, because the former bishop, Bishop Allen, insisted that anyone ever baptized in the Catholic Church be counted as Catholic even though he was such only nominally. This caused some exaggeration in early reports. It is safe to say, however, that half the figure here given would be no exaggeration for loss through migration.

The rural missions of Mon Louis and Chastang show losses. The people moved up to the cities; some remained in the cities, others moved elsewhere. Migration, however, does not fully explain a net loss of 90 reported from Chastang and its missions. Not many people have left this section. No explanation has been given for the loss indicated.

MISSISSIPPI—Short crops, the ravages of the boll weevil, and several successive storms have helped to swell the number of migrants from this state. Farming and industries in eastern Mississippi for a time were almost crippled; even the sawmill industry in the southern part of the state was reported as being seriously affected once the mass movement got under way.

The whole State of Mississippi felt the effects of the migration. Not all of the migrants, however, went to the North or West. Many went to the upper part of the Yazoo-Mississippi Delta in the northwestern part of the state; some went to Arkansas or other southern points either directly or after reaching Memphis, Tenn., which was a distribution center. Migrations of Mississippi Negroes in the past have always been much heavier to the West and even to the South than to the North. In 1910, Negroes born in Mississippi and living in the New England, the Middle Atlantic States, and the Middle West were less than one-sixth of the number of such Negroes living in the four States of Louisiana, Arkansas, Oklahoma and Texas. In Arkansas alone there were twice as many Negroes of Mississippi birth as in the whole of the northern territory mentioned above. In 1910 there were in southern states east of the Mississippi nearly three times as many Negroes born in Mississippi as there were of those Negroes in the entire North.

The colored missions in Mississippi were hard hit by the migration particularly the missions in Natchez and vicinity. Like Memphis, Tenn., and Mobile, Ala., Natchez was a point of distribution. In 1913 the Holy Family mission in Natchez had a congregation of 130 souls. In five years the number increased to 622, after which it dropped to its present number of 488. The annual turn-over in this parish has been large, although the net loss for the fifteen years is only 149. The towns of Biloxi, Pass Christian, and Pascagoula in this state are at a standstill, and the colored mission at each place is dwindling. Vicksburg, Jackson, Greenville, Meridian, and Camden, each having an exclusively colored mission, report no gain, although they do not give figures which would indicate how much they have lost. From Meridian 160 migrated; Jackson reports "they go as fast they come," and Greenville that "they have moved to Chicago and St. Louis."

3. WEST SOUTH CENTRAL GROUP

ARKANSAS—The Arkansas missions fared no better than did missions elsewhere. The pastor of St. Bartholomew's mission, Little Rock, reported "not much increase because people moved to northern states." "Not much" meant that although there had been 302 baptisms reported since 1918 the congregation numbered only 165 in 1928. Here is one classic example of results not being commensurate with labor expended. There was one colored Catholic in Little Rock in 1911 when Father Herman Patzelt, S.V.D., opened the mission. Since then 396 baptisms have been recorded. St. John the Baptist mission at Fort Smith, opened in 1917, reports a gain of 48, but St. Peter's at Pine Bluff shows a net loss of 125 in the same period. It is known that some people from this latter mission went as far as Brazil, South America, whence they wrote back telling friends how well they were treated and urging them to follow. Not a few have done so.

LOUISIANA—The migration from Louisiana is of particular interest because of the number of colored Catholics involved. There was a two-fold movement very noticeable in this state: one from rural sections to urban; another from the cities to other states. The general line of extra-state movement was in the direction of Texas and California, with a considerable number going to Chicago, Ill. It is of interest to note that of the ten parishes in the city of New Orleans only two indicated a loss: St. Katharine's parish is fast becoming commercial, and Holy Redeemer is scattered, many of the members attending white churches which are more convenient. In reality, therefore, it may be said that none of the city parishes have suffered.

The fact that four parishes in the city of New Orleans report a total net increase of nearly 8,000 souls unaccounted for by natural growth gives some indication of the extent of movement from rural sections. Not all of this increase, however, has come from the country. Many of the Negroes are natives of the city who formerly attended white churches or who did not attend church at all. Nevertheless, a very large number, because of the advantages offered, has come in from the rural missions and settled in the city replacing the city migrants who went to points in Texas and California. This is true also of Baton Rouge where St. Francis' mission has acquired a surplus of 614 in a fifteen-year period, an increase unaccounted for by natural growth. The fact is that Negroes are literally "flocking in from the surrounding country."

The extent of the intra-state movement is emphasized by the fact that nearly all the rural missions in the state report a loss. The missions at Lebeau, Donaldsonville, and Thibodaux all show a decrease. Lebeau lost 246, most of whom were driven out by the floods. Donaldsonville lost 186 who were driven out by high water, and Thibodaux indicates an unaccounted loss of 67. Breaux Bridge and New Roads, both of which have been opened since 1922, report a gain due mostly to reclamation work.

In the Diocese of Alexandria, La., the missions at Marksville, Isle Breville, and Alexandria all report losses. The mission at Shreveport alone shows a gain; it was opened in 1922. In the Diocese of Lafayette in the same state, the three

Josephite missions report gains, probably because they were founded after the migratory movement had almost ceased.

TEXAS—The State of Texas would seem to be the only southern state which has benefitted from the migration. The three missions at Beaumont, Houston, and Port Arthur report substantial gains; for a while the mission at Ames also shared in the general prosperity. Practically all the migrants to these missions were Louisianians. The three cities first mentioned are industrial developments. Beaumont and Port Arthur grew almost from nothing when the oil industry offered a golden opportunity to migrants; both cities ship huge quantities of petroleum products, and the district has become a great industrial center. The city of Houston would seem to be developing at the expense of Galveston. Seventeen railroads converge in Houston, which (though fifty miles from the sea) has become an important shipping port since the widening and deepening of the Buffalo Bayou and the San Jacinto River (1919).

The mission at Port Arthur, formerly attached to the Beaumont mission, reports a gain of 475 through immigration. In the past few years, however, a depression has been felt in this area. White laborers are now given precedence over the colored who are being discharged by the thousands;[1] many are returning to Louisiana whence they came. Even despite these adverse conditions, both Beaumont and Port Arthur missions have doubled their numbers in the past ten years; Beaumont now having 1,800 and Port Arthur 1,500. The development at Houston is more stable in that it does not depend on a single industry as do Port Arthur and Beaumont. The mission at Houston shows a net gain of 709, of which 631 is a natural gain by baptisms. This mission has grown from 800 in 1913 to its present 2,000.[2]

The other missions in Texas report a loss. Two exclusively colored missions in the city of San Antonio show a net loss of over 200 between them, although both have slightly in-

---

[1] Recent reports from Port Arthur indicate the arrival of a new era of prosperity consequent upon the development of civic improvements and the establishment of new industries.

[2] A new mission has since been established in Houston.

creased in actual numbers. This net loss is probably not so great if consideration be given to the fact that in former years many school children were baptized but did not persevere. The mission at Dallas, too, shows a net loss. Dallas was the "stopping-off" place for migrants to points west. Some of the loss which the mission shows comes from the fact that a boarding school is attached to it; accordingly, the return of pupils to their home states must be taken into consideration.

For a city which is normally quiet, Galveston lost many colored Catholics because for several years there was a strike of dock hands in the city. Many Negroes moved to Houston, which offered better opportunities. The Sacred Heart mission at Ames also reports a loss of several hundred, although at the beginning of the migration it received not a little increase. The boll weevil hit this section of Texas hard for several successive seasons, and many of the Louisianians returned to their former homes, taking with them some of the natives of Texas.

CHAPTER IX.

MIGRATION AND THE NORTH

It can hardly be said that as a whole the North has taught the South anything new in the handling of the race question. It is true that some bishops of the North have given considerable thought to the spiritual welfare of the Catholic colored migrants within the boundaries of their dioceses; it is equally true that other bishops seem to be unaware of such a problem. It is not without its irony that religious superiors should find it necessary to send out missionaries to "scout up" prospective missions in well-organized parishes and should there concentrate the energies and efforts of three or four missionaries for a period of several weeks so that faith already strong may be stirred up. In the meantime, what is happening to the colored Catholics in the diocese? In the following pages a sketch of the condition of Catholicism among the northern colored people is given in the hope that some idea of the enormity and seriousness of the situation may be grasped.

1. NEW ENGLAND STATES

In 1920 the New England States had a colored population of 80,000, which was an increase of 13,000 over that of 1910. The vast majority of migrants to the New England States came from Virginia, North Carolina, Georgia, South Carolina, and Maryland, in the order given.

MASSACHUSETTS—Since 1910, the State of Massachusetts has increased 20 per cent in Negro population. Boston, with a colored population of 17,000 (1920), is the only city in which there is anything like a special effort made to save Catholic Negro migrants to the Church. Strictly speaking, however, there is no colored mission in Boston. Some years ago a special Mass for the Negroes was started in old St. Patrick's Church, but whatever success was met with in the beginning, at the present time very few Negroes go to this particular Mass, most of them seeming to prefer to attend St. Philip's Church. The pastor of St. Philip's has jurisdiction over the Negroes of his parish only, there being about 350 in the parish. While the parish school is open to the colored children, only about a dozen children attend. The Sisters of the Blessed Sacrament have a Sunday school at which not more than 30 or 40 colored children attend. The Sisters also do social service work and have a sodality for Negro women, to which but a mere handful belong.

In the Diocese of Fall River, Mass., there are about 4,000 "bravas," the greater number living in New Bedford. Those not living in New Bedford are located in the small towns on Cape Cod. These "bravas" are Portuguese and cannot strictly be considered in our survey. In the Diocese of Springfield, Mass., there are not more than 75 colored Catholics.

CONNECTICUT—The State of Connecticut had 21,000 Negroes in 1920, which is a gain of 38.7 per cent over the number of 1910. The Right Rev. Bishop writes that the number of Negroes in the diocese is approximately 30,000, and of that number only about 500 are Catholics.

In the Diocese of Providence, which covers the State of Rhode Island, the number of colored Catholics does not exceed 100, although in 1920 the Negro population of the state was over 10,000. It is barely possible that there are a few more colored Catholics than this number, due to the fact that some genuine Africans attend one or two Portuguese churches where there are a handful of "bravas" from the Azores.

In Maine, New Hampshire, and Vermont there were 2,500 colored people in 1920. The number of colored Catholics is negligible.

2. MIDDLE ATLANTIC STATES

These States, with over 600,000 Negroes, have practically doubled their colored population since 1910. The majority of migrants were from the Atlantic seaboard states of the South.

NEW YORK—During the decade between 1910-1920, the State of New York had an increase of 47.9 per cent in its

Negro population. Three-quarters of the Negroes in the state live in the city of New York; the Dioceses of Rochester and Syracuse have few—not more than a hundred in both; the Diocese of Ogdensburg has few Negroes (due to the coldness of the winters) none of whom are Catholics.

In the Diocese of Buffalo there are about 250 colored Catholics living in three distinct districts: the city of Lackawanna has 50; the city of Buffalo, 200—divided into the Michigan-Williams district with 150, and the Jefferson-Utica district with about 50. The Church of St. Augustine, Buffalo, is the only exclusively colored church in the Diocese.

In the Diocese of Albany the Church of St. Mary (white), through its pastor, is sponsoring the work for the colored Catholics. Located in the lower part of Albany, St. Mary's has lost much of its white population which was replaced by colored. There are about 150 colored families within the territory. The parish volunteered to instruct in the Faith the colored Catholics of the city. As a result, St. Philip's Church was built for the exclusive use of the colored. Altogether there are about 4,000 colored people in the city of Albany, but at present not more than twenty or twenty-five families are Catholic.

The Diocese of Brooklyn has an estimated colored population of 85,000, according to Rev. Bernard Quinn, pastor of St. Peter Claver's Church. Most of these are West Indians— about 90 per cent. Of the colored population, Father Quinn estimates that about 12,000 are baptized Catholics, but not more than 1,000 attend St. Peter Claver's Church, the only exclusively colored Catholic church in the Diocese.

In the Archdiocese of New York there are 140,390 Negroes, according to the report from the Chancery Office. Of this number 13,800 are Catholics. This does not include the number of Negro Catholics in the Bahama Islands which are part of the jurisdiction of the Archdiocese. On the other hand, the annual report of the New York Urban League places much higher the Negro population of New York City alone. In the city of New York the League estimates there are 259,800 Negroes (early part of 1928). The annual report of the League points out that in 1910 the Negro population of

New York City was 1.9 per cent of the total and that today
it is more than 4 per cent, distributed as follows:

TABLE 11. DISTRIBUTION OF NEGROES IN NEW YORK CITY
Manhattan:
  Harlem 170,000
  Columbus Hill 10,000
  West Nineties 4,000
  East Nineties 4,000
  Longacre 5,000
  Kips Bay 1,500
  Greenwich 800
Bronx 8,000
Queens 15,000
Richmond 1,500
Brooklyn 40,000

The Harlem section of New York is practically owned
by Negroes. In that section alone there are 150 colored
churches, of which number 40 are Baptist, 25 Spiritualist,
22 Methodist, 1 Protestant Episcopal, 2 Congregational, 2
Presbyterian, 1 Moravian, 1 Christian Scientist, 2 Seventh
Day Adventist, 1 Hebrew, 1 Emmanuel, 1 Lutheran, and 7
African Orthodox, besides various other faiths that are off
the beaten paths of belief.

Within the past few years the colored population of Harlem has increased to such an extent that today, with its 170,-
000 souls, it is the most densely populated colored district in
the United States. At one time it was possible for St. Mark's
Church to care for the people of this section, but today a very
large number of former members have moved into better resi-
dential sections and attend the church of the parish in which
they are living. They are cared for by the priests of the
neighboring parishes of St. Aloysius, Resurrection, St. Thomas,
St. Charles, All Saints, and Our Lady of the Miraculous Medal.
In the Archdiocese it is understood that all churches are to
care for the colored people within their territories, even
though the church be not exclusively colored. Only two
churches in the Archdiocese are listed as being exclusively
colored: St. Mark's and St. Benedict the Moor's. The prospects in the city of New York are encouraging. It is a difficult
field, however, because of the constantly shifting population,
the awful conditions in which some of the people live, and the
large stream of unattached strangers, men and women, which

is always flowing into the town from the various parts of the country and the West Indies.

NEW JERSEY—The State of New Jersey, particularly the industrial centers of Jersey City, Newark, and Trenton, has had a substantial increase in colored population. In 1920 there were 117,132 Negroes in the state. While no reliable figures are at hand which would indicate the extent to which the influx of Negroes has changed the ratio of whites and colored since then, some idea of the problem may be had from the fact that in Jersey City there are in the neighborhood of 700 colored Catholics, while in Newark there is a large and growing contingent of colored folk of which approximately 400 are Catholics.[1]

The Diocese of Newark is industrial in character. The shifting changes from New York and Pennsylvania into New Jersey make a positive census of the colored Catholics a difficult task. A survey was begun the early part of 1928, but owing to the death of Bishop O'Connor and the installation of the new bishop, Bishop Walsh, it was temporarily postponed. Up to the time of interruption the census had listed some 700 colored Catholics in Jersey City alone.

In Atlantic City (Diocese of Trenton) there are about 600 colored Catholics. The only exclusively colored work is being done at St. Monica's, Atlantic City, at present only a welfare organization, but being developed into a parish. In the meantime, all the members attend the church of the parish in which they live. St. Monica's is attached to the Church of the Holy Spirit.

PENNSYLVANIA—The State of Pennsylvania received an increase of 46.7 per cent in its colored population during the period 1910-1920. In 1920 Pennsylvania had a colored population of 284,568. The city of Philadelphia contains 47 per cent of the Negro population of Pennsylvania, as compared with 21 per cent of the total population of the state. By adding the colored population of Pittsburgh, 60 per cent of the colored population of the state is accounted for. The only exclusively colored Catholic work is being done in these two

---

[1] The Chancery Office reported only 900 Colored Catholics in the Diocese of Newark.

cities. In the city of Philadelphia there are four exclusively colored parishes, each having a parochial school, while in Pittsburgh there is one colored church but no school.

Of the 500 Negroes living in the city of Altoona, only five are practical Catholics, two of these being converts of the past year. There are about 2,000 colored people in the city of Johnstown, yet only 20 or 25 are Catholics. The number of colored Catholics in the Dioceses of Erie and Scranton is negligible, although both have average colored populations.

In the Diocese of Harrisurg there are 94 adult colored Catholics, 49 children of school age, and 15 infants. In York City there are not more than 50 colored Catholics.

The colored work in Pittsburgh has a glorious record, having been one of the first undertaken after the Civil War. There are about 200 families scattered throughout the Diocese in addition to the 350 persons who attend the Church of St. Benedict, the only church in the city for the exclusive use of the colored.

In the Archdiocese of Philadelphia Table 12 will give some idea of the colored situation as far as the Church is concerned:

TABLE 12.—COLORED CATHOLICS IN ARCHDIOCESE OF PHILA.

I—*For the parishes outside the city*:

County	Colored Population 1920 Cens.	Catholic Families	Catholic Persons	Catholics in Paroch'l Schools	Negligent	Pervert
Berks	1,165	6	20		4	
Bucks	1,810	6	32	11	4	
Carbon ...	25	0	1	0		
Chester ..	25	11	36	7	4	4
Delaware	15,715	56	172	23	20	4
Lehigh ..	300	0	0	0		
M'tgom'y	8,326	37	167	35	18	2
N'tham'on	749	4	20	1	13	
Schuylkill	253	0	0	0		

II—*For the city of Philadelphia, outside the separate parishes for colored, the following are substantially accurate estimates*:

	134,229	40	200	20	50	150

III—*For exclusively colored parishes in the city of Philadelphia*:

		300	1500	600	no	figures
TOTAL	173,910	460	2148	697	113	156

[1] The above table was furnished by Rev. Vincent Dever, pastor of St. Ignatius' Church, at the request of Cardinal Dougherty.

3. EAST NORTH CENTRAL STATES

In this group, which includes the States of Ohio, Indiana, Illinois, Michigan and Wisconsin, there were 514,554 Negroes in 1920, which is a gain of 71 per cent between the years 1910-1920. Exclusively colored missionary work is being done in nine of the seventeen dioceses in these states.

OHIO—The State of Ohio shows an increase of 67.1 per cent in its colored population (1910-1920). Three cities in Ohio — Cleveland, Cincinnati and Columbus—account for 46 per cent of the total Negro population of the state, although these three cities contain only about 25 per cent of the total population of the State.

In the city of Cincinnati the work for the Negroes has been going on since the time of the Civil War, the parish of St. Ann having been established in 1862 by the Jesuit Fathers. Extremely slow progress seems to have been made in its earlier days, the Fathers having been able to devote only part of their time to the work. In 1909 Father Clery, a secular priest, took charge of the parish and did remarkable work. In 1926 the colored work in the Archdiocese was placed in charge of Rev. Leo Walsh. Of late years the population of Cincinnati has been moving to the suburbs. This took many Catholics from the parish of St. Ann, which is located in the "downtown" section. At the same time this movement affected Holy Trinity Church, a white church, located five blocks from the center of the city. Originally it was a German church, but with the development of the suburbs the German Catholics moved from the central city and their places were filled by incoming Negroes. This parish was taken over by the colored, and under the zeal of Father Walsh has grown larger than St. Ann's. The following statistics for the Archdiocese of Cincinnati have been supplied by Father Walsh:

TABLE 13.—COLORED CATHOLICS IN ARCHDIOCESE OF CINCINNATI

City	Total Colored Population	Practical Catholics	Fallen Away	In Catholic Schools
Cincinnati	43,000	500	400	523
Dayton	20,000	12	40	5
Springfield	11,000	7	20	4
Hamilton	7,000	3	?	0
Xenia	5,000	20	50	12
TOTAL	86,000	542	510	544

INDIANA—In 1920 the Negro population of this state was 80,810. In the Diocese of Indianapolis it is estimated that there are about 500 colored Catholics. St. Rita's Church, Indianapolis, the only exclusively colored church in the state, cares for about 175. In the Diocese of Fort Wayne there are 135 colored Catholics reported. The report indicates that 75 of these are in the city of Gary. According to the 1920 Government statistics, this latter city has a colored population of over 5,000, which is almost thirteen times as many as that of 1910.

ILLINOIS—In 1920 the total colored population of the State of Illinois was 182,274. The heavy migration of 1922-1924 to the Chicago district has considerably increased this number. Of this number, 60 per cent are centered in the city of Chicago, although this city contains only 42 per cent of the total population of the state. In Chicago the colored question is as great as it is in the city of New York. Ten years ago there were 40,000 Negroes in the city of Chicago, but the migration of 1916-1920 brought this figure up to an estimated 100,000. In 1922-24 another wave of migration swept this figure up to 165,000. There has been little migration since. According to the Chicago Urban League, whatever migration there has been since then has been offset by the departure of Negroes from Chicago to other cities. Of the Negroes in Chicago, about 3,000 are practical Catholics. Of this number, 1,700, including children, attend St. Elizabeth's Church, the only exclusively colored church in the city, while the other colored Catholics attend services in the white churches. In all, there may be 4,000 colored Catholics in the Archdiocese, although many are so only on the baptismal register.

In the Diocese of Springfield, Illinois, there is no colored church and only a limited number of colored families who attend the various churches of the whites. In July of 1927 an attempt was made to enlist the interest of the colored people of the city of Springfield. Rev. Edward Cahill, Diocesan Superintendent of the Catholic Bureau of Education, in company with a Jesuit Father, made a house to house visit in several of the Negro sections of Springfield for the purpose of interesting the colored people in a lecture on the Mass and the Life of Christ. While the effort was a failure, it led to the discovery of many colored Catholics who were not practising their religion. They were mostly from the city of St. Louis and the state of Oklahoma. In Springfield there is a large number of transient Negroes, one section of the city being composed entirely of such. There are in the city not over fifty colored people attending the Catholic Church. At one time there was a colored church in Quincy, the pastor being Rev. Augustus Tolton, the first colored priest in the United States. Meeting with no success Father Tolton later located in Chicago, where he died.

In the Dioceses of Rockford and Peoria there are practically no colored Catholics. At Belleville, in the Diocese of Belleville, an exclusively colored mission was begun seven years ago by the African Mission Fathers of the Irish Province. When they came to Belleville there was not even one colored Catholic to be found. Today there is a congregation of about 200.

MICHIGAN—In the State of Michigan there are 60,000 Negroes (1920). The city of Detroit, in which there are 41,000, accounts for 68 per cent, or two-thirds, of the total Negro population of the state. The industries of Detroit attracted the migrants and kept them centered in the city. There are two churches devoted to the exclusive care of the colored in the city, but the congregations of both do not exceed a total of 600. In the Diocese of Detroit it is estimated that there are from 1,000 to 10,000 colored people who should be Catholics. In the Dioceses of Marquette and Grand Rapids the number of colored Catholics is negligible.

WISCONSIN—With the exception of the city of Milwaukee, the State of Wisconsin has few colored people. Five thousand was the figure given in the 1920 census. In Milwaukee, the colored population of which is over the two thousand mark, there is a church and boarding school for the exclusive use of the colored. There are about 350 members in the congregation.

CHAPTER X

MIGRATION AND THE WEST

1. WEST NORTH CENTRAL GROUP

MINNESOTA—In view of the fact that the climate of Minnesota is so extremely severe in the winter time, very few Negroes have gone there. The Dioceses of Crookston, Duluth, St. Cloud, and Winona contain only small cities, and opportunities for work for the Negro in this part of the country are very limited.

In the city of St. Paul there are about 5,000 colored people, and in the city of Minneapolis about 6,500. These figures for the two cities were computed on the birth and death rates which were returned to the Chancery Office of the Archdiocese of St. Paul. Of the 5,000 in St. Paul, Rev. Stephen Theobald, pastor of St. Peter Claver's Church, says that 273 are Catholics, that is, members of his parish. Proportionately, there should be about 350 colored Catholics in the city of Minneapolis. These are the only two cities in the Archdiocese in which there is any considerable number of colored people. It is of interest to note that in the city of St. Paul there are 8 established non-Catholic colored churches: Baptist, 3; African Methodist, 2; Methodist-Episcopal, Episcopalian, and Presbyterian, 1 each. The Congregationalists, Adventists, and Pentecostal bodies also have missions in operation.

IOWA—There are few Negroes in the State of Iowa (2,000). Sioux City has 1,139, the largest number in any city in the state; about 25 of them belong to the Catholic Church. Some time ago a mission was given for the colored people of the city; although it was well advertised and the missioner who gave it was well acquainted with the Negro as a race, the mission was unsuccessful—not more than 75 people attended any exercise. It is estimated that there are about 63 colored Catholics in the whole state. No special work is being done.

MISSOURI—The colored population of the State of Missouri was 178,241 in 1920. Each of the three dioceses in the state is doing special work for the colored. In the city of St. Louis, with a population of 70,000 Negroes, there are 2,500 colored Catholics; about 500 other colored Catholics live elsewhere in the Archdiocese. There is one exclusively colored church in the city of St. Louis, St. Elizabeth's, one of the oldest colored churches in the country. St. Nicholas' Church cares for a number of colored Catholics, although it is not exclusively for their use.

In the Diocese of Kansas City there are 800 colored Catholics. Of these, about 500 are in the parish of St. Monica, Kansas City. To this parish is attached St. Monica's Girls' Home. In the Diocese of St. Joseph there are 107 colored Catholics. St. Augustine's mission in this city is attended from the Cathedral. Originally a Catholic Truth Club, started for the colored people in 1925, it later developed into a mission where Mass was celebrated each Sunday. The present mission church was erected in 1927.

NORTH AND SOUTH DAKOTA—Both of these states are sparsely settled even by the whites. They contain not more than 1,500 colored people. The states are strictly agricultural, and the climate is too severe for the colored man.

NEBRASKA—This state has a colored population of 13,242 (1920). In the Diocese of Omaha, the Rev. Francis Cassilly, S.J., Professor at Creighton University, who is in charge of the colored work in the city and vicinity, estimates that 161, including children, sometimes attend his Church of St. Benedict, which is exclusively colored. There are probably 100 more who have been baptized, but who on account of irregular marriages or lack of instruction never attend church. At Lincoln there is a good-sized colored community (896 in 1920), but hardly more than half a dozen Catholics. It is of interest to know that there is a colored sorority at the University of Nebraska. Scattered throughout the rest of the state there are not more than 50 or 60 colored Catholics.

KANSAS—In 1920 the State of Kansas had a colored population of 57,925. Outside of Leavenworth and Kansas City there are very few colored Catholics. In Leavenworth there is a colored church, home and school under the care of Monsignor Joseph Shorter. There are 181 in this parish. In Kansas City the Franciscans have a church for the exclusive use of the colored; there are 118 in the congregation.

2. THE MOUNTAIN STATES

In the Mountain States of Montana, Idaho, Wyoming, Colorado, New Mexico, Arizona, Utah and Nevada, there are altogether only 30,000 Negroes. With the exception of the Diocese of Denver, there are at most only a few colored Catholics. The nature of this section of the country does not appeal to the colored migrant. New Mexico, which, with Arizona, is the most southern state, is populated mostly by people of Spanish descent, or what is commonly called "Mexican," a class of people which works even cheaper than does the Negro.

3. PACIFIC STATES

The State of California has received the bulk of colored migrants who went west. The rapidly growing towns of California present glowing opportunity, and the mild climate is no little attraction. In the Archdiocese of San Francisco there are approximately 250 Catholic colored families. In the Diocese of Sacramento, one-half of which is in California and the other half in Nevada, there are 150 Negro Catholics. Of these, however, 140 are Portuguese-speaking natives of the Cape Verde Islands and their children, most of whom attend St. Elizabeth's Church for Portuguese. In the Diocese of Monterey-Fresno there is only a small migratory colored population of which not one is Catholic.

The Diocese of Los Angeles and San Diego drew heavily on the South. There are few colored people outside the city of Los Angeles: a small colony at Pasadena, with few Catholics, mostly "old-timers"; a small colony at San Diego, mostly drifters from Tia Juana, Mexico; a few truck farmers in the country; colored help in beach clubs and hotels, rather restricted, especially in certain places like Long Beach where opposition to the colored is very strong. Three years ago the colored Catholics of Los Angeles numbered 196 families with 748 persons, but this list was not complete or exact because many of the migrants drifted away from the Church and did not come to the attention of the pastors of the city churches; there were many omissions in this census, especially for the "east side," where the colored belt is located.

According to the survey of the Catholic Federated Charities, the colored population of Los Angeles is 50,000. The influx of Catholic Negroes was very noticeable during and after the War. The best estimate of the number of colored Catholics in the city is that given by Rev. Edmund Schlecht, S.M.A., pastor of St. Odilia's Church, Los Angeles, who puts the figure at 500 families, although less than 250 individuals attend the colored church of which he is in charge. In spite of the zealous efforts of this energetic missioner there is a tremendous leakage among the colored of the city, due largely to a disposition of the migrant to carry his new found feeling of freedom into church matters.

PART IV—EDUCATION

CHAPTER XI.

A RETROSPECT

Educational activities in behalf of the Negro before the Civil War may be divided into two rather well-defined periods. The first period would extend from the introduction of slaves into the colonies to the climax of the insurrectionary movement about 1835. During this period there was no general disposition to deny to the slaves what educational advantages they could get. After the year 1835, however, the general disposition would seem to have been that to educate the Negro would be to foment rebellion. This reaction against the liberal view was caused by the many insurrectionary attempts of ambitious Negroes who were encouraged to sedition by the Abolitionists.

Woodson[1] separates the early advocates of the education of Negroes into three classes, as follows: "First, masters who desired to increase the economic efficiency of their labor supply; second, sympathetic persons who wished to help the oppressed; and third, zealous missionaries who, believing that the message of divine love came equally to all, taught slaves the English language that they might learn the principles of the Christian religion." The early Spanish and French missioners receive unstinted praise from historians for their educational work among the Negroes. Their attitude was instrumental in causing other denominations in this country to take an interest in the education of slaves, for, as Woodson says, the Protestants were "put to shame by this noble example of the Catholics." In previous pages we have shown that Catholic slave-holders generally dealt with the situation in a commendable manner; in fact, if such masters wished to remain practical Catholics they had no other course than compliance with the oft-expressed desires of the Popes who had issued

---

[1] Woodson, *The Education of the Negro Prior to 1861*, p. 2.

numerous encyclicals on the matter of treating slaves as became Christians.

After 1835 the Negroes were strictly prohibited by law from taking advantage of educational opportunities. To get over these obstacles southern ministers began what was called "verbal instruction," or teaching the principles of Christianity by memory training. The Quakers and Catholics, however, openly defied the letter of the law and continued to instruct Negroes in reading and writing as a better means to teach their religion. Quoting the *Special Report of the U. S. Commissioner of Education, 1871*, Woodson writes: "They (the Catholics and Quakers) had for centuries labored to promote religion and education among their colored brethren. So earnest were these sects in working for the uplift of the Negro race that the reactionary movement failed to swerve them from their course. When the other churches adopted the policy of mere verbal training, the Quakers and Catholics adhered to their idea that the Negroes should be educated to grasp the meaning of the Christian religion just as they had been during the seventeenth and eighteenth centuries. This favorable situation did not mean much, however, since with the exception of the Catholics in Maryland and Louisiana and the Quakers in Pennsylvania, not many members of these sects lived in communities of a large colored population. Furthermore, they were denied access to the Negroes in most southern communities, even when they volunteered to work among the Negroes as missioners."[1]

In the year 1824 an effort had been made to found a sisterhood to do for the Christian education of Negro girls, most of whom were slaves, what the half dozen convent schools then in existence in this country were doing for the white girls. The attempt was made in Kentucky by Rev. Charles Nerinckx, founder of the Sisters of Loretto. Pitying the moral degradation and the mental neglect of the blacks in bondage, their spiritual desolation and their lack of industrial skill, Father Nerinckx planned the establishment of a branch of his institute to be composed of colored sisters devoted to the training of the young of their race and sex. With this

---

[1] *Op. cit.*, p. 183.

purpose in mind, he brought to Loretto, Ky., from farms in the surrounding region, a few talented Negro girls to be trained for the noble career he had planned for them. Some of them made such satisfactory progress in piety, learning, and industrial accomplishments that they were admitted to the Loretto society. In May, 1824, Father Nerinckx wrote: "Two days ago twelve young ladies offered themselves at Loretto for the little veil, among them our three blacks who received nearly all the votes. Their dress is to be different, also their offices and employment, but they keep the main rules of the society—they will take the vows, but not the perpetual ones before twelve years of profession." Subsequently two other colored postulants were received. The five lived apart from the white sisters in the novitiate, but they followed the same community exercises.

Later in the same year Father Nerinckx departed from Kentucky for Missouri, turning over to Bishop Flaget the sisterhood he had founded. The Bishop appointed the Rev. Guy Chabrat as ecclesiastical superior of the community, but the new director, persuaded that the time had not come for Afro-American religious, released the five Negro novices from their obligations and sent them back to their former homes.

At least it may be said that forty years before emancipation an endeavor had been made both to form a religious community of colored sisters and to educate the slaves. Had the times been more propitious the undertaking of Father Nerinckx might have had a development as fruitful as the congregation of the Oblate Sisters of Providence which was founded a few years later.

In Charleston Bishop England showed particular interest in the education of Negroes, both free and bonded. We have recounted how he taught Negroes, founding a school for boys under the care of a priest and a school for girls under the care of the Sisters of Mercy. He was compelled to suppress the slave schools by the passage of a law making it criminal to teach a slave to read or write, but he continued the schools for the emancipated blacks. [1]

At this time Maryland, long noted for its favorable atti-

[1] *Vide, infra,* p. 25.

tude towards the Negro, was not raising any particular objection to the instruction of slaves or free persons of color. Woodson remarks: "Most interest in the cause in Maryland was manifested near the cities of Georgetown and Baltimore. Long active in the cause of elevating the colored people, the influence of the revolutionary movement was hardly necessary to arouse the Catholics to discharge their duty of enlightening the blacks. Whenever they had the opportunity to give slaves religious instruction, they generally taught the unfortunates everything that would broaden their horizon and help them to understand life. The Abolitionists and Protestants were also in the field, but the work of the early Fathers in these cities was more effective. These forces at work in Georgetown made it, by the time of its incorporation into the District of Columbia, a center sending out teachers to carry on the instruction of Negroes. So liberal were the white people of this town that colored children were sent to school there with white boys and girls who raised no objection." [1]

In the District of Columbia several priests, one of whom was Father Leonard Neale, later Archbishop of Baltimore, established schools and gathered around them the ignorant and the poor, both white and black. In 1818, Father McElroy established a Sunday school for colored children in which for two hours each Sunday afternoon they were taught reading, writing, arithmetic and Christian doctrine. This was the first free school for Negroes established in the South. Young men and women of the first standing in Georgetown were the teachers. This school was maintained until 1822 when Father McElroy was transferred to Frederick, Md.

The Special Report of the United States Commissioner of Education for 1871 gives a fair and interesting account of Catholic educational activities for Negroes in the District of Columbia before the Civil War. It notes that the first seminary for colored girls was established in Georgetown, in 1827, under the special auspices of Father Vanlomen, then pastor of the Holy Trinity Church, who had for several years taught a school of colored boys three days a week, near Georgetown College gate, in a small frame house which was afterwards

---

[1] *Op. cit.*, p. 111.

famous as the home of the broken-hearted widow of Commodore Decatur. The seminary was under the care of Maria Becraft who was, to use the words of the Commissioner of Education, [1] "the most remarkable colored young woman of her time in the District, and, perhaps, of any time." At the age of fifteen years she had given herself to the work of a school for girls in Dunbarton Street, Georgetown. In 1827 Father Vanlomen took over this school and transferred it to a larger building on Fayette Street, opposite the convent of the Visitandines in Georgetown. There Miss Becraft opened a boarding and day school for colored girls which continued with great success until August, 1831, when she surrendered her little seminary to one of the girls she had trained in her school. In October of that year Miss Becraft entered the recently founded Oblate Sisters of Providence in Baltimore. The seminary averaged thirty to thirty-five pupils, girls from the best colored families of Georgetown, Washington, Alexandria and surrounding country.

The Sisters of the Visitation in the Georgetown Convent opposite the little seminary kept a watchful eye upon the enterprise. They rendered what help they could by giving Miss Becraft instruction and by helping with the children until such time as public opinion backed by the mob spirit forced them to discontinue their services. Previous to these mob outbreaks the Sisters had trained many colored girls in "the refined and solid attainments of a good education."

At this time several other colored schools in the District were being kept by Catholics, notably St. Agnes' Academy, located on what was known as "The Island." St. Agnes' was taught by Arabella Jones, who had graduated from the Oblate Sisters' Academy in Baltimore in 1851. About this time another colored school was opened in Georgetown by Nancy Grant, an aunt of Maria Becraft, who had been teaching privately as early as 1828.

A free school was established in 1858 and maintained by the St. Vincent de Paul Society, in connection with St. Matthew's Church. It was organized under the direction of

_____
[1] *Ibid.*, p. 204

Father Walter and kept in the Smothers' schoolhouse for two years. It was subsequently maintained for one year on a smaller scale in a house on L Street. The school was abandoned when the Society failed to give it the requisite pecuniary assistance after the breaking out of the Civil War. At the Jesuit Church of St. Aloysius there was also a large free school for colored girls in the parochial school building.

"The Negroes in Baltimore," writes Woodson, "were almost as self-educating as those of the District of Columbia. The coming of the refugees and French Fathers[1] from San Domingo to Baltimore to escape the revolution marked an epoch in the intellectual life of the colored people of that city. Thereafter their intellectual class had access to an increasing black population, anxious to be enlightened. Given this better working basis, they secured from the ranks of the Catholics additional catechists and teachers to give a larger part of illiterates the fundamentals of education. Their untiring co-worker in furnishing these facilities was the Most Reverend Ambrose Marechal, Archbishop of Baltimore from 1817 to 1828. These schools were such an improvement over those formerly open to Negroes that colored youths of other towns and cities thereafter came to Baltimore for higher training. The coming of these refugees to Baltimore had a direct bearing on the education of colored girls. Their condition excited the sympathy of the immigrating colored women."[2]

We have already described the founding of the Oblate Sisters of Providence in Baltimore by the Sulpician, Father Joubert, and three San Domingan ladies, with the subsequent opening of St. Francis' Academy for girls as the motherhouse of the Sisters in 1829. The Academy was first located on Richmond Street. Students were offered courses in all branches of "refined and useful education, including all that is usually taught in well-regulated female seminaries." This school was so well maintained that it survived all reaction-

---

[1] Evidently refers to the Sulpician Fathers who had come from France and had founded St. Mary's Seminary some years before the San Domingan refugees came to Baltimore.

[2] *Education of the Negro Prior to 1861*, p. 138.

ary attacks and was for many years the centre of enlightenment for colored women.

When the Josephite Fathers first arrived at Baltimore in
1871, they found a church, a convent, a convent academy or
boarding school, and a parochial school for the exclusive use
of the colored people. Yet, in all this noble work there was
no concerted action, no definite plan: a Sulpician has the immortal credit of founding the convent, a Redemptorist built
a house and founded a school for boys, a secular priest opened
one for girls, a Jesuit had purchased the parochial church.
As death, removal, sickness, change of place, or other cause
cut off the man, it stopped the work: a lay teacher went to
Rome and returned a priest, only to find that his school on
Clay Street had fallen; a Know-nothing rabble attacked another in South Baltimore; a third ceased when the devoted
religious, Father Greisen, C.SS.R., was transferred to New
Orleans. Individuals came and went, and with their going
went another venture in Negro education.

These many noble efforts on the part of zealous priests
and sisters to impart instruction, religious and secular, are
deserving of the highest praise. While for nearly half a century before the coming of the Josephites, the Oblates had carried on their work of instructing colored girls, fitful and temporary were the efforts to educate colored boys. The Josephites opened a school for boys and girls in connection with
St. Francis' Church. For seven or eight years no school was
available for the education of both sexes other than this
school in the basement of St. Francis' Church. About 1880
it was moved to a fine three-story brick building, for many
years occupied by the Christian Brothers for the male students of the Cathedral parish school.

The founding of the Sisters of the Holy Family in New
Orleans was a milestone in the progress of Catholic education
for colored youth. In 1842 three young ladies, Miss Harriet
Delisle, a native of New Orleans, Miss Juliette Gaudin, of
Cuba, and a Miss Alicot, of France, (they were later joined
by a Miss Josephine Charles), banded together for the purpose of instructing young girls of their race. For seven years
previous to this, they had been training in France. They

received the approval of Most Rev. Anthony Blanc, Achbishop of New Orleans, and were directed spiritually by the Vicar General of the Archdiocese, Father Etienne Rousselon. They were first established in a little house on Bayou Road, where they taught catechism, preparing young and old women for first Holy Communion. In 1848 they took charge of St. Bernard's Home for old and infirm women, and a few years later a new house was built on Bayou Road (or Street), between Rampart and St. Cloud Streets, where they received new inmates and continued teaching candidates for Confirmation and Communion. It was not until after the Civil War that the Society began to flourish. At that time Rev. Gilbert Raymond, V.G., took the Sisters under his care and received the assistance of Archbishop Perche. The Sisters continued to expand their works of charity, opening new schools for both boys and girls, as also an orphanage, and a home for the aged.

Immediately after the Emancipation Proclamation, January, 1863, schools for the education of freedmen were established in all parts of the South occupied by Federal armies. Schools thus multiplied in Virginia, North Carolina, South Carolina, Tennessee, Arkansas and Louisiana, and Negroes flocked to them. But they were individual, separate and distinct one from the other; there was no definite plan of action. It was only when the Federal Government took up the work of reconstruction after the close of the war and founded the Freedmen's Bureau (March 3, 1865) that there was anything like a system introduced—the first genuine public school system. Louisiana, in 1864, was the first of the seceded states to establish for freedmen a public school system supported by public taxation; in the same year Maryland did likewise; in 1865, Missouri; in 1867, Alabama and Tennessee; in 1868, Arkansas, Florida, and South Carolina; and in 1870, Georgia, Texas, and Mississippi followed suit. Kentucky did not progress so far until 1875, and Delaware, not until the following year.

In the five years of its existence the Freedmen's Bureau established 4,239 schools for colored people and expended for their education the sum of $3,500,000. Besides this direct result, by co-operating with benevolent and missionary associations, it assisted in establishing 13 colleges, graduates of which became the bulwark of Negro education when segregation forced white instructors out of the Negro schools. The first enrolment in public schools for Negroes in the sixteen former Slave States and the District of Columbia was made in 1876-77. It showed that 571,506 colored children were in the schools for that year.

The development of the Catholic mission school for the colored children was naturally more humble than was that of the more favored public school; efforts were necessarily individual and hampered by pecuniary difficulties. But the little mission school was not without its glory. For instance, Father Greene, S.S.J., writing in St. Joseph's Advocate in 1883 of the school tax in Kentucky, the only one of the late Slave States which threw the whole burden of colored schools on colored taxation, noted: "We know that long before this school law engaged the attention of the legislators, long before this anti-Catholic Commonwealth had ceased to frown upon every attempt to educate these poor people, they were the deep and anxious concern of the Kentucky clergy. So late a date as 1874 is that of its legislative recognition of the Creator's act—brains in a black head! In one Catholic corner of this diocese are to be found more Catholic schools for these poor people's children than in the entire belt of states from the Mississippi to the Atlantic immediately north of Mason and Dixon's line! We personally know those of Louisville, Bardstown, New Haven, Lebanon, Springfield, St. Mary and St. Charles, clustering, as it were, round the old chair of 1808 like sprouts from an invisible root. The first two are taught by the Sisters of Charity, that of Springfield by Dominican nuns, and the rest by those of Loretto, except, perhaps, that near St. Charles Borromeo's in which we meet only one lay teacher. What was our surprise, driving one day with a friend along a lonesome road cut through the woods of Washington County, to find a handsome buggy without horse or man, apparently abandoned on the public highway; and what to hear that this vehicle was brought to that identical spot every morning, left there all day and taken away in the evening?

In the adjacent field we noticed a solitary horse and a good one, browsing round a handsome frame building. That building was a colored school, into which we were cordially welcomed by two Irish ladies, white-robed daughters of St. Dominic, from the great convent and academy of St. Catherine, some two or three miles distant. Without fuss or feathers or sound of trumpet, here was a colored school in the woods of Kentucky, teeming with children, supplied with books and stationery and school furniture, two teachers qualified to instruct in the first academy in the land, and at their service a costly conveyance." [1]

Another such case in point was the school of St. Augustine, Louisville, of which Father Greene wrote: "Two Sisters of Charity, two of the best teachers we have ever met, have been engaged for many years without one dollar of salary or compensation otherwise. They preceded our advent more than a decade of years ago, with trudgings, every school day since, to and from their convent, of eighteen squares. Both at last actually 'fell in harness,' broken down with sheer toil, when two others of their heroic congregation stepped into the breach without the loss of a single day. We state a fact that time and again Protestant majorities could be seen in these schools, though cheek-by-jowl with one of the great sable palaces of the city school system." [2]

In 1877 a home for colored waifs was started by a colored woman in an alley of Baltimore. It grew and prospered until a large house was donated by a good Catholic lady. This was henceforth known as St. Elizabeth's Home. Once in the large house, the number of children outgrew the abilities of the colored matron, who urged the need of sisters to take over the work. The response came from the Franciscan Sisters of Mill Hill, England, a community of sisters founded by Cardinal Herbert Vaughan. Four sisters arrived in Baltimore on St. Stephen's day, 1881, the first white Sisters in America to devote themselves entirely to the welfare of the Negroes. St. Elizabeth's Home was soon supplemented by a new convent, St. Francis', where larger girls who have passed

[1] Vol. I, no. 4, p. 22.
[2] *Ibid.*, p. 23.

through St. Elizabeth's Home are prepared for domestic service. In 1895 a new St. Elizabeth's Home was erected, and the same year the American novitiate of the Sisters was canonically opened by Cardinal Gibbons. In a short time the Sisters opened schools in several other cities.

At this time there was in Corpus Christi, Texas, a Mrs. Margaret Murphy, widow of Hon. Judge I. B. Murphy, who had given up her private residence for use as a hospital, she herself helping to care for the sick. In 1888, while living in San Antonio, at the suggestion of the Oblate Fathers, who were then beginning to do some work for the Negroes of that city, Mrs. Murphy resolved to devote her all to the work of procuring for the poor colored children the benefits of Catholic instruction. Accordingly, she had built for them a church, and purchased four dwelling houses: one as a dwelling for herself and the teachers she gathered about her, and the others to be used as schools for the colored children.

To give to the Negroes only material aid did not satisfy Mrs. Murphy. With the consent of the Right Rev. Bishop John Neraz, Bishop of San Antonio, she associated with herself, under the title of "Servants of the Holy Ghost," a group of young ladies who desired to dedicate their lives to the welfare of the Negroes.

Since the foundation of the Servants of the Holy Ghost they have passed the hundred mark in numbers. They are no longer engaged exclusively in work among the Negroes, but have expanded their charity to include the Mexicans, of whom there are many in the cities of Texas.

In 1890 the Sisters of St. Francis (called Franciscans of Glen Riddle) came from Philadelphia and began work among the Negroes by taking over the school of St. Peter Claver, Baltimore, Md. At that time class was held in the basement of the church. The next work undertaken was that of St. Joseph's Home for Colored Orphan Boys, Wilmington, Del., an industrial school in charge of a Josephite Father. A few Sisters began there in 1892 with a small number of boys. Larger buildings were erected, the number of orphans increased, and the community of Sisters grew. Since then the Sisters of St. Francis have shown their zeal by undertaking many new schools and other works of charity for the Negroes.

In 1890, two years after the Commission for Mission Work Among the Negroes and Indians was established, it was able to report 99 mission schools with an enrolment of 6,093 colored children. In these schools the teachers belonged chiefly to the Sisters of St. Francis, Holy Ghost, St. Dominic, St. Benedict, Sisters of Mercy, of Charity, of St. Joseph, and of the Sacred Heart, as also the two colored sisterhoods—the Oblates of Baltimore and the Sisters of the Holy Family of New Orleans.

Encouraging as was this progress during a quarter of a century, the work was hardly begun. Summing up the pitiable conditions then existing, Father Chasse, Chancellor of the Archdiocese of New Orleans, wrote to the Commission in 1889: "There are one hundred and sixty thousand Negroes in this diocese, nearly all baptized Catholics. But for various reasons, especially for want of early religious instruction, the majority of them are lost to the Church. What we need most here is the establishing of Catholic schools to counterbalance the evil effects of the free public schools. Some progress has already been made in that line, and had we the means to push on the good work, each parish could have a free parochial school for the colored children. Could this be done, we certainly would have an immense number of children, born of Catholic parents and baptized Catholics, who now attend the free public schools and later on join the Methodists or Baptists. Race prejudice, although decreasing and disappearing, still exists, especially in country parishes. . . . The poverty of the great majority of our white Catholics makes it quite impossible for the pastors to have free colored schools. And, yet, without such schools these children will in all probability be lost to the Church." [1]

At that time sectarian efforts had succeeded in establishing not only innumerable primary and grade schools, but fully one hundred high schools supported mostly by northern Protestants. Besides these high schools there were not a few Protestant colleges and so-called universities with large enrolments. Claflin University, for instance, built by and named

---

[1] *Catholic World, March,* 1889, p. 729.

after a gentleman from Boston, during the scholastic year of 1886-87, had as many as 965 Negro youths.

For another quarter of a century the little colored mission school grew and waxed stronger. By 1915 the Commission for Mission Work Among the Negroes and Indians was able to report 140 Catholic schools for colored children with an enrolment of over 13,000. The work was well established. The Josephite Fathers and Mother Katharine with her Sisters of the Blessed Sacrament had revolutionized the mission educational program. Other sisterhoods took up the work, better equipment was made possible, standards were raised, and buildings modernized. While space forbids entering into the details of this development, in following pages we shall give an account of the present condition of Catholic education for Negroes in the United States.

CHAPTER XII.

THE SCHOOLS OF THE COLORED MISSIONS

1. IN GENERAL

To what may be attributed the remarkable progress that the Negro has made in the short span of half a century? The question is asked and answered in the *Survey of Negro Colleges and Universities,*[1] "No single factor," states the *Survey,* "has contributed more than education. When the Negro emerged from slavery, practically no private or public schools, except in isolated instances, existed for his enlightenment. Few Negro children were attending schools of any type. At that time 90 per cent of the entire population of the country was illiterate. Negroes now enrolled in the public schools number 2,150,000; the annual expenditures for Negro education amount to $37,000,000, of which $3,000,000 is derived from Negro sources; and illiteracy has been reduced to approximately 10 per cent."

Today no missioner properly visualizes his ultimate field of success without planning for adequate school facilities. The school factor is the very hope of future mission stability. Evidence of this is seen in the firm policy of supplementing churches and missions with suitable schools. In the colored mission field in the United States practically every mission has at least a primary school attached to it. Of their religious influence in the case of Catholic children nothing need be said. In most of these schools there is, however, an attendance of non-Catholic children. Non-Catholic colored parents are as a rule anxious to secure an education for their children; nor do they hesitate to send them to Catholic schools if there be one in the vicinity, even though they feel certain that the children will thereby become Catholics. From small beginnings most of the Catholic schools have developed into ably conducted

---

[1] Section of Bulletin, 1928, no. 7, p. 2.

grammar schools. Today better buildings with more ample accommodations are gradually replacing the pioneer type of school.

2. NON-CATHOLIC RESOURCES

All about us public and sectarian institutions of learning are springing into being and in many cases claiming Catholic colored children. No period of equal length has witnessed such wonderful strides in secular education in the South as has that of the past ten years. At the beginning of this decade the Southern States started a program of development in Negro education which previously had not been thought even remotely possible. Within that brief period eight of the states put into operation public school buildings for Negroes valued at $30,000,000.

With the advantages of vast sums of money and organized agencies liberally endowed, secular and sectarian schools are in the majority of cases able to offer greater material advantages in buildings and equipment. This necessitates the offering of similar inducements by the mission school, but manifestly this is often impossible, since expenditures are limited by the pecuniary difficulties in which most missioners find themselves. Where, for instance, have the missioners been able to rely on the stimulus, encouragement, and financial assistance of special funds, such as the General Education Board, the Ann T. Jeanes Fund, the John F. Slater Fund, the Julius Rosenwald Fund, the Pierre S. duPont Gift, the Duke Gifts, and many other special funds and donations founded by generous-minded men for the promotion of secular or sectarian education among the Negroes?

The General Education Board since its foundation in 1902 has contributed a total of $4,189,469 to aid the developing of common schools for Negroes, and $14,257,434 towards special projects. A grand total of $18,872,442 has been distributed by this Board which plans and directs the expenditures of all public and special funds for Negro education.

The Anna T. Jeanes Fund is a private endowment established in 1908 for the purpose of employing well-prepared Negro teachers, mostly women, "to help to encourage rural teachers; to introduce into small country schools simple home industries; to give lessons on sanitation, cleanliness, etc.; to promote improvement of school houses and school grounds; and to organize clubs for the betterment of the school and neighborhood." The original amount of the fund was $1,-000,000, the interest only to be available each year. Appropriations to 1928 have been $626,598.

The John F. Slater Fund for twenty-nine years aided church and private schools mainly. In 1911 it began to encourage what has been called County Training Schools. These are public county or district schools. Under certain conditions the Slater Fund gives $500 a year to each County Training School, the purpose being to develop high schools and to offer courses simple as possible in the basic industries of the community and in teacher training. In 1927 there were 308 County Training Schools in the South. Since 1912 the Slater Fund has contributed $347,080 to these schools. For all types of public education the Fund has given $1,039,943; for religious and private institutions $2,081,899.

The Julius Rosenwald Fund since its foundation in 1914 has contributed $3,333,852. Much of the valuable service rendered by the other foundations is in the field of organization, supervision, studying of needs, training of teachers, organizing schools, and the like. The Rosenwald Fund, however, aids the community in actually building the school house. In this it fills a long felt need. The total above given does not include many large contributions by Mr. Rosenwald to other educational and welfare projects for the Negroes.

Through the generosity of Pierre S. duPont every colored school district in the State of Delaware now has a modern school building on a minimum site of two acres in extent, with a cost, including the new high school for colored students in Wilmington, aggregating about $2,500,000, no part of which was raised either by the State or by the colored people.

The endowment provided for by Mr. J. B. Duke sets aside a certain annual income on about $1,600,000 for Johnson C. Smith University, North Carolina. Mrs. B. N. Duke has contributed large sums to Kittrell College, North Carolina College for Negroes, and other Negro institutions in North Carolina. No definite figures are available, but these gifts haye been estimated as more than $2,500,000.

3. CATHOLIC RESOURCES

So far all attempts to help the Negro educationally which have emanated from a Catholic source seem pitiably weak in comparison with the magnitude of the problem and the efforts put forth by others. In the field of private and personal endeavor but one Catholic name is outstanding; nowhere has the American Negro found a more practical and unselfish friendship than that which has been given by the Catholic branch of the Drexel family of Philadelphia. In a truly Catholic spirit these benefactors of the Negro—Mother Katharine Drexel, Mrs. Edward Drexel Morrell, and Mrs. Walter Drexel Smith (deceased)—have preferred not to let the right hand know what the left hand does. Their charities, amounting to millions, and presenting their whole fortune and life's work, are the only worth-while constructive efforts put forth by individual Catholics. We are not unmindful of individual contributions of relatively large sums of money: there is the gentleman from the West, for instance, who recently very unostentatiously gave a sum running into six figures; there is also one of nature's noblemen in Philadelphia who has already built ten mission chapels in the South; there are others, too, who prefer to do Catholic charity rather than public philanthropy, but in the main their number is small.

The Commission for Catholic Missions Among the Colored People and Indians does a great service through its disbursements of the annual collection taken up in the churches of the country. During the year 1928 it collected and disbursed the sum of $271,129. This is hardly a munificent sum, however, if one remembers that the Indian missions had a share in it. Relatively, it is insignificant. The 1928 report for a single white parish of the North, for instance, accounts for total receipts of $157,900, or nearly three-fifths of the total disbursements of the Commission.

The Catholic Board for Mission Work Among the Colored People, previously mentioned, also deserves great credit for its work in behalf of Catholic Negro education. The Board collects funds for distribution to such schools as cannot afford to pay the salaries of sisters and lay teachers. The annual amount so disbursed is approximately $75,000. The Board also finances the summer normal school for Sisters of the Holy Family at New Orleans, La.

Of the power of the school in the conversion of the Negroes, the Report of the Commission for Negro and Indian Missions (1926) observes: "A wedge can be driven into almost any non-Catholic district in the South by the establishment of a school as the nucleus of a mission. Experience has proved that this is a very effective means of getting into profitable contact with the Negro population. Non-Catholic children quickly flock to the well-conducted Catholic school. Even in well established parishes non-Catholic children are admitted to the schools in large numbers. The cry throughout the whole field is this: more and larger schools and additional teachers, for the schools everywhere are taxed to their utmost capacity. If we can only establish schools in new localities, enlarge those already in existence and help to support the teachers, the outlook for the conversion of the Negro is bright."

Table 14.   EDUCATIONAL ACTIVITIES ACCORDING TO STATES

	Children cared for	Grade schools	Complete high schools	Incomplete high schools	Sisters engaged	Lay teachers	Sisterhoods	Other Works
Alabama	1,489	13	1	1	29	16	Blessed Sacrament; Holy Family; Holy Ghost and Mary Immaculate; Holy Trinity	1 home
Arkansas	338	3	1	1	10	2	Benedictines; Missionary Servants of Holy Ghost	
California		1		1	3		Lady of Apostles	1 social service
Delaware	170				11	13	Franciscans (Glen Riddle)	1 industrial school
Florida	1,171	8			21	9	Holy Family; Holy Names; Mercy; St. Joseph	1 boarding school
Georgia	1,645	6	1	1	28	5	Blessed Sacrament; Missionary Franciscans	1 home
Illinois	1,461	2	1	1	43	6	Blessed Sacrament; Good Shepherd	1 industrial school; 1 social service
Indiana	65	1			2	1	Franciscans (III Regular)	
Kansas	260	2	1		22	1	Franciscans (III Regular); Oblates	1 home
Kentucky	597	8	1	1	25	6	Charity (Nazareth); Good Shepherd	1 industrial school
Louisiana	10,454	53	7	1	143	115	Ursulines; Blessed Sacrament; Divine Providence; Holy Family; Holy Ghost and Mary Immaculate	3 homes; 1 industrial school; 1 boarding school; 1 college

Table 14.   EDUCATIONAL ACTIVITIES ACCORDING TO STATES (*Continued*)

	Children cared for	Grade schools	Complete high schools	Incomplete high schools	Sisters engaged	Lay teachers	SISTERHOODS	OTHER WORKS
Maryland........ (and Dist. of Col.)	3,183	17	3	1	132	12	Madames of Sacred Heart Marianites Mercy Daughters of Charity Franciscans (Baltimore) Franciscans (Glen Riddle) Good Shepherd Immaculate Heart Mission Helpers Notre Dame Oblates Presentation	3 industrial schools 2 homes 2 social service
Massachusetts....	2,636	14	6	1	3 62	... 7	Blessed Sacrament Blessed Sacrament Holy Ghost and Mary Immaculate Missionary Servants of Holy Ghost	1 social service
Mississippi.......								
Missouri.........	664	4	...	...	32	6	Blessed Sacrament Charity (Leavenworth) Helpers of Holy Souls Oblates	1 home 2 social service
Nebraska........	102	1	...	...	2	1	Mercy Adorers of Precious Blood Blessed Sacrament Franciscans (Glen Riddle) Handmaids Heart of Mary	1 home 1 social service
New York........	1,233	5	...	...	67	6		

Table 14. EDUCATIONAL ACTIVITIES ACCORDING TO STATES (Continued)

	Children cared for	Grade schools	Complete high schools	Incomplete high schools	Sisters engaged	Lay teachers	Sisterhoods	Other Works
North Carolina	584	6	1	...	14	4	Franciscans (Baltimore) Immaculate Heart	
Ohio	759	4	...	1	20	...	Blessed Sacrament	
Oklahoma	337	2	...	1	8	...	Holy Ghost and Mary Immaculate	1 industrial school
Pennsylvania	604	6	...	1	33	1	Blessed Sacrament	
South Carolina	604	3	...	...	8	1	Oblates	
Tennessee	325	2	...	1	10	4	Blessed Sacrament Charity (Mt. St. Joseph) Dominicans	
Texas	1,759	11	2	1	46	5	Blessed Sacrament Holy Family Holy Ghost and Mary Immaculate	1 night school
Virginia	2,326	6	3	1	37	57	Blessed Sacrament Franciscans (Baltimore) Oblates	1 industrial and agricultural school 1 vocational and night school 1 boarding school 1 boarding school
Wisconsin	270	1	...	...	18	2	Dominicans	
								9 industrial schools 10 homes 8 social service 4 boarding schools
Total	33,036	179	28	13	829	279		

New schools have since been opened at Cairo, Ill., Greensboro, N. C., Helena, Ark., Shreveport, Church Point, and Rayne, La.

Table 15.   EDUCATIONAL ACTIVITIES ACCORDING TO DIOCESES

	Children cared for	Grade schools	Complete high schools	Incomplete high schools	Sisters engaged	Lay teachers	Sisterhoods	Other Works
Alexandria, La......	1,025	7	1		19	5	Sisters of Divine Providence	
Baltimore, Md......	3,183	17	3	1	132	12	Daughters of Charity; Franciscans (Baltimore); Franciscans (Glen Riddle); Good Shepherd; Immaculate Heart; Mission Helpers; Notre Dame; Oblates; Presentation	3 industrial schools; 2 homes; 2 social service
Belleville, Ill......	199	1			3	3	Blessed Sacrament	1 social service
Belmont Abbey, N.C.	34	2				2	Blessed Sacrament	1 social service
Boston, Mass....					3	1	Blessed Sacrament	
Brooklyn, N. Y....	136				5	1	Oblates	
Charleston, S. C...	604	3			8		Blessed Sacrament	
Chicago, Ill........	1,262	1	1		40	3	Oblates; Good Shepherd	1 industrial school
Cincinnati, Ohio....	490	2		1	9		Blessed Sacrament	
Cleveland, Ohio....	147	1			6		Blessed Sacrament	
Columbus, Ohio....	122	1			5		Blessed Sacrament	
Corpus Christi, Tex.	92	1	1		4		Holy Family	
Dallas, Tex........	302	1	1		6	1	Holy Ghost and Mary Immaculate	
Galveston, Tex.....	979	6	1		21	3	Blessed Sacrament; Holy Family	
Indianapolis, Ind...	65	1			2	1	Franciscans, (III Regular)	
Kansas City, Mo....	65	1			2		Charity (Leavenworth)	1 social service

Table 15. EDUCATIONAL ACTIVITIES ACCORDING TO DIOCESES (Continued)

Diocese	Children cared for	Grade schools	Complete high schools	Incomplete high schools	Sisters engaged	Lay teachers	Sisterhoods	Other Works
Lafayette, La.	3,690	19	5	1	43	39	Blessed Sacrament; Holy Family; Holy Ghost and Mary Immaculate; Madames of Sacred Heart; Mercy	1 industrial school
Leavenworth, Kan.	260	2	1		22	1	Franciscans (III Regular); Oblates	1 home
Little Rock, Ark.	338	3	1	1	10	2	Benedictines; Missionary Servants of Holy Ghost	
Los Angeles, Cal.					3		Lady of Apostles	1 social service
Louisville, Ky.	597	8	1		25	6	Charity (Nazareth); Good Shepherd; Ursulines	1 industrial school
Milwaukee, Wis.	270	1			18	2	Dominicans	1 boarding school
Mobile, Ala.	1,790	15	1	1	35	18	Blessed Sacrament; Holy Family; Holy Ghost and Mary Immaculate; Holy Trinity	1 home; 1 boarding school
Nashville, Tenn.	325	2		1	10	4	Mercy (Mt. St. Joseph); Blessed Sacrament; Dominicans	
Natchez, Miss.	2,636	14	6	1	62	7	Blessed Sacrament; Holy Ghost and Mary Immaculate; Missionary Servants of Holy Ghost	
New Orleans, La.	5,739	27	1		81	71	Blessed Sacrament; Holy Family; Holy Ghost and Mary Immaculate; Marianites	3 homes; 1 boarding school; 1 college

Table 15. EDUCATIONAL ACTIVITIES ACCORDING TO DIOCESES (Continued)

	Children cared for	Grade schools	Complete high schools	Incomplete high schools	Sisters engaged	Lay teachers	Sisterhoods	Other Works
New York, N. Y.	1,097	4			62	5	Adorers of Precious Blood Blessed Sacrament Franciscans (Glen Riddle) Handmaids Heart of Mary Holy Ghost and Mary Immaculate	1 home 1 social service
Oklahoma, Okla.	337	2		1	8		Mercy	
Omaha, Nebr.	102	1			2	1	Blessed Sacrament	
Philadelphia, Pa.	604	6	1	1	33		Franciscans (Baltimore)	1 industrial school
Raleigh, N. C.	550	4			14	2	Immaculate Heart	
Richmond, Va.	2,326	6	3	1	37	57	Blessed Sacrament Franciscans (Baltimore) Oblates	1 industrial and agricultural school (boys) 1 vocational and night school 1 boarding school (girls)
St. Augustine, Fla.	870	6			15	7	Holy Names St. Joseph	
St. Louis, Mo.	599	3			30	6	Blessed Sacrament Helpers of Holy Souls Oblates	1 home 1 social service
San Antonio, Tex.	386	3		1	15	1	Holy Family Holy Ghost and Mary Immaculate	1 night school
Savannah, Ga.	1,645	6	1	1	28	5	Blessed Sacrament Missionary Franciscans	1 home
Wilmington, Del.	170	1		1	11	13	Franciscans (Glen Riddle)	1 industrial school
Total	33,036	179	28	13	829	279		9 industrial schools 10 homes 8 social service 4 boarding schools

TABLE 16.—INSTITUTIONS IN CHARGE OF SECULARS

LOCATION: Diocese and Town	Pupils	Teachers and Instructors	REMARKS
BALTIMORE, MD. Ridge, Md.	56	8	Cardinal Gibbons Institute: academic courses, seventh to twelfth grades; industrial and agricultural courses; social service center.
KANSAS CITY, MO. Kansas City, Mo....	10	2	St. Monica's Girls' Home and social center, clinic and health center.
RICHMOND, VA. Richmond, Va.	220	30	Van de Vyver Institute, a vocational and night school; academic, commercial and industrial courses; conducted by Josephite Fathers in connection with St. Joseph's High School.
RICHMOND, VA. Rock Castle, Va....	150	17	St. Emma's Industrial and Agricultural Institute: academic, industrial and agricultural courses.
WILMINGTON, DEL. Clayton, Del.	73	8	Industrial school conducted by Josephite Fathers: academic and industrial courses.
TOTAL	509	65	

5. THE RURAL SCHOOL

The problem of the rural school deserves particular attention. Two-thirds of the Negroes in the United States live outside of cities, while in the South as a section this ratio is even higher, being three out of four. The rural school represents, therefore, the sole opportunity for education in the primary grades of a majority of all Negro children in the United States. The term rural mission school is used in contra-distinction to the graded parochial school with which most of the urban missions are equipped. Wherever the number of Catholic colored inhabitants in a southern rural community is large enough to encourage such an undertaking, a mission school is built. Under present circumstances the mission school is usually a humble building barely large enough to accommodate one or two teachers in charge of from twenty to a hundred colored children.

The rural mission school is an indispensable aid to breaking down prejudice against the Church. Through the children, many of whom are non-Catholics, the influence of the Church is felt in what would ordinarily be hostile homes. Numerous are the Negro adults who have been converted through the attendance of their children at the mission school.

The poverty of the rural missions is the reason why better educational facilities are not offered. Poor as these advantages are, however, in many sections of the South they represent the only opportunity for the rural Negroes to get the rudiments of an education. At Chastang, Ala., for instance, Rev. Sabino Grossi, S.S.J., saw but one way out of the difficulty of educating the children of his mission territory which, he writes, covers several hundred square miles. By his own labor he erected three buildings at his mother mission: two dormitories and a school building. Here many of the children are gathered together and given the advantages of an elementary education and boarded at the modest rate of five dollars a month. Few of those who attend ever pay the full tuition. By various means of conveyance, the children come from so far away as twenty-five or thirty miles on Monday mornings and stay at the mission until Friday. Father Grossi hopes in the near future to establish a little farm at Chastang where food products can be raised and a few cows kept, thus reducing the rate of tuition. Besides this central school, two other outlying mission schools are attached, each having a lay teacher. Altogether Father Grossi has 100 pupils taught by four lay teachers.

Many of the mission schools when originally established were not much better than shacks. At the West Mt. Vernon mission in Alabama, one of Father Grossi's, the original school was built of rough boards with slats nailed over the crevices to keep out the wind. At Crowley, La., Beaux Bridge, La., Pascagoula, Miss., and not a few other missions, conditions were or are not much better. The missioner is not long at his post, however, until more substantial buildings are erected, but generally speaking poverty continues to be the lot of the mission school.

In 1923 Mother Katharine Drexel brought great relief to the situation by establishing a system of rural schools in missions which ordinarily could not maintain such. Information at hand lists 18 such colored schools in the southern rural districts either partially or entirely supported by Mother Katharine in the system which she inaugurated.

Seldom is the little mission school able to offer more than five grades of curriculum. Often enough, full terms cannot be held because of the necessity of the children helping with the crops. For instance, at the mission school of St. Benedict the Moor, attached to the Thibodaux Mission and attended by Rev. Stephen Boysco, S.S.J., there is an enrolment of 120 pupils, but at the time of the report (fall of 1928) there were only 50 in attendance, due to the fact that it was the "grinding season."

Usually the little mission school is taught by lay teachers. These teachers fill a most important role in mission development. The lack of anything like a sufficient number of sisters to meet the demands of the schools is the reason why they are so necessary. Usually, too, the little mission school can support only one or two teachers. This would make impossible anything like a community life even were sisters available. While the lay teachers may capably perform this very necessary task of teaching in the rural schools, and while under present circumstances their services are indispensable, nevertheless, it cannot be expected that thy will exert the same influence that a religious would.

TABLE 17.—MISSION SCHOOLS CONDUCTED BY LAY TEACHERS

Location: Diocese and Town	Pupils	Teachers	Remarks
ALEXANDRIA, LA,			
Mansura, La.	120	2	
Marksville, La.	106	2	
BALTIMORE, MD.			
Morganza, Md.	57	2	
BELMONT ABBEY, N. CAR.			
Belmont, N. Car.	34	2	Two Schools
CHARLESTON, S. CAR.			
Ritter, S. Car.	52	1	
GALVESTON, TEXAS			
Pear Orchard, Tex.	44	1	

Table 17.—MISSION SCHOOLS CONDUCTED BY LAY
TEACHERS—Cont.

Location: Diocese and Town	Pupils	Teachers	Remarks
LAFAYETTE, LA.			
Abbeyville, La.	132	2	
Broussard, La.	114	2	
Carencro, La.	300	2	
Coulee Croche, La.	100	2	
Delcambre, La.	60	1	
Glencoe, La.	56	1	
Julian Hill, La.	95	1	Now in
Lebeau, La.	275	4	Charge of
Leonville, La.	116	2	Sisters of Holy Family
Olivier, La.			No Report
Prairie Basse, La.	78	1	
Rayne, La.	180	4	
Segura, La.			No Report
LITTLE ROCK, ARK.			
Pine Bluff, Ark.	60	2	
LOUISVILLE, KY.			
Lebanon, Ky.	38	1	
New Haven, Ky.	28	1	
New Hope, Ky.	14	1	
Raywick, Ky.	25	1	
St. Mary, Ky.	45	1	
MOBILE, ALA.			
Birmingham, Ala.	180	3	
Chastang, Ala.	126	4	
Fairfort, Ala.	33	1	
Little Chastang, Ala.	32	1	
Tuscaloosa, Ala.	119	3	
West Mt. Vernon, Ala.	24	1	
NATCHEZ, MISS.			
Harriston, Miss.	30	1	
Laurel Hill, Miss.	25	1	
Waltersville, Miss.	34	1	
NEW ORLEANS, LA.			
Bertrandville, La.	120	2	
Gretna, La.	60	2	
Klotzville, La.	40	1	
Mandville, La.	61	1	
Paillettown, La.	141	2	
Plaquemines, La.	167	3	
Point a la Hache, La.	245	5	Three schools
RALEIGH, N. CAR.			
Newton Grove, N. Car..........	22	1	
RICHMOND, VA.			
Columbia, Va.	46	1	
Rock Castle, Va.	25	1	
SAVANNAH, GA.			
Savannah, Ga.	135	3	
TOTAL	3,794	77	

6. Sisters

The alchemy which transforms the poverty of our mission schools into the vital spot of the missions is the supernatural love and devotion of the sisters who teach in them, unequalled as they are by any other body of teachers in the world. Because of her consecrated life, the sister takes a more personal interest in her pupils than could be expected of lay teachers. To the religious teacher, each child represents not merely a social animal but an immortal soul worthy of her best efforts. This attitude makes for a closer relationship than would be possible under ordinary circumstances. To the point is the following incident: a non-Catholic superintendent of a state-supported school for white girls was being shown through a House of the Good Shepherd for colored girls. In admiration of the work being accomplished, she turned to the Mother Superioress and said, "I suppose you are receiving a very munificent salary for the work you are doing in this institution." The Mother replied that she received nothing in the way of salary, but that she was bound by vow to a life of poverty and service to such girls as were being cared for in the institution. In amazement the non-Catholic woman exclaimed, "Why, how can you even do such work? I would not do it for a hundred dollars a day!" The Mother merely replied, "Neither would I do it for a hundred dollars a day." Such a life is a moral mystery beyond the comprehension of most non-Catholics and even many Catholics. It is such a spirit, however, which makes possible the Catholic educational activities on the Colored Missions.

In spite of the manifold difficulties which impede Catholic activity in the educational field of the Colored Missions, the priests and sisters have accomplished results which are truly marvelous. Non-Catholic schools and institutions have all the material advantages on their side, but there is nothing in the public or sectarian school system which can equal the tender love and devotion of the Catholic sisters. "The men and women on the missions are truly a credit to the Catholic Church," observes the *Report of the Commission for Negro and Indian Missions*, [1] "Their constancy, their courage, their

---
[1] 1926, p. 4.

zeal, their spirit of sacrifice are beyond doubt the chief assets of the work. Their temporal lot is indeed hard. Hardship and toil are the price they gladly pay for the salvation of the poor neglected souls for whom Christ also paid the price of His life."

There are thirty-two sisterhoods engaged in activities for the welfare of the Negro in the United States.[2] The activities of these communities are as varied as are the activities of the Catholic Church, ranging as they do from the kitchen to the college. Twenty-six communities teach in parochial schools, two are in charge of domestic departments in institutions preparing priests for the Colored Missions, three do social service work only, and one cares for delinquent colored girls. There are four communities engaged exclusively in work for the colored: three communities of colored sisters—the Oblates of Providence (Baltimore), Sisters of the Holy Family (New Orleans), and the Handmaids of the Most Pure Heart of Mary (New York); the Franciscan Sisters of Baltimore are the only white sisters engaged exclusively in work for the colored.

Besides the three communities of colored sisters already mentioned, a most remarkable development in religious communities for colored women is the foundation of colored Magdalens at the House of the Good Shepherd, Baltimore, Md. On April 24, 1922, His Grace, Archbishop Curley, ever a friend of the Negro, officially and personally opened the community. Ten months later four aspirants to the penitential life received the habit of the Magdalens from the hands of His Grace. This pioneer community has since grown to 15 members, further growth of the community being prevented by lack of housing facilities. Than the sight of this community of colored girls leading a life of penitential austerity, no more potent answer can be given those critics who question the native ability of the Negro to rise to a height of virtue equal if not superior to that of other races. By proving themselves capable of walking in the way of religious perfection, these Magdalens are harbingers of the dawn of a better day for the Negro race.

---

[2] The Sisters of the Holy Cross have since opened a school at Cairo, Ill.

TABLE 18. SUMMARY OF SISTERHOODS AND WORK UNDER THEIR CHARGE.

	Parochial schools	Complete high schools	Incomplete high schools	Homes	Industrial schools	Boarding schools	Social service	Lay teachers	Sisters	Children in charge	
Benedictine Sisters	1		2				2		2	55	
Blessed Sacrament, Sisters of the	31	5	2		1	1		79	220	10,123	1 college
Charity, Daughters of (Emmitsburg, Md.)	1								1	16	cf. note 1
Charity, Sisters of (Mt. St. Joseph, Ohio)	1	1							2	50	
Charity, Sisters of (of Leavenworth)	1	1						1	2	40	
Charity, Sisters of (of Nazareth)	2							1	6	225	
Divine Providence, Sisters of	5					1		3	17	771	
Dominic, Sisters of Saint	2		1	1				5	21	390	
Francis, Third Order of Saint	2	4		2				1	36	750	
Francis, Third Order Regular of Saint	2	1		1					5	207	
Franciscan Sisters of Baltimore City	4	4	1	4				14	62	2,031	
Franciscans, Missionary, of Immaculate Conception	3				3				20	872	
Good Shepherd, Our Lady of Charity of the									58	478	
Holy Cross, Marianites of the	1	1			1			1	1	75	
Holy Family, Sisters of the	16	4	4	4	1	1		11	153	3,581	colored
Holy Ghost and Mary Immaculate, Servants of the	16	2						4	67	2,586	
Holy Ghost, Missionary Sisters, Servants of the	6	6						3	50	1,819	
Holy Souls, Helpers of the							1				
Holy Names of Jesus and Mary, Sisters of the	2					1		3	18	263	
Immaculate Heart, Sisters, Servants of the	3								10	327	
Mercy, Sisters of	3							3	6	385	
Mission Helpers, Servants of the Sacred Heart					1	1			4	38	cf. note 2
Most Precious Blood, Sisters, Adorers of the									10	....	cf. note 3
Most Pure Heart of Mary, Handmaids of the	1						1		11	110	colored; day nursery

TABLE 18. SUMMARY OF SISTERHOODS AND WORK UNDER THEIR CHARGE (Continued)

	Parochial schools	Complete high schools	Incomplete high schools	Homes	Industrial schools	Boarding schools	Social service	Lay teachers	Sisters	Children in charge
Notre Dame School, Sisters of	5						1		10	420
Our Lady of the Apostles, Sisters of									3	cf. note 4
Presentation, Sisters of St. Mary of the									5	(colored; cf. note 5)
Providence, Oblate Sisters of	12	2	1	2				2	122	2,156
Sacred Heart, Religious of the (Madames of the)	1								3	125
St. Joseph, Sisters of	4		1				1	4	11	607
Trinity, Missionary Servants of the Most Blessed	2							2	2	116
Ursuline Nuns	1								2	117
TOTAL	128	26	10	10	6	4	7	137	940	28,733 cf. note 6

(1) New school opened at Greensboro, N. Car., 1928.
(2) Mission Helpers also do social service among the colored people in hospitals, prisons and at their homes.
(3) In charge of the domestic service at St. Joseph's Seminary, Baltimore, Md.
(4) In charge of the domestic service at Epiphany College, Newburgh, N. Y.
(5) The Oblate Sisters Community numbers 152 Sisters. They also do work in Cuba.
(6) The Sisters of the Holy Cross have since opened a school at Cairo, Ill.

CHAPTER XIII.

EDUCATIONAL ACTIVITIES

1. TRENDS

Two trends of thought would seem to predominate in discussing education for the Negro. Booker T. Washington saw salvation through industrial education of Negroes "in those arts and crafts in which they are now employed and in which they must exhibit greater efficiency if they are to compete with the white men." He argued that since the Negro had to toil he ought to be taught to toil skillfully. While not attacking higher education, he insisted that the education of the Negro should be planned with a view to his future. A youth, then, according to Washington, should not be educated away from his environment, but trained to lay a foundation on which he could build something above and beyond his beginnings. With the exception of a small minority, the Negroes regarded this policy as a surrender to the oppressors who desired to reduce the whole race to menial service; they branded Washington as a traitor to the cause of his people.

Against this plan for industrial education there have always stood forth some Negroes who would not yield ground. Outstanding were W. M. Trotter and W. E. B. DuBois. Such men have clung to the idea that recognition for the Negro must come through agitation for high education and political equality. What they demand for the Negro is the same opportunity and the same treatment generally given the white man. According to them, to accept anything else is treachery.

Carter G. Woodson[1] very appropriately points out that; "Washington's long silence as to the rights of the Negro did not necessarily mean that he was in favor of oppression of the race. He was aware of the fact that mere agitation for political rights at that time could not be of much benefit to the race, and that their economic improvement, a thing fun-

---

[1] Woodson, *The Negro in Our History*, p. 444.

damental in real progress, could easily be promoted without incurring the disapproval of the discordant elements in the South. . . . History will record that Booker T. Washington, in trying to elevate his oppressed people, so admirably connected education with the practical things of life that he effected such a reform in the education of the world as to place himself in the class with Pestalozzi, Froebel and Herbert. . . . Washington's advocacy of industrial education, moreover, in spite of all that has been said, was not a death blow to higher education for the Negro. That movement has lived in spite of opposition. Washington himself frequently stated that industrial education, as he emphasized it, was for the masses of the people who had to toil. Knowing that the race had to have men to lead it onward, he did not object to higher education."

While it is impossible at this time to share the sanguine optimism of those who believe that what is most necessary for a solution of the Negro problem is an accessible literary education for the mass of the race, it does not seem reasonable to base our educational program on the assumption that Negroes will never be other than hewers of wood and drawers of water; every race is entitled to have the constant opportunity of realizing those spiritual ideals that ultimately constitute its true destiny.

Any theory of Catholic education for the Negro should be built on two principles that must be looked upon as fundamental. The first is that our Catholic schools are not simply for the purpose of teaching the Catechism when other expedients might do as well. No matter how keenly religious and moral considerations enter into our educational ideals, our schools have carried and must carry the additional burden of fitting their pupils for secular life. The second fundamental principle upon which our educational program must be based is that the function of education is to help the human race in each of its generations to take at least one step in the direction of greater material prosperity, aesthetic enjoyment, and spiritual insight. Consequently, while doing all in our power to further the cause of higher education, we should not neglect the cause of industrial education.

168   CATHOLIC CHURCH AND AMERICAN NEGRO

2. COLLEGE EDUCATION

In 1925, 12,445 public high schools reported 396,003 graduates, of which number 126,782 went to college in 1926 and 54,-246 attended other institutions of higher learning.[1] In the *Survey of Negro Colleges and Universities* there are listed 79 institutions of higher learning for Negroes. The services rendered by these colleges and universities reach every section of the United States, January 1, 1926, there were 942,443 enrolled in colleges, universities, teachers' colleges, and normal schools attended primarily by whites, and 17,506 colleges, universities, teachers' colleges, and normal schools attended by Negroes. Accordingly, for every 10,000 whites, 90 white students were attending college; for every 10,000 Negroes, 15 were attending college.[2]

From 1854 to 1870 was the period in which were concentrated the pioneer efforts for Negro higher education. During those years 18 colleges were founded by white leaders from the North, with the co-operation of churches, missionary organizations, and philanthropists. During that time private agencies were the sole promoters of Negro higher education, the states having little interest in the matter. In the period 1870-1890, nine Negro land-grant colleges and 13 colleges under state-denominational (Negro) control were founded. Since then 39 state and denominational Negro colleges have been founded.[3]

The advisability of higher education for Negroes is indisputable. The latest available figures[4] show that in 1926 there were approximately 48,000 Negro teachers in the United States, including those teaching in elementary schools, high schools, and colleges. Of this number, 1,050 are teachers in institutions of higher learning and 46,950 in elementary and high schools. Upon the latter rests the responsibility of educating five million Negro youths under the age of nineteen years. The *Survey* notes that "a considerable portion of the

---

[1] "Biennial Survey of Education," Dept. of Education Bulletin, 1925, no. 25, p. 1044.
[2] *Ibid.*, p. 33.
[3] *Ibid.*, p. 34.
[4] *Ibid.*, pp. 2, 3.

46,950 teachers now giving instruction in Negro elementary and high schools are deficient in proper training. Many have not received more than a primary school preparation, while the training of a large number of others has been limited to one or two years in secondary work or graduation from a high school. A shortage prevails not only in the number of teachers but also in their quality." [1]

National social and economic life demands also the training of many more Negro professional and technical leaders. There are 3,500 Negro physicians and surgeons in the United States, or approximately one colored physician to every 3,343 Negroes, while the white race has a physician to every 553 persons. A serious lack of Negro dentists also prevails; there is only one to every 10,540 Negro inhabitants. In technical lines an even more pronounced shortage of trained men is revealed: there are in the United States only 50 Negro architects, 184 engineers, 145 designers, draftsmen, and inventors, and 207 chemists. These facts are incontestible arguments in favor of higher education for Negroes. As the *Survey* already referred to states: "Improvement of the economic welfare of the members of the race, protection of their health and physical well-being, their moral, intellectual, and aesthetic uplift are questions immediately affecting the other 91 per cent of the country's population. The attainment of these objectives can be accomplished only through higher education, through its upbuilding, expansion and development." [2]

Xavier University, New Orleans, La., opened in 1915, is the only Catholic representative in the field of higher education for Negroes. The fourteen years that have passed since then have witnessed a growth and development unparalleled in the history of schools for Negro youth. It was in response to the urgent request of the Most Rev. James H. Blenk, S.M., D.D., the late Archbishop of New Orleans, that the Sisters of the Blessed Sacrament took up the work of educating the colored Catholic youth of New Orleans. The buildings which had been vacated by Southern University upon its removal to Baton Rouge, in 1912, were purchased and renovated, and in

[1] *Ibid.*
[2] *Ibid.*, p. 4.

September, 1915, the high school department of Xavier was formally opened. In order to secure the standard of excellence required by the Faculty for graduation, students were not enrolled beyond the eleventh grade; therefore, the first Xavier High School graduates, twenty-five in number, received their diplomas in June, 1917. Since that time over three hundred have received diplomas of graduation from the high school.

In September of 1917 a normal department was opened to prepare students for the teaching profession. In September, 1925, this department expanded into a Teachers' College; at the same time the College of Liberal Arts was opened, and a Pre-medical Course was added to the curriculum. These courses provide for the higher education of young men and women of the colored race who aim to equip themselves for leadership in literary and scientific careers, or who wish to prepare for admission into recognized medical schools.

The urgent need of a standard college for the higher education of the colored youth of the South was recognized by the Sisters of the Blessed Sacrament shortly after the inauguration of their work in New Orleans· Accordingly, authorization to conduct college courses and to confer degrees was solicited in 1918. Under date of June 18 of that year, R. G. Pleasant, Governor of the State of Louisiana approved the Act passed by the General Assembly.

Although the term "university" is used in the charter, the school now uses the name "Xavier College," as the officers of the institution do not feel that they are justified in designating the work by so pretentious a title.

Xavier is a charter member of the South Central Association of Colleges for Negro youth. The Faculty is as follows:

President—Rev. E. G. Brunner, S.S.J., M.A.
Philosophy and Religion—Rev. E. V. Casserly, S.S.J., M.A., S.T.B.
Dean of College—Sr. M. Francis, S.B.S.
Dean of Pharmacy—Mr. Gaspar R. Bosetta·
Faculty—Five Sisters of the Blessed Sacrament and six lay teachers, as also a registrar, librarian and athletic coach.

The Dean of the School is the responsible administrative head.

The first class was graduated from the college department in June, 1928, when three young men and two young women received the degree of Bachelor of Arts.

At present the institution includes a four-year college, a school of pharmacy, and a high school. Extension courses for teachers are included in the college program. The enrolments for the several divisions on January 1, 1928, were as follows: the college, 37; the high school, 264; the extension courses, 28. The school of pharmacy enrolled 15. A class of eighth grade students is conducted for the purpose of enabling those who have had only seven grades of elementary instruction to meet the standards of the high school.

The high school and normal school were accredited by the Louisiana State Department of Education in 1922. During the past 10 years the high school graduates have been admitted without condition by a large number of leading colleges and universities both in the North and in the South.

The aim of the Sisters of the Blessed Sacrament in conducting Xavier College is to offer young men and women of the colored race an opportunity to receive a thorough, liberal education; to impart an education which will develop all the faculties of soul and body and find expression in clear thinking and right acting. A trained mind and a critical judgment, although essential to happiness and success, are of little avail unless controlled by a strong will and directed by a keen moral sense; hence, the Sisters of the Blessed Sacrament aim to supply an atmosphere favorable to the development of a sense of responsibility and the upbuilding of character. Consequently, in the form of discipline and the methods of teaching, they lay due emphasis on moral and religious agencies, ever striving for the realization of the Most Reverend John Lancaster Spalding's definition of education: "The soul's response to God's appeal to make itself like unto Him—self-active, knowing, wise, strong, loving and fair."

With justice, the *Survey of Negro Colleges and Universities* speaks of Xavier College in terms of praise, for "a careful study of the facts presented in this report and the observations made at the college, lead the survey committee to believe that Xavier College is rendering a needed service worthy of continued support. In the short period of twelve years, it has developed a well-attended high school and has found it necessary to expand its educational services in the fields of college and professional training. The committee is aware that the college and professional work of the institution is in a stage of transition and that it is working rapidly towards definite educational objectives and standards."[1]

While Xavier College is the sole Catholic endeavor for higher education among Negroes, it is an undertaking of which the Sisters of the Blessed Sacrament may well be proud. It is a beginning in the right direction. If the Catholic Church is to make that progress for which we have so long looked, it must train Catholic Negro leaders. The Hon. William D. Cunningham, at the Eighth Annual Convention of the National Council of Catholic Men,[2] pointed this out when he said: "There never has been a time in all the history of our Church when the necessity was so marked and the demand so inexorable as this day for Catholic laymen impelled and moved by an irresistible missionary impulse. The conditions to which I refer call upon us, the Catholic laymen of America, for affirmative and aggressive action."[3] In speaking of the obligation of the Catholic layman to see that our Faith and the truth be known, His Honor asks the question, "How is this to be done?" He answers it in these words: "Before we get leadership we must create the conditions which breed it. Most important is education. It is the power of intellect. . . . The future of the Church in this country depends upon the intelligence and the educated intellectuality of the Catholic lay body. We must create an educated body of youth—men and women—second to none in intellectual training and equipment."[4] Although spoken to Catholic laymen of the white race and of general conditions in the United States, not one

[1] *Ibid.*, p. 29.
[2] Cincinnati, Ohio, Nov. 18-21, 1928.
[3] "Lay Missionaries, the Need of the Hour," Catholic Defense and Exposition Series; National Council of Catholic Men, Dec. 1928, No. 2, p. 4.
[4] *Ibid.*, p. 9.

tittle of the honorable gentleman's advice need be changed
to apply to the necessity of intelligent Catholic laymen of
the colored race.

3. HIGH SCHOOLS

Educators recognize the importance of the high school
period in a child's educational life. They agree that the period
of adolescence is probably the most critical in his whole life.
That the relative importance of the secondary school training
during this period is being recognized is evident from the fact
that in 1926 the Bureau of Education had a record of 21,700
public high schools.[1] The 1926 Reports from State Departments of Education showed an enrolment in these high
schools of 3,757,466 pupils.[2] During the school year 1925-
1926, a total of 434,539 pupils were graduated from public
high schools, representing an increase of 92 per cent over the
graduation number in 1920.[3] Besides the public high schools,
there were, in 1926, 2,500 private high schools, 386 preparatory departments of colleges, and 125 secondary departments
in teacher-training institutions.

Secondary schools now enroll about 53 per cent of those
of secondary school age.[4] Private high school enrolments
number 295,625, preparatory enrolments 55,632, and secondary students in normal schools number 23,402, making a
grand total of 4,132,125.[5] These figures give some idea of the
role of the high school in the educational program of today.

That this progress in education has been shared to some
extent by the Negroes of the United States is evidenced by
the fact that almost all that has been done in the South to
provide public high schools for Negroes was done during
the decade 1918-1928. At the beginning of this period, outside of a few large cities and a small number of state institutions, there were no standard public high schools for Ne-

---

[1] Bulletin, 1928, no. 25, p. 1037.
[2] *Ibid.*, p. 1040.
[3] *Ibid.*, p. 1044.
[4] "Statistical Survey of Education, 1925-1926", Bureau of Education Bulle-
    tin, 1928, no. 12, p. 2.
[5] *Ibid.*, p. 12.

groes. The 1925-1926 Survey of Education [1] notes that there was a total of 423 public high schools for colored only, with an enrolment of 98,705 pupils. These figures include junior high schools. At the same time there were reported to the Bureau 103 private high schools and academies for Negroes with an enrolment of 10,261 pupils. This represents 430 per cent increase in enrolment over that of 1900. [2] Of the high schools for colored, 251 were accredited. [3] With very few exceptions these colored schools are measured by the same standards as the white schools. Most of the non-standard high schools were of four or less years' course, of which the majority are in process of development and will soon be standardized.

It is an undisputed fact that organizations making greatest progress in missionary work among the colored people are those which have the best system of high schools. In 1929, of the private and denominational institutions reporting some high school or higher work, the Baptist Church claimed 60, the different branches of the Methodist Church claimed a total of 38, the Presbyterian, 32, Congregational, 18, Episcopal, 7; and 26 others were distributed among other denominations. [4]

As George E. Haynes, Ph.D., points out, [5] in the educational field the white Protestant churches of the North have performed a real service since Negro high schools are largely dependent upon church agencies for support and supervision. The rapidly growing county training schools that are attaining high school standards have accelerated the sentiment among the whites for public support. The effect of the church support upon provision of high school opportunities for Negroes in the South is shown by the fact that in 1915 there were probably about 45 four-year course and 18 three-year course public high schools in 13 southern states. There were about 100 four-year course private high schools and a similar number of private schools offering some secondary work of three

[1] Bulletin, 1928, no. 5, p. 1068.
[2] Ibid., p. 1129.
[3] The American Negro; Annals of the American Academy, p. 214.
[4] Occasional Papers of The John F. Slater Fund, no. 20, 1929.
[5] Quoted in "The Church and Negro Progress"; The American Negro, Annals of the American Academy, p. 264.

years or less. At least three-fourths of these private high schools were church supported.

Quoting figures compiled by W. A. Robinson[1] for 1926-1927, Dr. Haynes shows that "for the sixteen southern states there were 167 public and 84 private state accredited four-year course high schools for Negroes. But these should be contrasted with 4,760 public and 547 private state-accredited four-year high schools for whites. In 1920 the Negro population of these states was 9,008,906, and the white population was 28,596,689. Meagre as it is, more than one-third of real secondary education among Negroes of the South today would disappear if high schools now supported by church educational and mission boards were discontinued."

Ten years ago (1919), a Catholic colored layman, speaking before a section of the Catholic Educational Association, could justly complain that "it gives us the greatest apprehension as to the future development of our colored people from the Catholic viewpoint that there should be just one standard high school in a population of two hundred and fifty thousand faithful, striving souls, and not a single college."[2] Today, however, we can count 13 full-course Catholic colored high schools accredited by the State Departments of Education, and 15 full-course Catholic colored high schools which have not yet been accredited. Most of the high schools in the latter group have not been accredited because of insufficient laboratory equipment. This is not strange, if one considers the outlay of money which complete laboratory equipment entails. Besides the high schools offering a complete four-year course, there are at least 13 as yet incomplete high schools; these are in progress of development and likely will be completed within the next five years. Two such incomplete high schools already have three-year courses; four have a two-year course, and seven have just started with the first year.

What becomes of the graduates of Catholic high schools for Negroes? A few notes concerning the 1926 and 1927 graduates of Xavier High School, New Orleans, La., will throw some light on the question. In 1926 Xavier High School

[1] *Ibid.*, p. 205.
[2] *Catholic Educational Association Bulletin*, Nov., 1919, p. 438.

graduates were 12 boys and 33 girls. Of the 12 boys: two entered Xavier College, one for a B.A. course, the other for a pre-medical course; one entered Xavier Commercial, which is a one-year course after the regular four-year high school course; another, who planned to study pharmacy, attended the extension courses of Xavier College while holding a position as porter in a bank; two other boys are on the road as traveling salesmen, another is an insurance agent, three are working as carpenters, and one is working at masonry with his father who is a prosperous contractor; the last boy in the class is driving a truck.

Of the 33 girls: 11 entered Xavier College, five entered other colleges, one entered Howard University (Washington, D. C.) to study music, one girl married, four obtained positions as teachers in rural schools, four are living at home with their parents, one is employed as a dressmaker, another sews at home, two are doing factory work, and three are doing housework.

In 1927 Xavier High School graduated 10 boys and 37 girls. Of the 10 boys: three entered Xavier College, two in the Pre-medical and one in the B.A. course; two entered other colleges, one New York City College, the other Straight College, New Orleans, La.; one is taking the commercial course at Xavier, one is an insurance agent, one is with his father in the stove business, one is an interior decorator, and one, a carpenter.

Of the 37 girls: 13 entered Xavier College, two in the Pre-medical, two in Pharmacy, three in the B.A. course in Education, six in the Arts course; four are taking a two-year normal course in Education at Xavier, one is taking the commercial course, three girls entered other colleges, four are teaching, two went in training to become nurses, one is in the printing business at home, six are living at home with their parents, and three are working in service.

The Catholic Church and her workers cannot hope to make rapid progress in their missionary endeavors until a stronger system of secondary and higher education is built up. American mission methods must prevail, and one tenet of the American creed is the importance of education. It is in the high school period of a child's life that the Church now loses so many potential Catholic leaders, because they are compelled to spend this critical period in non-Catholic or non-sectarian schools.

While the last decade has witnessed remarkable progress, Catholic secondary education is still largely a problem of tomorrow. The reasons for this are chiefly financial. Catholics in the North and West, upon whom the burden of building and operating such schools for higher education among the colored must in the long run fall, have been engrossed in creating a Catholic school system of their own. Furthermore, the charity of Catholics is more easily approached when there is question of the poverty-stricken mission school. The idea of higher education for the colored child is too new to find ready acceptance in the name of charity.

Considering the ever-present financial handicaps under which the workers on the colored missions are laboring, the record of Catholic high school development represents an era of remarkable achievement. It would be manifestly unfair to make a strict comparison between Catholic colored high school achievement and that of secular and sectarian education agencies. Given the millions of dollars which are pouring into public and denominational schools of the South, the Catholic high school would undoubtedly be an assured success; hampered as it is by the necessity of competing with these millions of dollars, its progress must by comparison seem meagre and slow.

We Catholics can profit, however, from a comparison with public and non-Catholic effort in the direction of higher education. We can profit to the extent of realizing that missionary activities of all denominations outside the Catholic Church would seem to be centered on higher education of the Negroes. If we Catholics are to hold our advanced colored laity and make their lives a factor in the conversion of the other eleven millions of colored people; if we are to make our Catholic people the motive power in the construction of the character of the race, we must give more concern to the means of influencing their thought and operation; in a word, we must go in for higher education. Practically, for the time being, we must develop the high schools; we owe this to the Negro and to the Church. Our aim must be to equip and staff our Catholic high schools as thoroughly and as competently as are the public schools. The criterion of this perfection is, of course, the state requirements for standard or accredited high schools. Only when our Catholic colored high schools meet these state requirements have we the assurance that we are not offering to our students an inferior intellectual training.

Our Catholic schools must, however, do more than secular schools. While it is true that an education promotes possibilities, it must also guide them; hence, the normal thing for higher schools is that they be of a denominational character, for the ethico-religious in education must ever be the core of the intellectual. That this phase of education is receiving universal attention is evident from the findings of the Commission of Education. From the *Biennial Survey of Education, 1924-1926*[1] we quote: "Religion in education has during the biennium been discussed to an extent that makes it almost take on the character of an important development . . . whatever the causes for revived interest in student religion. Studies show in state-supported, as well as in private and denominationally controlled institutions, that the number of courses in religion, in biblical literature, and in related subjects has been greatly multiplied."

In as much as Catholic schools have a peculiar and significant role of soul-training, they cannot be supplanted by any other kind of school. To establish the inner relationship between the religious instruction and the whole personal life of the student the specific character of the religious instruction must be made an integral part of the student's life; in other words, during his formative life the student should be taught in Catholic environment and under Catholic influences, otherwise Catholic morality will be to him only an imperfect application of vague and colorless generalities. Furthermore, the school can better co-operate with the home if both recognize the same religious basis. But even if the home has abandoned all, or never had any religious practices, the religious

---

[1] Bulletin, 1928, no. 25, p. 34.

Table 19. CATHOLIC HIGH SCHOOLS FOR NEGROES

STATE	CITY	DIOCESE	NAME	IN CHARGE	BOYS	GIRLS	SISTERS	LAY	REMARKS
Complete High Schools Approved by State									
Arkansas	Little Rock	Little Rock	St. Bartholomew	Servants of Holy Ghost	4	10	2	0	
Illinois	Chicago	Chicago	St. Elizabeth	Blessed Sacrament	22	57	4	0	2 years commercial course
Kentucky	Louisville	Louisville	St. Augustine	Charity (Nazareth)	7	6	2	2	Known as The Catholic Colored High School
Louisiana	Lafayette	Lafayette	Holy Rosary Institute	Holy Family	0	33	6	0	Industrial School
	Lake Charles	Lafayette	Sacred Heart	Blessed Sacrament	9	35	2	2	
	New Orleans	New Orleans	Xavier	Blessed Sacrament	113	151	7	7	1 year Preparatory; Commercial; vocational (40 women)
	Opelousas	Lafayette	Holy Ghost Train. Sch.	Holy Family	9	20	3	2	
	New Iberia	Lafayette	St. Edward	Blessed Sacrament	6	22	2	0	
Mississippi	Greenville	Natchez	Sacred Heart	Servants of Holy Ghost	20	32	2	0	
	Jackson	Natchez	Holy Ghost Institute	Servants of Holy Ghost	8	16	2	0	
	Vicksburg	Natchez	St. Mary	Servants of Holy Ghost	2	7	3	0	
Virginia	Rock Castle	Richmond	St. Francis Institute	Blessed Sacrament	0	149	17	0	1 priest; 1 year Preparatory Boarding School; Domestic Science
Alabama	Mobile	Mobile	Heart of Mary	Holy Ghost & Mary Immac.	18	36	2	0	
Complete High Schools Unapproved by State									
Georgia	Augusta	Savannah	Immaculate Conception	Missionary Franciscans	3	26	1	0	2 priests; application made for State approval
Kansas	Leavenworth	Leavenworth	Holy Epiphany	Oblates	3	13	1	0	1 priest; considered as branch of Immaculate H. S. which is State accredited.
Louisiana	Alexandria	Alexandria	St. James	Divine Providence	4	24	3	0	1 priest
	Lafayette	Lafayette	St. Paul	Holy Family					
Maryland	Baltimore	Baltimore	St. Francis Academy	Oblates	0	19	6	0	
	Baltimore	Baltimore	St. Francis Xavier	Franciscans (Baltimore)	3	7	2	0	
	Ridge	Baltimore	Card. Gibbons Inst.	Lay	30	26	0	8	Industrial and Agricultural; Boarding School.
Mississippi	Meridian	Natchez	St. Joseph	Servants of Holy Ghost	0	9	1	0	
	Bay St. Louis	Natchez	St. Rose of Lima	Servants of Holy Ghost	7	23	2	0	
	Bay St. Louis	Natchez	St. Augustine	Fathers of Divine Word	30				8 priests; prep. seminary for society of Divine Word.
North Carolina	Wilmington	Raleigh	St. Thomas	Franciscans (Baltimore)	5	10	2	0	
Virginia	Norfolk	Richmond	St. Joseph	Franciscans (Baltimore)	20	36	2	0	Application made for State approval.
Texas	Dallas	Dallas	St. Peter	Holy Ghost & Mary Immac.	1	22	2	0	1 Priest.
	Galveston	Galveston	Holy Rosary	Holy Family	5	17	2	0	
Virginia	Richmond	Richmond	Van de Vyver Inst.	Franciscans (Baltimore)	24	92	3	2	Commercial Course; Night School, Academic and Vocational
Incomplete High Schools									
Alabama	Tuscaloosa	Mobile	St. Mary Magdalen	Holy Trinity	2	5	1	0	1 Year
Arkansas	Pine Bluff	Little Rock	St. Peter	Lay					1 Year
Dist. of Columbia	Washington	Baltimore	St. Cyprian	Oblates	11	28	1	0	2 Years, to Prepare Students for Civil Service Exams.
Delaware	Clayton	Wilmington	St. Joseph	Josephite Fathers	6	0	0	1	Industrial School; Home; 6 Instructors.
Georgia	Savannah	Savannah	St. Benedict the Moor	Missionary Franciscans					3 Years
Louisiana	Crowley	Lafayette	St. Theresa	Holy Ghost & Mary Immac.			2		2 Years
Mississippi	Natchez	Natchez	St. Francis	Holy Ghost & Mary Immac.			2		3 Years
Ohio	Cincinnati	Cincinnati	Madonna	Blessed Sacrament	9	12	1	0	1 Year; Central High School
Oklahoma	Okmulgee	Oklahoma	Uganda Martyrs	Holy Ghost & Mary Immac.			1		2 Years
Pennsylvania	Cornwells Heights	Philadelphia	Holy Providence House	Blessed Sacrament					Industrial School
Tennessee	Jackson	Nashville	St. Joseph	Dominicans	2	2	1	0	1 Year
Texas	San Antonio	San Antonio	St. Catherine	Holy Ghost & Mary Immac.					1 Year
Virginia	Rock Castle	Richmond	St. Emma Indus. School	Lay	142	0	0	2	2 Years Industrial and Agricultural; Boarding School; 13 Instructors.

Children from the House of Good Shepherd, Louisville, Ky., attend St. Augustine's High School.
Children from St. Benedict's Home, Rye, N. Y., attend the city high school.

atmosphere of the school may remedy, to some extent, this deplorable condition. Because of its professed aim to develop the character as well as to cultivate the mind, the Catholic high school is, therefore, a most powerful instrument for the inculcation of that stamina so essential for the true progress of a race like the Negro, beset on all sides, as it is, by difficulties which tend to try the soul of any man and to submerge in pessimism the nobler aspirations of life. Not only to the Catholic Negro, but to the whole race, are we under obligation to develop untiringly our plans for a Catholic high school system equal, if not superior to, the Godless education offered by the public schools.

4. INDUSTRIAL SCHOOLS

A—Necessity of Industrial Training

While the necessity of stressing higher and secondary Catholic education for Negroes is evident, it is no less apparent that such education should be governed by a realization of the economic and psychological differences of the race as a whole and more particularly by the unequal advancement within the race itself. Where, for instance, is the congruity of giving a classical education to an excessively large group of Negroes if economic conditions are such as to stultify their abilities in the strife for existence? This is what Booker T. Washington called educating them out of their environment. Opportunities for advancement in the arts and professions are at present all too few for the "talented tenth" among our Negro population, much less for the mass of Negroes.

It is intelligible that educational leaders under the inspiration of high hopes should have with few exceptions failed to consider the needs of the mass. It is so easy to borrow in its entirety a scheme of education that has given good results under one set of circumstances and try to make it work in a set of circumstances entirely different. Culture is a thing to be highly valued even by the working man, but it is the end of education to assemble properly the cultural values, and so to impart them to the individual as to give him the free use thereof. An exaggerated conception of culture will necessarily entail an exaggerated estimate of the meaning and value of education.

The test of educational effort is always that it provides for the economic, intellectual and spiritual needs of the community. It is fatal to think that this ideal can be achieved by wholesale and immediate higher education of the colored race. Even the white race, with all its centuries of cultural advantages and ascendency, cannot yet claim as a mass to be educated. Already a reaction is setting in against the over-supply of "white-collar men." The *Statistical Survey of Education, 1925-1926*[1] observes that although secondary schools now enroll about 53 per cent of those of secondary school age, and still have room to grow, "the indication is that the rate of growth from now on will constantly decrease, provided social and economic factors remain relatively as at present."

A paper read before the now defunct Negro Section of the Catholic Education Association at its meeting in New York in 1920[2] in discussing the subject of industrial and agricultural schools observed rather keenly: "It is idle for a race to be dreaming of spiritual and intellectual utopias when its members are wrestling with the harsh inequalities of material life. . . . The number of Negroes in skilled occupations is negligible. An effective system of industrial education would benefit not only the colored, but would also bring greater prosperity to the Southern States and besides would go very much further towards more amicable race relations than all the blastings of editors and authors."

The strongest opposition to industrial education has come from the Negroes themselves. We can best understand their attitude from the experience of Booker T. Washington in founding Tuskegee Institute. While lauding his people for their high ambitions, Washington had to admit that many were under the impression that as soon as they had an education, in some inexplicable way they would be freed from most of the hardships of the world, or at any rate could live without the necessity of performing manual labor.[3] He stated

---

[1] Bulletin, 1928, no. 12, p. 3.
[2] vol. XVII, no. 1, p. 405.
[3] *Up From Slavery*, p. 81.

that, from his experience, he was convinced that the average
young man going to school intended to become a great law-
yer, or Congressman, and the girls planned to be teachers,
"but I had a reasonably fixed idea, even at that early period
of my life that there was need of something to be done to prepare the way for successful lawyers, Congressmen, and teachers." [1] Despite opposition to his plans, Washington was not
to be shaken from his purpose of industrial education. He
realized that although one may go into a community prepared
to supply the people with an analysis of Greek sentences, the
community may not be at the time prepared for or feel the
need of Greek analysis, but it may feel the need of bricks and
wagons. If a man can supply the latter, a demand for the
former will eventually follow, and with the demand will come
the ability to appreciate it and profit by it. [2]

Those who, with Washington, advocated industrial education for the Negro did not maintain that opportunity for
higher education should be altogether excluded. Frederick
Douglas, as far back as 1853, while stressing the utility of
industrial training for the masses did not deny the importance of professional training for the small minority who
would be able to use it to better adantage. He admitted it
is necessary that "we have orators, authors and other professional men, but these can reach only a certain class and
get respect for our race in silent circles." [3] At the same time,
he added, "we will need mechanics as well as ministers."

If for the time being we seem to ignore cultural education it is only because culture must have the foundation of
material success, for as Martin R. Delany wrote: "Let our
young men and young women prepare themselves for usefulness and business. . . . A people must be a business people
and have more to depend upon than mere help in people's
houses or hotels before they are either able to support or
capable of properly appreciating the services of professional
men among them. This has been our greatest mistake, we
have commenced at the superstructure of the building in-

[1] *Ibid.*, p. 93.
[2] *Ibid.*, p. 155.
[3] *The American Negro; Annals of American Academy,* p. 124.

stead of at the bottom. We should first be mechanics and common tradesmen, and professions as a matter of course would grow out of the wealth made thereby." [1] The lapse of three-quarters of a century has not altered the sanity of this advice.

The economic salvation of the Negro is dependent to a great degree upon his training in the field of agriculture and the mechanical arts and crafts. While 1,000,000 Negroes own or operate farms, there are 1,178,000 members of the race engaged in ordinary farm labor. The lack of training in the mechanical arts and crafts is indicated by the fact that only 56,000 Negroes are skilled craftsmen, as compared with 1,371,000 pursuing unskilled occupations or employed as day laborers. All states have established land-grant colleges which offer courses in agriculture, the mechanical arts, and home economics. In these colleges members of the race may prepare themselves not only to become teachers in their fields, but also to enter into those vocations with all the advantages of superior specialized knowledge. "If continued progress is to be made to higher economic levels," states the *Survey of Negro Colleges and Universities,* [2] "the Negro youth must take advantage of these opportunities. The untrained and unskilled occupations can not remain the goal of his ambitions."

Cardinal Gibbons clearly saw the necessity of industrial training for the Negro. On one occasion he said: "To be a factor in their country's prosperity, to make their presence felt and to give any influence whatever to their attempt to better their status, it is absolutely necessary that, besides a sound religious training, they should be taught to be useful citizens; they should be brought up from childhood in habits of industry. They should be taught that labor is honorable, that the idler is a menace to the commonwealth. Institutions should be founded wherein young men may learn the trades best suited to their inclinations. Thus equipped—on the one hand, well-instructed Christians, on the other, skilled workmen— our colored may look hopefully to the future." [3]

---

[1] *Ibid.,* p. 124.
[2] Section of Bulletin, 1928, no. 7, p. 3.
[3] *Journal of Negro History,* vol. II, Oct. 1, 1917, p. 407.

The advantages which would accrue to the Negro from industrial training are too obvious to need stressing. Were the advantages to be gained purely economic and social, we might leave industrial training to secular institutions. But the advantages of an industrial training under Catholic auspices are worth noting. Because many Negro homes are not prepared for the reception of the high ideals which Christianity associates with the home, it will be almost impossible to raise the Negro to a high moral and spiritual level unless at the same time we try to develop the home and to increase the colored man's industrial efficiency. How can the proper Catholic home life thrive in an environment that gives every opportunity for the growth of vice, and crime, and disease? Conditions of home life are closely related to the assurance of a decent and steady livelihood. With the assurance of economic independence, opportunity is given to develop those natural virtues of life which are absolutely essential to the growth of the supernatural life which the Church offers. While it is true that secular institutions for industrial training may give a basis for the development of natural virtues, Negroes will be better disposed to place a high value upon the supernatural life and to live up to the ideals of Christianity as taught by the Catholic Church if they be developed under Catholic auspices and concurrently with religious training. For this reason it is desirable that training in the trades go hand in hand with training in religious principles. The secular institution for industrial education of the Negro cannot directly affect the moral welfare of its students. Religion has no place in the secular scheme of training, whereas the professed aim of the Catholic institution for industrial training is to develop the spiritual life of its students while building up their economic and social life. For the same reasons that we are developing our Catholic parochial and high schools we must also develop our Catholic industrial schools; the Church has just as much need for Catholic artisans of the Negro race as it has for Catholic scholars.

B.—Catholic Efforts for Industrial Education

1. St. Emma's Industrial School, Rock Castle, Va.

January of 1895 marked the opening of the first industrial school for Negroes under Catholic auspices. St. Emma's Agricultural and Industrial Institute, Rock Castle, Va., was founded in that year by Mrs. Edward Drexel Morrell, of Torresdale, Pa. Named after her mother, St. Emma's was the result of Mrs. Morrell's realization of the good being accomplished for the Negro by such secular institutions as Hampton and Tuskegee. St. Emma's Institute now occupies the site of the Belmead homestead and plantation, at one time owned by Philip St. George Cocke who was a general during the Civil War. The site embraces 1,700 acres with a frontage almost two miles along the south bank of the James River. The Institute accepts colored youths of fifteen years of age or over who have completed the elementary course in English and the fundamental principles in Arithmetic. Non-Catholic students are not excluded.

The student's first year at the school is spent in the Agricultural Department. This is called the probation year. If his work be satisfactory during this year of probation, the student is permitted to pursue the trade which he has previously elected. A nominal tuition is charged those who are able to pay, but, in the event of inability to pay, the student is given opportunity to work out his tuition while pursuing his course. In the main, however, the upkeep of the school falls upon the charity of Mrs. Morrell. In 1928 there were 142 boys in attendance.

Realizing that the cultural side of life must not be neglected, a two-year high school course in the usual studies is provided under the supervision of four teachers. Until a few years ago the institution was in charge of the Brothers of the Christian Schools. Upon their withdrawal a secular faculty of whites was appointed. In 1928 a colored faculty was appointed, the Principal alone being white. At present there are thirteen instructors at the school. In the Industrial Department, representing the more important phase of training, the instructors are skilled artisans, well qualified to impart to the students the technique necessary to insure proficiency in the various branches taught.

Automobile mechanics, body-building, carpentering, cement and concrete work, electrical work, masonry, brick-laying and plastering, steamfitting and plumbing, wheelwrighting and woodworking are the principal trades taught. A course in mechanical drawing is also given to enable the students to understand thoroughly the drawing and reading of blue prints. The cooking and baking at the school are done by the students under the capable supervision of a chef and a baker. In addition to these trades, the students are also given a practical education in academic subjects in order to enable them to transact ordinary business affairs, and to cultivate an appreciation of the nobler aspirations of life.

Besides the executive and administration buildings, there is on the property an imposing group of buildings, comprising a church, dormitory, library and reading rooms, classrooms, kitchen, and dining hall. St. Edward's Memorial Church, the beautiful new chapel recently erected, is a memorial to General Edward Morrell, deceased husband of Mrs. Morrell.[1]

2. St. Joseph's Industrial School, Clayton, Del.

A second Catholic Industrial School was established in 1895 at Clayton, Delaware. In May, 1895, twenty-five boys left St. Joseph's Home in Wilmington, Delaware, to form the nucleus of St. Joseph's Industrial School. Father J. A. de Ruyter, a Josephite, was the founder of this institution. It was the outcome of his desire to take care of the boys at St. Joseph's Home who had reached the age limit but were at the same time too young to enter the world.

Here the name of Mother Katharine Drexel must be mentioned, for it was through her unbounded charity that Father de Ruyter was able to buy the property at Clayton. On the land, which consisted of about two hundred acres, was a large mansion in which the boys were housed until better buildings

---

[1] The Benedictine Fathers have taken over the management of St. Emma's Institute.

were provided. The boys were given work, and, under proper supervision, the land was made ready for cultivation.

Many improvements were made the following year. A large three-story building was erected on the east side of the original building. This was used for workrooms, assembly rooms and dormitories. On the west of the main building another was erected to accomodate the Sisters and to provide dining rooms and kitchens. Then followed a workshop and a large barn. The boiler room came next, furnishing steam, power, and heat for the entire plant.

All vegetables used at the institution are raised on the farm, and a fine herd of Holsteins supplies milk and butter. Most of the work on the farm is carried on by the boys. Modern methods in agriculture are used, and thus the boys are given a first-hand training in the proper tilling of the soil. Farming does not, however, appeal to them as do the trades, and it is in the industrial department that most of the boys are interested.

The printing department at St. Joseph's is one of the best in the state. The composing and press rooms are well-equipped with modern machinery. St. Joseph's is the home of St. Anthony's Monthly, of which thousands of copies are sent to subscribers in every section of the country. The boys also do commercial printing for busines houses in Clayton. This department is supervised by an experienced foreman.

There are also furniture, shoe, and tailoring departments in charge of experienced supervisors. Some of the boys work in the boiler room and are taught how to run the stationary engine, while others assist in the kitchen, bakery and laundry.

The boys at St. Joseph's pursue the regular grammar school course in studies. The academic course includes one year of high school. All have access to a well-stocked library and are encouraged to cultivate a taste for wholesome and helpful reading.

3. The Cardinal Gibbons Institute, Ridge, Md.

This Institute stands as a memorial to the zeal and interest of the late Cardinal Gibbons for the colored race. It is the only attempt that has been made to carry out the Hampton-Tuskegee plan of education north of the Potomac River. With the exception of the activities of Mrs. Morrell, it is the only considerable enterprise ever undertaken for the benefit of the colored people by any Catholic lay group. It is also the only institution for young men and women of the colored race under Catholic auspices to be entrusted entirely to a colored faculty.

The Cardinal Gibbons Institute is but a short distance from St. Mary's City, near the juncture of the Potomac River with Chesapeake Bay. This land was purchased by the late Cardinal Gibbons for a school for the colored race, but death prevented the realization of his hopes. Archbishop Curley brought to fruition the plans of his predecessor.

The institution started with an empty treasury and a group of thirteen very raw students. Yet in the few years that it has existed (it was incorporated under the laws of Maryland in 1922), it has developed, step by step, a strong program of academic, industrial, and extension work.

The Institute is open to both boys and girls of the colored race. Industrial work for the girls includes plain sewing, cooking, and the handicrafts. The girls do all the cooking and laundry work for the boarding department.

Beyond the direct agricultural demonstration that can be given on the farm, the boys' industries remain practically undeveloped because of lack of finances. As yet there are no workshops of any kind and no equipment, the boys are doing all the work on the farm and are maintaining the heating and water system. When the money can be raised, the Cardinal Gibbons Institute will be one of the finest trade schools in the country.

Nor is the Institute without its academic program. This is based on the religious, economic, and social needs of the people, extending from the first year of junior high school to a full four-year high school course. Weekly lectures in religion are given by a Jesuit Father who is chaplain of the institution.

The Board of Trustees of the Cardinal Gibbons Institute, with Archbishop Curley as President, is composed of prominent churchmen and laymen. Recently, a Cardinal Gibbons Institute Development and Maintenance Committee was named for the purpose of collecting funds. This committee is composed of leading Catholic men and women who have pledged their labor and support that this noble project for the advancement of the Catholics of the Negro race may prosper.

4. INDUSTRIAL TRAINING IN INSTITUTIONS UNDER DIRECTION OF SISTERS

Besides the institutions already mentioned, there are others which advance the cause of industrial education in various ways. There are the Sisters of the Good Shepherd, for instance, to the work of whom we shall have occasion to refer under a separate heading. Besides three Houses of the Good Shepherd exclusively for colored girls, there are five Houses of the Good Shepherd which have a large number of colored girls, not to mention the other Houses which have a few. Practically all the homes which care for colored orphans also give them at least a modicum of industrial training: there are eight institutions in charge of sisters which make a specialty of industrial training. St. Peter Claver's Industrial School and the Industrial School of Our Lady and St. Francis, Baltimore, Md., and the Holy Rosary Institute, Lafayette, La., are professedly industrial schools for girls. St. Benedict's Home, Rye, N. Y., Lafon Boys' Asylum, New Orleans, La., Guardian Angel Home, Leavenworth, Kan., Holy Providence House, Cornwells Heights, Pa., and St. Benedict the Moor's, Milwaukee, Wis., while not professedly industrial schools, include industrial training in their curricula.

The schools for girls, besides training students in the domestic arts, cooking, sewing, etc., teach the academic branches, which usually embrace all the subjects ordinarily taught in the grade schools. While this may not be industrial training in the strictest sense of the term, it is, nevertheless, a beginning in that direction.

At Van de Vyver Institute, Richmond, Va., adults are given opportunity for industrial training. A fully developed night school offers instructions to the women in practical nursing, beauty culture, dress-making, millinery, tailoring, etc. To the men are offered instructions in embalming, barbering, automobile mechanics, shoe-making, photography, bricklaying, plastering, and kindred trades. A well-equipped printing department is also part of the school. There are 30 instructors teaching and helping several hundred young men and women who are availing themselves of these opportunities. As an economic asset to community betterment Van de Vyver Institute may well be studied as a marvel in modern missionary methods which seek to better the soul by first bettering living conditions.

Xavier University, New Orleans, La., follows the same plan of offering opportunity for industrial training. Forty girls and women are enrolled in the industrial class. The practical arts are also taught to boys by competent instructors. Separate buildings are provided for the trades.

PART V.—SOCIAL WELFARE WORK

INTRODUCTION

Besides the development of religious and educational opportunities, there are many other features which should be an integral part of any missionary program for the Negroes in the United States. There is, for instance, the necessity of watching over recreational environment and of providing for orphans, the wayward, the sick—in a word, the weaker members of society. An intelligent approach to the problem of Negro evangelization necessitates the employment of the most efficient means at our disposal, not the least of which is social welfare work. While this feature is as old as the Church's charitable work, organized Catholic Welfare Work is a development of recent years. The results which have been produced by this concerted effort of organized charity have been so satisfactory as to win for it a place in practically every diocesan program.

Whatever may be said in favor of organized Catholic Welfare Work generally is true many times over when there is question of the Colored Missions in particular. Unfortunately, so great have been the demands upon the slender resources of organized Catholic charity that those in charge of such forces have not always been free or willing to give special attention to the peculiar problems which so frequently and inevitably arise in the promotion of the welfare of Negroes. This neglect has necessitated the development of independent social welfare work for the Negroes. While anything like an organized effort has thus far been out of the question, much in the way of institutional care for children has been accomplished in the past, and at present one sees an encouraging effort at further development of social welfare work along more modern lines.

It must be said that social welfare work comes highly recommended. If there is a tendency outside the Catholic Church to transform principles of belief into maxims of service it has led at least to a most far-reaching and effective service to the poor. Protestant sects have long since recog-

190

nized the appeal of social welfare work to the poor Negroes
and have used it with telling results. Even our own Catholic
foreign missioners have adopted it as an entrance wedge
among foreign peoples; witness the development of the Catholic Medical Missionary Movement. The results which organized social welfare work has produced in the way of conversions is its highest recommendation. A more extensive employment of social service action is, therefore, desirable in
our Colored Missionary program for, although the spiritual
interests of the poor are always the supreme concern of the
Church, social factors in morality are far-reaching. As Dr.
Kerby so well says :"If wholesome environment, effective
moral and mental training, vigorous home ideals and good
example are fundamental in all life, who shall measure the
extent to which lack of these results in every kind of delinquency that we find among the poor." [1]

---

[1] *Social Mission of Charity*, p. 53.

CHAPTER XIV.

NEGLECTED AND DELINQUENT NEGRO CHILDREN

1. CAUSES

The neglected and delinquent child has always given concern to the Catholic Church. The Negro child of today presents the age-old problem intensified by recent problems of group adjustment. The economic and social conditions which prevail in most Negro families lead to a considerable amount of neglect and consequent delinquency of children. While delinquency among white juveniles of the city is decreasing, "the figures for Negro children have been taking a contrary direction—the number of Negro juvenile delinquents has been increasing very rapidly." [1] Here, then, is a problem which demands the immediate and serious attention of those interested in the welfare of the Negro.

In the report of The Joint Committee on Negro Child Study in New York City, [2] the following are outstanding facts:

1. "In 1925, of a total of 11,512 cases in the New York City Children's Court, 890, or 8 per cent, were cases of Negro children; of these 61 per cent were delinquents; Negro boys brought into court for delinquency outnumbered the girls three to one.

2. "On the basis of population the proportion of juvenile delinquency among Negroes is considerably greater than among the whites, but whereas the most common charge against white boys is stealing, that against Negro boys is disorderly conduct; the offense second in importance among Negro boys is desertion of home, whereas among white boys who are brought to the Children's Court it is burglary.

3. "In approximately 85 per cent of the Negro girl delinquency cases the charge is ungovernable and wayward, or desertion of home.

[1] Report of Joint Committee on Negro Child Study in the City of New York, 1927, p. 12.
[2] Ibid., p. 6.

4. "Of the 890 Negro children arraigned, 802 were Protestants, 86 were Catholics, and in 2 cases the faith was not ascertainable.
5. "Of the 543 Negro children arraigned in 1925 as delinquents, 107, or approximately 20 per cent, were committed to institutions; of the rest some were placed on probation. Of 34 cases of assault one resulted in commitment; of 78 cases of stealing 14 were committed.
6. "Contributing causes of delinquency among Negro children the committee found to be:
   1. Lack of opportunities for supervised recreation.
   2. Lack of parental control, commonly where mothers work outside the home.
   3. Retardation in school and resulting tendency to truancy.
7. "The largest number of neglected Negro children were under seven years of age; the largest number of delinquents, boys and girls, were between 13 and 16 years of age.
8. "Of 50 cases picked at random only one child was found to have had any contact with organized recreation; in two-thirds of this group there was practically no attendance at Church or Sunday School by either child or parents.
9. "Whereas there is considerable provision for mild delinquents among the white children, there is less for colored children than for white, and even this limited provision is decreasing."

It is to be remembered that over 70 per cent of the Negro population of the country is rural; furthermore, the recent mass movement of Negroes was as much a movement from the country to the cities as it was from the South to the North. The complexities of city life disrupted the rural Negro's simple mode of living: rural life meant familiarity with rural methods, simple machinery, and plain habits of living; migration of farmers to the cities of the South and North meant the learning of new tasks. Even skilled craftsmen who migrated to northern cities had to relearn their trades when they were thrown amid the highly specialized processes of northern industries. Professional men, too, were faced with the necessity of re-establishing themselves. Most frequently it was the child upon whom the brunt of re-adjustment fell. The temptations of the city, the crowded and all too often immoral and unsanitary living conditions, an entirely different standard of living, the absence of both parents from the home until late in the day, meant weakening of family and religious control, and consequent neglect and delinquency of the children.

One of the chief causes of Negro child neglect and delinquency is the absence of both parents from the home until late in the evening. Not to mention the inequality of wages paid Negroes with those paid white workers, the inadequacy of such wages is a most significant influence in the cause of neglect and delinquency. Because a father is unable to earn sufficient to support a family, the mother is forced to secure employment. The Joint Committee on Negro Child Study noted prevalence of this unfortunate condition. The Report of the Committee states: "An indication of the severity of economic life pressure for Negro families is the extraordinary number of women forced to abandon home duties for outside work."[1] In the city of New York which the Report covers, the proportion of married colored women who work during the day is four times as great as that of native white women and five times as great as that of foreign-born women.[2] In the South, the percentage of Negro women who work for a living is about the same, being 41.3 for Negro females and 11.8 for white females.[3] "Negro Women in Industry"[4] notes that practically one-third of the Negro women whom it surveyed in industries were working ten hours or more a day; legislation to the contrary notwithstanding, in some industries they were working fourteen to sixteen hours a day.[5] In a survey of the tobacco industry in Virginia, in which industry about 60 per cent of the Negro working women are employed, the Bureau found that of a group of Negro women surveyed more than half of them were or had been married. Nearly half of these women had children who were entirely dependent upon their earnings. The number of de-

---

[1] p. 12.
[2] Ibid.
[3] Dowd, J., The Negro in American Life, p. 98.
[4] U. S. Department of Labor, Bulletin of the Women's Bureau, no. 20, p. 17.
[5] Ibid., p. 20.

pendent children ranged from one to four. Yet, nearly all these women with dependent children were in the wage group varying from $7 to $14 a week.[1] In 1928 a survey made in Richmond, Va., showed that of the 6,984 married working women in the city, 5,276 were Negroes.[2]

Neglect of home and family is even more pronounced in the case of Negro domestic servants who labor on an average of twelve hours a day for a nominal wage. In a study based on the *Records of The Domestic Efficiency Association of Baltimore, Maryland,* the Women's Bureau of the U. S. Department of Labor[3] found that of the Negro women reporting on conjugal condition in the records 54.2 per cent were married, while 10.7 per cent were widowed, separated, or divorced, making approximately two-thirds who were likely to have family and home responsibilities in addition to their domestic service. The largest proportion, as might be expected, was among those working by the day: 83.9 per cent of those reporting on conjugal conditions were married, widowed, separated, or divorced.[4] Probably family responsibilities were forcing most of these women to apply for work by the day rather than by the week.

Any condition that reacts on the family, that institution upon which the present and future welfare of the State and the Church rests, should be of vital interest to the State and the Church. The necessity of mothers of families working in order to help support the family leaves the children to the care of slightly older children or to the mercy of the neighborhood. This is fatal to the welfare of Negro children, as it would be to the children of any race, because it is chiefly upon the mothers of families that the molding of future citizens of the State and members of the Church depends. Bearing in mind the conditions noted, it is no cause for wonder that "the number of juvenile delinquents has been increasing very rapidly."

---

[1] *Ibid.,* p. 62.
[2] June P. Guild, "The Negro in Richmond, Va., *The Catholic Charities Review,* Jan., 1930, p. 7.
[3] Bulletin, no. 39, p. 29.
[4] *Ibid.,* p. 30.

2. CATHOLIC CHILD-CARING HOMES FOR NEGRO CHILDREN

This has often been called the century of the child because of the many agencies now under social control for promoting child welfare. The Catholic Church has by many years anticipated modern social welfare service in the care of neglected children; the orphan asylum was one of the earliest charitable foundations of the Church. With its sense of the value of one immortal soul it could not have been otherwise. Father Albert Muntsch, S.J.,[1] says: "Though the training given to children deprived of one or both parents in our orphan asylums may not meet all legitimate expectations, it has equipped many children for a useful career in after life, who without that training might have become a menace to society. The Catholic Church has deserved well of society for the many orphan homes in all sections of our country, generally conducted by women consecrated to this service for life."

Unlike certain other racial groups, the Negro has not yet reached that stage of economic well-being in which he can meet the social problems of his own race; consequently, he must depend upon society at large to solve his problems. Not the least of these problems is the care of orphaned, abandoned, and neglected Negro children for whom the orphan asylum is the only practical solution. In reference to colored children, however, the term "home" is more descriptive than "orphan asylum," since the children cared for are more generally neglected or abandoned. While both parents of a child may be dead, more frequently one or both are living. Illegitimacy, disrupted marriages, broken homes, and economic hardships are the usual reasons for abandonment of children.

Generally speaking, the ideal would be to find for each abandoned child a normal home with a Catholic family. The colored people are very charitable in this regard and most willing to care for orphaned or abandoned children, even at the cost of great personal sacrifice. An instance to the point is that of Henry Bush, of Port Tobacco, Md., a former slave,

---

[1] Muntsch-Spalding, *Introductory Sociology*, p. 242.

now ninety-one years of age, who during his life time has adopted and raised twenty orphan children, providing for them until they reached manhood and womanhood. As he said: "Thank God they all turned out well." Most frequently, however, economic conditions and questionable environment (conditions over which the Negroes have little control) impose the institution as the lesser evil.

To the sisters engaged in this work of caring for orphaned and abandoned colored children we can pay no more fitting tribute than did Archbishop Curley on the occasion of the blessing of the Day Nursery of the Mission Helpers at Baltimore, Md., when he said: "Whatever is done for the child is done for the family, whatever is done for the family is done for the nation at large." He then pointed out that the work is motivated by love: "With this doctrine of love the Church has taught the doctrine of the Master—love for all men. This doctrine of love is the fundamental doctrine of Jesus Christ. The Sisters of the Mission Helpers, Servants of the Sacred Heart, are simply continuing the mission of the Church of God; they have entered the field for our little colored children because in every child they see a figure of the Triune God and a soul redeemed by the Precious Blood of Christ. They love this work. That is the reason for this work."

Catholic child-caring work is listed on the following page.

St. Elizabeth's Home, Baltimore, Md., is a nursery and home conducted by the Franciscan Sisters of Baltimore City, the only white sisterhood in the United States which is exclusively devoted to the care of Negroes. The Sisters care for colored girls (and boys under seven years of age). Small appropriations are received from the City of Baltimore and from the State of Maryland, but more than half of the support comes from charity.

The Industrial School of Our Lady and St. Francis, Baltimore, Md., is a home for girls in charge of the Franciscan Sisters of Baltimore. It is an industrial school in which the girls are taught the domestic arts. Upon completion of the training period the girls are placed in private homes.

St. Peter Claver's Industrial School for Colored Girls, Baltimore, Md., is in charge of the Mission Helpers, Servants

TABLE 20.—CATHOLIC CHILD-CARING HOMES FOR NEGRO CHILDREN

Name & Location	In Charge of	Sisters	Lay	Boys	Girls	
St. Elizabeth's, Baltimore, Md.	Franciscans (Balto. City)	16	0	42	162	
Our Lady and St. Francis, Balto., Md.	Franciscans (Balto. City)	17	1	0	35	industrial
St. Peter Claver's, Baltimore, Md.	Mission Helpers	4	0	0	38	industrial
St. Joseph's Clayton, Delaware	Josephites and Franciscans (Glen Riddle)	4	2	75	0	agricul'al industrial
St. Monica's, Kansas City, Mo.	Lay	0	2	0	10	
Guardian Angel's, Leavenworth, Kan.....	Oblates	11	0	68	0	agricul'al industrial
Holy Epiphany, Leavenworth, Kan.....	Oblates	4	0	0	50	
Zimmer Memorial, Mobile, Ala.	Holy Ghost	4	0	16	13	
Lafon Asylum, New Orleans, La.	Holy Family	5	0	49	0	
St. Francis', Normandy, Mo.	Oblates	13	0	0	123	
St. Benedict's, Rye, N. Y.	III Order St. Francis (Glen Riddle)...	15	2	70	83	industrial nursery
St. Francis', Savannah, Ga.	Missionary Srs. of the Immac. Heart ...	3	0	0	35	
Mission Helpers' Day Nursery, Balto., Md....	Mission Helpers					day nurs.
St. Benedict's Nursery, New York, N. Y........	Handmaids of Most Pure Heart of Mary					day nurs.
St. Benedict the Moor Milwaukee, Wis.	Dominicans					nursery

of the Sacred Heart. Here also the girls are taught proficiency in the industrial arts. Since this survey the buildings of the school have been enlarged to accommodate fifty girls.

St. Joseph's Industrial School, Clayton, Del., is a home for boys, owned and conducted by the Josephite Fathers. The Franciscan Sisters of Glen Riddle are in charge of the domestic department. The boys are taught industrial trades and help to care for the farm which is worked in connection with the home. The home is partly self-supporting, but depends mostly on charity.

St. Monica's Home for Girls, Kansas City, Mo., is conducted by St. Monica's parish. Two lay matrons are in charge. At the time of this survey there were 10 girls in the home, although the capacity is 30.

The Guardian Angel Home for Boys, Leavenworth, Kan., owes its existence to the interest of Rt. Rev. Monsignor Joseph Shorter, LL.D. Formerly the Oblate Sisters of Providence (Baltimore, Md.) had a residence adjoining Holy Epiphany Church, Leavenworth, where they cared for a few orphans. Monsignor Shorter interested himself in the work, and the number of orphans increasing, he purchased for them a home outside the city. The property now consists of 80 acres of land, with buildings to accommodate 75 boys. The ordinary branches of grammar school are taught. The boys range in age from four to sixteen years. Besides helping on the farm, they are taught cooking, repairing, and laundering.

Holy Epiphany Girls' Home, Leavenworth, Kan., is another institution which owes its existence to Monsignor Shorter, pastor of Holy Epiphany Church for colored. Adjacent to the church a large brick building was erected to serve as a home for destitute colored girls. The home has a capacity of fifty and is in charge of the Oblate Sisters of Providence.

Zimmer Memorial Institute, Mobile, Ala., is a diocesan orphanage. At the time of this survey it was in charge of the Sisters of the Holy Family, but has since been taken over by the Sisters of the Holy Ghost (San Antonio, Texas). It receives children of both sexes.

Lafon Orphan Boys' Asylum owes its origin to a wealthy colored gentleman, Anthony Lafon, who left a legacy for the purpose. It is located on a farm outside the city of New Orleans, and is supported by the diocese and by charity. The boys attend regular grammar school classes, take care of the home, and help with the farming.

St. Benedict's Home for Colored Orphan Children, located at Rye, N. Y., is under the direction of Monsignor Mallick Fitzpatrick, Director of the Mission of The Immaculate Virgin for the Protection of Homeless and Destitute Children in the City of New York. It is a nursery, home, and industrial school for colored orphans of both sexes. It is a diocesan institution supported by charity, and is conducted by the Sisters of the Third Order of St. Francis (Glen Riddle).

St. Francis' Home, Savannah, Ga., owned by the Diocese of Savannah, is conducted and supported by the Missionary Franciscan Sisters of the Immaculate Conception. It receives girls only. There are fourteen Sisters in the convent, eleven of whom teach in St. Benedict's parochial school, Savannah. Three Sisters are in charge of the orphanage. The orphans attend St. Benedict's parochial school.

St. Francis' Home, Normandy, Mo., is in charge of the Oblate Sisters of Providence. There are 123 inmates in the asylum, 97 of whom are orphans. Girls only are admitted between the ages of two and twelve years.

3. DAY NURSERIES

The Mission Helpers' Day Nursery, Baltimore, Md., was opened in November, 1928. Colored children not of school age whose parents are employed during the day may be left at the nursery in the morning and called for in the evening. They are given medical attention, three meals, special care when required, kindergarten training, and recreation. Children of school age are also received; they go from the nursery to school, and at noon are given a hot lunch at the nursery, after which they again go to their respective schools. School being over, the children return to the nursery where they engage in supervised recreation until such time as they are called for by the parents. Careful supervision is exercised over all the children, and each child receives a physical examination and medical care when necessary. In the course of time it is hoped to extend the facilities of the nursery so as to include other branches of social service.

St. Benedict's Day Nursery, New York City, conducted by the Handmaids of the Most Pure Heart of Mary, was opened in the latter part of 1923 to care for the children of Harlem, whose mothers are obliged to work. In connection with the nursery the Sisters conduct a kindergarten.

A nursery for boarding and day children three years of age and over is also maintained by the Institute of St. Benedict the Moor, Milwaukee, Wis. It is conducted by the Dominican Sisters.

4. HOUSES OF THE GOOD SHEPHERD

Colored girls should receive the same moral protection that white girls receive. The prejudice against colored girls who are ambitious to earn an honest living is unjust; such an attitude frequently drives them into immoral surroundings. They need special care and protection on the maxim that it is the duty of the strong to protect the weak. Any effort therefore to improve conditions should provide more wholesome surroundings for colored girls.

The House of the Good Shepherd is the practical solution of the Catholic Church for the problem of delinquent girls. In such Houses the charges are girls placed in the care of the Sisters by the courts, Catholic Charities, social agencies, or State Departments of Health; some of the children are "preservates," that is, girls taken from evil environment with a view to preserving them from immoral associations. There are three Houses of the Good Shepherd exclusively for colored girls. Four other Houses, though not exclusively for colored, have a considerable number of colored girls.

As to school grades in Houses of the Good Shepherd, it is difficult to give exact information, since the children are committed at varying ages and for varying periods of time. At the time of commitment the scholastic standing of the girls varies from primer to high school grades. As a rule short terms of commitment prevent much academic advancement. In several of the houses vocal and instrumental music, elocution, dramatics and physical culture are added to the curriculum.

Besides regular classroom work, the girls are trained in the domestic arts: cooking, sewing, laundry work, etc. Attention is called to the very meagre allowance which municipal authorities make for the support of the inmates of the Houses. This usually necessitates reliance upon laundry work as a means of support.

At Louisville, Ky., the "preservate" children are permitted to attend the Catholic Colored High School. At Hot Springs, Ark., the colored children are day scholars, not inmates. Connected with the House of the Good Shepherd in

Table 21.   HOUSES OF GOOD SHEPHERD

	Sisters	Exclusively colored	Average yearly number cared for	Preservates	Delinquents	Age limit	Court commitments last year	Court allowance for support	No. years grammar school	Remarks
Baltimore, Md.	23	yes	200	0	72	7–21	70	$16.50 month	6	
Chicago, Ill.	18	yes	173	100	0	6–16	12	$15.00 month	8	industrial training only
Louisville, Ky.	17	yes	105	0	0	.....	...	......	..	
Carthage, Ohio	..	no	170	90	80	no limit	50	......	8	commercial
Germantown, Phil., Pa.	..	no	81	0	81	12–18	20	$15.00 month for girls under 16	8	
Hot Springs, Ark. (¹)	..	no	35	...	...	.....	...	......	...	children from town attend school only.
New Orleans, La.	..	no	260	0	31	10–	120	$8.00 month	3–8	5 grades usually because of short commitments.
New York, N. Y.	..	no	125	0	125	12–16	52	$24.00 month	8	commercial
			1149	190	389					

(¹) Conducted by Religious of Our Lady of Charity of Refuge.

New York are social welfare workers who follow up the girls after they leave the House.

In their own quiet, unostentatious way the Religious of Our Lady of Charity of the Good Shepherd are a tremendous factor in the welfare of the colored race. With a love heretofore alien to the lives of the girls committed to their care, they teach them by word and example to live upright, honest, and pure lives. Not all the girls are Catholics, or even Christians, when they come to the Sisters. No force is used except that of good example; yet, it causes no surprise that most of the non-Catholic girls become converts before they leave the House. Besides the art of right living the girls are taught the science of useful living. Habits of industry are engendered so that when the girls are ready to leave they are well fitted to walk in the path of virtue as useful members of society and an honor to their race.

CHAPTER XV.

SOCIAL SERVICE CENTERS

1. NECESSITY

The problem of the Negro is largely a material one; perhaps in our zeal for his soul we have lost sight of the demands of his body. A letter from a Catholic colored woman gives a glimpse of how some Negroes regard our zeal for their souls. Among other disagreeable things she wrote: "Sometimes I get so tired of hearing about saints, and prayer, and spiritual food. Those things help little when we are face to face with the struggle for even a miserable living. Does knowledge of the pricelessness of chastity fill the hungry girl's stomach? No. You must help us to live first, then teach us how to live." Speaking to a prospective convert one day, a priest was asked by him: "What will I get if I join the Catholic Church?" Asked what he expected, the would-be Catholic replied: "Well, the church I belong to now got me my job, gave clothes to my children, and takes care of my mother."

Indicative of the necessity for social service work are the conditions revealed by a recent survey made in Richmond, Va. About sixty per cent of over 1,000 Negro families interviewed during the survey (1928) had from all sources, including income from husband, wife, children, and lodgers, less than $20 a week upon which to live. Over 40 per cent of the wage earners lost over one month from work during 1928. Approximately 10 per cent were out of employment at the time visited, although Richmond was enjoying fair prosperity at the time. [1] In New York a recent survey disclosed the fact that although the average family income per Negro family was only $85 a month, the average rent per month was $40. Housing conditions were much the same as in Richmond, where of approximately 1,000 families, 277 were living in three rooms, 55 in two rooms, 12 in one room. Typical families living in such small quarters are: man, wife, four children

---

[1] Quoted in "The Negro in Richmond, Virginia," *The Catholic Charities Review*, Jan., 1930, by June P. Guild.

and two lodgers in one room; woman, grown son, small daughter, two lodgers living in two rooms; man, wife, and eight children living in three rooms. [1]

Admirably well has Dr. Edward Murphy stated the case for social service. [2] Speaking of the poverty of the Negro, he says: "The decencies of existence in which the flowers of the Faith so readily take root are often wholly lacking. . . . What with the pre-occupation of their experiences with race exploitation, discrimination, disease and sin, our colored brethren have often been as burdened in seeking the Church as the Church has been in reaching them. Bodily slavery is dead, but other forms are as alive as ever. Much social debris must be cleared away before the way will be widely open to Catholic approach; an evidence that the minds and hearts of aspirants to the apostolate should be enriched with a good sociological instruction and stimulation in the seminary course of training. Quite understandable is the Negro's demand for 'a religion which fills not only his soul but also his stomach, clothes and shelters his body and employs his hands.' " Well has it been remarked that the best thing which could at present happen to the Catholic missionary movement among the Negroes would be a liberal injection of the spirit that inspired the monks of the early Middle Ages to pray, to preach, and, above all, to drain swamp lands.

2. WELFARE WORK FOR SICK AND AGED NEGROES

Under the direction of Rev. Thomas Lenahan, pastor of St. John's (white) Church and St. Mary Magdalen's (colored) Church, Tuscaloosa, Ala., the Catholic Association for Non-sectarian Welfare and Charity Work opened a hospital for colored in connection with the Church of St. Mary Magdalen. The hospice is under the supervision of Sister M. Matthew, M.S.B.T. It provides for a limited number of aged colored people who have no home or relatives to care for them. A practical nurse is in charge. The hospice is also a center to

---

[1] *Ibid.*
[2] *Ecclesiastical Review*, Nov. 1928, p. 504.

which the needy come for aid in sickness, and relief in poverty. Benefactors keep the hospice supplied with simple remedies for the sick and clothing for the destitute. In connection with the hospice a class in practical nursing is conducted.

The school children of the parish have organized a club as an aid to the hospice. "The Missionary Club," composed of the younger members of the school, meets weekly and reports cases of sickness and poverty. After council is held, the cases reported are investigated by members of the club under the guidance of the Sister who is in charge of the welfare work. The club treasury is frequently called upon to aid needy cases.

At New Orleans, La., the Sisters of the Holy Family conduct the Lafon Home of the Holy Family for aged men and women. Here 30 men and 75 women are cared for. The home is diocesan property supported by charity.

In the care of the aged, credit must be given to the Little Sisters of the Poor who, while they have no home exclusively for aged Negroes, care for them whenever they present themselves. The Little Sisters of the Poor recognize no distinction of color.

At Chicago, Ill., the Techny Sisters of the Holy Ghost have purchased a large piece of property in the "Black Belt," and are now engaged in a campaign to raise funds to build a modern and well-equipped hospital to care especially for the Negroes of Chicago. It is confidently expected that the hospital will be a reality within a few years.

At present hospital service for Negroes is negligible. Statistics furnished by The American Medical Association show that there are available for Negroes only 210 hospitals of all kinds, with a total bed space of 6,870, or an average of one bed for each 1,941 persons. As compared with bed space for whites, the average of which is one bed for each 139 of the population, this is extremely low if consideration be given to the susceptibility of the Negro to diseases, particularly diseases of the more infectious variety. Discounting the admirable though feeble effort being made at St. Mary's Hospice, Tuscaloosa, Ala., there is no Catholic hospital exclusively for the use of Negroes. In the past, at least three futile efforts were made to establish an exclusively colored hospital under

Catholic auspices: one at Memphis, Tenn., another at Pine Bluff, Ark., and the latest at Greenville, Miss. While no information is available as to how many of the 612 Catholic hospitals provide bed space for Negroes, it is definitely known that many of them refuse their ministrations to Negroes. While many Catholic hospitals receive Negroes in their wards, unofficial inquiries from a number of missioners brought to light knowledge of only one Catholic hospital with a total of two private rooms for Negroes. Even these two rooms are maintained on an endowment founded by a Negro. Sad to relate, it has even occurred that colored sisters were forced to accept hospitalization in wards, the sentiment against a colored person occupying a private room being such as to forbid privacy even to the consecrated spouses of Christ. More could be said; further comment is deemed unnecessary. It is certain that the Catholic hospital for Negroes which is now in a fair way to become an actuality in Chicago will fill a long-felt need.

3. SOCIAL CENTERS

Besides the institutional social welfare work for Negroes already noticed, there are several social service centers scattered throughout the country. The Mission Helpers, Servants of the Sacred Heart, render such service to the Negroes of Maryland. While not laboring exclusively for the welfare of the Negro, the work of the Mission Helpers in Baltimore and vicinity is largely for the benefit of the colored race. Theirs is a work of instruction and reclamation; in a large measure preventive, yet to a great extent reconstructive. They gather the children of the Jesuit Missions in Maryland for instruction, prepare them for the reception of the Sacraments; by means of house-to-house visits they seek careless, negligent, and fallen-away Catholics, encouraging them to return to their duties and to attend to the religious education of their children. The Mission Helpers go through the wards of public hospitals, almshouses, penal institutions, and reformatories, seeking those in need of spiritual assistance and instruction. Needless to say, they do not give spiritual ministrations at the expense of the physical. Theirs is truly the

Christian concept of the social mission of charity—a spiritual apostolate by means of the corporal works of mercy.

At the Cardinal Gibbons Institute, Ridge, Md., a program of social service has been organized which is bound to produce results of a most far-reaching nature. It is the only work for the general social and cultural welfare of the American Negroes which has been undertaken under Catholic auspices. Besides the academic and industrial work which we have previously noticed, the Institute conducts extension social work, work which for sheer possibilities is staggering in comparison with our other feeble efforts at social welfare work.

The extension work includes, yearly, two semi-annual Farmers' Conferences, a Health Campaign of two months' duration, a Children's Day, two Dental Clinics, a Farmers' Institute under state supervision, and a County Fair. In addition, there are weekly illustrated lectures and special classes in home-nursing and handicrafts for the farm women. The combined minimum attendance for one year is 2,500. The 1927 Health Campaign covered ninety miles of territory and counted a thousand families as active participants in cleaning, screening, repairing, and planting for health improvement.

In Philadelphia, Pa., St. Agnes' Guild for Catholic Working Girls has recently opened a home for colored working girls. The venture was made possible through the generosity of an anonymous friend. The purpose is to offer colored Catholic working girls a place where they may live under the care and protection of the Church. At Boston, Mass., the Sisters of the Blessed Sacrament conduct a social service center. Three Sisters visit the sick, instruct the ignorant, and provide food and clothing for the poor, besides conducting a sodality and sewing circle for colored women. At Los Angeles, Calif., three Sisters of Our Lady of the Apostles perform the same services in connection with St. Odilia's Colored Church. At Atlantic City, N. J., there is also a social service center, which for the time being serves as a nucleus for a parish in the formation. At St. Louis, Mo., the Helpers of the Holy Souls conduct a social center for colored women and also visit the sick poor, both Catholic and non-Catholic, in their homes and hospitals. The

Helpers of the Holy Souls perform the same services in San Francisco, California.

Undoubtedly there are other social service centers scattered throughout the missionary field, in their own quiet way doing very efficient work. These few instances are deserving of notice as being outstanding examples of the application of modern missionary methods to the problem of the Negro.

4. CATHOLIC SOCIETIES FOR NEGROES

The "Federated Colored Catholics of the United States" was organized to bring the colored Catholics of the United States into closer co-operation with one another and with the white workers in the field. It aims to federate all Catholic organizations and individuals of the race into one comprehensive organization and to focus their attention upon the single purpose of improving the temporal and spiritual conditions of the Catholic Negroes. This organization is not intended to supplant any existing organization, or to compete in any way with other Church organizations. Its sole purpose is to weld all into a solid unit for race betterment.

The Knights of St. Peter Claver is a fraternal organization of Catholic Negroes. It is composed of fifty-five councils with a total membership of approximately 2,500. The object of the Society is the same as other fraternal organizations, but it also renders aid to the mission to which it is attached, local councils giving financial assistance in so far as they are able and their means permit. The Knights of St. Peter Claver has also a Ladies' Auxiliary.

The Knights of St. John is not exclusively for the colored. It is a military benefit society, the aim of which is to care for the sick and the needy, and to hold before its members the spirit and practices of the "Knights of St. John Hospitalers." The society issues insurance and maintains a Widow and Orphan Department organized on the mutual insurance plan. There are 22 commanderies for colored with a membership of approximately 1,400.

PART VI.—OBSTACLES TO GREATER RESULTS

We have sketched the history of the Colored Missions in the United States and have recounted the "tremendous trifles" which have been accomplished. Truly tremendous are the results if thought be given to the pathetically small number of zealous pioneers who gave their all to the cause. Their story is one of persistent strivings, of a long drawn-out effort on their part, and of a struggle on the part of the members of the race itself. Individually, theirs was a success given to few missioners. The results were none the less trifling if we bear in mind that of the millions of Afro-Americans, constituting one-third of the Negroes to be found outside of Africa itself, at the beginning of this century more than half had no church affiliation whatsoever; of the other half, not two hundred thousand belonged to the Catholic Church.

Today, those pioneer missioners of another year might well lift up their silvered heads and glimpse the dawn of a new tomorrow breaking upon the skyline of the South. The past three decades have witnessed a steady advance painstakingly won from a begrudging world; won step by step, it is true, but none the less a most remarkable advance. From Texas to Massachusetts, from New York to California, the Cross of Christ now yearningly stretches toward the heights of heaven in earnest pleading for dusky congregations which find a home within the Catholic Church. In smug retrospection we might rest were not this glorious scene darkened by an ominous shadow which still enfolds 11,000,000 souls in a gloomy fastness of spiritual desolation. Eleven million souls! What means this endless flood of souls arriving who knows whence, departing who knows whither? Will the Catholic Church, that Citadel of Truth and Tower of Strength, stand idly by and proffer no assistance? Two hundred thousand American Negro Catholics is hardly a fitting tribute to lay at the feet of a King Who claims by right the soul of every man,

210

no matter what the chance of birth or hue of skin bequeathed as his portion.

Divinely commissioned as it is to teach the Gospel to all men, why has the Catholic Church not had a greater reaping?

CHAPTER XVI

EXTERNAL DIFFICULTIES

1.—PREJUDICE AGAINST THE CHURCH

Speaking in a general way, a universal obstacle to better results is the social stigma usually attached to profession of the Catholic Faith in most parts of the South. The last presidential election brought to the surface some tangible evidence of the opposition which the Church in the South must meet and beat to the ground. In the thoroughly Protestant sections—notably Virginia, North and South Carolina, Georgia, Florida, Tennessee, Arkansas, and the northern parts of Alabama, Mississippi, and Louisiana—Catholic influence in general is very weak; there is no outstanding accomplishment of the Church which would give to it the prestige so necessary to gain the esteem of the southern people. The Protestant Churches, on the other hand, have all the advantages of social preferment, and are in a position to offer not a few other inducements of no little value.

As far as the southern Negro is concerned (and he forms a majority of the race), if he be more inclined to one religion than to another, that one is certainly not the Catholic religion. His environment has always militated against the Catholic Church. If the light-skinned portion of the South, with all its opportunities for better knowledge, has so much ill-feeling towards Catholicity, what can we look for from the colored man whose every effort is in imitation of the white? Turn back the pages of American history as far as we will, the story ceaselessly dinned into the ears of the Negro pictures the Catholic Church as anything but the Bride of Christ or the Kingdom of God.

Were it possible to reach Negroes unaffected by denominational influence, we might be able to judge how the truths of the Catholic Faith would appeal to them, but where in the

South are we to find minds or hearts unswayed by the anti-Catholic influence of their surroundings? While it is true that the majority of the Negro race is unaffiliated with any of the sects, the millions which constitute that majority are not segregated from their Baptist or Methodist neighbors; consequently, their opinions of the Catholic Church are but reflections of Baptist or Methodist thought. There is no more difficult task for the priests laboring on the Colored Missions than the uprooting of prejudice. Years of struggling effort are required to remove the barnacles of misrepresentation and misconception. Since bigotry and prejudice are without doubt the greatest barriers to a greater success in the work of the Colored Missions, the conversion of the Negro must be regarded in the same light as the conversion of whites living in the same sections: where there is a strong Catholic influence and the Church is prosperous, the Negro will naturally be attracted to it; where missionary conditions still prevail, it is more difficult to persuade the Negro to join the Catholic Church.

2.—DISCRIMINATION

The method of the Church is not fiery, nor does it believe in dashing its foot against a stone. It accepts conditions, but always strives to mold them with higher principles. At the same time, the Catholic Church has a right to expect its members to adhere steadfastly to the principles laid down by Christ. The law of Christian Charity explicitly declares that, according to a prudent order, everyone must be treated at least neighborly. "By this shall all men know that you are My disciples, if you have love, one for another." [1] In the new Dispensation, according to St. Paul, "there is neither Jew nor Greek, there is neither bond nor free, there is neither male nor female; for you are all one in Christ Jesus." [2] St. Paul, by these words, means to indicate the levelling of all distinctions of class, color, and creed which would divide the followers of Christ into hostile camps, destroying that amity of charity which Our Lord obtained by the shedding of His Blood. The

[1] *St. John*, XIII, 35.
[2] *Galatians*, III, 28.

Catholic Church teaches this Pauline equality. Certainly, then, it is not the fault of the Catholic Church or of its doctrines that the Negro is discriminated against.

If the Catholic Church be free from blame, the same may not be said of all its members. It is idle to deny that many Catholics discriminate against Negroes. And here we do not mean merely that discrimination in social circles which is based upon our social system of caste. The necessity of exclusively colored churches throughout the South is mute evidence of a more pervading presence of race prejudice. Indeed, at least one Catholic divine has felt the necessity of publishing a book in an effort to "examine the discriminations against the Negroes in terms of strict obligation; to determine not only the heroic works which a Christian should perform in order to be perfect, but the actions which must be fulfilled if the Christian would attain eternal life." [1]

Most white people in the South, and elsewhere, too, are seemingly unaware of the inconsistency of Christian profession with their treatment of the Negro. If they do think of such incongruity (and not a few do), they justify it on the grounds of racial differences. Dr. Gilligan, in his commendable treatise [2] observes that: "If this fundamental doctrine of Christianity (the essential equality of all men) is applied to the American Race Problem, the white Christian must admit that the natural rights of the Negro are identical in number and sacredness with the natural rights of the white man. No matter how strong the prejudice, no matter how consistently throughout history he may have been regarded as the hewer of wood and the drawer of water, his natural rights must be respected as those of the white man. For natural rights are rooted not upon membership in one nation or upon membership in the white race but upon the sacredness which the individual enjoys because of his end."

One of the most sacred natural rights which any man enjoys is that of worshipping God. The Catholic Church has legislated that this right is to be exercised on certain days and in a definite manner. When racial prejudice becomes an

---

[1] Gilligan, S.T.D., Rev. F. J., *The Morality of the Color Line*, p. x.
[2] *Ibid.*, p. 41.

obstacle to the exercise of this right or to its exercise in the manner prescribed under pain of mortal sin, then this prejudice is doubly wrong. The plea of social necessity may palliate the custom of separating the white from the colored portion of the congregation in a mixed church, but certainly it cannot condone reservation for the colored of what is usually a totally *inadequate* number of pews in the rear of the church. If today a major portion of the work of many missioners is reclamation of fallen-away colored Catholics, it is due to this relegation of the colored to the inadequate "Jim Crow" section of the church.

Conditions in the North are more hopeful. Heretofore undisturbed by the presence of any large number of Negroes, the North has for the most part been serenely unconscious of the perplexing problem of the Colored Missions in the South. With the recent Negro hegira the people of the North have had this problem brought forcibly home to them. While it is encouraging to note the alacrity with which some northern bishops have grappled with the problem, so far only the surface has been touched. The people must be educated by their priests to realize that right here is a mission problem which they can do much towards solving.

At heart most Catholics are missioners and respond readily when their pastors call attention to a need. This is admirably demonstrated in the conduct of the members of St. Mary's Church, Albany, N. Y., who have concerned themselves practically with the care of the Negroes of the city. Surely in every section of the country there are well organized parishes which can turn some of their extra energy into a local Negro apostolate. Or if there be no need for local missionary work, surely such wealthy parishes should feel no hesitation in following the example of many Protestant congregations of means: supporting a poor mission in the South, or founding a scholarship for the education of a missioner. The people would quickly respond to such a suggestion. Parochialism is a sin of pastors, not of people.

3.—LACK OF PRIESTS

Despite race prejudice and a general apathy towards the work of the Colored Missions, undoubtedly it would show more gain if there was anything like an adequate supply of priests. In his report to the American Board of Catholic Missions, Archbishop John Shaw, New Orleans, La., lists lack of missioners as first among the causes of loss of Faith among the Negro slaves and their descendants. By way of remedy Doctor Edward Murphy, S.S.J., suggests: "The day may come when our hierarchy will find it feasible and desirable to supply the dioceses of the country from central seminaries. The inter-diocesan idea is not counter to the provisions of the Council of Trent, and Italy has already given an illustration of its worth and practicability. In our country it would have the effect of remedying the condition of relative over-supply in some states and tragic lack in others. Also, the policy of young men studying for particular, favorite dioceses, and, consequently, throughout their years of training, banefully limiting their vision of the needs of the Church to mere spots in the Vineyard, would be in the past tense. A more catholic spirit would obtain. Then, incidentally, the enterprise of Negro evangelization as well as many another essential project could be much more effectively advanced; for the bulk of our colored population is in the South, and the number of southern priests has, up to date, been far from adequate. With a better distribution of diocesan clergy, delocalized and missionary-minded, the colored would at least have a real spiritual chance."[1]

As a matter of fact, have we thus far had any real missionary work on a large scale among the colored people of this country? It is too true that the men in the work have had to bear all the hardships of missionary life, but has not the bulk of the work so far been of a parochial nature? Most of the colored parishes and missions are offshoots of mixed parishes, the missioner simply relieving such parishes of their colored element, forming of it distinct parishes which function much as do white parishes. Convert classes are formed and, while in places the number enrolled is larger than in

---

[1] *Ecclesiastical Review*, Nov. 1928, p. 502.

white parishes, the manner of working is the same in both. It is true that this has been the only feasible plan heretofore, but the fact remains that it has not resulted in a satisfactory increase in the number of Negro Catholics. Considering the relatively large number of priests now working exclusively for the colored people, as compared with the few of forty years ago; bearing in mind the many mixed parishes still existing, and the natural increase in the population of the Negroes, we have a right to look for better results.

Apart from the gallant effort of a few missionary organizations, why has there been no real missionary effort made in behalf of the Afro-American? One reason is the sharp line of distinction between the diocesan clergy and the missionary societies. It is the mind of the Church that there be such a distinction: parish work, be it white or colored, rightly belongs to the diocesan clergy. Because of circumstances in the South, however, missionary organizations have had to do the parish work for the colored. Yet, this is not the chief purpose of their existence. If the missioners were relieved of the burden of too much parish work, their energies would be available for the extremely necessary work of itinerant mission giving, a necessity which in present circumstances must be largely foregone. Then, too, the missionaries would be free to work out into new mission fields, founding missions which, when organized as parishes, would be handed over to secular parish priests. This plan is being partially worked out in the Diocese of Raleigh by Rev. Charles Hannigan, S.S.J., with the aid of the Passionist Fathers.

But it would seem that the diocesan clergy are more or less exclusively mindful of their white charges, and the concerns of the colored people are left almost entirely to missionary priests. The attitude that the Negroes are the responsibility solely of certain priests has resulted in a shifting of the responsibility for the whole colored question to the shoulders of two or three missionary organizations which are doing most of the work, and these few organizations have had to bear the onus usually attached to pioneer work. This relegation of responsibility to a few missioners is hardly consistent with the Divine command given to the Apostles and their successors. Responsibility for the solution of the Negro problem in this country, as far as the Catholic Church is concerned, rests squarely on the shoulders of the American Hierarchy. All other agencies are subservient.

4.—FINANCIAL

The financial handicaps of the Colored Missions are all too patent. The late Bishop Russell, of Charleston, S. C., once wrote: "From my way of looking at it, after my experience in the Southland, the conversion of the colored people is chiefly a matter of dollars and cents." The Negro and Indian Commission for 1929 reported collections, gifts, and bequests as amounting to $267,751.41. It is worthy of note that our largest cities, with one or two exceptions, "have contributed no more, and in most cases much less, than many a Christmas collection in a single church." The American Board of Catholic Missions, which is in charge of the distribution of the home mission share of the income of the Propagation of the Faith, from July 1, 1928 to July 1, 1929, reported receipts of $375,787.03. This sum is to be distributed among all the home missions, white and colored. It is not known what portion of it will find its way to colored missions, since a rule of the Board is that only bishops may petition for help.

If missioners are forced to spend much of their time begging or devising ways of raising money with which to carry on their work, they have just so much less time to devote to the work of the ministry. We are accustomed to regard tne missioner as one who can conjure mission plants and schools out of thin air. That satisfactory results may be thus secured in the wilderness or jungle we are not in a position to know, but it is certain that the American standard is high and that American missions must meet it if success is to be had. It is a matter of no little mystery how many missioners in the South are able to maintain an American standard of living on weekly collections that all too frequently do not average the wage of a sexton. Let it not be thought that the missioners among the colored people of the South are unwilling to embrace the hardships of the mission life; they recognize these as inevitable adjuncts of their vocation.

While not all missioners are in needy circumstances, is it fair to expect any of them to produce well-nigh miraculous results in the face of enormous state appropriations for public schools and equally large Protestant expenditures for mission purposes? Small wonder that some of the missioners are unable to meet the competition. "The multiplication of public schools is telling on the parochial," writes a New Orleans missioner of more than three decades' experience; "The equipment of the public schools is such that competition is out of the question. Happily the teaching staffs are largely Catholic."

While Catholic gratitude is due the colored people who generously contribute from their slender means, as also to the Catholic laity at large whose willingness to assist has been attested over and over again, there must be some way out of this haphazard method of mission support. The Commissions already existing are adequate mechanical means, and it is a matter of experience that where the people can be reached they respond generously. Are we, despite the piteous pleading of the Church which we profess to love, willing to ignore the prompting of charity and let the work of evangelizing the Negroes be handicapped and dragged on indefinitely? If not, the degree of indifference shown to any appeal for funds for mission work among the colored citizens of the United States, than whom no people have prior claim to our charity and interest, should cause a blush of shame.

CHAPTER XVII

INTERNAL DIFFICULTIES (REMOTE)

1.—NEGRO RELIGION

When we consider the Negro in relation to the Catholic Church, we are confronted by so many and such varied difficulties that it would seem well-nigh impossible to pick our way through the maze of explanations for the seeming failure of Catholic missionary effort in his behalf. We do not relish the thought of failure, yet who can rightly claim success when today the number of colored Catholics is hardly larger than it was forty years ago? Bearing in mind that they had then received but scant attention, albeit the voices of Plenary and Provincial Councils had published their needs, now, after the lapse of two-score years, we are very far from the glorious achievement for which so many had hoped and so few have striven. Without detracting one scintilla from the the credit due the many earnest priests who have labored among the Negroes, the facts of the case would seem to favor the conclusion that the Catholic Church has not made the progress which it has a right to expect.

A.   The Negro Church; Its Rise

One reason why the progress of the Catholic Church is so slow may be found in the past religious experiences of the Negro. It is often forgotten that the rise of the Negro Church was a curious phenomenon. It really represented all that was left of African tribal life, and was the sole expression of the organized efforts of the Negroes. It was natural that any movement among the Negroes should center about their religious life, the sole remaining element of their former tribal system. [1] Before the Civil War the religion of the slave, if he had any at all, was usually that of a master who had long

---

[1] DuBois, W. E. Burghardt, *Philadelphia Negro*, p. 197.

since learned that coincidence of religious beliefs on the part
of slave and master was a necessity in the economy of the
slave-holding states. Since masters did not look with favor
upon the proselytizing of their slaves by ministers whom they
would not have as their own spiritual advisers, Catholic missioners, even where available, had little access to the slaves.

In early days the slaves constituted a part of a mixed congregation: where the number was small, they were allowed
to attend the services held for the masters, although they
were segregated in the gallery or in certain pews; if the number was large, separate buildings were usually provided, or
they were permitted to use the church of the whites at different
hours.[1] Later, there was not much commingling of the two
races in the same meetings; then, white ministers preached
to the Negroes in their own special meetings, or provided
some approved Negro preacher of power to supply that need.

Much conflicting evidence has been adduced concerning the
care of masters for the spiritual welfare of their slaves. It
is safe to say that the religious condition of the slaves de-
pended upon the moral calibre of masters, among which there
were the good and the bad. It is certain, moreover, that previous to the Civil War there was no distinctly Negro Church.
After the emancipation the freedmen presented a fertile field
for the best missionary efforts of practically all non-Catholic
bodies. While most of the religiously inclined Negroes retained their adherence to the Baptist and Methodist Churches,
with which during the days of slavery they had been closely
connected through their masters, changed conditions necessitated an adjustment in church relations of whites and Negroes; accordingly separate churches were formed.[2] Thenceforth the rise of the Negro Church was rapid.

Writers have advanced various reasons to explain the pre-
dominance of the Baptist Church among the Negroes.[3] It
has been said that the Baptist Church offers broader opportunity to develop the tendency to excitement, a remarkable
feature of the Negro's piety. It has been said also that in

---

[1] Woodson, *History of the Negro Church*, p. 132.
[2] *Journal of Negro History*, vol. XI, p. 434.
[3] *Ibid.*, p. 437.

the constitution of the Baptist Church, which is organized along strictly democratic lines, each congregation being a law unto itself, is found the source of attraction; especially would this be the reason where persons preferred a career in the ministry to more laborious employment, since fitness for the ministry turned upon the issue of personality rather than of training. Probably both reasons have a share in explaining the large membership of the Negro Baptist Church. For much the same reasons membership in the Methodist Church is a close second to that of the Baptist.

Be the explanations what they may, it is a fact that the Baptists and Methodists were first to reach the Negro with an extensive missionary program. All recognize that the majority of Negroes attended these Churches previous to the Civil War; they had a body of itinerant preachers who went out into the wilderness to find the people and bring them into the Church. Other Churches, the Catholic Church included, did not have "the emotional character of experimental religion"—their appeal was too intellectual. "While the good Presbyterian parson was writing his discourses, rounding off sentences, the Methodist itinerant had traveled forty miles with his horse and saddle bag; while the parson was adjusting his spectacles to read his manuscript, the intinerant had given hell and damnation to his unrepentant hearers; while the disciple of Calvin was waiting to have his church completed, the disciple of Wesley took to the woods and made them re-echo with the voice of free grace." [1] So great was the hold of evangelism on the Negroes that more doctrinal religions, like Catholicism and Episcopalianism, could have had but scant appeal, even had they the missioners to make the effort.

It was not long, consequently, before the South was dotted with churches (in most cases merely shacks) professing allegiance to the evangelical bodies. Wherever a handful of Negroes were so inclined, they formed a church of their own —a minister was the least difficult acquisition.

[1] Woodson, *History of the Negro Church*, p. 98.

B. Emotional Religion

The religious experience of the Negroes was emotional rather than rational, many obtaining their first religious experience at a camp-meeting or revival. As such assemblages were social as well as religious, and frequently partook of a festive nature, the Negroes easily became attracted to this more liberal method of promoting the cause of Christ. [1]

"While an Episcopal clergyman with his ritual and prayer book had difficulty in interesting the Negroes," writes Woodson, [2] "they flocked in large numbers to the spontaneous exercises of the Methodists and Baptists, who, being decidedly evangelical in their preaching, had a sort of hypnotizing effect upon the Negroes, causing them to be seized with emotional jerks and outward expressions of an inward movement of the spirit which made them lose control of themselves."

That the power of the emotions is well grounded in the religion of the Negro is evident. Howard Odum had this to say:

"In spite of pretensions and superficiality, there is nothing so real to the Negro as his religion, although it is a different 'reality' from that which we commonly find in religion. The Negro is more excitable in his nature, and yields more readily to excitement than does the white man. The more a thing excites him, the more reality it has for him. So, too, the quality of arousing emotions, of moving or exciting him, has as much to do with his belief in a thing as does the quality of giving pleasure and satisfaction; they also are very much aroused in their worship. Their belief in the reality of religion is, then, almost a natural acquirement. And although the greater part of the religion of the Negro is pleasurable excitement, it is nevertheless, perhaps on that very account, the reality of realities to him; his faith comes in this way rather than by knowledge." [3]

Speaking of the conversions resulting from emotional experiences, Woodson writes:

"Statistics, however, show that such a conversion of people who were given no opportunity for mental development amounted to very little in the edification of their soul. Not long after these exciting camp meetings and protracted efforts had passed over, many of these persons who had been most vociferous in their praise of God for cleansing them of their many sins, readily fell thereafter by the wayside in engaging in what is known as pleasurable evils. Baptists and Methodists during this period

---

[1] *Ibid.*, p. 142.
[2] *Ibid.*
[3] *Social and Mental Traits of the Negro*, p. 88.

insisted that dancing was an evil, but how could the plantation Negro resist the temptation when he heard the clapping of the hands and the tune of the banjo? It became fashionable, therefore, for a person to be converted several seasons, sometimes once every four or five consecutive summers, before his feet could be completely taken out of the mire and the clay and placed upon the solid rock where the wind might blow and storm might rise, but none should frighten them from the shore."[1]

The soul-stirring reunion of the Baptists differed little from the camp-meeting of the Methodists; the Negroes became seized with hysteria, and interest in the work passing from one to another spread almost like a contagion, moving whole communities to seek salvation. As Woodson writes:

"Persons passing as sinners were made to feel that they were wretches in the sight of God and that direful punishments awaited them as the lot of the wicked. Their state was awful to behold, and their opportunities were swiftly passing away. That moment was the accepted time; for their delay would mean damnation. Persons fell helpless before the altar of the church and had to be carried out to be ministered unto, and when they emerged from their semi-conscious state they came forward singing the song of the redeemed who had been washed white in the blood of the Lamb."[2]

The power of the emotional appeal has only been strengthened by the traditional teachings of the race. Through his whole history the Negro has been taught to fear the powers of the spirit world; from African days unseen powers have been the directing and controlling forces in his life. It is but natural that the tendency of his religious teaching now is to keep alive the feeling of dependence upon divine powers. No doubt the disposition of primitive people is to interpret everything mystically, particularly if the thing be strange or inexplicable to them. This may account for a great deal of superstitition, conjuring, voodooism, and magic generally found among the Negroes of the United States, more especially in rural districts where opportunities for education are less frequent.

With the coming of the new, free, and evangelistic types of Christianity—the Baptists and the Methodists—the masses of the colored people, that is the plantation Negroes, found a form of Christianity which they could make their own and

---

[1] *Op. cit.*, p. 144.
[2] *Ibid.*

develop along lines of mysticism towards which they were inclined. The religion of the plantation Negroes was then, as it is today, of a primitive sort. Furthermore, there was considerable difference in the intellectual status of the different regions of the South, and these differences were reflected in the Negro churches.

The religious concepts of the Negro are perhaps best preserved in his plantation melodies. In the imagery with which the Negro chose to clothe his hopes and his dreams we have reflections of his imagination and various temperaments. While the sentiments contained in the spirituals occasionally rise to sublime heights, for the most part they are characterized by an emotionalism which would seem to be omnipresent in the religious experiences of the Negro.

While it is true that the outbreaks characteristic of Negro meetings in general would seem to be subsiding somewhat, even yet they are sufficiently characteristic of the Negro's religion to make it difficult for a more dignified and doctrinal religion like that of the Catholic Church to have appeal for the masses. There are thousands of meeting places scattered throughout the country in which the poor people, led by wandering preachers, express their religion in frenzied shouts, maniacal gesticulations, and ecstatic visions, if we can believe the accounts of those who profess to have first-hand knowledge.

W. E. Burghardt Du Bois, himself an educated Negro, gives his own impression of such a meeting:

"A sort of suppresed terror hung in the air, and seemed to seize us— a pythian madness, a demoniac possession, and that lent terrible reality to song and words. The black and massive form of the preacher swayed and quivered as the words crowded to his lips and flew at us in singular eloquence. The people moaned and fluttered, and then the gaunt-cheeked brown woman beside me suddenly leaped straight into the air and shrieked like a lost soul, while round about came wail and groan and outcry and a scene of human passion such as I had never before conceived." [1]

Such wild excitement meant little in the spiritual uplift of the slaves. There remained throughout the South, however, a few denominations, including the Catholic, which still adhered to the idea that the slaves should be given practical in-

---

[1] *Souls of Black Folk*, p. 190.

struction in religion. Even after laws forbidding the instruction of slaves had been placed on the statute books of most southern states, many masters and some few ministers of the Gospel defied the law. But, as Woodson remarks: "The more the Negroes were instructed by these rather intellectual denominations, however, the less they, as a group, seemed inclined to join their fortunes with those persons who were disposed to lay a foundation for an intensive spiritual development." [1]

It is clear that the concept of religion as an emotional experience will of necessity have greater appeal to a race, the majority of which have not as yet passed the "child stage" of intelligence, than will an intelligent religion such as Catholicism. Catholics were early concerned with the amelioration of the condition of the Negro and were found among the first to bear testimony against slavery, as Woodson so fairly states. [2] But our success has not been phenominal. Only a relatively small number of Negroes have profited by our heroic efforts. In extenuation it may be said that the Catholic Church stands not alone in its failure to reach this emotional people; other religious bodies experience the same difficulty of "too much intellectuality."

C. Social Religion

Apart from the emotional aspect of the Negro's religion, there is also the social, a characteristic of all Negro churches, particularly those of the better class. While the Church of the Negro has always been a social institution, that particular feature would seem to predominate in proportion as the emotional character is forced into the background. Because they present the one common ground for meeting, particularly in the South where there are not so many public amusements offered to the Negro, the churches are centers of social life to an extent not true of white churches anywhere. The best expression of the life of the better class of Negroes is in the church where their social life centers and where they discuss their situations and prospects. It is natural, then,

[1] *Op. cit.*, p. 145.
[2] *Ibid.*, p. 98.

that the function of the Negro Church is rather to give expression and satisfaction to social and religious emotions rather than to direct moral conduct.

Du Bois thinks that the Negro Church is the peculiar and characteristic product of the transplanted African and as such deserves special study.[1] As a social group, the Negro Church may be said to antedate the Negro family on American soil. As such, it has preserved, on the one hand, many of the functions of tribal organization; on the other hand, it retains many of the family functions. Its tribal functions are shown in its religious activities, its social authority, and general guiding and co-ordinating work; its family functions are shown in that the church is the center of social life and intercourse. The local church of the Negro acts as newspaper and intelligence bureau, is the center of amusements—indeed, is the world in which the Negro moves and acts.

The Church as center for the social life of the race is not new. Prior to the emancipation it was the only institution which offered an avenue for the expressional activities of the race.[2] Not only education found its basis in the Church, but fraternal organizations developed therefrom; business and enterprise accepted it as an ally, and professional men often became dependent on it. Most movements among the Negroes, moreover, have owed their success to the leadership of Negroes prominent in the Church.[3]

Since the Civil War the Negro Church as a factor of general uplift has become what the oppressed Negro longed to make of it prior to that conflict.

"In the first place, Negroes regularly attend church whether Christians or sinners. They have not yet accumulated wealth adequate to the construction of clubhouses, amusement parks, and theaters, although dance halls have attracted many. Whether they derive any particular joy therefrom or not, the Negroes must go to church to see their friends, as they are barred from social centers open to whites. They must attend church, moreover, to find out what is going on, for the race has not sufficient interests to maintain in every locality a newspaper of its own, and the white dailies generally mention Negroes only when they happen to commit crimes against white persons. The young Negro must go to

---

[1] *Philadelphia Negro*, p. 201.
[2] Woodson, *History of Negro Church*, p. 266.
[3] *Ibid.*, p. 267.

church to meet his sweetheart, to impress her with his worth, and woo her in marriage; the Negro farmer, to find out the developments in the business world; the Negro mechanic to learn the needs of his community and how he may supply them." [1]

During the past few decades the Negro Church has assumed a broader aspect in its social service. While retaining its former character of center in the social life of the colored community, it has developed more along the lines of modern social service. Social welfare agencies now find in it a powerful ally; wherever these social welfare agencies have succeeded in carrying out a program of improvement, it has been with the aid of church organizations. Of necessity the church assumed this more extensive form of social service; it had to provide for the social needs of its members or see them go over to the more progressive churches and agencies which catered to the social instincts of the race. As Woodson remarks:

"In case some social uplift agency failed to attract the youth, they too often drifted to the dance halls or places where their needs were supplied in the midst of vices. Many churches have, therefore, modified their program. Seeing that the young Negro is decidedly social and hoping to save him, they have done what many formerly questioned. The Negro Church, moreover, has become in many respects a welfare agency itself, doing in several communities so much of this work that it has been necessary for the national agencies to invade some of their parishes with an intensive program." [2]

No doubt many Negroes of today attend church for the single purpose of religious worship, but a majority go with the expectation of meeting friends and making acquaintances. Besides, the preaching services, the Sunday school, prayer meetings, class meetings, and the like, attract special groups. On week days and evenings, lectures, debates, socials, entertainments, musicals, and festivals provide numerous occasions for frequent social gatherings. In this way the social life of the Negro centers in his church: baptism, wedding, burial, gossip and courtship, friendship, and intrigue—all lie within the church walls.

The rapid growth of Negro Church membership during the

---

[1] *Ibid.*
[2] *Ibid*, p. 275.

past thirty years, in the face of multiplying distractions of modern living and changed conditions of urban residence, is practically explained by the Church as a field for leadership excluded from other avenues, and by the motivating force of emotional and imaginative self-expression in Negro Church exercises. [1] To the Church all Negroes ambitious for independent leadership must look, in as much as other institutions touching the life of the Negro are more or less completely controlled or directed by whites. With the development of the professions, however, the Church as an avenue for leadership is becoming less necessary. Nevertheless, it not infrequently happens that the social status of the Negro is fixed by his standing in the local church. In this way the Negro Church not only gives social compensation for the restrictions of the segregated, handicapped life of Negroes in America, but it gives a certain social prestige to many who have ambition to become leaders.

The phenomenal growth of the Negro Church, accordingly, means more than the establishment of many places of worship. The Negro is, to be sure, a religious creature (most primitive folk are), but his rapid and even extraordinary founding of churches is not due to this fact alone; rather it is a measure of his development and an indication of the increasing intricacy of his social life. The multiplication of the organ which is the function of his group life — the church — is but a consequence. [2] Working along social lines of endeavor the Negro Church has a better chance for success in making its evangelical appeal to the people than it would have if it attempted to deliver its message to individuals not bound together by a bond of communal social life.

D. The Negro Preacher

While the colored preachers of the Baptist and Methodist Churches have not cared or have not been able to conform to the strict requirements of the churches controlled by whites, not a few are really quite gifted. There would seem to be no doubt, however, that the better trained preachers are in the

[1] *The American Negro;* Annals of the American Academy, p. 271.
[2] Du Bois, *The Philadelphia Negro,* p. 201.

churches of other denominations. In the colored Episcopal, Presbyterian, or Congregational Churches, for instance, today one will usually find a high type of church service, but almost invariably with a small congregation. If one would see the typical colored congregation, one must go to the Baptist or Methodist Church—as a distinct institution they are typical.

In the past it would seem that too few Negro ministers have been concerned about the spiritual welfare of their charges. The ministry was too often used as a stepping stone to a political career,[1] or as a means towards the material uplift of the race.[2] There is no objection to the use of the Church in these spheres provided such practice does not entail neglect of spiritual duties. One suspects that frequently such was the case. This is not surprising in view of the fact that: "The great mass of the colored preachers of the South are extremely ignorant; many of them, we are assured by the best testimony, do not know enough of the Gospel to lead a poor inquiring sinner to Jesus Christ for salvation."[3]

The Negro Church can scarcely be said to have a theology. Its teachings are the traditional doctrines of the white church accepted without any effort to establish their truth or identity. What the average Negro wants is not to test by rational standards the truth of a proposition or its tenableness, but to hear an effective sermon. He is willing to accept as true what others say so long as his minister can use it effectively. This disposition of the people to be content with bombastic verbosity has had its effect upon the ministry of the Negro Church:

"I have talked with many of the best trained preachers of the colored race," writes J. J. Watson, Ph.D.,[2] "and I have yet to find one who in any way is bothering himself with the current problems of theology. One of these men told me that it would do no good to keep up with current questions as his people were not interested in them and could not profit by their discussion. What pleases the average congregation is

---

[1] Woodson, *History of the Negro Church*, chap. XI.
[2] *Ibid.*, chap. XII.
[3] *Journal of Negro History*, vol. XI, no. 3, p. 445; *cf. also*, Thomas, William H., *The American Negro*, pp. 151, 152.
[4] *Churches and Religious Conditions;* Annals of the American Academy, vol. XLIX, Sept., 1913, p. 124.

the recital of Bible stories, and the preacher usually conforms to this demand."

The colored pastor, as a general rule, has little religious or lay learning; if he has, the tendency is to lose it when surrounded by a people largely ignorant.[1] The Chicago Commission on Race Relations[2] found that among the ministers of 147 Negro churches in Chicago only twenty-two had had special training. Six of these were graduates of recognized northern institutions for whites, while fourteen were graduates of Negro institutions; some of the others had not even a grammar-school education. Dowd quotes Corrothers, himself a Negro minister,[3] as saying that:

"The majority of ministers were sadly lacking in education, quite often far more so than some of the gambling Negro ruffians whom I had known on the boat. When I added their mental unpreparedness to their other unlovely personal traits, I could not see in them enough of those better qualifications which fit men for a holy calling or for leadership."

Woodson, in the History of the Negro Church,[4] is kinder. He writes:

"Some young Negroes have learned to look upon the calling as a necessary nuisance. Except in the church schools where the preparation for the ministry is an objective, it has often been unusual to find one Negro student out of a hundred aspiring to the ministry, and too often those who have such aspirations represent the inferior intellect of the group." Further he states: "Because Negroes now realize how limited the opportunity for the race is in politics and some of the professions, however, the ministry will doubtless continue, as it has since the Reconstruction, a sort of avenue through which the ambitious youth must pass to secure a hearing and become a man of influence among his people. This does not mean that irreligious men will masquerade as spiritual advisers, but that, inasmuch as the church as an institution is considered a welfare agency as well as a spiritual body to edify souls, some Negroes, interested in the social uplift of the race, are learning to accomplish this task by accepting leadership in the churh."

There are, of course, certain ministers of the more serious type who have been able to form an ideal of religion other than one of emotionalism. This is possible to them by reason of continued contact with whites, or by reason of their affilia-

---

[1] *Ibid.* p. 260; also, *Negro in American Life*, Dowd, p. 181.
[2] *Negro in Chicago*, p. 146.
[3] *Negro in American Life*, p. 80.
[4] p. 300.

tion with doctrinal churches, such as the Episcopal. These ministers are not usually they who attain great success in religion; they play much the same role that intellectual Negroes play in the civic life of the people.[1]

Of the types of Negro ministers, the intinerant is the lowest; he is usually found in camp-meetings and "shack missions" with all the accoutrements of a savage emotionalism. Higher in the scale of attainment is the average minister; if not a man of at least some little learning, certainly one who knows his Bible and is an appealing preacher. Finally, there is the educated minister, in number all too few. The possession of a D.D., however, does not necessarily entitle one to classification in this group. Personal acquaintance vouches for the example of a Negro minister who received his B.A. degree only after four years' attendance at a northern Catholic college, yet a course of four months at a recognized southern Negro university of reputed standing sent him home a Doctor of Divinity.

The preacher plays an important role in the life of a Negro community—an importance often beyond his worth. Concerning Negro ministers, Odum has this to say:

"Among the Negroes there is much respect for all the minister says in public and private: his actions are sanctioned. He carries with him a sanctity frequently ill-deserved and ill-won . . . He seldom cares for high principles in his life. Many cases of gross immorality among Negro preachers have been noted, which though of the lowest and most corrupt nature, elicit no surprise among the Negroes, for it is not expected that the average Negro preacher will be pure in life; rather his position gives him freedom to do as his inclination dictates . . . The ignorance, too, of most Negro preachers is appalling; many are without accurate knowledge of the simplest truths of the Bible. But it may be assumed for the time, that the notable exceptions, of which there are many, constitute the majority, and that the Negro preacher only reflects one phase of the weakness of the race."[2]

Du Bois admits that:

"The Negro preacher is primarily an executive officer, rather than a spiritual guide. If one goes into any great Negro church and hears the sermon and views the audience, one would say: either the sermon is far below the calibre of the audience, or the people are less sensible than they

---

[1] Warrington Dawson, *Le Negre Aux Etats-Unis*, p. 259.
[2] *Op. cit.*, p. 88.

look; the former explanation is usually true. The preacher is sure to be a man of executive ability, a leader of men, a shrewd and affable president of a large and intricate corporation. In addition to this he may be, and usually is, a striking elocutionist; he may also be a man of integrity, learning, and deep spiritual earnestness; but these last three are sometimes all lacking, and the last two in many cases. Some signs of advance are here manifest: no minister of notoriously immoral life, or even of bad reputation, could hold a large church in Philadelphia without eventual revolt. Most of the present pastors are decent, respectable men; there are perhaps one or two exceptions to this, but the exceptions are doubtful, rather than notorious. On the whole, then, the average Negro preacher in this city is a shrewd manager, a respectable man, a good talker, a pleasant companion, but neither learned nor spiritual, nor a reformer." [1]

There is hope in the fact that "probably the most promising aspect (in the progress of the Negro church) is that Negro ministers of today measure up to a higher standard than formerly." [2] Unquestionably, there are many Negro ministers of exceptional worth as spiritual leaders of their people; but somehow or other the impression still prevails that when it comes to actual religious instruction given and the motive power for better living, as Odum puts it: "The greatest need of the church seems to be for preachers whose lives do not give the lie to their teachings, and who realize the responsibility resting upon them. As a rule the average pastor does not begin to grasp the situation or recognize the crying needs of his people." [3]

---

[1] *The Philadelphia Negro*, p. 206.
[2] Woodson, *History of the Negro Church*, p. 311.
[3] *Ibid.*, p. 87. Concerning the Negro preacher, *vide* any Negro newspaper: e.g., *Afro-American*, Nov. 23, 1929, p. 1.

CHAPTER XVIII

INTERNAL DIFFICULTIES (REMOTE, *Continued*)

2.—NEGRO MORALITY

It has been suggested that with honorable exceptions the Negro's concept of morality is too loose to permit ready acceptance of the high standard of morality imposed by membership in the Catholic Church. Even if true (though apparently supported by social statistics, it is subject to debate), this charge should not be levelled at the Negro—the Negro has a history.

A. *Heredity and Morality*

It is conceded that the moral heritage of the Negro has been determined mainly by the influence slavery has exerted upon it. [1] While slavery may have been less brutal in some sections of the South and under some masters, usually the institution exerted a degrading, dehumanizing influence upon the slaves. Family life among the slaves generally disintegrated because of the emphasis planters placed on the breeding of slaves for the markets, after unscientific agriculture had impoverished the lands; this induced a laxity in sexual relations between slaves. In general, too, slaves were not permitted to hold property; hence, they had no opportunity to develop respect for property rights, as is evidenced by the amount of petty pilfering charged against them. The slave was subject, furthermore, to despotic rule and arbitrary punishment without an unbiased hearing; so he developed the vices of deception and outright falsehood in order to escape corporal punishment. Moreover, the Negro gambled and drank, because the white people whom he took as models practised these things. [2] In general, there prevailed the low condition of morals which should be expected in a barbarous people forced to labor in a strange land. [3]

[1] Thomas, *op. cit.*, p. 107, 361.
[2] *Journal of Negro History*, vol. XI, no. 3, p. 454.
[3] Du Bois, *The Philadelphia Negro*, p. 15.

Referring to the slow moral growth among the Negroes, the American Missionary Association expressed alarm over the condition of Negro women. At first seriously concerned over the emotional religion and intemperance of the freedmen, the Association, in its Report for 1869, noted that, "Slavery systematically attempted, and with terrible success, to obliterate (from the minds of Negro women) the instinct of chastity." [1] As a result, destitution quickly drove many to sexual immorality as a means of support. Some years later, the Rev. A. Binga, Jr., a Negro minister of Manchester, Va., expressed alarm over the moral condition of the Negroes; he thought they had deteriorated below the standard of native Africans. "Among the Negroes here," he said, "vice has been enthroned and virtue debased." [2] Since Negro men had not been taught to regard the marriage vows as sacred, or the protection of their wives and daughters a duty, what better could be looked for?

To the already heavy burden of his own troubles, animality added what Du Bois describes as "The red stain of bastardy, which two centuries of systematic legal defilement of Negro women had stamped upon his race, (and which) meant not only the loss of ancient African chastity, but also the hereditary weight of a mass of corruption from white adulterers, threatening almost the obliteration of the Negro home." [3] Before the evidence of a long, long chain of mulattoes, "quivering with discontent and the tragedy of belonging to both races without being quite acceptable to either," it must not be forgotten that the Negro's vices are in a large measure a legacy bequeathed to him by the white man, while his virtues are his own.

The laws of heredity are as yet incompletely known. In physiological heredity the true nature and cause of heredity is that the child's organism is a continuation of that of the parents; hence, the body of the offspring is bound to have some characteristics of the bodies of the parents. How this development works is obscure and not now to our purpose;

---

[1] *Quoted from Journal of Negro History*, vol. XI, no. 3, p. 454.
[2] *Ibid.*, p. 456.
[3] Du Bois, *The Souls of Black Folk*, p. 9.

it suffices to apply these laws to the Negro whose immediate ancestry goes back to the cruel days of slavery. Can anyone who is familiar with the literature of those days deny that certain physical modifications were then produced which will require more than a few generations to be eliminated from the race?

The physical deterioration resulting from the transmission of real diseases, exaggerated tendencies, nervous conditions, etc., all have manifold and extensive moral implications in possible hysteria, temporary insanity, kleptomania, and hypersexuality; while mental and emotional deterioration may find moral implication in the possible transmission of feeble-mindedness, and a tendency to develop certain wrong inclinations due to the over- or under-development of certain organs or parts of organs.

Psychological heredity is more subtle. While transmission of mental characteristics cannot be direct, because the soul of the parent has nothing to do with that of the child, nevertheless, psychological heritage rests indirectly on the physical in that with certain physical organs over- or under-developed, the activities of the mental and spiritual machinery are necessarily impaired. Pertinent, too, is the transmission, through tradition, of certain concepts of morality begot in slavery which now exert an indirect, but no less terrible, hereditary influence on the lives of the Negroes.

Of the influence of heredity in free and moral acts, we must note that ancestry of a low type, such as that of most Negroes, may create physical deterioration of organism, as also mental and emotional deterioration. Unquestionably, these influences have a marked effect upon the moral status of the present-day Negro.[1] Even to those Negroes who, by the grace of God and their own efforts, have climbed high in the way of upright living, they present obstacles which must be given ample consideration.

Difficult indeed was the task of any Church to remedy conditions. Because of the undeveloped state of the freedom, it could not be expected that in a short while they would become models of morality. Faced with the sudden readjust-

---

[1] Thomas, *op. cit.*, p. 139, also, pp. 176-188.

ment coming with emancipation, the Negro was asked to change from a position of irresponsibility to one of responsibility; to take his place in a society already well organized, when he had no previous training; to adopt a new standard of ethics and make it effective in his life, when his traditions and inbred inclinations made that well-nigh impossible. Small wonder that most Negroes failed to find any secure moral or religious footing. Accordingly, in judging the slow growth of Catholicism among the Negroes, we must bear in mind that the Negro home and the stable marriage state, absolute essentials in the Catholic scheme of life, are for the mass of colored people a new social institution, the slave family having been dependent in morals as well as in work upon the master. If the great weaknesses of the Negro family are still lack of respect for the marriage bond, inconsiderate entrance into it, bad household economy, and worse family government (and Du Bois assures us these are),[1] they are largely the after-effects which would be produced by any sudden social revolution—a strain upon the strength and resources of the Negro: moral, economic, and physical.

B. *Environment and Morality*

In most cities the Negro quarters are adjacent to the worse "red light" districts of the whites. Since the examples which environ Negro youths are mostly those of evil, they are early initiated into a life of sensuality.[2] Home conditions all too frequently are but reflections of the environment. Because of the low moral state of the Negro's family life, Thomas, a Negro author, believed that it would be a good thing to separate all Negro children from their parents and raise them in orphanages.[3] Du Bois rates environment a greater evil than slavery and emancipation with their attendant phenomena of ignorance, lack of discipline, and moral weakness.[4]

With the recent migration, the pressure of sudden increase

---

[1] *Philadelphia Negro*, p. 72; *cf. also* Thomas, *op. cit.*, chap. VII, also p. 126.
[2] Dowd, *op. cit.*, p. 99.
[3] *Op. cit.*, p. 386.
[4] *Op. cit.*, p. 284.

in the population of Negro communities created many new problems, but seldom did this increase bring into existence any new large Negro quarters; rather, it resulted in an expansion and increased density in areas in which Negro groups already lived. While many Negroes of the better class have succeeded in building up respectable neighborhoods, the vast majority of urban Negroes are still crowded into narrow streets, dingy courts, and dirty alleys.

Such severe over-crowding, both in neighborhood and home, results in rent exploitation and serious disorganization of home life. Housing is always an important element in the environmental causes of immorality, particularly so in the Negro situation, for vice districts and the Negro residence districts are now and have long been close together. The Chicago Vice Commission disclosed that: "In addition to this proximity to immoral conditions, young colored girls are often forced into idleness because of prejudice against them, and they are eventually forced to accept positions as maids in houses of prostitution. Employment agents do not hesitate to send colored girls as servants to these houses. . . . The apparent discrimination against colored citizens of the city in permitting vice to be set down in their very midst is unjust and abhorrent to all fair-minded people." [1]

To environmental difficulties must be added the lodging system, a direct effect of rent exploitation. Desire for proximity to church and work, and restriction of selection to segregated districts make available for Negroes only a limited number of houses. Shortage of housing facilities, in turn, necessitates the payment of high rents. As a consequence, Negroes who are unable to afford the full rent (and they form a large part of the race) [2] must take in lodgers if they would meet the exhorbitant demands of rapacious house owners. This means undesirable crowding and the sacrifice of privacy. Commenting on the moral aspect of the lodger system, Du Bois writes: "The result is, on the whole, pernicious,

---

[1] *The Negro in Chicago*, p. 343.
[2] In Richmond, Va., for example, of the families surveyed by the Richmond Council of Social Agencies in the 1928 Negro Welfare Survey of Richmond), 38 per cent kept lodgers, 15 per cent unrelated lodgers.

especially where there are growing children . . . The lodgers are often waiters, who are at home between meals, at the very hour when the housewife is off at work, and growing daughters are left unprotected. In some cases, though this is less often, servant girls and other female lodgers are taken. In such ways the privacy and intimacy of home life is destroyed, and elements of danger and demoralization are admitted." [1]

Odum uses very strong language in describing the home life of many Negroes. He writes: "Growing out of this disorder, confusion and lack of home training two things must be expected: immorality and crime, on the one hand, and disease on the other. Such is the case. The indiscriminate mixing in the home leads to bad personal habits; the utter lack of restraint deadens any moral sensibilities that might be present. Nowhere in the home is there restraint; the contact and conduct of its members belong to the lowest classification. There is little knowledge of the sanctity of the home or marital relations, consequently little regard for them. The open cohabitation of the sexes related by no ties of marriage is a very common practice, little is thought of it as it relates to the race; there is apparently no conscience in the matter." [2]

Fortunately, there is a brighter side to the picture. Not all environment is equally disorderly; there are many neighborhoods to be found which show marked pride and do credit to the residents. Even in cases where Negroes own their own homes and keep them clean, where the best influences of the home are represented, and where children give promise of growing up to be virtuous men and women, general conditions of environment over which they have little or no control, make it very difficult for Negro youths to develop into what they give promise to become. [3]

This we must know in regard to the Negro if we would study his social condition: his strange social environment must have an immense effect upon his thought and life, his work and crime, his religion and his soul. That this environment

[1] *Op. cit.*, p. 194.
[2] *Op. cit.*, p. 163, *cf. also* Thomas, *op. cit.*, p. 177.
[3] *Ibid.*, p. 175, *cf. also* Thomas, *ibid.*, p. 179.

differs, and differs broadly, from the environment of his white fellows we all know, but we do not know just how it differs. Du Bois tells us: "The real foundation of the difference is the widespread feeling all over the land, in Philadelphia as well as in Boston and New Orleans, that the Negro is something less than the American and ought not to be much more than what he is. Argue as we may for or against this idea, we must as students recognize its presence and its vast effects." [1]

Environment may influence the morality of the Negro in three ways: it may supply him with convictions and prejudices which form the basis for much of what little moral knowledge he has; it may, and frequently does, copiously supply him with occasions and friendships which tend to arouse the baser emotions; finally, it is an important contributing factor in the creation of habits or acquired dispositions which may impair moral activity. While good environment in itself would not make the Negro good, it would serve as an antidote to the poisonous influence of heredity and be a strong support in his struggle to overcome his handicaps. [2]

The evil influence of unwholesome environment may be overcome by education; but a purely secular education does not give the Negro a moral training sufficient to overcome the ever-present influence of his environment. Example, too, is an antidote against bad environment; but to whom can the average Negro look for example? Discipline is another check against the influence of evil environment, but who is to apply the proper kind of discipline? The police? Lynching? His church? So far none of these have had the desired effect. The Catholic Church is the answer. But with social forces such as they are at present, the work of the Catholic Church is excessively hindered.

C. Poverty and Morality

The low estate of our colored brethren is another social obstacle to a more flourishing Catholicity in the Colored Harvest. While poverty may be an unmitigated blessing for

---

[1] *The Philadelphia Negro*, p. 284.
[2] *Cf.*, Thomas, *op. cit.*, p. 204-206.

many, the same may not be said of the Negro; emptiness of stomach with fulness of soul is quite other than emptiness of both. The poverty which most colored families know is such that "the decencies of existence in which the flowers of our Faith so readily take root are often wholly lacking." Ordinary conveniences, considered essentials by the average white family, are most frequently lacking; the necessity of taking in lodgers makes anything like privacy rare, and suggests probable injury to health or morals, and sometimes both; high rents and low incomes leave little or nothing for anything more than bare necessities of existence.

At the close of the Civil War there were two classes of Negroes, each widely set apart in economic status and opportunity. In one class, a small minority, were the sons and daughters of free parents; they constituted the aristocracy of the colored population and, for the most part, usually were mulattoes of some education. The second class comprised the great mass of slaves who had little opportunity for advancement. After the war class distinction ceased—all were under the common ban of color.

Today the economically independent Negroes form a distinct, though not always clearly defined, class as apart from the more impecunious members of the race. Often lost sight of in discussing the Negro, as a group this class feels strongly the centrifugal forces of class repulsion among their own people; indeed, they are compelled to feel it in sheer self-defense.[1] Shrinking from the free and easy worship of most Negro churches, even more than the rest of the race they feel the difficulty of getting on, for their higher standard of living makes heavier drain upon their resources. Nevertheless, they enjoy a pleasant home life, and among them at least the natural virtues have found surprising development.

Most truly representative of the Negro race is the hard laboring class. The Negroes in this class live with a degree of respectability which is good on the average and roughly equivalent to the status of the poor class among the whites. They

---

[1] Du Bois, *The Philadelphia Negro*, p. 177.

live in houses fairly well furnished, but while they spend considerable for food, dress, church, and beneficial societies, their home life lacks many pleasant features of good homes. Traces of plantation customs still persist, and there is the widespread custom of seeking amusement outside the home. Two great hindrances affect this class: low wages and high rents. Low wages make it imperative for the mother of the family to work until late in the evenings, leaving the children without guidance or restraint for the better part of the day. High rents result in the lodger system, the evils of which we have noticed.

To the third and lowest class of Negroes belong the inefficient, unfortunate, and improvident who barely manage to exist. Even in this class there are degrees: the poor but decent, the indigent, and the outcasts. The conditions in which this class lives is what might be called, according to our standards, abject poverty. Occasionally, but not often, a Negro family manages to escape from such wretched living conditions and to purchase a home in a more reputable Negro section of the town.

If the poverty of the Negroes who occupy the more crowded quarters of our cities is so devastating, "volumes could not express the limitations of the poor black's existence in the rice-swamps of the Carolinas, the sugar-bottoms of Louisiana, or the corn-fields of Mississippi." Yet, three-quarters of the Negroes in the United States live in rural sections of the country.

In childhood, neglected because of the absence of both parents from the home; in adolescence, employed in sundry menial occupations when they should be in school; in maturity, unable to secure economic independence, the moral idea has been made almost impossible to countless numbers of Negroes. With the home frequently failing in its spiritual role, it is not surprising that "since it is equal to none of the tasks of time, it falls short often of meeting those of eternity."

A normal home presupposes "a comfortable house, adequate room space to protect privacy and morality, decent surroundings, intelligent parents, protected childhood, sufficient wholesome food, freedom from unreasonable fear, and the experience of peace, affection, and hope. A home involves a moral unity between parents and children that is the basis of continuity of life, a source of motive and aspiration and affective discipline that prepares one for the wider relations of life. Through this moral unity of life experience is assured in thoughtfulness, renunciation, obedience, respect for duty, and the memory of a thousand joys that are dear to the affection, and are the enduring springs of noble impulse later." [1] When the home lacks these qualifications it ceases to be a nursery for the development of those virtues which make for a full realization of the human and divine purposes in life.

Ordinarily, poverty is not an insurmountable obstacle to the missioner seeking souls, because our Faith has a special appeal to the blessed poor; but "among the Negroes who occupy the more crowded quarters of our cities the conditions of life are such as to render very difficult the development or preservation of any human virtues." [2] It is upon such an untilled ground that the missionary sower must cast the seed of the Gospel. While all things are possible to Him who gave the command to preach the Gospel to every nation, in the course of human events the supernatural has a better chance to flourish when nature has already done something constructive, or has provided at least a base upon which to build.

D. Emotion and Morality

Frequently lost sight of in considering the Negro is the great influence of the emotions on his life. [3] Morally speaking, we know that emotion augments the intensity of an act but diminishes freedom, sometimes even destroys it. Being more excitable in his nature, the Negro yields more readily to emotion than does the white man; the more a thing excites him, the more reality it has for him. [4] The sense emotions, being more vivid, naturally, have a greater appeal than have intellectual things; wherefore, the quality of arousing emo-

---

[1] Kerby, *The Social Mission of Charity*, p. 29.
[2] Dowd, *op. cit.*, p. 99.
[3] Du Bois, *The Philadelphia Negro*, p. 209, *et sq.*
[4] *Ibid.*, p. 189.

tions, of moving, or of exciting the Negro, has as much to do with his belief in a thing as has the quality of giving pleasure. "It is not surprising, then," observes Odum, "that the Negro's religion is not one of practical application, and that a scarcity of thoughtfulness and will power is everywhere predominant . . . The attitude of both races is to take it for granted that all Negroes may be morally unaccountable." [1]

The moral implication of the high degree of emotionalism in the Negro is that it frequently lessens the liberty of his actions, for if more attention be given to the pleasurableness of an act, less can be given to its moral aspect. The emotionalism of the Negro makes more vivid this pleasureableness, because it is referred to his sense appetition, whereas the morality of the act is referred to the moral law, a more abstract and remote reality. The influence of the emotions in the moral life of the Negro may even be so great as to destroy entirely his liberty. While this condition of irresponsibility is not readily to be admitted in normal persons, it must be admitted that not a few actions of many Negroes, especially those of the less intellectual type, are purely instinctive and have no morality at all.

There can be little room for doubt that his view of religion as an emotional experience only has had a detrimental effect upon the character of the Negro. It constantly stimulates the lower emotions at the expense of the higher, so that frequently when a crisis is presented to him the emotions predominate at the expense of that clear, calm judgment so necessary for the proper evaluation of moral standards.

The Negro like the child must be taught morality effectively if he is to be held strictly accountable for his acts. Where, unless to his Church, is he to look for this moral training? Yet, we are assured by many Negro writers, the Church of the Negro is, as Du Bois puts it: "to be sure a social institution first, and religious afterwards. . . . The chief function of these Churches in morals is to conserve old standards and to create about them a public opinion which shall deter the offender, and in this the Negro Churches are peculiarly

---

[1] Odum, *op. cit.*, p. 88; Thomas, *op. cit.*, p. 153.

successful, although naturally the standards conserved are not as high as they should be." [1]

Applying Catholic notions of morality to the Negro, we find that owing to a mistaken psychology those who sit in judgment over him most frequently suppose that the moral sense is a basic primitive impulse in man. It is not. Moral goodness or evil are qualities not directly perceived in an act, but are ascribed to it through moral reasoning. It is for this very reason that children must be given moral training, and unless they are taught morality effectively, they may grow up to be immoral—or rather unmoral. The Negro, with, of course, honorable exceptions, has not had the religious training so necessary to develop a high moral standard. In the absence of this training, how can the Negro have that knowledge without which there is no moral freedom and, consequently, no basis for moral imputation?

A criterion of morality being a process of growth, the Negro cannot be expected within the short span of half a century to have attained a standard for which even God prepared the world by centuries of patient training. On the whole, the Negro has done remarkably well in so short a time, and much better than anyone has a right to expect of him. Nevertheless, we cannot fail to take cognizance of the fact that his parcular lack of moral perspective, excusable as it may be, is an obstacle to his more rapid conversion to Catholicism.

---

[1] *The Philadelphia Negro*, pp. 205, 206.

Chapter XIX

INTERNAL DIFFICULTIES (IMMEDIATE)

History records the conversion of peoples far lower in the scale of culture than are the Negroes, but vastly different were the circumstances. In the United States there were no tribal chiefs to lead the Negroes after them under the yolk of Christ, but there were non-Catholic masters who gave to their vast holdings of slaves a membership in the Baptist, Methodist, and other evangelical Churches. Even today, conditions over which neither the Negro nor the Catholic Church has control, make it as difficult for the Negro to find the Catholic Church as it is for the Church to interest the Negro. On the one side is poverty with her daughters of heredity, race-exploitation, discrimination, disease, and sin; on the other, the Church of Rome with her meagre financial resources but a high standard of morality.

1.—Two Idealisms

It is quite understandable that the Negro's notion of doctrine is confined to some few hazy ideas about God's care for the needy, the atonement of Christ, and what we would term the verbal inspiration of the Bible—traditional relics of whatever religious instruction he received in the days of slavery. It is understandable, too, that the form of the minister's discourses usually is an attempt to offset the discouraging thoughts accumulated during the week; to bring to lives accustomed to harshness and injustice some few glimpses of comfort. The lot of the Negro, whether in Africa or America, has never been an easy one, and his daily needs have driven him to feel the need of heaven as a place for the righting of all wrongs and for the enjoyment of all things denied him here. To the mind of the average Negro the Church is the medium of attainment of all these desires. [1]

---

[1] Thomas, *op. cit.*, p. 148.

At the same time, to the Catholic missioner approaching the work of Negro evangelization, it should be plain that he must discount two fond idealisms which formerly dominated, and even yet to some extent, dominate Catholic thought. The first idealism which must go is that the Negro is naturally religious. He is not essentially so, if by religion we understand a moral religion entailing much mortification of the senses.[1] That approximately half the race is under no apparent religious control is sufficient indication of the situation; that of the other half, the majority are under questionable religious control is more than sufficient indication of the seriousness of the situation. The other idealism which must go is that the Negro is to be won to the Catholic Church through his senses—that he must have plenty of sound and color. While the importance of the emotional appeal of the Catholic ritual is not to be under-estimated, at the same time, anything like a wide application of that form of appeal would produce results questionable, if not positively harmful. The Negro must be converted as all other people have been converted: by the slow and laborious process of training his intellect, forming his will, and guiding his emotions. This method alone will insure permanency of conversion.

2—THE EMOTIONAL TENDENCY OF CATHOLIC NEGROES

The Negro has often been criticized for his emotionalism, and the Negro preacher has been roundly scored for appealing to it in his sermons, but it has been seriously questioned if the bulk of the race is prepared for anything else. While there are many Negroes, particularly among the better educated class, who can appreciate an intellectual sermon, there are few congregations composed of such. Even among colored Catholics who have been trained to some appreciation for a religion of the spirit, the response at times is disheartening. A powerful voice and sweeping gesticulations will most certainly result in the commendation that, "Father sure is a most powerful preacher"; whereas a simple and un-

---

[1] *Ibid.*, p. 165.

affected explanation of some elementary Catholic doctrine will invariably produce a "sonorous" apathy. Yet, the missioner who would build up a congregation with some stability in the Faith must lay a doctrinal foundation. It is one thing to make colored converts, quite another to make colored Catholics. While a mission with all its "revival" adjuncts has the necessary emotional appeal, the long weeks of instruction classes, insistence on the fulfilment of the religious obligations of attendance at Mass, Confession, and Communion, etc., require a moral stamina which is far above the requirements of more comfortable "religions."

On the other hand, it must be said that when well instructed, Negroes make loyal Catholics and compare very favorably with other Catholics as to quality. Among them, as among all congregations, there are the good, indifferent, and bad; their classification depending to a considerable extent on their environment and the interest taken in them. When properly instructed the colored people generally take a livelier interest in things Catholic than do most white people, and remarkable examples of attachment to the Faith are not rare among them.

While it is true that the Catholic Church with its vestments, candles, pictures, and ceremonial has all the material equipment to reach the soul of the Negro through the senses, at the same time, the organization of the Catholic Church as we know it in this country is such that the members of the congregation are assigned a passive part in the service and very little, if any, voice in the management of parish affairs. Congregational singing has been found to help, but it is not an all-sufficient vent for the suppressed emotions of the average Negro. Forced to assume a place of inferiority during his week's work in the world, compelled by necessity to contain himself even under provocation, always "held down," what the Negro seeks most in his religion experience is relief from pent-up emotional strain. It is this appeal to the emotions which makes the Negro churches and meetings so dear to the heart of the colored man; the church is the one place where he can pour out his soul and revel in the unchecked flow of feeling and sentiment. The Negro members of the Catholic

Church, on the contrary, hear but do not shout, see and reflect, and carry from the services a dignity and restraint which decidedly increase their worth—but such passivity is hard on the instinct for action. Unquestionably, a religion such as that found in the Catholic Church is of incalculable worth in the uplift of the Negro race: it teaches that emotional restraint so necessary for advancement be it material or spiritual; but at the same time, it must be recognized that to the non-Catholic Negro this religious decorum is not exactly an inducement to favorable consideration of the claims of the Catholic Church.

3.—LACK OF SOCIAL LIFE IN THE CHURCH

Besides the difficulties which arise from the disposition of the Negro to view religion as an emotional experience, there are also the practical difficulties which arise from his regarding the church as a social center and religion as a factor in his social life. The Negro does not easily perceive the distinction between the religious and the social phases of religion, and frequently he merges their identities. In the Catholic Church religion is primarily a matter of worship, at least so far as attendance at church services is concerned. In Negro churches, as we have seen, religious worship is frequently subordinated to the social. To the average white Catholic attendance at church services is a matter of conscience: there is little or no lingering at the church door after services; and if there be any social function held in connection with the church, it is only as an incidental to parish life. To the Negro, on the other hand, attendance at church services is more than a mere religious duty—it is frequently the only opportunity he has for social contact with most of his friends.

Perhaps the nearest approach to the social religion of the Negro is that of rural Catholics in sparsely settled districts. Such Catholics, cut off as they are from ordinary social intercourse with one another, find weekly attendance at Mass an opportunity for friendly gathering and mutual intercourse. While frequently what little social life rural Catholics have is centered around the church, still there is always a clear line of demarcation between the religious and the social. Catholics have been taught so to regard their religion, whereas the Negro has always been so situated that church to him frequently connotes little more than a meeting place.

Realizing the need of some social life in their missions, Catholic priests laboring for the welfare of the colored people strive to supply it in the form of frequent social affairs. These affairs serve as occasions for friendly contact in places where a more pretentious social club is out of the question. Some of the more prosperous missions have such Catholic clubs; as a rule, however, the financial outlay which these ventures entail forces the pastor to be satisfied with the ordinary parish societies and sodalities. Supervised dances go a long way towards solving the social problem of the missions. Under the watchful eye of pastor and omnipresent "committee," young couples are brought together by the appeal of a common pastime. Besides the pecuniary advantages of such occasional dances, no insignificant benefit is derived therefrom in that Catholic marriages are thus fostered. Practically, however, the only frequent occasion which the missioner has at his command for social intercourse with his parishioners is the few minutes spent in exchanging words of greeting with them on the church steps after the Sunday services; and even this opportunity must be curtailed in the larger city churches because of the closeness with which one Mass follows another.

On the whole, it cannot be said that there is anything in the Catholic religion as such which favors the demands of the Negro for a social religion. This demand must be met in the parish activities which in turn depend to a considerable extent on the resourcefulnes and ingenuity of the missioner. Even at its best, such resourcefulness is a variable quantity.

4.—SECRET SOCIETIES

We are told that secret societies are a hindrance to conversions. Doubtless this is frequently the case, but it is by no means so frequent as might be imagined. The number

of those who give up membership in secret societies as a condition precedent to reception into the Church is as great,
if not greater, than of those who are unwilling to do so.
Furthermore, we must not think that all Negroes belong to
forbidden societies. It is perfectly true that there is a fond-
ness for the gaudy trappings of a great diversity of benevolent
societies and social organizations, but most Negroes are content with local societies or country-wide organizations which
in no way affect religion. While in some sections of the
mission field proscribed secret societies have a considerable
following among the colored, in general the number who are
unwilling to sacrifice membership in distinctly non-Catholic
and condemned societies is comparatively small. It must be
said that we have had too few opportunities for forming a
conclusive judgment in the matter. Bitterness and prejudice
against the Church might be a better explanation. How this
ill will towards the Church is to be contravened is a question
perplexing the entire Church in the United States, not merely
those engaged in the work of the Colored Missions. Ways
and means must be found for the enlightenment of all who
misunderstand and, consequently, dislike the Church. When
found, the remedies will apply equally to all races.

5.—Mixed Marriages

To the claim that mixed marriages are an obstacle to a
more rapid conversion of Negroes to the Catholic Church,
it is to be observed that such marriages are to be regarded
rather as cause of defection from the Church. The difficulty
is not so much of winning the non-Catholic partner over to
the Faith, as it is of saving the Catholic party to the Church.
The question more properly belongs to "leakage from the
Church," and will be discussed presently.

On the other hand, it cannot be denied that illegitimate
unions frequently prevent otherwise well-disposed persons
from being received into the Church. Marital entanglements
inconsistent with the demands of Catholic morality are frequent enough in the experience of any missionary.

6.—CLASS DISTINCTIONS WITHIN THE RACE

Another internal difficulty which confronts the missioner to the Negro is the existence of classes within the race. To the casual observer the colored people of the United States form but one homogeneous group. The actual condition is quite different. In a general way, it may be said that there are at least two great distinctions within the race: that based on culture and economic independence, and that of blood (including all those who may roughly be classed at mulattoes). Foremost in the first group is the "talented tenth," representing the best culture that is in the race. Naturally, this group resents inclusion with the mass of colored people, who are considered inferior. Because of the peculiar social environment in which they find themselves (and which touches this highest class at most points and tells upon them most decisively), they live a life apart from the rest of the race, have their own social life, their own churches, neighborhoods, and clubs; they have their own social difficulties, too, differing from those of other classes and from those of the whites of a corresponding class. By mental attitude, moral standards, and economic status, they stand a group apart from the rest of the race, separated by a chasm as wide as that between themselves and the white race.

Closely allied with this group, although not of it in the social sense, is that large group of colored people who resent anything which even remotely smacks of segregation; they fight against churches for the exclusive use of their people, and prefer to go to no church at all in the event that they are unable to attend a church used by white people. They adhere to the principle that because the Catholic Church teaches there is no distinction between its members so far as it is concerned, it has, therefore, no right to acquiese to prevailing social conditions by the establishment of race churches. So far as this class is concerned, although Catholic in name, rather than submit to what they conceive to be segregation, they would prefer to see prevailing conditions which drove thousands of their brethren out of the Church.

Concerning the mulatto class, estimated as forming one-fifth to one-third of the total Negro population, it must be said that they form an important element within the race. They, too, have their peculiar social difficulties and problems. In many cases this class overlaps the cultural group, for: "There is seldom a sharply marked separation on the basis of color alone. It is rather that there is a high percentage of mulattoes in certain social classes and occupational groups and a preponderance of the unmixed Negro type in the others. In general, the economically prosperous, the socially prominent, and the educated, intellectual, and professional groups are chiefly mulatto, while the poor, ignorant, religious, and socially disadvantaged classes show relatively little trace of white admixture." [1]

Since the mulattoes, generally speaking, have been the superior individuals of the race, the group had, and still has, a great cultural advantage over the unmixed Negroes. In the present day they have as a group more education, more property, more self-consciousness and self-respect. Two states of mind are discernible in this group. To one belong those mulattoes who accept identification with the Negro race. They have developed a personal life organization within the traditional and institutional restrictions, ceasing to struggle against segregation. Within the race they have an assured position. "Their white ancestry gives them a certain prestige, and the tradition of mulatto superiority gives a self-confidence rare in the Negro group. They form the small aristocracy and are the local leaders of the masses." [2] The other group is characterized by a point of view which makes them unable and unwilling to accept classification with the backward group as inevitable; hence, they will not accommodate themselves to the accepted social rules, but hold themselves apart from and superior to the Negroes as such. The intolerant edict of the majority prevents their being white, and their own personal ideals and aspirations prevent their being black. Therein lies their tragedy.

To the missioner working on the Colored Missions these groups frequently present most intricate problems. Realiz-

---

[1] *The American Negro;* Annals of the American Academy, p. 37.
[2] *Ibid.,* p. 40.

ing that the Catholic Church recognizes no distinction as to color or caste, and that he is sent to save the souls of all men, the missioner must tactfully steer his bark through the maelstroms of social feuds which are brought over into the church. He must scrupulously refrain from seeming to favor one group rather than the other, lest he injure the cause for which he is working. Theoretically, he may know what to do; practically, he is frequently at a loss as to how to compose the different elements into a peaceful flock led by one shepherd. In the doctrines of the Church he has the means to accomplish this fusion, but in the social animosities which have their sources outside the church he has his difficulties.

7.—RACE CONSCIOUSNESS

Besides affecting the various groups within the race, race consciousness, or consciousness of kind, affects the race as a whole. Consciousness of kind binds people of like race into a sympathetic union; at the same time, it awakens in them a social aversion to people of a different race. Psychologists regard this consciousness of kind as the most fundamental of sociological facts. Ray Stannard Baker takes cognizance of this in *Following the Colour Line*. He writes: "One of the natural and inevitable results of the effort of the white man to set the Negro off, as a race, by himself, is to awaken in him a new consciousness—a sort of racial consciousness. It drives the Negroes together for defense and offense. Many able Negroes, some largely of white blood, cut off from all opportunity of success in the greater life of the white man, become of necessity leaders of their own people. And one of their chief efforts consists in urging Negroes to work together and to stand together. In this way they are only developing the instinct of defense against the white man which has always been latent in the race. This instinct exhibits itself in the way in which the mass of Negroes sometimes refuse to turn over a criminal of their colour to white justice . . . I don't know how many Southern people have told me in different ways of how extremely difficult it is to get at the real feeling of the Negro, to make him tell what goes on in his clubs and his churches or his innumerable societies." [1]

The priests laboring on the Colored Missions have experienced difficulties arising from this "consciousness of kind." Their chances of success are very hopeful if they give their whole time and devotion to the Negroes, but no divided allegiance must be theirs if they would do well the work committed to their care. This demand of exclusive devotion by the colored people—an imperative demand for undivided allegiance to their cause—necessitates the missioner to a voluntary ostracism from his own kind. Occasionally, a missioner has found to his chagrin that even a small social intermingling wich white friends has worked his undoing. One of the most successful missioners among the colored people has admitted that during fifteen years he had entered the homes of but three white families.

This "consciousness of kind" has engendered a "chip-on-the-shoulder" attitude. Developed, no doubt, by historical grievances, and perpetuated even in the face of earnest efforts to render racial benefits, it is an argument in favor of race clergy. Unquestionably, priests of their own race could understand better the thoughts of their own people and could sympathize more readily with their grievances. This does not mean that white priests working among the Negroes cannot understand or sympathize with them; the success which has rewarded the consecrated services of white missioners in the Colored Harvest is ample testimony to the contrary. But it does mean a recognition of the fact that the social segregation of white and black in the United States has driven the Negroes "together for defense and offense." For long has the Negro been defensively secretive. Slavery made him that. "In the past the instinct was passive and defensive; but with growing education and intelligent leadership it is rapidly becoming conscious, self-directive and offensive." [2] And right here lies an important difficulty in the work of the Colored Missions.

Perhaps a consequence of this "race consciousness" is the apparent tendency of Negro Catholics to protest to higher

---

[1] p. 38.
[2] Baker, op. cit., p. 39.

authorities, frequently without justification. Whether this tendency is an inheritance of a once needed racial defense immediately necessitated by conditions following the acquisition of freedom, or a disposition acquired by reason of their previous participation in the affairs of Negro non-Catholic church government, the fact is that protests are written to higher authorities upon the least provocation, real or imagined. So small a reason as a difference of opinion over the management of a parish society has given occasion for more than one protest to the powers that be. While the principle of right of appeal to higher authority is always to be admitted, the abuse of the privilege has not infrequently been the source of annoyance, if not of positive harm, for most frequently these protests are made under the form of anonymity, with subsequent injustice to a zealous missioner properly offering himself in consecrated service.

8.—IRREGULARITY IN CHURCH ATTENDANCE

A difficulty common to both whites and colored, but more pronounced with the latter, is that of irregularity in church attendance and practices. This would seem to be a habit brought over from former church affiliation. In non-Catholic Churches there is no obligation to attend Sunday services with unfailing regularity: attendance is a matter of inclination. In the Catholic Church, on the contrary, weekly attendance at Sunday Mass is of grave obligation. Yet, flimsiest reasons are offered in excuse for non-attendance. A picnic or a light rain shower will be sufficient cause to reduce by half attendance at Sunday Mass. We are not unaware of the many Catholic Negroes who are most scrupulous in their observance of the laws of the Church, nor are we unaware of the many difficulties which may present themselves to rural Catholics who would be considerably inconvenienced were they to attend regularly; but even when due allowance is made for legitimate non-attendance, the number of those who absent themselves for no reason other than slight inconvenience or a minor indisposition is abnormally large. Of course, the economic status of Negroes in general is still that of service; early and long hours of work unquestionably have their effect on attendance at Mass, Confession, and Communion. But even where the hours of service are so arranged that few would be seriously inconvenienced, carelessness in the fulfilment of serious religious obligations is often quite marked.

Another reason for haphazard attendance at church services is personal attitude towards the pastor: freely deciding church obligations on the basis of like or dislike for the priest. While not peculiar to the Negro, in his case this disposition has been intensified perhaps by his former church affiliation. In non-Catholic churches for Negroes the personality of the preacher is a deciding factor in the size of the congregation. If the minister of one church is not to a member's liking, it is a simple matter to join another church. In the Catholic concept of things, on the contrary, the personality of the priest is a very minor consideration. Of course, all priests strive to be all things to all men; yet, missioners have been known to fail in holding their people despite the fact that they were excellent priests.

The difficulties which we have noted in the preceding pages, while not in themselves serious, are undoubtedly obstacles in the way of a more numerous colored membership in the Catholic Church. The passing of a few generations will likely find the Negroes a more thoroughly Catholic-minded people. Considering the previous lack of training of colored Catholics in general, bringing as they do their non-Catholic customs and notions with them into the Church, one cannot help but feel that much has been accomplised in the way of laying a solid foundation for greater future success. If the number of colored Catholics is not so large as some would wish, it must not be forgotten that the colored Catholics of today are of a type far superior to that of a generation ago. The mission equipment is now of a type better suited than that of a few decades ago to produce intelligent Catholics able to give a reason for that faith which is in them. On the whole, it must be said that the present is bright and the future auspicious.

CHAPTER XX

DEFECTIONS FROM THE CHURCH

Thus far we have been discussing the various obstacles which militate against Catholic success in winning converts among the Negroes in the United States. A correlative question is that of defection, or "leakage," among colored Catholics. It might properly be asked: is the difficulty so much that of making converts as it is of holding the Negroes already Catholic? In a sense, the problem of defection from the Church might be considered as of even more importance than convert making, for unquestionably the first duty of a mother is towards those of the household. In discussing the question of leakage much that has already been said must again be alluded to, even at the expense of tiring the reader, for basically the conditions affecting both questions are the same.

1.—LEAKAGE

A. Existence

Of the fact of leakage there can be no doubt, either in the past or in the present. That in the past many Catholic Negroes were lost to the Church is evident from the amount of reclamation work now being done in certain sections of the South. In one section of Louisiana alone, for instance, it was reported that as many as 65,000 fell away from the fold in the years immediately following the Civil War.[1] In some parts of the South where at one time the majority of Negroes were members of the Catholic Church today a scattered handful is all that claims allegiance to it.

That there is some leakage going on even at this late date of organized missionary activity would also seem to be true, although the evidence supporting the conclusion is less indicative of complete loss than of temporary aberration due

---

[1] *Colored Harvest*, Oct., 1892, p. 3; *vide, infra*, p. 42.

to unsettled conditions. When one studies the statistics of certain parishes and missions which during the past two decades have reported converts sufficient in number to double the present membership, one must perforce admit some leakage. Unsettled conditions due to the recent migration together with a shifting of local centers of Negro population are the main explanations of such statistical losses. Whether or not such losses are absolute is difficult to state definitely, since the evidence at hand would seem to indicate that many Catholic Negroes are finding places in white churches where the color of members is not reported. On the other hand, evidence may be adduced to show that many Negroes who should belong to the Catholic Church are affiliating with non-Catholic sects or attending no church at all.

B. Extent

The extent of defection of Catholic Negroes from the Church in the past cannot be measured with exactness because of the absence of anything like satisfactory statistics with which to make accurate comparisons. The only statistics available for the past are those of the Commission for the Catholic Missions Among Negroes and Indians. A study of the figures contained in the reports of the Commission shows that, excepting those of very recent years, their accuracy is open to serious doubt. As a matter of fact, until recent years there was no way of knowing with an assurance of even approximate correctness the number of Catholic Negroes in any diocese, much less in the United States. A census was out of the question for the reason that the work was unorganized. We can be certain of only one fact: in the past there has been a large defection of Catholic Negroes from the Church. This fact is attested to by the reclamation work being done by missioners. Beyond a mere statement of the fact, however, we may not go with safety.

2.—CAUSES—Past

First among the past causes of defection of Catholic Negroes from the Church must be rated the general feeling of irresponsibility which followed the granting of liberty to the millions of bondmen. In the years following the emancipation the interests of the Church and religion found little place in the confusion of the new-found freedom. Unprepared for the responsibilities of self-government and self-direction which were suddenly thrust upon him, the Negro was engulfed in a sea of conflicting emotions which perforce must run riot until, in the general plan of reconstruction, religious influences should re-assert themselves and bring out of spiritual chaos some semblance of order, understanding, and morality.

Real religion played little part in Negro life prior to the emancipation. Despite the fact that in many instances Catholic masters watched over the religious interest of their slaves, the majority of Catholic slaves were Catholic in little more than name. Whatever they may have been quantitatively, qualitatively their religion had few of the deeply rooted principles which alone can influence the entire life of a man. Those who were well grounded in the truths of the Faith, and consequently dominated by sound moral principles, were comparatively few, and almost to a man remained loyal through all the turmoil of war and reconstruction.

Call it what we will, a natural inclination to religion, a craving for the mysterious, a groping after anything that held out a ray of hope for ultimate freedom, an emotionalism that gave solace in the suffering and bitterness of bondage, or things similar, could have no stability unless grounded upon faith which meant more than formal regeneration in the laver of Baptism. In the religion of the slave, as we have alluded to elsewhere, this faith, except in rare instances, was lacking. And when freedom gave a fuller outlet for unrestrained emotion expressive of joy in release from servitude, no longer did the groping after freedom, no longer did the prayer, the tear, or the sigh in fettered existence serve as a guiding star towards things of the spirit. Material comfort and the means to attain it became the motivating force in the lives of the Negroes; the Church was relegated to a relatively low place in the scheme of his daily life.

Free as their former masters from whom they had taken their religion, the Negroes could now go whither they chose.

Especially attractive to them were the services of the evangelical sects in which the old emotionalism could find vent in new expression. How many resented the restraints of the Catholic Church and quitted its portals never to return it is not possible to say. That the number was large must be admitted, for the Church, with its doctrinal system and moral code, could not have the drawing power of those less formal sects with their emotional unrestraint, their lack of any definite system of dogmatic teaching, and their easy-going rules of conduct. Nor were such sects slow to see the oportunity and to seize upon it. When the Catholic Church, hampered as it was at the time, did finally come into a position where it could do something positive for the Negro, it was too late—the damage had already been done. Men and means had been pouring in from every side to get and to hold a large membership in the evangelical sects. Came too the colored minister and preacher, generally uneducated, occasionally with a smattering of knowledge, rarely with a real education; yet, all found ready success because they were of one blood with their congregations and knew best how to play upon their minds, and their hearts, and their prejudices.

Meanwhile, what could the Catholic Church do to hold its Negro members? We know how few Catholics there were in the South, the internal difficulties which the Church was experiencing, and the handful of priests which the southern Hierarchy could command—insufficient to care properly for their regular charges much less the colored freedmen. The task of the clergy became increasingly difficult after the war because of the impoverished condition of the South; and among the poorest of the poor were the Catholics. With the possible exception of Louisiana, the Church in the southern states was in sore straits. Where before it might count on Catholic masters to hold the Negroes to the practice of their religious duties, now even Catholics, living among the charred embers of an aristocratic past, ate the bread of the Gospel with the ashes of hate. Before the Proclamation the law alone drew a line between the races; now, with the birth of freedom, there was drawn in the hearts of the South a line deeper and deadlier than ever a pen could trace.

Outstanding were the efforts of the few priests for the welfare of the Negro at this time; their light seems all the brighter to us now because it shone in stygian darkness. Unfortunately, in cannot be said of all the priests of the South that they were zealous with a zeal that looks not to color. Living in the South, some had, consciously or otherwise, imbibed the spirit of the South. At any rate, the effort put forth was not commensurate with the needs of a people suddenly thrust upon their own resources and ready to grasp at anything which even remotely seemed likely to add to their material well-being.

Finally, came priests to labor for the Negro alone. From 1871 to 1900 their number was few and their best efforts seemed barren of results, if we are to measure success by statistics. Cold figures, however, do not record the many who were brought back to the Church by these pioneer missioners. Feeling the warmth of the welcome extended to them by these missioners who were all things to all men, untold numbers of straying sheep returned to the Fold. On the minds of others, however, it could not be impressed that the Church was not responsible for existing conditions. They saw only the fact and the humiliation—they were lost to the Church forever.

3.—CAUSES—*Present*

A—*Where no special priests are assigned to the Negroes*

Where there are no special priests assigned to the care of Catholic Negroes, they must attend local white churches. In the North, where the number of Catholic Negroes is relatively small and scattered, there is no difficulty. In the South, where the church has been built and maintained by the whites, the Negroes are segregated in what is usually an inadequate number of rear pews, or in the gallery. It is not now our purpose to discuss the morality of this arrangement, [1] but the results of the practice are such as to favor defection, particularly of those who are more sensitive to the implied humiliation of in-

---

[1] cf. Gilligan, S.T.D., Rev. Francis, *The Morality of the Color Line*, pp. 208-210.

feriority. That the harm is not lightly to be estimated is evident from the words of the Rev. Joseph Eckert, S.V.D., who feels the baneful influence of such segregation as far north as Chicago. "Often I have heard from leading and highly educated Negroes in Chicago, as answer to my well-meant invitations to come to our services: 'We Negroes are not wanted in the Catholic Church.' Then they prove their statement by pointing out the condition of segregation of both races in the churches and schools of the South; they cite numerous instances where, even in the North, Catholic Negroes are constantly being snubbed, by both clergy and laity, by being frankly told 'go to their own church,' though 'their own church' may be far distant; where they are directed to seats on the side of the church; or where people refuse to join with them before the communion rail." [1] In previous pages we have sufficiently discussed the enormous evils arising from "jim crowism" in the Catholic Church, and while instances could be multiplied indefinitely, there is no need now to labor the question. There can be little doubt that where no priest is specially charged with the care of the Catholic Negroes the practice of segregation is a great leak in the walls of the Catholic Church.

B—Where special priests are assigned

Where there are priests devoting their whole time and energy to the welfare of the Catholic Negroes it is to be expected that defections from the Church will be reduced to a minimum.

(a) Migration

First among the root-causes of leakage from the churches of the Colored Missions must be rated the migrations which occurred between the years 1913 and 1923. These mass movements stirred the missions to their very depths; they tore unnumbered families from old and secure moorings and cast them into strange and troubled waters. While it is evident from the otherwise inexplicable accretions to some missions, particularly those of the North and West, that many of

---

[1] *The White Harvest*, edited by Rev. J. A. O'Brien, Ph.D., p. 97.

these migrants found a haven in the Catholic churches of the cities to which they went, it is equally certain that a vast number floundered about and were eventually engulfed in muddy waters. It is no exaggeration to say that in many cities where there were no special facilities to handle the influx of Catholic Negroes during the migrations a majority, taking with them the inherited traditions of the South, drifted into what they thought to be more welcome coves of denominational churches for their own kind.

A letter from a priest in the West throws some interesting light on what became of many Catholic migrants. In a city with a colored population of more than fifty thousand, this missioner began a mission in the hope of saving to the Church the Catholic Negroes who had come to the city. He writes: "The start was very hard for several reasons peculiar to the colored people here, but especially since some did not want a church or a priest. So-called representative Catholics from a distinctly Catholic section of the South were my worst enemies. The figures I give in the accompanying questionnaire represent active church members; viz, people who have expressed their will to worship in my church, who attend services habitually, and who shoulder the financial obligations. But these people do not constitute the whole Catholic colored population of the city. I have a list of thirty-eight colored families before me. Some live within a stone's throw of the church. I visited them time and time again, yet they remain unresponsive to all advances. There are at least fifty families who are opposed to a colored church and who attend other churches more or less regularly. Then there is a large floating population of which no one can keep trace. Few of them go to Church. Finally, there is a huge crowd of fallen-away Catholics. I use the word "huge" purposely, because the number of these unfortunates coming to my attention increases daily. Right on my street are six families; all my endeavors to bring them back are useless. These one-time Catholics join Baptist and Methodist churches, and a few the Episcopal, but the greater number have no religious affiliation whatsoever. The reason for this wholesale apostasy is not lack of sympathy for the Negro. First, all coming here are not desirable; too many come here because they had to leave home for one reason or another. Others come here through desire to gain more money, and they have no time for religion; this is particularly true of those who are better off in this world's goods. Finally, among some it would seem to be a mark of distinction to change their religion when leaving the South, just like shedding the garment of servitude. They glory in the fact of having been leaders in their home parishes (mostly a fact), and then gaily join any church in town; or if some scruple holds them back, they go occasionally (two or three times a year) to some other Catholic Church, but with no reception of the Sacraments." If such conditions prevail in a city where at least one priest is giving his whole time to the care of Catholic Negroes, what must be the sad state of affairs where no attention is given them?

(b) *Environment*

Perhaps the two local causes most productive of defection of Catholic Negroes from the Church are harmful environment and mixed marriages. Elsewhere we have noted the harmful effects of the usual environment in which the Negro must live. Forced to breathe in an atmosphere more deadly to spiritual than to physical welfare, his every step dogged by dangers kept far from the feet of the white man, the marvel is not that so many stray from the Mother of Nations as that so many hold fast to the things that are taught them.

(c) *Mixed Marriages*

As regards the effect of mixed marriages upon the chances of the Catholic Negro for ultimate perseverance, there is no doubt in the minds of any priest, much less those engaged in the work of the Colored Missions, that many mixed marriages result in indifference to religion and eventual loss of faith. That the cause given in so many applications for dispensations for mixed marriages is "periculum matrimonii coram praecone" is ample evidence that ecclesiastical authority views with alarm the danger of many incurring the excommunication attached to such a procedure. At the same time, it is evident that strength of faith is lacking in just so many cases as are so dispensed. We might here remark that the pre-nuptial promises, which are always demanded in such cases, usually have little weight among the Negroes once the marriage has taken place.

The number of converts made through mixed marriages is negligible, while the number of Catholic Negroes who are lost to the Faith by such unions is a cause of great concern to the missioners. Little or nothing can be done by way of remedy if one considers the relative disproportion between Catholic and non-Catholic Negroes. That the situation is not exaggerated may be seen from the annual reports of the missions in some of which there has not been a straight Catholic marriage for six or seven years. When, over a period of ten years, the number of Catholic marriages in an average of 75 missions was 2,528, as compared with 5,020 mixed marriages, one realizes the seriousness of the problem.

If thought be given to the prevailing utter disregard for any marriage ceremony at all, the situation becomes more serious. We quote here an excerpt from the letter of a missioner in a presumably Catholic state. The letter reads: "When I came here I found 115 illegitimate unions out of 150 families. Since then, several of my good Catholic families have migrated to Texas. To make matters worse, the list of illegitimate unions has gone up to 130. My mission is listed for 1,000 Catholics; yet, the fact of the matter is that there are only about 100 who might be called 'pretty good.' Of course my work here is one of reclamation. Materially, I have made good progress; spiritually, I cannot say the same. I find that nothing can be done with the older generation; my hope is with the younger element. If I can only get them to enter Catholic unions, I may be able to save them as well as reclaim others. At the present rate of illegitimate unions, however, this mission has a long, hard road to travel." The conditions described in the letter are, no doubt, extreme, although they are known to be true of the particular mission.[1]

---

[1] cf. also The White Harvest, op. cit., pp. 97, 98.

(d) Insufficient Instruction

It has been said that did the priests on the Colored Missions sufficiently instruct prospective converts their defection would not be so likely. While in isolated cases it cannot be denied that blame for hasty or insufficient instruction may be laid at the door of the priest, the consensus of opinion among those who should know is that such reprehensible methods are too rare to deserve serious consideration. At a recent conference of missioners it was decided that weekly (in some cases twice weekly) instructions for a period of six months was the minimum of instruction to be given. Such was the practice of all the Fathers present. Even where insufficient instruction is the probable cause of future defection, in most instances the missioner can be absolved from blame. Two facts must be borne in mind: that instructing converts is only one of the manifold and multiplex duties of the missioner (not the least of which is to raise funds sufficient to keep open the mission) and that the average mission has only one priest. If, as is generally true, the greater part of the missioner's time must be spent in devising ways and means to secure a bare sufficiency to maintain the mission, while not neglecting the routine work connected with its management, it is hardly cause for blame if on occasion he finds that human limitations make imperative a curtailment of the time spent in instructing converts.

Might not such a busy missioner protract the period of instruction? He could, and many do. Experience, on the other hand, has shown that the average Negro lacks the stability and pertinacity necessary to make such a plan workable. Is it not preferable to losing the convert that he be given the essentials and received into the Church with the hope, even remote, that as time goes on he will learn more about the truths of religion and get a better appreciation of the workings of divine grace?

Nor must it be forgotten that lack of even rudimentary education frequently renders it difficult for the convert to grasp elementary and fundamental truths. Lack of facility of comprehension is not to be imputed to their fault, and it is not the mind of the Church that when the heart is strong but the head slow the arm of God should be shortened.

While the facts in the case do not warrant a blanket exoneration from blame of all missioners, neither do they justify a wholesale indictment. The evidence at hand would indicate that lack of sufficient instruction of prospective converts as a cause of their subsequent defection must be considered as exceptional, and even then not often a contributing factor of major importance.

4.—Inefficiency in Schools

The schools of today hold the promise of tomorrow. If the Catholic colored child is well grounded in his religion and trained to walk in the way of Catholic moral practices, there is every hope for his ultimate perseverance. While many of the schools of the Colored Missions are equal, if not superior, to the public schools for colored children, there are some which have not been able to meet the accepted standard. Beset by financial difficulties which even an abundance of good will cannot overcome, they are shaping themselves to desired perfection as rapidly as is possible. While such schools may be still far from the acme of perfection, as compared with the public schools under the same conditions they are not one wit inferior.

The importance of the school in the question of defection is not so much that of equipment as of policy. The charge may be formulated thus: Non-Catholic children are permitted to so over-crowd our limited school facilities as to render inefficient the work of the sisters and so prepare the way for subsequent defection of the Catholic children. As formulated, the objection is invalid because it is based upon two erroneous assumptions; viz, that the normal conditions of Catholic schools for Negroes is such as to render the teacher inefficient, and that even an over-crowded school is necessarily a preliminary to defection.

A study of school statistics reveals the fact that in the schools of the Colored Missions (1928) the average load per teacher was 31.3 pupils. In the public school system (white and colored) the ratio of the number of pupils to the number of teachers in the elementary and secondary schools was 28.7;[1] in elementary and secondary private and parochial schools, 31.9;[2] and in elementary and secondary public schools for colored (1926) the load was 33 pupils.[3] These figures dispose of the objection that the teachers in the Catholic schools for colored children are reduced to inefficiency by overloading.

Does the acceptance of numerous non-Catholic children in the schools of the missions make for subsequent defection from the Church? In other words, if the sisters concentrated their efforts on their Catholic charges to the exclusion of non-Catholic children would the Catholic colored child have better promise of ultimate perseverance? All things being equal, there can be no doubt that any child who receives more personal attention during the years of childhood has a better chance for ultimate perseverence than has a child who must share his opportunities with many others. But on the Colored Missions all things are not equal. Who can measure the eighteen or nineteen hours of daily influence exerted by the child's home life, environment, and (later, and most frequently) mixed marriage against the transient five or six hours of influnce which the sister exerts on her charges, and that, for the majority of the children, over a period varying from four to eight years only? It is true that the teacher's influence is exerted over the plastic years of the early life, but it must not be forgotten that, except where high school facilities are available, that influence is terminated at the very age when new and strange experiences beset the feet that hitherto have walked only in the paths of childish innocence.

As against this problematical degree of safety which more personal attention during the years spent in the grade schools might add to future chances of ultimate perseverance, there are the unquestioned advantages of experience to be weighed and considered. It is on the school that missionary organizations have learned to base their prime hopes for the upbuild-

---

[1] *Biennial Survey of Education*, 1924-1926, p. 358.
[2] *Ibid.*, pp. 615, 616.
[3] *Ibid.*, p. 162.

ing of a mission. Knowing full well that the ways of God are not the ways of men, who are they to close the doors of their school to the insistent clamor of non-Catholic parents who seek for their children the advantages of the sister's loving devotion? If non-Catholic parents see in the religious air of the mission school a "something" which they sense is lacking in the public schools, shall the missioner stand in the way of what he knows is the working of a Providence Who watches over even the sparrows of the air? Even supposing that the missioner does over-crowd his school in order to accommodate as many non-Catholic children as is possible, is he required to forego a positive good which experience has taught to result from such generosity in favor of a problematical good which the same experience has shown to be questionable?

Father Eckert, S.V.D., presents the case for the practice of admitting even numerous non-Catholic children to share in the advantages of our Catholic schools. He writes: "Our parish in Chicago began to take on new vigor and life when our efforts were concentrated on the school work. Today we have almost 900 children in our school. Half of them are non-Catholic children . . . Up to the present time this has met with no objection; the non-Catholic parents fully realize the intrinsic value of religious instruction for their children. . . . What are the results of our school work for convert making? We do not admit a child to Baptism unless he has made good in every way, and has obtained the written permission of his parents and the parents' promise that they will continue to send their children to our school in the future. Our lower grades are stocked with Protestant children, while in the higher grades there are more Catholic children; indeed, the last grade consists of Catholic children who were nursed in our Faith, from the first grade onward. These children are loyal and faithful in their religious duties, though they may be the only Catholics in their respective families.

"On the other hand, those children who do not join our Church during the school term—because their parents object, or because they have already been taken into a Protestant Church—retain a kindly feeling towards the Church. Later, when they are of age, these also usually join the Church.

Others again will visit our church regularly, even every Sunday, and contribute generously for church needs. Gradually the grace of God works its way with them also.

"Through the children we reach the children's parents. As has already been mentioned, many parents appreciate greatly the sacrifices and efforts of the sisters. They soon notice the good effects of the Catholic school-training upon the moral character and manners of their children. . . . The parents and their relatives, after a time, grow inquisitive concerning the Church. They occasionally accompany their children to our services. . . . I have found that this procedure causes a wholesome relationship to spring up, as it were, between the Church and the parents, resulting sometimes in the conversion of whole families." [1]

On the whole, it must be said that the present policy in force in the schools of the Colored Missions makes for the greatest good for the greatest number of souls.

5.—CONCLUSION

Finally, it should be noted that where missionary organizations may seem to be retaining certain small and unsuccessful missions at the expense of more fertile fields, it is not they who dictate policies in the various dioceses. When and where a mission is to be opened remains for the Ordinary of the diocese to say—missionary organizations are helpers, not dictators.

In conclusion, it must be said that against the work of the Colored Missions as it is now being carried on there is little room for criticism other than what might reasonably be made against any mission work, be it home or foreign, white, black, red, or yellow. Not even a work which bears the mark of divine approval is perfect so long as it is left to human hands to do it. The human element connotes imperfection. The errors and mistakes which may be imputed to the missioners are such as would inevitably occur in blazing a trail through any expanse as large and bewildering as the Colored Missions.

---

[1] *The White Harvest*, op. cit., pp. 102, 103.

Experience is teaching rapidly and mistakes are being corrected as quickly as circumstances permit. At the same time, not all the experience of the past generation of missionary pioneers in the Colored Missions will guarantee immunity from error to future generations—leakage will continue to flow from the Colored Missions just as it now does from well established white parishes.

CHAPTER XXI

CONCLUSION

1. GENERAL

Those who have not kept pace with the march of events in the past few decades are probably unaware that a new Negro has developed in our country—the "talented tenth," some are pleased to call this new type. The respect of the civilized world is challenged by the tremendous progress which he has made in industry and education, in art and creative literature, in social and cultural life, in ethical and moral standards. A new race pride is developing; memory of the tragedies of slavery which have made for an inferiority complex is being replaced by a pride in the ancient history of the race as well as in its present day accomplishments.

With new achievements comes a new and healthy race consciousness; the Negro is developing a spirit that frees itself from a provincial and subjective view of the race and is taking on a more scientific attitude. As H. W. Bond, of Fisk University, writes: "Race oppression accordingly comes to be a phenomenon to be studied and even to be laughed at, rather than a monstrous imposition calculated to stir one's soul to bitter anger." [1] In every department the song of the new Negro is one of progress.

The mass of Negroes, too, has made tremendous advances. In the past, agriculture was the forte of the Negro population; today it is becoming industrialized. Limitation of immigration which checked the flood of European unskilled laborers gave an opportunity long looked for, and the fleeing of conditions always felt intolerable resulted in the migration of thousands from the tenant cotton farms and the alleys of the South to the cities of the North and West. No longer may it be said the Negro is solely a "southern problem."

[1] *The American Negro;* Annals of the American Academy, p. 24.

Of recent years, it has been found necessary to reverse or even to discard old theories concerning the Negro; a new approach to the problem is not only desirable but imperative. Of course, this rearrangement of our ideas as to the proper "place" of the Negro gives a severe shock to our preconceived notions and considerably disorganizes our present missionary methods. On both sides of the "color-line," it is true, there are various types of agitators, all suffering from distortions; but while we Catholics are trying to collect our wits, a more aggressive Socialism is making strong bid for the allegiance of the Negro, particularly the more intelligent of the race. As the intelligent leaders go, so goes the mass.

In the past, the American Negro unquestioningly accepted religion as a panacea for healing abrasions caused by race friction. Religion was acceptable and welcome because, as a recent writer put it: "The thing he (the Negro) needs most is wise counsel, encouragement to work and find his place, and a solace and resignation which he can only find in the Christian religion, whose first virtue is humility." [1] The new Negro, however, refuses to keep "his place," he does not ask for solace, and he has no time for the virtue of humility. His tendency is to discard religion as a deadweight against progress. Dubois, a representative of the new type of Negro, writes accusingly: "This country professes loudly and blatantly a religion of mercy, humanity and sacrifice; we profess to regard all men as brothers, and teach that we should turn the other cheek to evil; and that all human distinctions, not based on individual character and desert, are false and wrong. Yet, at the mere presence of a colored face, again and again our whole moral fabric falls, fails and collapses, in simple matters of human intercourse, in larger matters of social service and in the very pews of the church itself." [2]

Small wonder that the more intellectual Negro is dissatisfied with religion. By the very token of his intelligence he should be dissatisfied with what for the most part he has known as religion. By the very same token of intelligence the Catholic Church is given opportunity to present to this

---

[1] Aswell, *Commonweal*, Nov. 21, 1928.
[2] *The American Negro;* Annals of the American Academy, p. 8.

new Negro, and through him to the Negro race, an intelligent religion—the religion of Jesus Christ as preserved intact and unvitiated by the Catholic Church alone. The Catholic Church is admirably fitted for just such mission: at once it is broad enough to accommodate the highest intelligence of the most learned and the simple faith of the unlettered; it is human enough in its ceremonial to appeal to the dramatic instincts of the emotional man, and, at the same time, it is rational enough in its theology to give satisfaction to the intellectual man.

It is not without significance that very few recent accounts of the Negro in relation to his Church make mention of the work of the Catholic Church. They assume that the Catholic Church has done nothing towards solving the problems of the race. Through whole pages of facts and figures one looks in vain for so much as even a single mention of the word "Catholic." This attitude is neither fair nor scholarly, yet it is indicative of the low regard, even disdain, in which the Catholic Church is held by many race leaders. Reasons of an extenuating nature are not wanting in explanation of our past inability to meet the situation adequately, but the present is time for action if we would remain faithful to the Divine command to teach *all* nations. Confident in its ability to offer to the American Negro a more hopeful message than Socialism or any of the existing emotional religions can give, the Catholic Church must find its place in this renascence of a race.

At the same time, it is felt that the Catholic Church is not achieving the degree of missionary success which might reasonably be expected. In making this statement, however, a sharp line of cleavage must be drawn between the missioners who are laboring on the Colored Missions and those whose duty it is to support them both morally and materially. There is probably no body of men in the whole world who have so persistently carried on in the face of at times almost insurmountable obstacles as have the priests engaged in mission work among the colored people of this country. Unheralded and unsung, they have gone into a section of the country which was born in prejudice and reared in suspicion of the Church. But much more heroism is required to work on in the face of obstacles which a little consideration from those whose duty it is to be considerate would overcome. All glory and honor is due the missioners who have borne the heats and burdens of the day in the Southland. When one considers the difficulties of the work, one must marvel that so much has been accomplished.

If, on the other hand, one considers what has been done in relation to what might have, and should have, been done, one perforce wonders at the degree of indifference usually exhibited towards this field of Catholic missionary activity. Here in our own country we have a vast mission field of 12,000,000 colored citizens; a field which is in danger of being overlooked in the wave of mission enthusiasm now sweeping America and tending to become a foreign mission movement exclusively. No less than an Archbishop decries this condition of indifference on the part of American Catholics. In a personal letter dated December 7, 1927, His Grace writes: "It is hard to believe that among the 12,000,000 American Negroes in the United States there should not be more than 200,000 Catholics. I do wish with my whole heart that in the near future all our organizations working on the Colored Missions will start a steady and lively 'agitation' in favor of these missions. Why should we send men and women and money to the foreign missions, and neglect 12,000,000 American citizens who are ready to come to us if we show them the way?"

It is to be fervently hoped that there will be no lessening of the foreign mission movement, for it has ever been the history of the Catholic Church that the light of the Faith is brought to a people by missioners from a foreign land. This was the case even in our own country of America, until recently a missionary country in the truest sense of the word. At the same time, as His Grace, Archbishop Curley, in the 1926 Appeal for the Negro and Indian Missions, rightly observed: "Whilst every priest and layman is expected by very reason of his faith to have a deep interest in the work of the foreign missions, it is evident that his interest in the missions at home should certainly not be less than his interest in the faith of far-away lands. Here in our own America we have not less than 12,000,000 of our colored people, of whom not quite a quarter of a million know Christ and His teaching in His Church."

More recently, the Denver Register (Colorado) quoted Bishop McCort, of Altoona, Pa., as having said that in his estimation American Catholic leaders will be held responsible by Almighty God because they have not done more for the conversion of the Negroes, which would be "A comparatively easy task if we provide the men and means necessary."

There was a time when it was considerate, and, perhaps, imperative, not to press mission problems on an American Catholic public that was struggling through days of parish and school organization on a large scale. Surely the days when such delicacy might be reasonably expected are nearly over for a large part of the country. The burden of the mission problem should be more evenly distributed, consequently, instead of falling on the relatively few as at present; it should be a part of normal Catholic functioning, and such is undoubtedly the mind of the American Hierarchy.

If we are to bring into the Catholic Church the millions of Negroes in the United States, the work must be the work of all American Catholics. While the actual mission work may be done by individuals and societies, all Catholics must have a share in it: hierarchy, clergy, and laity. No bishop can look upon it as being beyond his sphere and dismiss it with a prayer for success. As a member of the American Hierarchy, each Bishop is an integral part of that body to whom, as successors of the Apostles, the destinies of the Church in the United States have been entrusted; he is, therefore, bound to take an active interest in all apostolic works.

So, too, must every priest in the United States do his share. The fact that some may be affiliated with a particular diocese does not mean that all their priestly efforts must remain circumscribed by diocesan boundaries. They are priests, not of a diocesan church, but of the Catholic Church, and while their activities may be chiefly diocesan, even parochial, there should be no limits to the priestly zeal which yearns and sighs for souls in distress. Prayers for the missions, fostering of vocations for the missions, encouragement of their people to support both missionaries and missions—these are but a few of the many ways in which priests can help the Cause of Christ in the Colored Missions.

As for the laity: if it were not for their generosity there would be no Colored Missions. While recognizing the tremendous influence of their charity in the past, we have reason to fear for the future; not that their charity will be any less, but because organized mission movements are directing it into certain definite channels which would seem to be ignoring more or less the work of the Colored Missions. General mission collecting agencies of late have developed the mechanics of specialized advertising to a heretofore unheard of degree. One result of this development is that today the American people hear and know more about missions in general than ever before. On the other hand, missionary organizations which have been spending all their time and money on the actual work of the Colored Missions have been unable to meet the competition; consequently, they have been relegated to a comparatively insignificant place in the publicity campaign.

The priests laboring on the Colored Missions have known, too, the experience of hopes dashed to the ground because donations and vocations have been diverted elsewhere by individuals who did not fancy the Negro. So long as we have conditions such as these, so long do we lack the true spirit of Christ. If we are to be apostles in any sphere of the Church's activities, we must first grasp the Church's broadness: it cannot be circumscribed by racial or territorial lines—it is, and ever must be, the same for white and black and red and yellow, because Christ is catholic and rules over all men without distinction as to color or country.

While recognizing the past accomplishments and the future possibilities of the Colored Missions, we are not of the number of those who can see but one side of the question. In our admiration for certain deep-rooted religious traits of the Negro we do not care to close our eyes to the fact that with his religion are to be found mingled rank superstition and distorted ideas of even the most fundamental truths of Christianity. Nor can we go so far as some zealous men have gone and say that the race is entirely free from prejudice against the Church. The fact that priests laboring on the Colored Missions have had a relatively phenomenal success does not necessarily lead to the conclusion that the problem is solved any more than does the relatively little being done on the Colored Missions give ground for the assertion that the Catholic Church is doing nothing.

At the same time, we are thoroughly convinced that, as a recent correspondent put it: "I consider your task one of the most praiseworthy and beneficial that is being undertaken today in these United States, for the reason that the Negro question will become one of the most serious to be dealt with by the Catholic Church and the American people as the colored population increases in numbers. I have little knowledge of what the different Protestant sects are doing for the Negro, but if the leaven of Communism should permeate the minds of a large fraction of the Negro population, what do we face? There is but one weapon with which to fight Communism, and that is Christianity. Catholicity must show how the battle is to be fought, and your Society should be one of the most powerful weapons. In your attempt to save souls you are likewise building up a bulwark for the preservation of the Republic."

Of course, the emergence of a race from a status of slavery to a high degree of moral and intellectual enlightenment of necessity will be a slow process. The Church works slowly and orderly; not anarchistically overthrowing customs and institutions which however indefensible have their seat in tradition and a long course of social observance. The Mother of all peoples, in the winning of one the Church must be careful not to lose the other, for its first duty is to those already of the Faith.

While praying for a more positive interest on the part of many Catholics in the spiritual welfare of the Negroes, we cannot fail to take notice of a tendency on the part of some Catholic race leaders to exaggerate conditions of neglect under which the race labors. A certain element, for instance, would have us believe, and that in the face of facts, that the number of colored Catholics has decreased tremendously in late years. This is not so. In the first place, what statistics there were (those of the Commission for Negro and Indian Missions) would indicate a steady annual gain in the number of colored Catholics. Furthermore, opposed to the gratuitous assertion that the number of colored Catholics is steadily decreasing are the incontestable facts shown by the annual reports of societies engaged in colored missionary activity. With the development of the colored missionary movement during the past twenty-five years, these reports indicate an increasingly large number of baptisms and converts, not to mention the large number of reclamations. The Josephite Mission reports, for example, indicate that in the past fifteen years alone the Josephite Fathers have baptised 33,274, have had 10,319 converts, and now have in their charge congregations numbering 58,948, and schools enrolling 11,613 pupils, as opposed to 15,-284 and 3,855, respectively fifteen years ago. These figures would not indicate that the work is retrograding, and they represent the work of only one society in the field.

What is true is that immediately after the Civil War and before the inauguration of the concerted missionary movement in behalf of the Colored Missions, there would seem to have been a tremendous loss. Conditions having been as they were at the time, it could not have been otherwise. It is true also that, as we have previously suggested, the number of colored Catholics has not increased *relatively* to the increase in the total colored population of the United States. But there is a vast difference between the assertion that the Catholic Church is not making a reasonable progress and that the Catholic Church is actually losing ground. The first statement would seem to be true; the second is not true.

If a fair estimation is to be placed upon the work which the Catholic Church is doing for the Negroes in the United States, another fact which must be borne in mind is that such an estimation will not be based upon a comparison of Catholic membership with the membership of non-Catholic church bodies. When quantitatively the Catholic Church is compared with non-Catholic Negro bodies it must be remembered that qualitatively membership in the Catholic Church makes demands upon a member far greater than the demands of non-Catholic Negro churches.

The two paramount difficulties of work for the Negroes are lack of men and means—vocations to the missionary priesthood and means to train and support them. Realizing that the Catholic Church has made the worth of its priesthood, so far as that worth is answerable to human effort, depend upon seminaries, mission societies must have ample material means for developing in their subjects all the traits which should characterize men of priestly rank. A few years ago, St. Joseph's Society opened a new modern and well-equipped preparatory college at Newburgh, N. Y. More recently, the Society has erected a new St. Joseph's Seminary at the Catholic University, Washington, D. C. Other societies laboring on the Colored Missions have likewise been under the necessity of expanding their student-training facilities. These improvements are bound to have a decided effect upon the future success of the Colored Missions.

But of what use is even the most excellent material equipment if vocations are lacking? We believe that the sons and the daughters of the Church in the United States are brave enough to suffer the hardships of the Colored Missions for the benefit of the souls of their fellow citizens. We believe also that the Lord of the Vineyard would not fail to send laborers to carry on a work which gives promise of such great abundance. It is not expected that the South will produce many vocations for work among the Negroes; consequently, the burden is shifted to the North and the West. With practically all the missioners laboring in the South, anything like personal contact between the missioners and prospective candidates for the mission life is immediately eliminated. Ultimately, then, vocations to the work of the Colored Missions must depend upon the interest of northern and western clergy who can, if they will, encourage vocations to the work.

In some sections of the country the cry is not where shall we get priests, but what shall we do with them. Does it mean nothing to the clergy of such favored sections of the country that 12,000,000 American souls are wandering as sheep with-

out a shepherd? In the words of the Fathers of the Third
Plenary Council of Baltimore: "The Divine commission to
the Church stands forever: 'go, teach all nations, preach
the gospel to every creature,' and every one who desires the
salvation of souls should yearn for its fulfilment and consider
it a privilege to take part in its realization. The more we
appreciate the gift of Faith, the more must we long to have
it imparted to others. The Missionary spirit is one of the
glories of the Catholic Church and one of the chief characteristics of Christian zeal."

If the years that have passed would seem to have produced
results less than those looked for, let it be remembered that
poverty has always been a check on the extension of the
Colored Missions program. Of all the missions in the South,
not one outside of the larger cities is self-supporting; and
even of those in the cities, many must rely on outside help.
Missioners have been compelled to spend in raising funds
much time that could have been devoted to the spiritual side
of the work were it better situated financially. The financial
situation has always been a serious one The people are as
poor as their priests, and while this cannot be imputed to their
fault, it is a fact which may not be ignored, since it demands
the expenditure of time and energy in the quest for funds
with which to carry on the work.

The ultimate solution of the Colored Mission problem must
have foundation in the Negroes themselves. When it comes,
it will be based upon Pope Pius' encyclical, *"Rerum Ecclesiae,"*
that remarkable document in which Our Holy Father so well
lays plans for the solution of the problems of the foreign
missions. The procedure advised in that document is very
similar to that which was followed by the Baptist and other
evangelical sects that have had so much missionary success in
dealing with the Negroes in the United States.

While the nucleus of the various non-Catholic colored sects
was laid in the establishment of separate churches by the
Negroes themselves before the Civil War, the break which
came after the emancipation was not necessarily a declaration
of war between the whites and the Negroes. As a matter
of fact, the ties which bound the Negro Church organizations

to the whites were such as could not be severed by a mere change in the management of church affairs. There still remained among northern whites numerous philanthropists who helped the Negroes in the promotion of religion and morality. From this group came numerous Christian workers supported by funds freely contributed to the cause. The Baptists, Methodists, Presbyterians, and Congregationalists, who had had a considerable number of communicants among the Negroes prior to the Civil War, took the lead in this movement to educate the Negroes as a means to spread the Gospel through an intelligent ministry. Many universities and theological seminaries were founded, and numerous mission boards were established for the support of schools and scholars. The missionary teachers from the North came with a determination to train the Negroes to care for themselves. With all these workers in the field promoting religious education without regard to creed, the Negro Churches soon had a much larger number of men equipped to extend their work. Given such an impetus the work of the Negro Church was rapidly carried forward. Within a few years the neglected masses of freedmen were being evangelized by their own ministers and provided with some sort of religious instruction in their own churches, both preachers and missions being subsidized by white missionary organizations; many are still so supported.

While we believe that a similar plan of action, based upon the encyclical of Pope Pius, can eventually be pursued to advantage by the Catholic Church, of necessity it would have to be put into effect only gradually and with much greater caution than was demanded of the sects. The sects could afford to be free and easy in their requirements for the ministry: they were not doctrinal religions, nor were their organizations hierarchical, nor had their ministry any permanent and indelible character. Like their churches, the Negro ministers were a law unto themselves.

In the Catholic Church, on the contrary, religion is essentially doctrinal; in organization there is no room for the multiple and diverse factions that characterize non-Catholic Negro sects; many years of training are required to prepare a candidate for the priesthood; and, finally, after ordination he is a priest "in aeternum." Conditions being such, the exercise of the greatest care is required in training and ordaining priests, a caution which sharply restricts the immediate general practicability of the plan. Nevertheless, the time will come when white priests now laboring on the Colored Missions must to a great extent gradually withdraw from the work and leave to a Negro clergy the spiritual concerns of the race. Until that day, however, the greatest needs of the Colored Missions are men to do the work and generous Catholics to subsidize it.

In the meantime, Catholic as we are, it is our duty to recognize what is true: that the soul of the Negro is as valuable as is that of any other race of men. This recognition, however, is theoretical and has always been admitted by Catholics. Of far greater importance is the practical recognition of our duty to bring to that race the uplifting influences of the Church; to discover and to develop such qualities as tend to its improvement; to help a people that is down-trodden by giving to them the opportunities of freedom, religion, and education; in a word, it is our duty, not only as Catholics but as Christians, to do something positive towards the solution of the race problem, never forgetting, and never hiding the fact, and never fearing to say that the Negro is our brother in the fellowship of Christ and the fatherhood of God.

2.—RECOMMENDATIONS

1. *An Episcopal Statement.* The great body of anti-Negro public opinion, preserved in the traditions and literature of the white race, has exercised a persistent and powerful effect, both conscious and unconscious, upon the thought and behavior of white Catholics generally. Indifference and positive misunderstanding have been fostered by the antipathy and ignorance of white Catholics concerning the application of the principles of fraternal charity as enunciated by Christ and taught by the Catholic Church, which recognizes no caste or color, race or nation. Well-intentioned Negroes misinterpret

this attitude of individual Catholics as being that of the Catholic Church.

The Fathers of the Second Plenary Council of Baltimore in no uncertain terms expressed the attitude of the Catholic Church as regards the Negroes of the United States. The Fathers of the Third Plenary Council in more forceful language appealed "by the bowels of the mercy of God" for a more Catholic interest in the welfare of the Negroes. While the acts of neither of these Councils have been abrogated, a new age has come upon us, and a new generation has grown up among us; consequently, the lapse of a long period of time has had the effect of enshrouding in oblivion the heart-rending appeals of the Fathers of the Councils. From time to time, individual Bishops raise their voices for a more Catholic attitude towards the Negroes, but an authoritative re-affirmation of the thoughts of the Fathers of the Councils of Baltimore by the entire body of the American Hierarchy assembled in meeting would go far towards reminding this new generation of Catholics in general, and convincing this new generation of Negroes in particular, of the Church's real and continued interest in the 12,000,000 colored people in the United States.

2. *Greater Co-operation.* The intense individualism of institutional and geographic units of the Church's life has exerted a marked influence on the development of its missionary activities. Parishes, dioceses, religious communities, civic and lay organizations are units of consciousness and centers of responsibilities in Catholic life, but there is a tone of individuality about the average Church group which isolates it from missionary activities. Practically, there is a tendency to limit the needs of the Church to those within the confines of the group. But the true spirit of Catholicism will prevail only in so far as larger purposes tend to overcome the habit of isolation, and as the problems of the Church are looked upon as the concerns of the Church as a whole rather than as of any particular unit. All Catholics, all parishes, all dioceses, and all religious societies, consequently, should regard the work of the Colored Missions as being partly under their responsibility and care.

Much could be gained from well organized methods of co-operation among missionaries engaged in the work of the Colored Missions; there is no hurt to prestige, no surrender to individualism; there is nothing but the greatest good to be derived therefrom. It is ardently to be desired that the near future will see the establishment of conferences between the members of organizations working on the Colored Missions.

3. *Lack of Priests.* The small number of priests laboring among the Negroes of the United States is entirely inadequate to the demands of the situation. The outlook for an immediate increase in the number of such laborers is not too bright. At the same time, some religious societies which are blessed with a more abundant supply of priests would seem to be adverse to undertaking any work for the Negroes. If Rome found it expedient to solve the foreign mission problem by the division of missionary countries into districts cared for by definite religious orders, it would not be without its advantages that the same policy be pursued as regards the Colored Missions. As it exists in the United States, the Negro problem is too big to be relegated to a few small societies. If all religious societies were willing to participate in the work, the problem would undoubtedly find a quicker solution.

Furthermore, some favored dioceses in the country would seem to have an over-supply of priests. A term of years spent in the work of the Colored Missions would serve the double purpose of better fitting young priests for work in the dioceses of their adoption and of relieving the situation in the South.

4. *Colored Clergy.* A native priesthood is the general desire of the Holy Father. Colored America will be no exception. The proposal, however, calls for adequate solution with due regard to the matter of fact difficulties as related to existent American society, difficulties patent to those acquainted with the work of the Colored Missions. We may not walk blindly in the face of these facts, no matter how high our aspirations may be.

The colored priest must belong to either a diocese or a community. If a diocese, the problem of his placement ends; if to a community, it only begins, for the Superior of a community is dependent upon the will of bishops for the acceptance of priests to labor within their dioceses. Under such circumstances, a community fostering colored vocations may clearly be confronted with the impossibility of placing its colored priests.

This situation can be met, so it would seem, by the establishment of a Pontifical Seminary for the colored priesthood in America, the seminary to be maintained by the Hierarchy or the likely diocesan beneficiaries. Assignment from the seminary would be made upon request of the Bishops or through the Apostolic Delegate.

5. *Education.* In increasing numbers the Negroes in the United States are becoming educated. Thomas, himself a Negro, believes that "Whatever possibilities there may be in Negro awakening, it is the child that today represents the 'promise and potency' of racial achievement—the may or may not of actual regeneration, the trend and the status of the future man or woman. All rational faith, then, working towards the awakening and uplifting of the freed people, should center in child culture." [1] As he well states: "What the Negro stands in absolute need of is such a renovating education as will implant within his untutored nature high ideals of sound sentiments respecting manhood and womanhood, and, at the same time, will train his mind, enlighten his soul, and discipline his body in every essential function of wholesome living." [2] He further states: "The Negro needs to be taught how to create and maintain a home in honor and purity, and to that end he requires the influence of wholesome example and the inspiration of supervising contact. But no substantial moral elevation of the Negro is possible without the intervention and cooperation of highly qualified women, such as are thoroughly capable, painstaking, and God-fearing teachers of truth and righteousness." [3] The Catholic school system, staffed as it is with consecrated teachers and exemplars of righteous living, can properly train the Negro youth.

While encouraging a continuation of the present policy of mission schools, Catholic high schools for colored youths

---

[1] *The American Negro*, p. 386.
[2] *Ibid.*, p. 204.
[3] *Ibid.*, p. 205.

should be further developed to enable them to meet the requirements of State Boards of Education. At the same time, another college or two would go a long way towards meeting the demands of the race for higher education under Catholic auspices. The North and the Middle West both could afford a Catholic college for Negroes.

6. *Financial.* If the Negro race is ever to be converted to the Catholic Church, it will not be under the present system of haphazard mission support. There should be some way of subsidizing the work of the Colored Missions. That non-Catholic religious bodies have found a way of subsidizing their missions gives proof of the feasibility of such a procedure.

Three Boards have been erected officially to assist in the collection and disbursement of funds for the Colored Missions. The Commission for Catholic Missions Among the Colored People and Indians, The Catholic Board for Mission Work Among the Colored People, and The American Board for Catholic Missions. The first named disburses the annual collection ordered by the Third Plenary Council of Baltimore, the second, collects and disburses its own funds, while the last named disburses to both white and colored missions the allotment of the Society for the Propagation of the Faith. With three boards functioning for the same purpose, there is an inevitable overlapping of appeal and a consequent dissipation of effort. The three Boards might be amalgamated to form one Board performing the three functions: disbursing the annual collection taken up in all the churches, collecting and distributing funds independently of any other board or collection, and allocating the funds apportioned to the Negro Missions by the American Board for Catholic Missions. It must be emphasized, however, that the functions of none of the boards should be abolished— present funds are all too inadequate.

7. *Social.* The social life of Catholic Negroes should be more extensively developed. Realizing the necessarily scant opportunities of the Negro for developing a wholesome social life, as also his previous experience of associating social activity with the religious, the missioners on the Colored Missions should leave untouched no opportunity for a more varied parish social life. Parish social life is an essential which of ne-

cessity must be more or less subordinated to the exigencies of church and school building; nevertheless, if we would hold our Colored Catholics we must make an effort to offer them social inducements as good as, if not better than, they have been accustomed to in their former church affiliations. This program of social betterment will entail the inclusion of club houses and social centers as integral parts of the complete mission unit. A greater social life under Catholic auspices would have the advantage of providing greater opportunities for the encouragement of Catholic marriages.

8. *Emotional.* The emotional life of the Negroes should be given more consideration. By nature and former church affiliation Negro Catholics are inclined to the emotional. Passive assistance at the beautiful services of the Catholic Church is not sufficiently satisfying. More widespread use of congregational singing might help considerably to relieve the situation. The people should be taught and encouraged to sing at every service possible. They need it, and they want it; they should have it.

BIBLIOGRAPHY

General

American Board of Catholic Missions, Report of, from Sept. 1925 to June 1928, Chicago, 1928.

American Church History, Thomas O'Gorman, New York, 1895.

Bibliography of the Negro In Africa and America, compiled by Monroe N. Work, New York, 1928.

Catholic Church in the United States, DeCourcy, Henry—Shea, John G., New York, 1856.

Catholic Church in the United States, undertaken to celebrate the Golden Jubilee of His Holiness, Pope Pius X, 3 vols., (Cardinal Edition), published by The Cath. Editing Co., New York, 1913.

Catholic Directory, The Official, 1928, 1929, New York

Catholic Encyclopedia, New York, 1914.

Catholic Year Book, The Official, New York, 1928.

History of the People of the United States, John Bach McMaster, 6 vols., New York, 1895.

Jesuit Relations, New York, 1847.

Negro and Indian Missions; Annual Reports of the Secretary of the Commission for the Catholic Missions Among the Colored People and Indians, 1890-1929, Washington, D. C.

Negro Year Book, 1925-1926, edited by Monroe N. Work, Tuskegee, Ala., 1925.

World Almanac and Book of Facts, New York, 1927.

PERIODICALS

Advocate, St. Joseph's, formerly edited and published quarterly by the Fathers of St. Joseph's Foreign Missionary Society of the Sacred Heart, Baltimore, Md.

Augustine's Messenger, St., published quarterly at St. Augustine's Seminary, Bay St. Louis, Miss.

Colored Harvest, The, edited and published bi-monthly by St. Joseph's Society of the Sacred Heart, Baltimore, Md.

Colored Man's Friend, The, published quarterly in the interest of Holy Rosary Institute, Lafayette, La.

Colored Missions, Our, published monthly by "The Catholic Board for Mission Work Among the Colored People," New York, N. Y.

Council Review, The, formerly the official organ of the Federated Colored Catholics of America, Washington, D. C.

Negro History, The Journal of, published quarterly by The Association for the Study of Negro Life and History, Inc., edited by Carter G. Woodson, Washington, D. C.

Historical

Adams, Nehemias, *A South-Side View of Slavery: or Three Months in the South in 1854*, Boston, 1854.

American Historical Association, *Annual Reports for 1897, 1898, 1899*, 2 vols., Washington, D. C.

Brackett, Jeffrey R., *The Negro in Maryland; A Study of the Institution of Slavery*, Baltimore, 1889.

Channing, William E., *Slavery*, (fourth edition), Boston, 1836.

Flemming, Walter L., *The Civil War and Reconstruction in Alabama*, Cleveland, 1911.

Goodell, William, *The American Slave Code in Theory and Practice; Its Features Shown by Its Statutes, Judicial Decisions, and Illustrative Facts*, New York, 1853.

Grimke, A. E., *Letters to Catherine E. Beecher, in reply to an Essay on Slavery and Abolitionism*, Boston, 1838.

Guilday, Ph.D., LL.D., Rev. Peter, *Life and Times of John Carroll*, New York, 1922.
Life and Times of John England, New York, 1927.

Hughes, Rev. Thomas, S.J., *History of the Society of Jesus in North America*, 2 vols., New York, 1917.

Johnson, Sir Harry H., *The Negro in the New World*, New York, 1910.

Kemble, Frances Anne, *A Journal of Residence on a Georgian Plantation in 1838-1839*, New York, 1863.

Maze, Cornelius P., *Life of Rev. Charles Nerinckx and Early Catholic Missions of Kentucky*, Cincinnati, 1880.

Messmer, Most Rev. Sebastian G., *John England's Works*, Cleveland, 1908.

McConnell, John P., *Negroes and Their Treatment in Virginia from 1865 to 1867*, Pulaski, Va: 1910

Mercy, A Member of the Order of, *A Catholic History of Alabama and the Floridas*, New York, 1908.

O'Connell, O.S.B., Rev. J. J., *Catholicity in the Carolinas and Georgia*, New York, 1879.

Paxton, J. D., *Letters on Slavery, addressed to the Cumberland Congregation, Virginia*, Lexington, Ky., 1833.

Reily, Rev. John S., *Recollections in the Life of Cardinal Gibbons*, Martinsburgh, W. Va., 1892.

Russell, Rev. W. T., *Maryland, The Land of Sanctuary*, Baltimore, 1907.

Shea, John Gilmary, *History of the Catholic Church in Colonial Days*, New York, 1886.
Life and Times of Archbishop Carroll, New York, 1866.
History of the Catholic Church in the United States, 1815-1843, New York, 1888.
History of the Catholic Church in the United States, 1844-1866, New York, 1892.

Sneed-Cox, J. G , *Life of Cardinal Vaughan*, 2 vols., London, 1910.

Spalding, Rt. Rev. M. J., *Sketches of Life, Times and Character of Rt. Rev. Benedict Flaget*, Louisville, 1852.

Sketches of the Early Catholic Missions of Kentucky, Louisville, 1844.

Stroud, George M., *A Sketch of the Laws Relating to Slavery in Several States of the United States of America,* (second edition), Philadelphia, 1856.

Treacy, Rev. William P., *Old Catholic Maryland and Its Early Jesuit Missionaries,* Swedesboro, N. J., 1888.

Trial of John Ury "for being an ecclesiastical person, made by authority pretended from the See of Rome, and coming into and abiding in the Province of New York," and with being one of the Conspirators in the Negro Plot to burn the City of New York, 1741. Philadelphia, 1899.

Will, Allen S., *Life of Cardinal Gibbons,* Baltimore, 1911

Williams, George W., *History of the Negro Race in America,* 2 vols., New York, 1883.

Williams, Gomer, *The Liverpool Privateers,* London, 1897.

Webb, E. J., *Centenary of Catholicity in Kentucky,* Louisville, 1884.

Woodson, Carter G., *The Negro in Our History,* (fifth edition), Washington, 1928.

PAMPHLETS

American Anti-Slavery Society, *Letter to Louis Kossuth concerning Freedom and Slavery in the United States,* Boston, 1852.

Anderson, Osborne P., *A Voice From Harper's Ferry; Narrative of Events at Harper's Ferry,* Boston, 1861.

Bassett, John Spencer, *Anti-Slavery Leaders of North Carolina* Johns Hopkins University Studies in Historical and Political Sciences, Baltimore, 1898.
Slavery and Servitude in the Colony of North Carolina, Johns Hopkins University Studies in Historical and Political Sciences, fourteenth series, Baltimore, 1896.

Beard, A. F., *Sketches from the South,* New York.

Brackett, Jeffrey R., *Notes on the Progress of the Colored People of Maryland Since the War,* Johns Hopkins University Studies in Historical and Political Sciences, eighth series, Baltimore, 1890.

Carolinian, A, *Slavery in the Southern States,* Cambridge, 1852.

Child, L. Maria, *The Right Way the Safe Way,* New York, 1862.

Helper, Hinton Rowan, *Compendium of the Impending Crisis of the South,* New York, 1860.

Hickok, Charles T., *The Negro in Ohio, 1802-1870,* Cleveland 1896.

Ingle, Edward, *The Negro in the District of Columbia,* Johns Hopkins University Studies in Historical and Political Sciences, eleventh series, Baltimore, 1893.

Leo, XIII, Pope, *Letter to the Bishops of Brazil on the Church and Slavery.*

Trial of John Sims, on an Issue of Personal Liberty on the Claims of James Potter, of Georgia, Boston, 1851.

Strayer, Jacob, *My Life in the South*, Salem, Mass., 1890.
Steiner, Bernard C., *History of Slavery in Connecticut*, Johns Hopkins University Studies in Historical and Political Sciences, eleventh series, Baltimore, 1893.

ARTICLES

Anonymous, "The Baltimoreans from San Domingo," *Baltimore Sun*, Sept. 1, 1929.
Dickens, Elizabeth, "Estevan—Early American Negro," *Commonweal*, Aug. 14, 1929.
Foster, Katharine R., "A Moses in War-time Maryland," *Baltimore Sun*, April 21, 1929.
Whitmore, C. W., "Emancipation a la Maryland," *Baltimore Sun*, Feb. 10 1929.

Race

The Annals of the American Academy of Political and Social Science; "The American Negro," Philadelphia, 1928.
   "The Negro's Progress in Fifty Years," Philadelphia, 1913.
Baker, Ray Stannard, *Following the Colour Line; An Account of Negro Citizenship in the American Democracy*, New York, 1908.
Brawley, Benjamin, *A Social History of the American Negro; being a History of the Negro Problem in the United States*, New York, 1921.
Chicago Commission on Race Relations, *The Negro in Chicago; a Study of Race Relations and a Race Riot*, Chicago, 1922.
Dawson, Warrington, *Le Negre Aux Etats Unis*, Paris, 1912.
Dowd, Jerome, *The Negro in American Life*, New York, 1926.
Du Bois, W. E. Burghardt, *John Brown*, Philadelphia, 1909.
   The Gift of Black Folk, Boston, 1924.
   Darkwater, New York, 1920.
   The Souls of Black Folk, fourteenth edition, Chicago, 1924.
Haynes, Elizabeth, *Unsung Heroes*, New York, 1921.
Johnson, Julia, *The Negro Problem* (selected articles), New York, 1921.
Mathews, Basil, *The Clash of Color; A Study in the Problem of Race*, New York, 1924.
Morton, James F., *The Curse of Race Prejudice*, New York.
Rogers, J. A., *As Nature Leads; an informal discussion of the reason why Negro and Caucasian are mixing in spite of opposition*, Chicago, 1919
Seligman, Herbert J., *The Negro Faces America*, New York, 1920.
Skaggs, William H., *The Southern Oligarchy; an Appeal in Behalf of the Silent Masses of our Country Against the Despotic Rule of the Few*, New York, 1924.
Thomas, William Hannibal, *The American Negro*, New York, 1901.
Washington, Booker T., *The Story of the Negro; the Rise of the Race from Slavery*, 2 vols., New York, 1909.

Up From Slavery; an Autobiography, New York, 1901.
The Future of the American Negro, Boston, 1899.
Weale, B. L., *The Conflict of Color*, New York, 1910.
Weatherford, W. D., *Present Forces in Negro Progress*, New York, 1912.

PAMPHLETS

Barrows, Isabel C., Report of The First Mohonk Conference on the Negro
    Question, held at Lake Mohonk, Ulster County, New York, June 4-6,
    1890, Boston, 1890.
Dillard, James H., *Booker T. Washington, A Christian Philosopher*, Found-
    er's Day address, delivered at Tuskegee Institute, April 5, 1925.
Gaines, Bishop W. J., *The Negro and the White Man*, Philadelphia, 1897.
Haynes, Rev. John, *The Disfranchisement of Negroes*, Washington, D. C.
*Proceedings of the National Conference of Colored Men of the United
    States*, held in the State Capitol at Nashville, Tenn., 1879. Wash-
    ington, D. C., 1879.
Slater Fund, Trustees of the John F., Occasional Papers of the:
    Gannett, Henry, *Statistics of Negroes in the U. S.*, paper No. 4.
    Gilman, Daniel, *A Study in Black and White*, paper No. 10.
    Johnson, James Weldon, *Native African Races and Culture*, paper
    No. 25.
    Locke, Alain, *A Decade of Negro Self Expression*, paper No. 26.
    *Five Letters of the University Commission on Southern Race Ques-
    tions*, paper No. 24.
Work, J. W., *Folk Songs of the American Negro*, Nashville, 1915

ARTICLES

Anonymous, "The New Emancipation," *Commonweal*, Sept. 5, 1928.
Connolly, Myles E., "The Black Man," *America*, May 1, 1920.
Haygood, Atticus G., "The Black Shadow in the South," *Forum*, Oct., 1893.
La Farge, Rev. John, S.J., "The Immediate Negro Problem," *America*,
    Dec. 24, 1921.
    "Full Measure for the Negro," *America*, Dec. 17, 1921.
    "The Crux of the Mission Problem," *America*, No. 6, 1926.
    "Jordan River," *America*, March 5, 1927.
    "The Unknown Field of Negro History," *America*, July 21, 1928.
    "Opportunity for the Negro," *America*, Feb. 2, 1929.
Locke, Alain, "The High Cost of Prejudice," *Forum*, Oct. 1927
McKinny, Ernest R., "Race Solidarity," *The World Tomorrow*, Jan. 1929.
Morse, George C., "A Negro Answers," *Commonweal*, Dec. 26, 1928.
Murphy, Rev. Edward, S.S.J., Ph.D., "Dusky Progress," *The Sign*, Oct. 1928.
    "Darkness to Light," *The Sign*, Jan. 1929.
    "Fairness First," *The Sign*, Aug. 1929.
    "The Rising Shadow," *Commonweal*, Jan. 9, 1929.
Negro Question, The, Letters on, "Communications," *America*, April 1,
    1922.

Pules, L. W., "The Southern Problem," *A. M. E. Church Review*, vol. V, No. 4, April 1889.
Thoma, Theo A., "Changing the Color Line," *Extension*, Feb. 1929.
Sheehy, Maurice S., "New Light on the Color Question," *America*, Dec. 8, 1929.
Stoddard, Lothrop, "The Impasse at the Color Line," *Forum*, Oct. 1927.
Sunday Visitor, Our, Whole Issue of Nov. 29, 1925.
Weil, Elsie, "The Negro's Place in the Sun," *Commonweal*, June 19, 1929.

Social and Economic

Dardano, Ven. Archpriest Lorenzo, *The Elements of Social Science and Political Science*, translated from the Italian by Rev. William McLoughlin, Dublin, 1909.
Du Bois, W. E. Burghardt, *The Philadelphia Negro; A Social Study*, together with a *Special Report on Domestic Service*, by Isabel Eaton. Publication of the University of Pennsylvania series in Political Economy and Public Law, No. 14, Philadelphia, 1899.
Kerby, Ph.D., LL.D., Rev. William J., *The Social Mission of Charity; a Study of Points of View in Catholic Charities*, New York, 1924.
McCullough, James E., *Battling for Social Betterment; a Report of the Southern Sociological Congress, Memphis, Tenn., 1914*, Nashville, 1914.
Muntsch, Albert, S.J., and Spalding, Henry, S.J., *Introductory Sociology*, Boston, 1928.
Odum, Howard W., *Social and Mental Traits of the Negro; Research into the Conditions of the Negro Race in Southern Towns; a Study in Race Traits, Tendencies, and Prospects*. Studies in History, Economics, and Public Law, edited by the Faculty of Political Science of the Columbia University, vol. XXXVII, No. 3, whole No. 99, New York, 1910.
Spalding, Rev. Henry S., S.J., *Chapters in Social History*, New York, 1925. *Introduction to Social Service*, New York, 1923.

PAMPHLETS

Hobson, Mrs. E. C. and Hopkins, Mrs. C. E., *A Report Concerning the Colored Women of the South*, Trustees of the John F. Slater Fund, Occasional Papers, No. 9.
National Child Labor Committee, *Child Labor Facts*, New York, 1928.
Negro Child Study in the City of New York, Joint Committee for, *A Study of Delinquent and Neglected Negro Children Before the New York Children's Court*, New York, 1927.
Urban League, "A Challenge to New York"; *Annual Report of the New York Urban League*, New York, 1927.
Women's Bureau, United States Department of Labor, *Negro Women in*

Industry, Bulletins Nos. 20, 22, 24, 29, 32, 35, 37, 39, 40, 41, 42, 43, 44, 48, 49, 51, 54, 55, 56, 57, 59, 62, 63, 64, 67, 68, 69, 70, 71.

ARTICLES

American Labor Legislation Review, "The New Industrial South," March, 1928.

Baltimore Catholic Review, "A Day Nursery for Colored People"; an account of the dedication of the Mission Helpers' Day Nursery, Baltimore, Md., Nov. 9, 1928.

Crabites, Pierre, "White South or Black? The Fears of an Eminent Southerner," *The North American Review*, March, 1929.

Dickerson, W. P., "A Plea for Social Justice," *The Catholic Educational Association Bulletin*, Nov. 1919.

Garvey, Marcus, "The Negro's Greatest Enemy," *Current History Magazine*, Sept. 1923.

Guild, June Purcell, "The Negro in Richmond, Virginia," *The Catholic Charities Review*, January, 1930.

Literary Digest, The, "Why Lynching Has Slumped," July 28, 1913.

Murphy, S.S.J., Ph.D., Rev. Edward, "Colored Care," *The Catholic Charities Review*, January, 1930.

New York Times Book Review, "Through the South Unsentimentally," a book review of *Darker Phases of the South*, by Frank Tannenbaum, March 23, 1924.

Scarborough, Dorothy, "Now the Negro Shifts From Agriculture to Industry," a review of *The American Negro*, New York Times Book Review, Jan. 13, 1929.

Topeka Plain Dealer, The, "What the Catholic Church is Doing for the Colored Race," an account of the activities of Rt. Rev. Msgr. J. Shorter, at Leavenworth, Kansas; issue of Oct. 12, 1928.

Winston, Robert Watson, "Should the Color Line Go?" *Current History Magazine*, Sept. 1923.

Migration

Joseph, Society of Saint, Annual Reports, 1913-1928.

Woodson, Carter G., *A Century of Negro Migration*, Washington, 1918.

PAMPHLETS

Epstein, Abram, *The Negro Migrant in Pittsburgh*, Pittsburgh, 1918.

Labor, United States Department of, *Negro Migration in 1916-1917*, Wash.-ington, 1919.

Recent Northward Migration of the Negro, Washington, 1924.

ARTICLES

Commerce, United States Department of, Bureau of the Census, "Center of Negro Population, 1920," press release Oct. 11, 1921.

"Negro Migration," press release Dec. 17, 1921.

"Population of the United States by Color or Race," press release Sept. 26, 1921.

Fortson, Blanton, "Northward to Extinction," *Forum*, Nov. 1924.

Harris, A. L., "Negro Migration to the North," *Current History Magazine of the New York Times*, Sept. 1924.

Hill, J. A., "Recent Northward Migration of the Negro," *Monthly Labor Review*, March 1924.

Labor, United States Department of, "Inclusion of Negro Workers into Northern Industries," press release July 9, 1923.

Labor Review Monthly, "Negro Migrant in Pittsburgh," Feb. 1928.

"Negro Migrants in Philadelphia," Nov. 1924.

"Negro Migration," June 1923.

"Negro Migration in 1923," April 1924.

"Negro Migrations and Migrants," Jan. 1922.

Literary Digest, "Another Negro Exodus to the North," Feb. 17, 1923.

"Economic Causes of the Negro Exodus," Aug. 18, 1923.

"Johnstown Flood of Negro Labor," Oct. 6, 1923.

"South Calling Negroes Back," June 23, 1917.

"Why the Negroes Go North," May 19, 1923.

Moses, Kingsley, "The Negro Comes North," *Forum*, Aug. 1917.

Pickens, William, "Northward to Fuller Life," *Forum*, Nov. 1924.

Saunders, W. O., "Why Jim Crow is Flying," *Collier's*, Dec. 8, 1923.

Schieffelin, W. J., "Harmful Rush of Negro Workers to the North," *New York Times Magazine*, June 3, 1917.

Shaffer, E. T. H., "A New South: The Negro Migration," *Atlantic Monthly*, Sept. 1923.

Snyder, Howard, "Negro Migration and the Cotton Crop," *North American Review*, Jan. 1924.

Waldron, Eric D., "Negro Exodus from the South," *Current History Magazine*, Sept. 1923.

Religious

Anciaux, S.S.J., Rev. Joseph, *De Miserabili Conditione Catholicorum Negrorum in America* (private printing).

Anonymous, *The Negro Pew*, Boston, 1837.

Armitage, Rev. Thomas, *History of the Baptists*, New York, 1887.

Gilligan, S.T.D., *Rev. Francis J., The Morality of the Color Line*, Washington, 1928.

Woodson, Carter G., *History of the Negro Church*, Washington, 1921.

PAMPHLETS

Cunningham, Honorable William D., "Lay Missionaries, the Need of the Hour," Catholic Defense and Exposition Series, No. 2, Dec. 1928; National Council of Catholic Men, Washington, D. C.

Laures, Rev. John, S.J., *The Friend of the Colored Man; with an after-*

word on The Race Problem in the United States, New York.
Joseph's Seminary, Saint, *The Catholic Church and the Colored Race.*
The Catholic Colored Missions in Statistics.
St. Joseph's Society of the Sacred Heart.

ARTICLES

Anonymous, "Christianity versus Slavery," *The Catholic Mind,* April 8, 1921.
"The Negroes and Indians," *Ecclesiastical Review,* March, 1890.
"The Negroes and Indians," *The Catholic World,* March, 1889.
Aswell, E. C., "The Church and the Negro," *Commonweal,* Nov. 21, 1928.
Butsch, Rev. Joseph, S.S.J., "Negro Catholics in the United States," *Catholic Historical Review,*" April, 1917.
"Catholics and the Negro," *Journal of Negro History,* Oct., 1917.
Carroll, Rev. Charles B., S.S.J., "Evangelizing the Negroes," *The Missionary,* Oct. 1904.
Duffy, Rev. Thomas, S.S.J., "The Negro in America," *The Mission Movement in America,* Washington, 1906.
Guilday, Rev. Peter, Ph.D., LL.D., "The Catholic Church and the Slave Question," *"The Catholic Question in the United States,"* article XXV.
Haas, Rev. Florence J., S.V.D., "The Mysterious 250,000 Colored Catholics," *Our Missions,* May, 1928.
Meehan, Thomas F., "Mission Work Among Colored Catholics," *The Catholic Mind,* April 22, 1922.
Moroney, T. B., "The Condition of Catholic Colored Mission Work in the United States," *Ecclesiastical Review,* Dec. 1919.
Murphy, Rev. Edward, S.S.J., Ph.D., "The Colored Harvest," *Ecclesiastical Review,* Nov. 1928.
Murphy, Miriam, "Catholic Missionary Work Among the Colored People," *Records of the Catholic Historical Society of Philadelphia,* vol. XXXV, No. 2.
Tennelly, Rev. J. B., S.S., S.T.D., "Apropos of The Mysterious 250,000 Colored Catholics," *Our Missions,* July, 1928.
Theobald, Rev. Stephen, "Catholic Missionary Work Among the Colored People of the United States," *Records of the Catholic Historical Society of Philadelphia,* vol. XXXV, No. 4.

Education

Woodson, Carter G., *The Education of the Negro Prior to 1861; a History of the Education of the Colored People in the United States From the Beginning of Slavery to the Civil War,* (second edition), Washington, 1919.
Willmartin, Otto, *The Science of Education in Its Sociological and Historical Aspects,* 2 vols., translated by Rev. Felix Kirsch, O. M., Cap., Beatty, Pa., 1922.

PAMPHLETS

Benedict the Moor Institute, Catalog of Saint, Milwaukee, Wis.

Blessed Sacrament, Sisters of the, *Xavier High School Bulletin*, 1927-1928, New Orleans.

Xavier College Bulletin, 1927-1928, New Orleans.

Education, Bureau of, Washington, D. C.:

> *Annual Report of the Commissioner of Education for the Fiscal Year, June 30, 1926.*
>
> *Biennial Survey of Education for 1920-1922.*
>
> *Biennial Survey of Education for 1922-1924.*
>
> *Biennial Survey of Education for 1924-1926.*
>
> "Colored Education," *Report of the U. S. Commissioner of Education for 1893-1894.*
>
> "Higher Education," *Biennial Survey, 1922-1924*, Bulletin, 1926 No. 20.
>
> "History of the Schools for the Colored Population in the District of Columbia," *Report of the U. S. Commissioner of Education for 1871.*
>
> "Legal Status of the Colored Population in Respect to Schools and Education in the Different States, *Report of the U. S. Commissioner of Education for 1871.*
>
> "Recent Progress in Negro Education," Bulletin, 1919, No. 27.
>
> "Schools for the Colored Race," reprint of Chapter XXXVIII from *Report of the U. S. Commissioner of Education* for 1910.
>
> *Secondary Schools of the Southern Association*, Bulletin, 1928, No. 16.
>
> *Statistical Survey of Education, 1925-1926*, Bulletin, 1928, No. 12.
>
> *Statistical Summary of Education for 1923-1924*, Bulletin, 1926, No. 19.
>
> *Survey of Negro Colleges and Universities*, Bulletin, 1928, No. 7.

Embree, Edwin R., *Julius Rosenwald Fund*, a review to June 30, 1928, Chicago, 1928.

Emma's Industrial and Agricultural Institute, Catalog of Saint, Rock Castle, Va.

Dillard, James H., "Fourteen Years of the Jeannes Fund, (1909-1923)." Reprint from the *South Atlantic Quarterly*, July 1923.

The Portal of a New Life; A National School for Colored Youth. Cardinal Gibbons Institute, Ridge, Md.

Johnson, William D., *Lincoln University; or the Nation's First Pledge of Emancipation*, Philadelphia, 1867.

Joseph's Seminary, Saint, *The Catholic School for Colored People*, Baltimore.

Miller, Kelly, "The Education of the Negro," chapter XVI of the *Report of the U. S. Commissioner of Education for the year 1901.* Washington.

Sumner, Charles, Esq., *Argument of Charles Sumner Against the Constitutionality of Separate Colored Schools, Before the Supreme Court of Massachusetts, Dec. 4, 1841*, Boston, 1849.

Slater Fund, Trustees of the John F., Occasional Papers of the:
 Brawley, Benjamin, "Early Efforts for Industrial Education," paper No. 22.
 Curry, J. L. M., "Education of the Negroes Since 1860," Paper No. 3.
 "Difficulties, Complications, and Limitations Connected with the Education of the Negro," paper No. 5.
 "Proceedings and Report for the years ending Sept. 30, 1924, 1925, 1926, 1927, 1928."
 "Reference List of Private and Denominational Southern Colored Schools," (fourth edition, 1929), paper No. 20.
 Williams, W. T. B., "Report on Negro Universities and Colleges," paper No. 21.

ARTICLES

Catholic Educational Association Bulletin:
 Bustin, Rev. J. T., "Primary Education Among the Colored People," Nov. 1920.
 Dickerson, W. P., "Urgent Need of More High Schools for Colored Catholics," Nov. 1922.
 Florence, Brother, O. F. M., "The Little Mission School," Nov. 1922.
 Hannigan, Rev. Charles, S.S.J., "High Schools for our Colored Catholics," Nov. 1921.
 Moroney, T. B., "Catholic Secondary Education for Negroes," Nov. 1920.
 Turner, Thomas W., "Actual Conditions of Catholic Education Among the Colored Laymen," No. 1919.
Census, Bureau of the, Department of Commerce, "Illiteracy of Native and Foreign-born Whites and Negroes," press release Oct. 15, 1921.
La Farge, Rev. John, S.J., "An American Folk School," reprint from *Southern Workman*, Jan. 1928.
Williams, Daniel B., "The Colored American and Higher Education," *A. M. E. Church Review*, April 1891.

INDEX

A.

Abbeyville County, S. C., 112.

Abolition Movement: effect on early N. education, 24; on Bishop England's school in Charleston, 25; and early N. education, 137.

Adorers of the Precious Blood, Sisters, 153, 157, 164.

African Mission Society: priests working for N., 79, 129; Rev. Joseph John, member of, 86.

Aged: home for, Sisters of Holy Family, New Orleans, 141; Cath. welfare work for sick and aged N., 205-207.

Agricultural: efforts of Fathers of Holy Ghost, 41; and high schools, table 19 *facing* 179; Cardinal Gibbons Institute, 187.

Akron, Ohio: concentration of N. in, 100; migrants from Alabama, 115.

Alabama: slaves in, 23; Jean Chastang, 23; Creoles, 24; opposition to Cath. Church in, 35; N. Caths. (1893), 42; N. Caths. (1928), 50; distribution of N. Caths. in, 52; concentration of N. in, 54; missionary work in, 59; Government statistics for Cath. N. work in, 61; unlisted mission for Cath. N. in, 67 (footnote); and early migrations of N., 96; loss through migration, 98, 102; effect of migration on missions in, 102, 115, 116; migrants from, 103; public school for freedmen, 141; Cath. educational activities in, 152; Rev. S. Grossi and rural education in, 159; mission schools conducted by lay teachers in, 161; Cath. high schools for N., table 19 *facing* 179; prejudice against Cath. Church in, 212.

Albany, N. Y.: N. Caths. in Diocese of, 48; Cath. mission for N. in, 57, 67; Cath. N. and work for in Diocese of, 123, 215.

Alexandria, La.: N. Caths. in Diocese of, 48; missionary work for N. Caths. in Diocese of, table 4 *facing* 58; effect of migration on missions in city and Diocese of,

118; Cath. educational activities in Diocese of, 155; mission schools conducted by lay teachers in, 160; Cath. high school for N. in, 179.

Alexandria, Va., St. Joseph's mission, 111.

Aloysius, Church of St., Washington, D. C., and N., 29.

Altoona, Pa., N. Caths. in Diocese of, 48, 126.

Amarillo, Texas, Diocese of, 48.

American Board of Catholic Missions: collection (1929), 218; a recommendation, 288.

American Hierarchy, The: statistics given by, 46; appeal in behalf of the Negro and Indian missions, 107, 108; on duty of Caths. towards N., 277; an episcopal statement from, 284, 285.

American Missionary Association: in Virginia, 34, 35; opposition to Cath. Church in Alabama, 35; on morality of N. women, 235.

Ames, Texas, Sacred Heart mission, 120.

Ann, Church of St., Cincinnati, Ohio: early N. Caths. attend, 31; given over to N. Caths., 127.

Anthony's Mission House, St., Tenafly, N. J., priests at, 79.

Apostles, Sisters of Our Lady of the: 152, 156, 165; social work in Los Angeles, 208.

Appalachicola, Fla., Holy Family Missions, 114.

Arizona: earliest N. in, 10; N. Caths. in state, 50; no mission activity, 61; N. in, 132.

Arkansas: N. Caths. in state, 50; distribution of N. Caths., 52; concentration of N. in state, 54; missionary work in, 59; Government statistics for Cath. N. work in, 61; loss through migration, 98, 102; effect of migration on missions in, 102, 117; migrants from Mississippi in, 116; public schools for freedmen in, 141; Cath. educational activities in, 152; mission school taught by lay teachers, 161; Cath. high school in, table 19 *facing* 179; prejudice against Cath. Church in, 212.

Athens, Ga., early Caths. in, 21.

Atlantic City, N. J.: Cath. mission in, 57, 60, 67, 125; social work, 208.

Augusta, Ga.: Immaculate Conception Mission, 113.

Augustine, Church of St., Louisville, Ky, 39; Washington, D. C., 39.

Augustine, Seminary of St., Bay St. Louis, Miss.: priests at, 79; students at, 87; high school of, table 19 *facing* 179.

Ayllon, Vasquez de, and N. at Guandape, 10.

B.

Badin, Rev. Stephen, 20.

Baltimore, Archdiocese of: N. Caths. in, 48; missionary activity for N. in, 58; effect of migration on missions in, 110, 111; Cath. educational activities for N. in, 155; mission schools conducted by lay teachers in, 160; Cath. high schools for N. in, table 19 *facing* 179; Cardinal Gibbons Institute, 186-188; industrial training by sisters, 188; Cath. institutions for N. children in, 197, 198, 200; social service of Mission Helpers in, 207; social service of Cardinal Gibbons Institute, 268.

Baltimore, City of: arrival of San Domingan refugees, 15; interest of Sulpicians in N. of, 16; founding of Oblate Sisters, 16; progress of Oblates, 27; first Cath. church for N. in U. S., 29; first Cath. slave taken from, to Richmond, 31; arrival of first Josephites in, 40; center of missionary activity, 46; N. priests ordained in, 85, 86; N. population of, 104; early N. education in, 137, 139, 140; N. education upon arrival of Josephites, 140; St. Elizabeth's Home, 143, 144; Franciscan Sisters (Glen Riddle) begin school work in, 144; married N. women working in, 195; house of Good Shepherd, 202.

Baltimore, Plenary Council of: plea of Second, for N., 36, 40; plea of Third, for N., 36; Third, establishes Commission for Catholic Missions Among the Colored People and Indians, 43; Third, on zeal for souls, 282; re-statement of sentiments of Second and Third, recommended, 285.

Baker City, Oregon, 48.

Baptism: of slaves and Churches, 11; Spanish and French missionaries and, 11; in Georgia, 21; majority not baptized, 33; according to dioceses, table 4 *facing* 58; number of (1927), 64-66; admission of children to, 270; Josephite mission reports show gain in, 280.

Baptist Church: colored, of the South associates with that of North, 30; Free Will, in Virginia, 34; American Baptist (African) Missionary Convention, 35; N. membership in, 55; Cath. children attend schools of, in New Orleans, 145; high schools of, 174; influence on N. estimation of Cath. Church, 213; emotional appeal of, to N., 221-224; preachers in, 229; and lost Caths., 264; and "Rerum Ecclesiae", 282; and N. ministers, 283.

Bardstown, Ky., Caths. at, 19.

Baton Rouge, La., St. Francis Mission, 118.

Beaumont, Texas, Blessed Sacrament Mission, effect of migration on, 119, in city of, 119.

Becraft, Maria, and early N. education in District of Columbia, 138.

Belleville, Ill., Diocese of: N. Caths. in, 48, 129; missionary work for N. Caths. in, table 4 *facing* 58; Cath. educational activities for N. in, 155.

Belmont Abbey, N. Car.: Cath. N. in abbatia, 49; missionary work for Cath. N. in, table 4 *facing* 58; Cath. educational activity for N. in, 155; mission schools conducted by lay teachers in, 160.

Benedict the Moor, Church of, Charleston, S. C., 41.

Benedict, Sisters of St.: in schools (1893), 42, 145; educational work for N. according to states, table 14, 152, according to dioceses, 155; work of, for Cath. N., 164.

Benedictines: in Charleston, S. C., 41; missions in charge of, in 1893, 42; priests working for N., 79; take over St. Emma's Industrial School, 185 (footnote).

Bergier, O. S. B., Rev. Gabriel, 41.

Bessemer, Alabama, distribution point for N. migrants, 115.

Biloxi, Mississippi, Cath. mission for N. at, 117.

Binga, Rev. A., on moral condition of slaves, 235.

Birmingham, Alabama: effect of migration in, 102, 115; on Immaculate Conception mission, 115.

Bismark, N. Dak., 48.

Bladen, Governor, of Maryland, warns Caths., 14.

Blanc, Rt. Rev. Anthony: founds Sisters of Holy Family, 30; approves Sisters of Holy Family, 141.

Blessed Sacrament, Sisters of the: foundation, 44; educational activities according to states, 152, according to dioceses, 155; work of, for N., 164; Xavier College, 169-172; high schools for N., table 19 facing 179; social service in Boston, 208.

Boarding schools: according to states, 152 et sq., according to dioceses, 155, et sq., according to sisterhoods, 164; and high schools, table 19 facing 179.

Boise, Idaho, 48.

Bond, H. W., on race oppression, 273.

Boston, Mass., Archdiocese of: Cath. N. in, 31, 48; work for N. Caths. in, 57, 67, 121, 122, 155; social work of Sisters of Blessed Sacrament in, 208.

Boysco, S.S.J., Rev. Stephen, 160.

Bravas, 49 (footnote), 122.

Breaux Bridge, La., school at, 159.

Brooklyn, N. Y., Diocese of: Cath. N. in, 48; work for N. Caths. in,

table 4 facing 58, 123; West Indians in, 60, 123; loss of Cath. N. migrants in, 106; school for Cath. N. in, 155; number of N. in Diocese, 123, in borough, 124.

Brothers of the Christian Schools, in charge St. Emma's Industrial School, 184.

Brunner, S.S.J., Rev. Edward, president Xavier College, 170.

Brunswick, Ga., early Caths. in, 21.

Buffalo, N. Y.: Cath. N. in Diocese of, 48, 123; missionary work for N. Caths. in, table 4 facing 58; concentration of N. in city of, 100.

Burgess, C.S.Sp., Rev. John, N. priest, 86.

Burke, Rev. John, 45.

Burlington, Vermont, 48.

C.

Cahill, Rev. Edward, 128, 129.

Cairo, Ill.: mission in, 67 (footnote); school in, 154 (footnote), 165.

California: Cath. N. in, 50; distribution of Cath. N. in, 52; missionary work in, 59, 132; migrants from Louisiana in, 103, 118; Cath. educational activity for N. in, 152.

Camden, Miss., 117.

Cantonment, Fla., 114.

Capuchin: founds Christian Doctrine Society, 18; priests working for N., 79.

Carolinas: early Cath. in, 20; slaves in, 22.

Carroll, Rt. Rev. John, "Relation of Religion in United States," 14.

Casserly, S.S.J., Rev. Edward, 170.

Cassilly, S.J., Rev. Francis, 131.

Catholic Board for Mission Work Among the Colored People: formation, 45; disbursements towards N. education, 150, 151; a recommendation, 288.

Catholic Church, The: ignorance of writers on work of, for N., XIII; and neglect of N., 13; U. S. Commissioner of Education on fairness of, in District of Columbia, 28; first Cath. church for N. in

U. S., 29; opposition to, after emancipation, 35, 36; Cath. reaction to Protestant opposition, 36, 37; churches for N. in 1871, 38, 39, in 1893, 42; and slavery, 76-78; migration makes new problem for, 105-108; and education of N., 134 et sq.; and higher education for N., 172, 176, 177; advantages of industrial training to, 183; and industrial education, 184-189; and child-caring homes for N. children, 196 et sq.; N. not naturally inclined to, 212; teaching of on color-line, 213, 214; lacks emotional appeal, 222-226; and N. morality, 237, 245; and N. environment, 240; and N. poverty, 240, 243; value of Cath. ritual, 247, 248; defections from, 258 et sq.; versus Socialism, 274, 275; and the new N., 274, 275; mother of all peoples, 279; and solution of N. problem, 283, 284.

Catholic Hill, Ritter, S. C., 113.

Catholic Negroes: population in 1888, 1, in 1928, 1; gain, 1890-1928, 1, 2; Bishop England on, 25; treatment of, in District of Columbia, 28, 29; in Richmond, Tennessee, Boston, New York, New Jersey, Philadelphia, St. Louis, and Cincinnati, 31; after emancipation, 33-35; in 1893, 42; present type of, 46; national census of, 47-50; distribution of, in relation to total population, 51-57; in white parishes, 58, 64; missionary work for, according to dioceses, table 4 facing 58; according to states, 59; summary of Government statistics for, 61, 62; erroneous impression from Government statistics, 62-64; distribution by sex, 64; converts and baptisms, 64-66; advantages to, of separate churches, 69-71; opposition of, to separate churches, 71-73; Cath. migrants, 102; number Cath. of migrants, 104; migrants must be cared for, 106-108; emotional tendency of, 247-249; attendance of at church, 256, 257; defection of from Church, 258 et sq.; demands on, 280, 281.

Catholics: accused in Maryland, 14; percentage of, in South, 54; and

slave labor, 77; and the color-line, 76-78; and education of N., 134 et sq.; individual contributions of to N. education, 150; delinquents in New York City, 193; and discrimination, 213-215; and finances for N. work, 218, 219; early concerned with care of N., 11, 226; indifference of, 276, 277; duty of towards Colored Missions, 108, 277, 284.

Chabrat, Rev. Guy, 136.

Charity, Sisters of: in schools (1893), 42; in Kentucky, 142, 143; work of, tables 14, 15, 18, 19.

Charleston S. C.: Cath. N. in, 20, 24; free N. in, 34 (footnote); churches for N. in, 38; Benedictines begin work for N. in, 41, 42; missionary work for N. in Diocese of, table 4 facing 58; effect of migration in city of, 102, on missions in Diocese, 112; early educational efforts in, 136; Cath. educational activities for N. in Diocese, 155; mission schools conducted by lay teachers in Diocese, 160.

Chastang, Alabama: foundation of, 23; mission at, 116.

Chastang, Jean, marries slave, 23.

Cheyenne, Wyoming, 48.

Chicago, Ill.: N. Caths. in Archdiocese, 48; missionary work done in, table 4 facing 58; Rev. Augustus Tolton, 85; concentration of N. in district of, 99, in city of, 100; migrants from Louisiana and Alabama to, 103, 108, 115; N. population of, 104; migration and work for Cath. N. in, 128; Cath. educational activity in Archdiocese, 155; Cath. high school for N., table 19 facing 179; house of Good Shepherd 202; plans for Cath. N. hospital in, 206.

Chicago Urban League, 128.

Child Welfare: sisters doing, 163 et sq.; delinquency, 192 et sq.

Christian Doctrine Society, 18.

Churches: and baptism of slaves, 11; slaves attending, 12; N. attending, in Washington, D. C., 28, 29; first Cath. church for N. in U. S., 29, 30; effect of emancipation on, 33; established in Virginia, 34; Rt. Rev. J. J. Kain, on separate, for N., 36; exclusively for N. in 1871, 38, 39; for N. at time of establishment of American Josephites, 42; affiliation of N. to, 55; survey of exclusively N. Cath., 57, 58; for N. according to dioceses, table 4 *facing* 58; according to states, 59; for N. in New Orleans, 60; Government statistics on Cath. churches for N., 61 et sq.; exclusively for N., 67-78; affiliation of delinquents, 193; discrimination in, 215; the N., and its rise, 220 *22*; emotional character of N. 223-226, 244; social character of N., 226-229, 244; preachers of the N., 229-233; and N. morality, 236, 237; irregularity in attendance at, 256, 257.

Church Point, La., 154.

Cincinnati, Ohio: early N. Caths. in city of, 31, in Archdiocese, 48; missionary work for Cath. N. in, table 4 *facing* 58, 127; concentration of N. in district of, 99, in city of, 100; migrants from Alabama to, 115; Cath. educational work in Archdiocese, 155, high schools, table 19 *facing* 179; house of Good Shepherd (Carthage), 202.

Civil War: conditions before, 10-31, after, 32 et sq.; education for N., before and after the, 134 et sq.; religion of slaves before, 220, 221, 227; classes of N. at time of, 241; defection of Cath. N. after the, 261, 280.

Claflin University, 145, 146.

Classes: among N., 241, 242; within the race, 252-254.

Cleveland, Ohio: N. Caths. in Diocese of, 48; missionary work in Diocese, table 4 *facing* 58; beginning of Church of Our Lady of the Blessed Sacrament, 74; concentration of N. in city of, 99, 100; migrants from Louisiana and Alabama to, 103, 115; N. population of, 127; Cath. educational work for N. in Diocese of, 155.

Code Noir, in Louisiana, 17.

Colleges: Protestant, for N., 145, 146; Cath., 152, 156, 164; Trotter and Du Bois on, 166; Cath. higher education for N., 169-173.

Colorado, 50, 132.

Colored Clergy: discussion on, 85-93; an argument for, 255; and ultimate solution of N. problem, 284; a recommendation on, 286.

Color Line: in church, 68; Murphy, on, 69, 71; Rt. Rev. Bishop Janssens, on, 72; opposition to, 71-76; the Cath. Church and the, 76-78; priests and the, 84; Northern Caths. more liberal on the, 107; none in schools in District of Columbia, 137; teaching of Cath. Church on the, 214, 215; within the race, 252, 253.

Columbus, Ohio: N. Caths. in Diocese of, 48; missionary work in Diocese of, table 4 *facing* 58; concentration of N. in district of, 99, in city of, 100; N. population in, 127; Cath. educational work for N. of, 155.

Commercial courses in high schools, table 19 *facing* 179.

Commission for Cath. Missions Among the Colored People and Indians: N. population in 1888, 1; formation of, 43; report on Cath. schools for N. in 1890, 145; on schools in 1915, 146; disbursements (1928), 150; on the sisters of the Colored Missions, 162, 163; collection of (1929), 218; past statistics and defections, 259; a recommendation, 288.

Communism versus Catholicity, 279.

Concordia, Kansas, 48.

Conditions, Past: from 1619-1829, 9-45; in general, 11-14; in Maryland, 14-16; in Louisiana, 16-19; in Kentucky, 19, 20; in Georgia and the Carolinas, 20-22; in Virginia, 23; in Alabama, 23, 24; from 1829-1866, 24-31; from 1866-1871, 32-39; after the Civil War, 34-36; Cardinal Vaughan on, 37; in N. education, 134-146; in the N. churches, 220 et sq.; and N. morality, 234 et sq.

Conditions, Present: 46, et sq.; number of N. Caths., 47-50; distribution of N. Caths., 51-57;

Cath. churches for N., 57-76; priests for Cath. N., 79-93; effects of migration on Cath. missions, 94-133; education, 134-189; social work, 190-209; of neglect, exaggerated, 279, 280.

Congregational Church: high schools of, 174; N. preachers in, 230; and N. ministers, 283.

Connecticut, 50, 122.

Consciousness of kind: Murphy on, 69, 71; and the color-line, 76; in northern cities, 101; and Cath. N., 254-256; new race consciousness, 273.

Converts: number reported, 64-66; to emotional religions, 223-225; through mixed marriages, 266; insufficient instruction of, 267, 268; Josephite mission reports show gain in, 280.

Co-operation, a recommendation, 285.

Corpus Christi, Texas, Diocese of: Cath. N. in, 48; mission work in, table 4 facing 58; Rev. Joseph John in, 86; Cath. educational work for N. in, 155.

Corrothers, James D., on N. preachers, 231.

Cote d'Afrique, La., 67 (footnote).

Covington, Ky., Diocese of: Fathers of the Holy Ghost in, 41; N. Caths. in, 48; missionary work in, table 4 facing 58; effect of migration on missions in, 114.

Creole, in Alabama, 23 (footnote), 24.

Crookston, Minn., 48, 130.

Crowley, La., 159.

Culture, and industrial training, 179.

Cunningham, Hon. William, on need of Cath. leaders, 172.

Curley, Most Rev. Michael J.: and colored Magdalens, 163; and Cardinal Gibbons Institute, 187; on sisters caring for N. children, 197; on interest in Colored Missions, 276.

D.

Dallas, Texas, Diocese of: N. Caths. in, 48; missionary work in, table 4 facing 58; effect of migration on missions in, 120; Cath. educational work in, 155; Cath. high school in, table 19 facing 179.

Davenport, Iowa, 48.

Dayton, Ohio, 67, 100, 115.

De Courcy, Henry, 28.

Defections of N. Caths. from Church: 2, 258-272; in Carolinas, 20, 25; after the Civil War, 33, 35, 42, 280; in rural areas, 55; and migration, 66, 103; reasons for, 68, 71; of Cath. migrants in North, 106; on Josephite missions, 109; in South Atlantic States, 109-114; in Los Angeles, 133; in New Orleans, 145; in non-Cath. schools, 148; leakage, 258-268; existence, 258; extent, 259; past causes, 259-262; present causes, 262-268.

Delany, Martin, 181.

Delaware: Cath. N. in, 50; distribution of Cath. N. in, 52; concentration of N. in, 54; mission work in, 59; effect of migrations on mission in, 109, 110; public schools for N. in, 141; du Pont contributions to, 149; Cath. schools for N. in, 152; high school, table 19 facing 179; St. Joseph's Industrial School, 185, 186.

Delinquency: sisters working for delinquent girls, 163 et sq., 192 et sq.; work of Good Shepherd Sisters for, 201, 203; environment and, 237-240.

Denver, Colorado, 48, 132.

Derrick, Rev. W. B., condemns efforts of Cath. Church, 36.

Derricks, Rev. Augustine, N. priest, 86.

de Ruyter, S.S.J., Rev. J., founds St. Joseph's Industrial School, 185.

Des Moines, Iowa, 49, 100.

de Soto, Hernando, and slaves, 10.

Detroit, Michigan: Cath. N. in, 49, 129; missionary work in, table 4 facing 58, 129; Rev. Norman Duckette, 86; concentration of N. in district of, 99, in city of, 100,

101; migrants from Louisiana and Alabama in, 103, 115.

Dever, Rev. Vincent, 126.

Difficulties of the N. Problem: due to lack of literature, 5; due to distribution of N. population, 54 et sq.; external, 212 et sq.; internal, 220 et sq.

Discrimination: by Caths., 213-215; and defection, 261-263.

District of Columbia, vide, Washington, D. C.

Divine Providence, Sisters of, activities of, for N., 152, 155, 164.

Divine Word, Society of the: priests working for N., 79; and N. clergy, 87; preparatory high school, table 19 facing 179.

Dominic, Sisters of St.: in schools (1893), 42; in Kentucky, 142, 143; educational activities for N., 154, 156, 157, 164; nursery of, 198, 199, 201.

Donaldsonville, La., 118.

Donelan, Rev. John, and N., in District of Columbia, 29.

Dorsey, S.S.J., Rev. John, N. priest, 85.

Douglas, Frederick, on industrial training, 181.

Dowling, S.S.J., Rev. Cornelius, 40.

Drexel, Miss Katharine, founds Sisters of Blessed Sacrament, 44; vide, Katharine, Mother, and Blessed Sacrament, Sisters of.

Du Bois, W. E. Burghardt: on higher education for N., 166; on emotional religion of N., 225; on social religion of N., 227, 244; on N. preachers, 232; on N. morality, 235; on N. environment, 237, 240: on lodgers, 238, 239; and religion, 274.

Dubourg, Rt. Rev. William, and Baltimore, N., 16.

Dubuque, Iowa, 48.

Duckette, Rev. Norman, N. priest, 86.

Duffy, S.S T., Rev. Thomas, acknowledgement, xv.

Duke Funds, for N. education, 149, 150.

Duluth, Minnesota, 49, 130.

Du Pont, Pierre S., contribution to N. education, 149.

E.

East North Central States: N. Caths. in, 50; Cath. churches for N. in, 67; missionary work in recent years, 106; effect of migration in, 127-129.

East St. Louis, migrants from Alabama in, 115.

East South Central States: N. Caths. in, 50; effect of migration in, 114-117.

Eccleston, Most Rev. Samuel, on lack of missioners, 28.

Eckert, Father, in Charleston, 41.

Eckert, S.V.D., Rev. Joseph: on discrimination by Caths., 263; on non-Cath. children in Cath. schools, 270, 271.

Economic: advantages of separate churches for N., 70; causes of migration, 95; conditions in North differ from South, 101; cause of migration in Georgia, 113, in Mississippi, 116, to Texas, 119; welfare of N. and higher education, 169; salvation of N. and industrial training, 182; conditions and delinquency, 194 et sq.; division of N. classes, 241, 252, 253; condition of N. and effect on church attendance, 256, 257.

Education: of slaves, 12; in Louisiana, 17; prior to 1829, 24; after 1829, 24; Bishop England and, 25, 136; in Tennessee, 31; in Virginia, 34; foundation of industrial and agricultural school by Holy Ghost Fathers, 41; Benedictine Fathers and work for, 42; schools in 1893, 42; schools for Cath. N. according to dioceses, table 4 facing 58, according to states, 59; schools for N. in New Orleans, 60; Government statistics on Sunday school attendance, 61, 62; educational value of separate churches, 69; of priests for N. missions, 80-85; of N. candidates for priesthood, 86-89; educational causes of migration, 96; Cath. educational activities for N., 134-189; a retrospect of, 134-146;

early advocates of, 134; prohibited by law, 135; verbal instruction, 135; efforts of Father Nerinckx for, 135, 136; early efforts in Maryland for, 136, in District of Columbia, 137-139; sisters take up work of, 142 et sq.; schools of the Colored Missions, 147 et sq.; and N. progress, 147; development of public school system, 148; Cath. educational activities for N., according to states, table 14, 152, according to dioceses, table 15, 155; the problem of the rural school, 158-161; Cath. educational activity for N., according to sisterhoods, table 18, 164; trends in, 166, 167; foundation of Cath. education for N., 167; Cath. college for N., 169-173; Cath. high schools for N., 173-179; industrial, 179-189; of N. preachers, 229-233; and N. environment, 240; superior education of mulattoes, 253; of N. ministers after Civil War, 283; a recommendation on, 287.

Education, United States Commissioner of: on N. in District of Columbia, 28; on efforts of Caths. and Quakers for early N. education, 135; on schools in District of Columbia, 137.

El Paso, Texas, 49.

Emancipation: Lincoln signs Proclamation, 32; Cath. labor, a contributing cause of, 77; effects of, on Cath. Church, 33-35, on Cath. N., 260, 261.

Emma's St., Industrial and Agricultural School: and Holy Ghost Fathers, 41; beginnings and work of, 184, 185.

Emotion: in early N. Baptist churches, 221, 222; emotional character of N. religion, 223-226; N. preacher and, 230-233; and morality, 243-245; emotional tendency of Cath. N., 247-249; a recommendation, 289.

Employment: helped by separate churches, 70; and migration, 95; of N. mothers outside home, 194, 195.

England, Rt. Rev. John: conditions in Charleston on arrival of, 20; champion of N. cause, 24-27; and

sisterhood for N., 25; and N. education, 25, 136; O'Connell, on, 26; excerpts from diary, 26.

Environment: and prejudice of N. against Cath. Church, 212; and morality of N., 237-240; social, and class distinctions, 252; and defection from Church, 265.

Epiphany Apostolic College: foundation, 41; priests at, 79; Rev. Charles Uncles, S.S.J., at, 85; and N. priests, 86; new building, 281.

Episcopal Church: high schools of, for N., 174; lack of emotional appeal in, 223; N. preachers in, 230, 232; and lost Caths., 264.

Erie, Pennsylvania, 49, 126.

Escambia, Florida, 114.

Estevan, N. slave, 10.

Evangelistic Churches: emotional appeal for slaves, 222-226; preachers of, 229-233; and Cath. N. after Civil War, 261.

F.

Fall River, Massachusetts, 49, 122.

Fargo, North Dakota, 49.

Fawcett, Rev. Benjamin, address to N. in Virginia, 23.

Federated Colored Catholics in United States, 209.

Financial: value of church edifices and expenditures in Cath. work for N., Government statistics, 61; effect of migration on, 102; poverty and establishment of free schools for N. in New Orleans, 145; expenditures for public schools, 147; Non-Cath. resources for education, 148, 149, Cath. resources, 150; poverty of rural schools, 159; poverty of sisters, 163; difficulties of Cath. high schools, 177; difficulties of Cardinal Gibbons Institute, 187; difficulties of Cath. work for N., 218, 219, 251, 281; recommendation, 288.

Fitzpatrick, Msgr. Mallick, 200.

Flaget, Rt. Rev. Benedict: in Kentucky, 20; and Father Nerinckx's N. sisters, 136.

Fleming, Walter, on Protestant opposition to Cath. Church in Alabama, 35.

Florida: N. Caths. in (1893), 42, in 1928, 50; distribution of N. Caths., 52; concentration of N. in, 54; mission work in, 59; Government statistics for Cath. work in, 61; and slavery, 77; and extent of migration, 96; loss through migration, 98, 102; destination of migrants from, 103; effect of migration on missions in, 113, 114; migrants from, to Alabama, 115; public schools for freedmen in, 141; Cath. educational activities for N. in, 152; prejudice against Cath. Church in, 212.

Fort Smith, Arkansas, 117.

Fort Wayne, Indiana, 49, 128.

Fort Worth, Texas, 67 (footnote).

Francis Xavier, Church of St.: first Cath. church for N., 29, 38; given to Josephites, 40; school, 140.

Francis, S.B.S., Sister, Dean, Xavier College, 170.

Francis, Sisters of St.: in schools in 1890, 145; in 1893, 42.

Francis, Sisters of St., Baltimore City: take over St. Elizabeth's Home, 143, 144; educational activities of, 153, 155, 164, 179, 197, 198; work exclusively for N. 163.

Francis, Sisters of St., Glen Riddle: take up N. work, 144, 145; educational activities of, 152, 155, 164, 198, 199.

Franciscan, priests working for N., 79.

Franciscans, Third Regular, educational activities of, 152, 155, 164.

Franciscans, Missionary, educational activities of, 152, 155, 164, table 19 facing 179.

Franklin, Louisiana, 67 (footnote).

Freedmen: majority not baptized, 33; number at emancipation, 34; wealth of, 34 (footnote).

Freedmen's Aid Society, The New England, activities after emancipation, 34.

Freedmen's Bureau, The, and schools for N., 141, 142.

Froman's Creek, Kentucky, early Caths. at, 19.

Furfey, Rev. P. H., 5.

G.

Galveston, Texas, Diocese of: N. Caths. in, 49; missionary work in, table 4 facing 58; effect of migration on missions in, 119; Cath. educational work for N. in, 155; mission schools conducted by lay teachers in, 160; Cath. high school for N. in, table 19 facing 179.

Gary, Indiana: mission, 67 (footnote); concentration of N. in, 100; growth of N. population in, 128.

General Education Board, resources of, for N. work, 148.

Georgetown, early N. education in, 137.

Georgia: and slaves, 20-22, 77; N. Caths. in, 50; distribution of N. Caths. in, 52; concentration of N. in, 54; Cath. missionary work for N. in, 59; Government statistics for Cath. missionary work in, 61; priests working for N. in, 79; and early migrations, 96; loss through migration, 98, 102; destination of migrants from, 103; effect of migration on missions in, 113; migrants from, to Alabama, 115; public schools for freedmen in, 141; Cath. educational activities for N. in, 152; mission schools conducted by lay teachers in, 161; Cath. high schools for N. in, table 19 facing 179; prejudice against Cath. Church in, 212.

Gibbons, Cardinal: on number of Cath. N., in 1892, 1; and Josephites, 41; approves formation of American Josephites, 44; forms Catholic Board for Mission Work Among Colored People, 45; ordained Rev. Charles Uncles, 85, Rev. John Dorsey, 85; and Franciscan Sisters, 144; on industrial training, 182.

Gibbons, Cardinal, Institute, The: 186-188; social service of, 208.

Gilligan, Rev. Francis, 214.

Good Shepherd, Sisters of the: activities for N., 152, 155, 162-164, 201-203; and industrial training, 188.

Gore, S.S.J., Rev. James, 40.

Grand Island, Nebraska, 49.

Grand Rapids, Michigan, 49, 129.

Grant, Nancy, and early N., education in District of Columbia, 138.

Great Falls, Montana, 49.

Green Bay, Wisconsin, 49.

Greene, S.S.J., Rev. John, 38, 142.

Greensboro, N. Carolina, 67 (footnote), 154 (footnote), 165.

Greenville, Mississippi, 117, 207.

Greenville County, S. Carolina, 112.

Greisen, C.SS.R., Rev., and school for N. in Baltimore, 140.

Grossi, S.S.J., Rev. Sabino: mission territory, 56; rural education, 159.

Guilday, Rev. Peter, on care of N., 39.

H.

Hagspiel, S.V.D., Very Rev. Bruno, 87.

Handmaids of the Most Pure Heart of Mary, activities of, 153, 157, 163, 165, 198-201.

Hannigan, S.S.J., Rev. Charles, 217.

Hardin's Creek, Kentucky, early Caths. at, 19.

Harlem: Cath. churches for N. in, 61; N. in, 124; Protestant churches in, 124; St. Benedict's Nursery, 201.

Harrisburgh, Pennsylvania, 49, 126.

Hartford, Connecticut: N. Caths. in, 49; concentration of N. in, 100.

Haynes, George E., on church high schools, 174.

Helena, Arkansas, 154 (footnote).

Helena, Montana, 49.

Helpers of the Holy Souls: activities of, 153, 157, 164; social service work in St. Louis, 208, in San Francisco, 209.

Heredity and N. Morality, 234-237.

Higher Education: need and advisability of, 168, 169, 177; Xavier College, 170-173; industrial training versus, 179-182; a recommendation on, 287; vide, Colleges.

High Rents, 238, 242.

High Schools: Protestant, for N., 145; Cath., according to states, 152, according to dioceses, 155, according to sisterhoods, 164: graduates of public and private, 168; Xavier, 170; Cath. high schools, 173-179; a recommendation on, 287.

Holy Cross, Sisters of the, 165 (footnote).

Holy Family, Sisters of the: foundation, 30, 31, 140, 141; in schools (1893), 42, in 1890, 145; summer school of, 151; educational activities of, 152, 155, 164, table 19 facing 179; institutions for N. children, 198, 199; home for aged N., 206.

Holy Ghost, Sisters of the, in schools, 42, 145.

Holy Ghost, Sisters, Servants of the: foundation of, 144; educational activities of, 152, 155, 164.

Holy Ghost and Mary Immaculate, Sisters of the: educational activities of, 152, 155, 164, table 19 facing 179; home for N. children, 199.

Holy Ghost, Missionary Servants of the: educational activities of the, 152, 155, 164, table 19 facing 179; plans for Cath. hospital for N., 206.

Holy Ghost, Society of the: begin work for N., 41; priests working for N., 79; Rev. John Burgess, member of, 86.

Holy Names, Sisters of the, educational activities of, 152, 157, 164.

Holy Trinity, Sisters of the Most: educational activities of, 152, 156, 165, table 19 facing 179; welfare work at Tuscaloosa, 205.

Home, The Negro: Odum on, 239; poverty of the, 241-243.

Homes for Negro children: accordto states, 152, according to dioceses, 155, according to sisterhoods, 164; industrial training in,

188; social service of, 196 et sq.; *vide*, Orphanages.

Housing Problem: 204; and environment, 238.

Houston, Texas, effects of migration in, 119.

I.

Idaho, 50, 132.

Ignatius, Church of St., Baltimore, used by N., 30.

Illinois: N. Caths. in state of, 50; distribution of N. Caths. in, 52; missionary work for N. in, 59, 67 (footnote), migrants from Alabama in, 115; migration and Cath. work for N. in, 128, 129; Cath. educational activities for N. in, 152, table 19 *facing* 179.

Illiteracy, percentage of N., 147.

Immaculate Heart, Sisters of the, educational activities for N., 153, 155, 164, 198, 199.

Indiana: N. Caths. in, 50; distribution of N. Caths. in, 52; missionary work for N. in, 59, 67 (footnote); migration and work for Cath. N. in, 128: Cath. educational activity for N. in, 152.

Indianapolis, Indiana: N. Caths. in Diocese of, 49, 128; missionary work for N. in Diocese, table 4 *facing* 58; concentration of N. in district of, 99, in city of, 100; St. Rita's Church, 128; Cath. educational activities for N. in Diocese of, 155.

Industrial School: by Fathers of Holy Ghost, 41; by Benedictines in N. Car., 41; Slater Fund and, 149; according to states, 152, to dioceses, 155, to sisterhoods, 164; Booker T. Washington on, 166, 167; Woodson on, 166; and high schools, table 19 *facing* 179; necessity of, 179-183; advantages of Cath., 183; Cath. efforts for, 179-189; the industrialized N., 273.

Immoral Conditions: and delinquency, 194; of slaves, 234-236; environment, 237 et sq.

Iowa, 50, 130.

Isle Breville, La., 118.

J.

Jackson, Mississippi, 117.

Jackson, Tennessee, 115.

Jacksonville, Florida, 113.

Janssens, Rt. Rev. F.: on need of priests for N. work, 37; on separate churches for N., 72.

Jeanes, Anna T., Fund, resources of, for N. education, 148.

Jersey City, New Jersey, 125.

Jesuits: and N. in Maryland, 15, 30, in Louisiana, 15-18, in District of Columbia, 29, in St. Louis, 31, in Cincinnati, 127; work of, 38, 42, 79, 80, 140; and early N. education in District of Columbia, 139; chaplain to Cardinal Gibbons Institute, 187.

John, Knights of St., 209.

John, Rev. Joseph, N. priest, 86, 90.

Jones, Arabella, and early education of N., in District of Columbia, 138.

Joseph, Church of St., Philadelphia, 31.

Joseph, Seminary of St., Baltimore: opened, 41; priests at, 79; in Washington, D. C., 281.

Joseph, Sisters of St., educational activities for N., 42, 145, 152, 157, 165.

Joseph, Society of St. (Josephite Fathers): arrival in United States, 39-41; opens St. Joseph's Seminary and Epiphany College, 41; missions in charge of, in 1893, 42; formation of American branch urged by Cardinal Vaughan, 43; separation made, 44; conversions and baptisms on missions of, 65, 66; priests of, working for N., 79; and N. priests, 85, 87; condition of education upon arrival of first Josephites, 140; home for orphans, Wilmington, 144; influence on N. education, 146; high schools of, table 19 *facing* 179; St. Joseph's Industrial School, 185; and N. children, 198, 199; mission reports of, show gain, 280.

Joseph's Industrial School, St., Clayton, Delaware, 185.

Joubert, Rev. Nicholas: and N. in

Baltimore, 16; and the Oblate Sisters, 27.

K.

Kain, Rt. Rev. J. J., on condition of N., 36.
Kansas City, Kansas: concentration of N. in, 100; missionary work for N. in, 132.
Kansas City, Missouri: N. Caths. in Diocese of, 49, in state of, 50; distribution of N. Caths. in, 52; missionary work in, table 4 *facing* 58; and early migrations, 96; concentration of N. in district of, 99, in city of, 100; work being done for Cath. N. in, 59, 131, 132, 155; Cath. educational activity for N. in, 152, table 19 *facing* 179; St. Monica's Home, 198.
Katharine, Rev. Mother: founds Sisters of Blessed Sacrament, 44; and education of N., 146; financial help for N. education, 150; and rural schools, 160; aids in establishing St. Joseph's Industrial School, 185.
Kentucky: early Caths. in, 19; treatment of slaves in, 19; Fathers of Holy Ghost begin work in, 41; N. Caths. in, 50; distribution of N. Caths. in, 52; concentration of N. in, 54; missionary work for N. in, 59; Government statistics for Cath. missionary work for N. in, 61; loss through migration, 98, 102; effect of migration on missions in, 114; migrants from Alabama in, 115; effort to found N. sisterhood in, 135; public schools for N. in, 141; Father Greene on Cath. schools for N. in, 142, 143; Cath. educational activity in, 152; mission schools conducted by lay teachers in, 161; Cath. high school for N. in, table 19 *facing* 179.
Kerby, Rev. William: on statistics, 6, 7; on social service, 191.
Ku Klux Klan, kidnaps Father Warren, 70.

L.

La Crosse, Wisconsin, 49.
Lafayette, Louisiana, Diocese of:

N. Caths. in, 49; missionary work for N. in, table 4 *facing* 58; effect of migration on missions in, 118; mission schools conducted by lay teachers in, 161; Cath. high schools for N. in, table 19 *facing* 179; industrial training by sisters in, 188.
Laube, S.M.A., Rev. Alfred, 113.
Lay Teachers: in schools (1893), 42; number of, according to states, 152, according to dioceses, 155; institutions in charge of, 158; schools conducted by, 160; employed by sisters, 164; in high schools, table 19 *facing* 179; at St. Emma's Industrial School, 184; at Cardinal Gibbons Institute, 186; in child-caring homes, 198, 199.
Lead, S. Dakota, 49.
Leakage, *vide* Defection.
Leavenworth, Kansas, Diocese of: N. Caths. in, 49; missionary work for N. in, table 4 *facing* 58, 132; Cath. high school for N. in, table 19 *facing* 179; industrial training by sisters in, 188; institutions for N. children in, 198, 199.
Lebeau, Louisiana, 188.
Lenahan, Rev. Thomas, 205.
Leo XIII, Pope, on slavery, 77.
Leonardtown, Maryland, N. in (1636), 15.
Lexington, Kentucky, 114.
Lincoln, Abraham, 32, 33, 78.
Lincoln, Nebraska, 49, 131.
Literature on the Negro Problem: a contribution to, xv; lack of literature of investigation, 6, of interpretation, 7, of direction, 7.
Little Rock, Arkansas. Diocese of: Fathers of Holy Ghost in, 41; N. Caths. in, 49; missionary work in, table 4 *facing* 58; effect of migration on missions in, 117; mission school conducted by lay teachers, 161; Cath. high school for N. in, table 19 *facing* 179; House of Good Shepherd, 202; effort to establish Cath. hospital for N. in, 207.
Little Sisters of the Poor, 206.
Locust Grove, Georgia, 21.

Lodgers: in Virginia, 204; and N. morality, 238, 239; result of high rents, 242.

Loretto, Kentucky, efforts to found first N. sisterhood at, 136.

Loretto, Sisters of; and N. sisters, 135; in Kentucky, 142.

Los Angeles, California, Diocese of: N. Caths. in, 49, 132, 133; missionary work in, table 4 *facing* 58; concentration of N. in city of, 100; social work of Sisters of Our Lady of Apostles, 208.

Louisiana: early work of Cath. Church for N. in, 16-19; de Courcy, on religion of N. in, 28; free N. in, 34 (footnote); N. Caths. in. 50; distribution of N. Caths. in, 52; concentration of N. in, 54; missionary work for N. in, 59, 60, 67 (footnote); Government statistics for Cath. missionary work in, 61; slavery in, 77; priests working for N. in, 79; and early migrations of N., 96; loss through migration, 98, 102; migrants from, to other states, 103, 110, 118; Mississippi N. living in, 116; effect of migration on missions in, 102, 117, 118; Cath. efforts for N. education in, 135; schools for freedmen in, 141; Cath. educational activities for N. in, 152; mission schools conducted by lay teachers in, 160; Xavier College, 169 et sq.; Cath. high schools for N. in, table 19 *facing* 179; Xavier and industrial training in, 189; prejudice against Cath. Church in, 212; defection of Cath. N. in, 258.

Louisville, Kentucky: masters and slaves in, 19; church of St. Augustine, 39, 42; N. Caths. in Diocese of, 49; missionary work in Diocese of, table 4 *facing* 58; effect of migration on missions in, 114; mission schools conducted by lay teachers, 161; Cath. high school for N. in, table 19 *facing* 179; house of Good Shepherd in, 202.

Low Wages. 242.

Lynch, Rt. Rev. Patrick, 38.

M.

Macon, Georgia, 113.

Magdalens, Colored, 163.

Maine, 50, 122.

Manchester, New Hampshire, 49.

Marechal, Most Rev. Ambrose, and early N. education in Baltimore, 139.

Marianites of the Holy Cross, Sisters, educational activities for N., 153, 157, 164.

Marksville, Louisiana, 118.

Marquette, Michigan, 49, 129.

Marriages: Cath., fostered by social life in church, 250; mixed, 251; mixed and defection of N. Caths. 265, 266.

Married Women, working, 194.

Mary's Church, St., Alexandria, Virginia, and treatment of N., 29.

Maryland: and N. in, 14-16; Jesuits and N. in, 15; Cath. migrants from, to Kentucky, 19, to Georgia, 21; Maryland N. in Charleston, 24; Archbishop Whitfield on N. Caths. in, 28; de Courcy on religion of N. in, 28; N. Caths. in, 50; distribution of N. Caths. in, 52; concentration of N. in, 54; missionary work in, 59; Government statistics on Cath. missionary work in, 61; and slavery, 77; priests working for N. in, 79; Jesuits in southern, 79; effect of migration on missions in, 110; Cath. efforts for education of N. in, 135, 137, 153; public schools for freedmen in, 141; Cath. high schools for N. in, table 19 *facing* 179; Cardinal Gibbons Institute, 186-188.

Massachusetts: N. Caths. in, 50; distribution of N. Caths. in, 52; mission work in, 59, 121, 122, 153.

Matthew's Church, St., Washington, D. C.; and early N., 29; and early N. education, 138.

Matthew, Father, and N. in District of Columbia, 29.

Maysville, Alabama, 67 (footnote).

McCort, Rt. Rev. John, on Cath. indifference, 277.

McElroy, Father, and education of N. in District of Columbia, 137.

Memphis, Tennessee: Cardinal Vaughan on conditions in, 37; effect of migration on St. Anthony's mission in, 60, 114; point of distribution for migrants, 114, 116, 117; effort to establish Cath. hospital for N. in, 207.

Mercier, Rev. le, and baptism of slaves, 22.

Mercy, Sisters of: in schools in 1893, 42, in 1890, 145; and Sisters of Blessed Sacrament, 144; and early N. education in Charleston, 136; educational activities for N., 152, 156, 164.

Meridian, Mississippi, 117.

Methodist Church: opposition to Cath. Church, 35; N. membership in, 55; Cath. children attend schools of, in New Orleans, 145; high schools for N., 174; influence of, on N. estimation of Cath. Church, 213; emotional appeal to slaves, 222-224; preachers of, 229; and lost Caths., 264; and N. ministers, 283.

Michigan: N. Caths. in, 50; distribution of N. Caths. in, 52; missionary work in, 59, 129.

Middle Atlantic States: N. Caths. in, 50; Cath. churches for N. in, 67; migrants to, 103, 111; missionary work in recent years, 106; Mississippi N. living in, 116; effect of migration in, 122-126.

Migration: effect on distribution of N. population, 56, 57; nature of, 56; and New Jersey, 60; effect on baptisms and conversions, 66; migration of church members, 69; the recent migration, 94-133; in general, 94-108; number of migrants, 94, 95; causes of, 95, 96; character of, 96, 118; extent of, 96-99; concentration of N. migrants in districts, 99; concentration in cities, 100; adjustment of migrants, 101; effect on missions, 101-105; number of migrants, 104; loss of Cath. migrants, 106, 259; migration and the South, 109-120; and the North, 121-129; and the West, 130-133;

and delinquency, 193, 194; and N. environment, 237, 238; and defection of Caths., 263-265.

Miles, Nicholas, settles in Kentucky, 19.

Miles, Rt. Rev. Richard: in Kentucky, 20; in Tennessee, 31.

Miller, S.J., Rev. Peter, and labors for N. in Baltimore, 30.

Milwaukee, Wisconsin: N. Caths. in, 48; missionary work in, table 4 facing 58, 129; concentration of N. in city of, 100; industrial training by sisters in, 188; nursery, 198, 201.

Minneapolis, Minnesota, 100, 130.

Minnesota: N. Caths. in, 50; distribution of N. Caths. in, 52; missionary work in, 59, 130.

Mission Helpers of the Sacred Heart: activities for N., 153, 155, 164; Archbishop Curley on, 197; institutions for N. children, 197-200; social service in Baltimore and vicinity, 207.

Missionaries: Catholic, and baptism of slaves, 11; lack of, 27, 28, 104, 216-218; Protestant, after the war, 34; and past statistics, 63; and separate churches, 73; necessity of trained, 80-85; arm-chair, 82; requirements of, to the N., 82-84; early, and N. education, 134; and financial handicaps, 218, 219; no access to slaves, 221; two idealisms, 247; and social life in churches, 250; personal attitude of N. towards, 257; and work done for N., 275.

Missionary: effective mission methods, XIII, 4; Protestant missionary societies, 5; Protestant, after emancipation, 34, 35; centers, 46; work concentrated in South, 54; work according to dioceses, table 4 facing 58, according to states, 59; work for N., 79; societies and a colored clergy, 91, 92; effect of migration on southern work, 101-105; activity for the migrant in the North, 106-108; American Hierarchy on missionary work for N., 107, 108.

Mississippi: N. Caths. in, 50; distribution of N. Caths., 52; concentration of N. in, 54; missionary work in, 59, 61; Government statistics for Cath. missionary work in, 61; and early migrations of N., 96; loss of N. through migration, 97, 98, 102; effect of migration on missions in, 102, 117; migrants to Alabama, 115; public schools for freedmen, 141; Cath. educational activities for N. in, 153; Cath. schools conducted by lay teachers in, 161; Cath. high schools for N., table 19 *facing* 179; prejudice against Cath. Church in, 212.

Missouri: N. Caths. in state, 50; distribution of N. Caths. in, 52; missionary work in, 59, 61, 131; public schools for freedmen, 141; Cath. educational activity for N. in, 153.

Mobile, Alabama, Diocese of: N. Caths. in, 42, 49; missionary work in, table 4 *facing* 58; effect of migration on missions in, 114, 115; point of distribution for migrants, 116; mission schools conducted by lay teachers in, 161; Cath. high schools for N., in, table 19 *facing* 179; institutions for N. children in, 198, 199; welfare work at Tuscaloosa, 205.

Moine, Abbe la, 21.

Mon Louis, Alabama, 116.

Montana, 50, 132.

Monterey, Fresno, California, 49, 132.

Montgomery, Alabama, 102.

Moral: values in N. problem, 3-5; condition of slaves, 234; idea impossible to many N., 242.

Morality of N., 35, 234-245.

Morrell, Mrs. Edward Drexel: contributions for N. education, 150; founds St. Emma's Industrial School, 184; erects memorial to General Edward Morrell, 185.

Mose, N. settlement at, 22.

Mountain States, 50, 132.

Mulattoes, and class distinctions, 252, 253.

Murphy, Mrs. Margaret, founds Sisters, Servants of the Holy Ghost, 144.

Murphy, Rev. Edward: on the colorline, 69, 71; on priests for N., 81; on clerical interest, 84; on poverty of the N., 205; on lack of priests for N. work, 216.

N.

Narvaez, Panfilo de, and Estevan, 10.

Nashville, Tennessee, Diocese of: free school for N. in, 31; N. Caths. in, 42, 49; missionary work in, table 4 *facing* 58; effect of migration on missions in, 114, 115; Cath. high school for N., table 19 *facing* 179.

Natchez, Mississippi, Diocese of: N. Caths. in, 49; missionary work for N. in, table 4 *facing* 58; effect of migration on missions in, 116, 117; mission schools conducted by lay teachers in, 161; Cath. high schools for N. in, table 19 *facing* 179; effort to establish Cath. hospital for N. in Greenville, 207.

Neale, Most. Rev. Francis, and N. in District of Columbia, 29, 137.

Nebraska: N. Caths. in, 50; distribution of N. Caths. in, 52; missionary work in, 59, 131, Cath. educational activity for N. in, 153.

Neglected and Delinquent Negro Children: 192 et sq.; child-caring homes for, 196 et sq.

Negro Year Book: on extent of migration, 97, 98; on destination of migrants, 99.

Neraz, Rt. Rev. John, 144.

Nerinckx, Rev. Charles, and colored sisters, 20, 135, 136.

Nevada, 132.

Newark, New Jersey: N. Caths. in, 49, 125; missionary work in, table 4 *facing* 58; concentration of N. in, 100.

New Bedford, Massachusetts: concentration of N. in city of, 100; bravas in, 122.

Newbern, N. Carolina: Passionists in charge of mission in, 79 (footnote), 112.

New England States: N. Caths. in, 50; migrants to, 103, 111; Mis-

sissippi N. living in, 116; effect
of migration in, 121, 122.
New Hampshire, 122.
New Jersey: N. Cath. in, 31, 50;
distribution of N. Caths. in, 52;
missionary work in, 59, 125; and
migration, 60, 125; migrants from
North Carolina to, 112.
New Mexico, 10, 50, 132.
New Orleans: San Domingans in,
18; Christian Doctrine Society in,
18; Sisters of Holy Family in, 30,
140, 141; N. Caths. in, 42, 48, 104;
center of missionary activity, 46;
missionary work in, table 4 facing
58; organization of N. work in,
60; effect of migration on missions in, 102, 118; conditions in
(1889), 145; mission schools conducted by lay teachers in Archdiocese, 161; Xavier College in,
169 et sq.; Cath. high schools for
N. in, table 19 facing 179; industrial training by sisters in, 188;
institutions for N. children in
Archdiocese, 198; house of Good
Shepherd in, 202; home for aged
N. in, 206.
New Roads, Louisiana, 118.
Newton Grove, N. Carolina, 79 (footnote), 112.
New York: Caths. from, in Georgia,
21; de Courcy on religion of N.
in, 28; N. Caths. in city of, 31,
in Archdiocese of, 48, in state of,
50; distribution of N. Caths. in,
52; missionary work for N. in,
table 4 facing 58, 122-125; effect
of migration, 60, 122-125; West
Indians in, 60; Cath. churches
for N. in, 61, 121; concentration
of N. in district of, 99, in city of,
100; loss of Cath. migrants, 106;
migrants from N. Carolina in,
112; Cath. educational activities
for N. in, 153; industrial training by sisters at Rye, 188; neglected and delinquent children
in, 192; homes for N. children in,
198-201; house of Good Shepherd,
202.
New York Urban League, on N. in
New York, 123.
Night Schools, table 19 facing 179;
at Van de Vyver Institute, 188.

Noonan, S.S.J., Rev. James, 40.
Norfolk, Virginia: mission at, 42;
Father Warren's Band, 70; effect
of migration, 111.
North Carolina: N. Caths. in state,
50; distribution of N. Caths. in,
52; concentration of N. in, 54;
missionary work for N. in, 59;
Government statistics for Cath.
missions in, 61; and early migrations, 96; loss through migration,
98; destination of migrants from,
103; effect of migration on missions in, 112; public schools for
freedmen in, 141; Duke contribution for N. education in, 149;
Cath. educational activities for N.
in, 154; mission schools conducted by lay teachers in, 160; Cath.
high school in, table 19 facing
179; prejudice against Cath.
Church in, 212.
North Dakota, 50, 131.
Notre Dame, School Sisters of, educational activities of, 153, 155,
165.
Nurseries, Catholic, for N. children, 198-201.

O.

Oakland, California, 100.
Oblate Fathers, 144.
Oblate Sisters: founded, 16; canonically erected, 27; in schools, 42,
145; and effort to establish first
colored sisterhood, 136; Maria Becraft enters, 138; St. Francis'
Academy, 139; educational activities according to states, 152, to
dioceses, 155; work of community, 165; high schools in charge
of, table 19 facing 179; institutions for children in charge of,
198, 199.
Obstacles to greater results, 210 et
sq.
O'Connell, O.S.B., J.J., on Bishop
England, 26.
O'Connor, S.J., Rt. Rev. M., begs for
St. Francis' Church, 30.
O'Connor, Rt. Rev. James, and Sisters of Blessed Sacrament, 44.
Odum, Howard: on emotional character of N. religion, 223, 244; on

N. preachers, 232, 233; on home life of N., 239.

Ogdensburgh, New York, 49, 123.

Oglethorpe Expedition, 22 (footnote).

Ohio: N. Caths. in, 50; distribution of N. Caths. in, 52; missionary work in, 59; Government statistics for Cath. mission work in, 61; migration and Cath. mission work in, 127; Cath. educational activities in, 154; Cath. high school for N. in, table 19 *facing* 179.

Oklahoma City, Diocese of: N. Caths. in, 49; missionary work in, table 4 *facing* 58; N. from, in Springfield, Illinois, 129; Cath. high school for N. in, table 19 *facing* 179.

Oklahoma, State of: N. Caths. in, 50; distribution of N. Caths. in, 52; concentration of N. in, 54; missionary work in, 59; Government statistics for Cath. mission work in, 61; loss through migration, 98; effect of migration on missions in, 102; Mississippi N. living in, 116; Cath. educational activities for N. in, 154.

Omaha, Nebraska: N. Caths. in Diocese of, 49; missionary work for N. in, table 4 *facing* 58; concentration of N. in city of, 100; effect of migration in, 131.

Opposition: to work of Cath. Church, 35, 36; to separate churches, 71-76.

Oregon City, Oregon, 48, 50.

Orphanage: care of orphans, 31; opened in New Orleans, 141; beginning of St. Elizabeth's Home, Baltimore, 143, 144; St. Joseph's, Wilmington, 144; according to states, 152, to dioceses, 155, to sisterhoods, 164; Cath., for N. children, 196 et sq.

P.

Pacific States, 50, 132, 133.

Paddington, Rev., 85 (footnote).

Parochial Schools: development of the, 142 et sq.; according to states, 152, to dioceses, 155, to sis-

terhoods, 164; the problem of the mission school, 158-161; mission schools conducted by lay teachers, 160.

Pascagoula, Mississippi, 117, 159.

Pass Christian, Mississippi, 117.

Passionist Fathers, 79 (footnote), 217.

Patrick's School, St., Washington, D. C., 29.

Patzelt, S.V.D., Rev. Herman, work in Little Rock, 117.

Pennsylvania: N. Caths. in, 50; distribution of N. Caths. in, 52; missionary work for N. in, 59; Government statistics for Cath. mission work in, 61; priests working for N. in, 79; loss of Cath. migrants in, 106; migrants from N. Carolina in, 112, from Alabama in, 115; migration and work for Cath. N. in, 125, 126; Quaker efforts for N. Education in, 135; Cath. educational activities for N. in, 154; Cath. high school for N. in, table 19 *facing* 179.

Pensacola, Florida, 113.

Peoria, Illinois, 49, 67 (footnote), 129.

Peter Claver: Chapel of Blessed, Baltimore, 30; Church of St., Charleston, S. Carolina, 38; Knights of St., 209.

Philadelphia: N. Caths. in, 31, 48, 126; Fathers of the Holy Ghost in, 41; missionary work for N. in, table 4 *facing* 58, 125, 126; concentration of N. in district of, 99, in city of, 100; N. population of, 104, 125; Cath. high school for N. in, table 19 *facing* 179; industrial training by sisters in, 188; house of Good Shepherd, 202; social work of St. Agnes' Guild, 208.

Pine Bluff, Arkansas, 117.

Pittsburgh, Pennsylvania: N. Caths. in Diocese of, 49; missionary work for N. in, table 4 *facing* 58, 125, 126; concentration of N. in district of, 99, in city of, 100.

Popes: and treatment of slaves, 134; Pius II and education of slaves, 77; Pius IX and first Josephites, 40; Pius X requests formation of

Cath. Board for Mission Work Among Colored People, 45; Pius XI approves St. Augustine's Seminary, 87, on native clergy, 87, 88, 282, 283.

Plantvigne, S.S.J., Rev. Joseph, N. priest, 86.

Population: of N., Cath. N., and gain in, 1, 2, 11; N. in Maryland, 14, Charleston, 20, 24, 25, Virginia 27; at emancipation; survey of Cath. N., 47-50; distribution of Cath. N. in relation to total, 51-57; map, 53; Federal census of N., 54; concentration in rural areas, 55; effect of migration on, 56, 96-102; concentration in districts, 99, in cities, 100; number of migrants, 104; increase in N., in southern cities, 104, 105; N. in New England states, 121, 122, in Middle Atlantic, 122-126, in East North Central, 126-129, in West North Central, 130-132.

Porras, Blessed Martin, 39.

Port Arthur, Texas, 119.

Portland, Maine, 49.

Pottinger's Creek, Kentucky, early Caths. at, 19.

Poverty: and Morality, 240-243; and N. missions, 282.

Preacher, The Negro: condition after emancipation, 34; in the rural community, 56; and rise of N. Church, 221, 222; and emotional religion, 225, 229-233, 244; and defections from Cath. Church, 261.

Prejudice, against Cath. Church in South, 212, 213.

Presbyterians: in Virginia, 34; high schools for N., 174; N. preachers, 230, 283.

Presentation, Sisters of the, activities, 153, 155, 165.

Prevot, Mme. de, and baptism of slaves, 22.

Priests: Archbishop Whitfield on lack of, for N. missions, 27; and care of N. after emancipation, 34; need of, for N. missions, 36, 37; Cardinal Vaughan on indifference of, 37; lack of, in rural areas, 55, 104; working for N., according to dioceses, table 4 facing 58, to states, 59; for N. in New Orleans,

60; and mixed congregations, 68, 69, 73; working on the Colored Missions, 79-93; summary of survey on, 79-80; necessity of trained, for N. work, 80-85; armchair missioners, 80; requirements of, for N. work, 82-84; colored clergy, 85-93; lack of, for N. work, 216, 218, 228, 281; personal attitude of N. towards, 257; and defections of N., 261, 262; duty of, towards N. missions, 277; a recommendation on, 284, 286.

Problem, The Negro: existence, 1-3; nature, 3-5; slowness of Caths. to recognize the, 3; spiritual and moral values in the, 3-5; literature of the, 5-9; no longer a southern problem, 273; the Cath. Church and the solution of the, 283.

Protestants: exclude N. from churches in Washington, 29; activity of, after emancipation, 34; oppose Cath. efforts for N., 35, 36; strength in South, 54 et sq.; Caths. versus, in missions, 107; early, and education of N., 134-137; and verbal education, 135; schools for N., 145, 146; churches and high schools, 174; and social welfare, 190; delinquents, 193; and racial advantages in South, 212; and finances for N. work, 219.

Providence, Rhode Island, 49, 122.

Public Schools: formation of public school system, 141, 142; N. enrolled in, 147 et sq.; remarkable growth of, 148; teachers versus sisters, 162, 163; graduates of, 168; enrolments in public high schools, 173, 174; versus mission schools in New Orleans, 219.

Q.

Quakers: and care of slaves, 11; in Virginia, 34; and education of slaves, 135.

Quincy, Illinois, 129.

Quinn, Rev. Bernard, 123.

R.

Raleigh, N. Carolina, Diocese of, N. Caths. in, 49; mission work in, table 4 facing 58, 67 (footnote), mission school, 161; Rev. Charles Hannigan, 217.

Raymond, Rev. Gilbert, 141.

Rayne, Louisiana, 154 (footnote).

Reclamation work in Louisiana, 60.

Recommendations, 284-289.

Redemptorists: work of the, 38; at Newton Grove, N. C., 79 (footnote); and early N. education in Baltimore, 140.

Religion: of masters and slaves, 13; of N., and Cath. progress, 220 et sq.; of slaves before Civil War, 220, 222; emotional character of N., 223-226, 244; social character of N., 226-229; religious concepts of N., 246; and the new N., 274, 275.

Rerum Ecclesiae, on native clergy, 87, 282.

Rhode Island, 50.

Richmond, Virginia: first Cath. slave in, 31; mission in, 42; N. Caths. in Diocese of, 49; missionary work in, table 4 facing 58; effect of migration on missions in, 111, 112; mission schools conducted by lay teachers in, 161; Cath. high schools for N., in, table 19 facing 179; St. Emma's Industrial School, 184; Van de Vyver Institute, 188; social survey in city of, 204; lodgers in, 238.

Rochester, New York, 49, 123.

Rock Castle, Virginia, 112.

Rockford, Illinois, 129.

Rosenwald, Julius, Fund for N. education, 149.

Rousselon, Rev. Etienne, and Holy Family Sisters, 30, 141.

Rural: concentration of N. in, 55; migration from, 56; Government statistics for Cath. mission work for N. in, 61, 62; population in North, 99, in South, 101; effect of migration on the rural problem, 104, 105, 118; lack of priests for missions in, 104; the problem of the rural school, 158-161; rural schools conducted by lay teachers, 161; children and delinquency, 193, 194; emotional religion of rural N., 224; poverty of rural N., 242; social life in rural churches, 249.

Russell, Rt. Rev. William, on financial handicap of N. missions, 218.

Ryan, Most Rev. P. J., approves Sisters of Blessed Sacrament, 44.

S.

Sacramento, California, 49, 132.

Sacred Heart, Sisters of the, educational activities, 42, 145, 153, 156, 165.

Salt Lake, Utah, 49.

San Antonio, Texas, Archdiocese of: N. Caths. in, 48; missionary work in, table 4 facing 58; effect of migration on missions in, 119, 120; foundation of Sisters of Holy Ghost, 144; Cath. high school for N., table 19 facing 179.

San Domingans: arrival of, in Baltimore, 15; arrival in New Orleans, 18; in Georgia, 20, 21; in Charleston, 25; and early N. education in Baltimore, 139.

San Francisco, California, Archdiocese of: N. Caths. in, 48, 132; social work in, 209.

Santa Fe, New Mexico, 48.

Savannah, Georgia, Diocese of: N. Caths. in, 49; missionary work in, table 4 facing 58; effect of migration in, 102, 113; mission school, 161; high schools, table 19 facing 179; home, 198, 200.

Schlecht, S.M.A., Rev. Edmund, 133.

Schools: Catholic, for N. in Charleston, 25, 136; in Alabama, 35; in District of Columbia, 137; for freedmen in South, 141; development of Cath. mission school, 142, 143; need of schools for N. in New Orleans, 145; of the Colored Missions, 146 et sq.; influence of, 147, 151 ; need of, 151; according to states, 152, to dioceses, 155, to sisterhoods, 162; the problem of the rural, 158-161; sisters in Cath., 162-165; foundation of Cath. 167; Xavier College, 169-173; Cath. high schools, table 19 facing 179; industrial, 179-189; and defections, 268-271; the hope of the missions, 269, 270; a recommendation, 287.

Scranton, Pennsylvania, 49, 126.

Seattle, Washington, 49.

Secular Priests: for the N. 79; increasing in number, 85; and colored clergy, 91, and school for N. in Baltimore, 140; attitude of, towards N. work, 216, 217.

Sejour, Victor, 18.

Sex: distribution of Cath. N. by, 64; cohabitation of, 239.

Shaw, Most. Rev. John, on lack of priests for N. work, 216.

Shorter, Msgr. Joseph, work for N., 132, 199.

Shreveport, Louisiana, 118, 154.

Sick, Cath. welfare work for aged and, 205-207.

Sioux City, Iowa, 49, 130.

Sioux Falls, S. Dakota, 49.

Sisters: first colored, to receive veil, 20; Bishop England and, 25; Oblates, 16, 27; founding of Sisters of Holy Family, 30, 31, 140; in schools, 42, 145, 152, 155, table 19 *facing* 179; founding of Sisters of Blessed Sacrament, 44; first effort to found colored, 135, 136; in Kentucky, 142, 143; Franciscans come to Baltimore, 143; foundation of Sisters of Holy Ghost, 144; on the Colored Missions, 162-165; industrial training by, 188; Archbishop Curley on sisters, 197; and care of neglected and delinquent children, 192 et sq.; of the Good Shepherd, 201-203; overloading of, and defection, 268-271.

Skidaway Island, N. Carolina, 41.

Slater, John F., Fund for N. education, 149.

Slavery: the Cath. Church and, 76, 77; effects on N. morality, 234, 235.

Slaves: religion and churches of, 10 et sq., 220-222; emotional character of religion of, 223-226; social character of religion of, 227; moral conditions of, 234-236.

Smith, Mrs. Walter, 150.

Social: life, fostered by separate churches, 70; expediency as temporary justification of slavery, 77; pressure, use of by Cath. Church, 78; education of the N. and the trained priest, 83; life in N. churches, 83, 84; conditions and a colored clergy, 90-92; causes of migration, 96; conditions in North differ from South, 101; conditions in New York city, 124;

character of N. religion, 226-229; condition of N. affected by his environment, 239; lack of social life in Cath. Church, 249; a recommendation, 288.

Social Service Work: in Atlantic City, 60; centers of, according to states, 152, to dioceses, 155, to sisterhoods, 163; of Cath. Church for N., 190 et sq.; importance of, 190, 191; for neglected N. children, 196 et sq.; centers of, 204 et sq.

Socialism and the new N., 274, 275.

Societies: Cath. for N., 209; effect of secret, 250, 251.

Sociology and the N. problem, 3-5.

South Atlantic States: N. Caths. in, 50; distribution of N. Caths. in, 52; migration and the, 109-114.

South Bend, Indiana, 67 (footnote).

South Carolina: first N. in, 10; prohibitive legislation in, 12; N. Caths. in, 50; concentration of N. in, 54; missionary work in, 59; and early migrations of N., 96; loss through migration, 98, 102; destination of migrants from, 103; effect of migration on missions in, 112; public schools for freedmen in, 141; Cath. educational activities in, 154; mission schools by lay teachers, 160; prejudice against Cath. Church in, 212.

South Dakota, 50, 131.

Spalding, S.J., Rev. Henry, 4.

Spalding, Rt. Rev. John L., 39.

Spalding, Most Rev. Martin: plea for N., 36; and first Josephites, 40.

Spaniards and N., 10.

Spokane, Washington, 49.

Springfield, Illinois: N. Caths. in, 49, 128; first N. priest ordained for, 85.

Springfield, Kentucky, Father Miles at, 20.

Springfield, Massachusetts: N. Caths. in Diocese of, 49; concentration of N. in city of, 100.

St. Augustine, Florida: slaves in, 22; N. Caths. in Diocese of, 49; missionary work in Diocese of, table 4 *facing* 58; effect of migration on mission in, 113.

Statistics: reliability of chancery,

XIV; source of, on Cath. N. in
U. S., 46, 51, 57; of Government
misleading, 62-64; misrepresentation of, 279, 280.

St. Cloud, Minnesota, 49, 130.

St. Joseph, Missouri, Diocese of: N.
Caths. in, 49, 131; missionary
work in, table 4 *facing* 58.

St. Louis, Missouri: N. Caths. in
Archdiocese of, 31, 48; missionary
work in, table 4 *facing* 58, 131;
concentration of N. in district of,
99; N. from, in Springfield, Ill.,
126; home for N. children (Normandy), 198, 200; social work in,
208.

St. Paul, Minnesota, Archdiocese of:
N. Caths. in, 48; missionary work
in, table 4 *facing* 58, 130; Rev.
Stephen Theobald in, 86.

Sulpicians: and N. in Baltimore,
15; M. Dubourg starts catechism
class for N., 15; M. Tessier founds
Oblates, 15, 30; Father Greene on,
38; and early N. education in Baltimore, 139, 140.

Superior, Wisconsin, 49.

Syracuse, New York, 49, 123.

T.

"Talented Tenth": and opportunities, 179; progress of, 273.

Tennelly, S.S., Rev. J. B., 43.

Tennessee: free school for N. in,
31; N. Caths in, 50; distribution
of N Caths. in, 52; concentration
of N. in, 54; missionary work in,
59; Government statistics on
Cath. mission work in, 61; loss
through migration, 98; effect of
migration on missions in, 114,
115; public schools for freedmen
in, 141; Cath. educational activities for N. in, 154; high school
for N. in, table 19 *facing* 179;
prejudice against Cath. Church in,
212.

Tessier, Rev. John, 16.

Texas: N. Caths. in, 50; distribution of N. Caths. in, 52; concentration of N. in, 54; missionary
work in, 59, 67 (footnote); Government statistics on Cath. mission work in, 61; priests working
for N. in, 79; and early N. migrations, 96; loss through migration,
98,102; effect of migration on mis-

sions in, 102, 119, 120; migration
from Louisiana to, 103, 118, 119;
Mississippi N. living in, 116; public schools for freedmen in, 141;
Cath. educational activities for N.
in, 154; mission school by lay
teachers, 160; Cath. high school
for N. in, table 19 *facing* 179.

Theobald, Rev. Stephen, N. priest,
86, 131.

Thibodaux, Louisiana, 118, 160.

Thomas, William, on N. family life,
237.

Toledo, Ohio: N. Caths. in Diocese
of, 49; missionary work in, 57,
table 4 *facing* 58, 67; concentration of N. in district of, 99, in
city of, 100.

Tolton, Rev. Augustus, N. priest,
85, 129.

Trenton, New Jersey, Diocese of, N.
Caths. in, 49, 125.

Trinity, Order of the Most Holy,
Rev. Augustine Derricks, member
of, 86.

Trotter, W. M., on higher education
for N., 166.

Tucson, Arizona, 49

U.

Uncles, S.S.J., Rev. Charles, N.
priest, 85.

Ursulines, educational activities of,
152, 156, 165.

Utah, 50, 132.

V.

Vanlomen, Rev., 37.

Van Lommel, Rev., 29.

Vaughan, His Eminence, Cardinal:
letter to Cardinal Gibbons, 1; on
condition of N. in the South, 37;
and arrival of first Josephites, 40;
urges formation of American Josephites, 43; and Franciscan Sisters, 143.

Verbal Instruction, of slaves, 135.

Vermont, 50, 122.

Vicksburg, Mississippi, 117.

Vigeront, S.S.J., Rev. Charles, 40.

Vincent, Abbey of St., Benedictines
from, in Charleston, 41.

Vincent de Paul, Society of, and
early N. education in District of
Columbia, 138.

Vincentians, priests working for N., 79.

Virginia: first N. in, 10; slaves in, 23; Archbishop Whitfield on N. in, 27; first Cath. slave in, 31; Protestant missionary work in, after emancipation, 34; missionary work for N. in, 42, 59; Caths. in, 42, 50; distribution of N. Caths. in, 52; concentration of N. in, 54; Government statistics on Cath. mission work for N. in, 61; loss through migration, 98, 102; destination of migrants from, 103; effect of migration on missions in, 111, 112; migrants from N. Carolina in, 112; migrants from Alabama in, 115; schools for freedmen in, 141; Cath. educational activities for N. in, 154; mission schools by lay teachers in, 161; Cath. high schools for N. in, table 19 facing 179; St. Emma's Industrial School, 184; Van de Vyver Institute, 188; married N. women working in, 194; prejudice against Cath. Church in, 212.

Visitation, Sisters of the, 138.

Vocational Training: table 19 facing 179; by sisters in, 188; vide Industrial Schools.

Vocations: plea of Third Plenary Council of Baltimore for, 36; to work of N. Missions, 281.

W.

Walsh, Rev. Leo, 127.

Walter, Rev. 139.

Warren, S.S.J., Rev. Vincent, and work in Norfolk, 70.

Washington, State of, 50, 104.

Washington, Booker T., and industrial education, 166, 167, 179, 180, 181.

Washington, D. C.: treatment of N. in, 28, 29; Church of St. Augustine, 39; N. Caths. in, 50, 60; distribution of N. Caths. in, 52; concentration of N. in, 54; missionary work in, 59; advantages of mission work in, 60; Government statistics for Cath. mission work in, 61; priests working for N. in, 79; effect of migration on missions in, 110, 111; early N. education in, 137, 138; Cath. educational activities for N. in, 153;

high school for N. in, table 19 facing 179.

Washington, N. Carolina, Passionists in charge of mission in, 79 (footnote).

Washington, Tennessee, 67 (footnote).

West, Mr., 13.

West Indians, in New York, 60, 123.

West North Central States, 50.

West South Central States: N. Caths. in, 50; effect of migration on missions in, 117-120.

West Virginia: N. Caths. in, 50; distribution of N. Caths. in, 52; concentration of N. in, 54; effect of migration on, 112; migrants from N. Carolina in, 112; migrants from Alabama in, 115.

Wheeling, West Virginia, 49, 112.

White, Rev. Charles, 39.

Whitfield, Most. Rev. James: on lack of missionaries, 27, 28; approves Oblate Sisters, 27.

Wichita, Kansas, 49.

Wilmington, Delaware: Diocese of, N. Caths. in, 49; missionary work for N. in, table 4 facing 58; effect of migration on St. Joseph's mission, 109; St. Joseph's Home for orphans, 144; St. Joseph's Industrial School (Clayton), table 19 facing 179, 185, 198; Du Pont contribution for N. education in city of, 149.

Wilmington, N. Carolina, 112.

Winona, Minnesota, 130.

Wisconsin, State of: N. Caths. in, 50; mission work for N. in, 129, 130, 154.

Wissel, Rev. Raphael, 41.

Woodson, G. Carter: on early advocates of N. education, 134, in Maryland and District of Columbia, 137, in Baltimore, 139; on Booker T. Washington, 166; on emotional character of N. religion, 223-226; on N. preachers, 231.

Wyoming, State of, 50, 132.

X.

Xavier College, 169-173.

Y.

Youngstown, Ohio, 99.